MENLO SCHOOL

founded 1915

MENLO COLLEGE

GIFT OF

A. H. BRAWNER, SR.

The Bakufu in Japanese History

The Bakufu
in Japanese History

Edited by JEFFREY P. MASS and
WILLIAM B. HAUSER

Stanford University Press 1985
Stanford, California

Stanford University Press, Stanford, California
©1985 by the Board of Trustees of the Leland Stanford Junior University
Printed in the United States of America

CIP data appear at the end of the book

Map reprinted by courtesy of Yale University Press from John W. Hall and Jeffrey P. Mass, eds., *Medieval Japan: Essays in Institutional History* (1974)

Published with the assistance of Stanford University's Japan Fund, the Japan Foundation, and the University of Michigan's Center for Japanese Studies

To John Whitney Hall, teacher and friend,
on his seventieth birthday

Preface

In 1974, a panel on shogunates in Japanese history was held at the annual convention of the American Historical Association. Chaired by Professor John Whitney Hall of Yale, it generated considerable interest and the hope that it might lead to an expanded conference. Unfortunately, such a gathering never took place, and the idea of using shogunates as a bridge between periods was temporarily put aside. Yet the notion of analyzing the warrior epoch as something coherent retained its earlier appeal. The present collection is an outgrowth of Professor Hall's original idea.

In fact, it was Hall's own *Government and Local Power in Japan, 500-1700* (Princeton, N.J., 1966) that provided the initial model for a scholarly enterprise transcending the traditional sub-periods of the larger age. It is fair to say that this work has become a kind of "sacred text" that in hindsight helped to legitimize a new field. At any rate, the contributors to the present volume—the students of Professor Hall and the students of his students—hope that the essays offered here will promote the field that our *sensei* so ably pioneered.

J.P.M.
W.B.H.

Contents

Contributors

Peter J. Arnesen is assistant professor of history at the University of Michigan and the author of *The Medieval Japanese Daimyo* (New Haven, Conn., 1979).

Harold Bolitho is professor of Japanese history in the Department of East Asian Languages and Civilizations, Harvard University, and the author of *Treasures among Men: The Fudai Daimyo in Tokugawa Japan* (New Haven, Conn., 1974), among other studies.

Suzanne Gay received her Ph.D. from Yale University in 1982 on the completion of her dissertation, "The Muromachi Bakufu in Medieval Kyoto." She teaches at John Carroll University in Cleveland, Ohio, and is the author of "The Kawashima: A Warrior-Peasant of Medieval Japan," *Harvard Journal of Asiatic Studies* (forthcoming, 1986).

Andrew Goble is a Ph.D. candidate at Stanford University and is completing a dissertation entitled "Go-Daigo and the Kemmu Restoration." He is the author of "The Hojo and Consultative Government," in Jeffrey P. Mass, ed., *Court and Bakufu in Japan* (New Haven, Conn., 1982).

Lorraine F. Harrington received her Ph.D. from Stanford University in 1983 on the completion of her dissertation, "Regional Administration under the Ashikaga Bakufu." She is the author of "Social Control and the Significance of *Akutō*," in Mass, ed., *Court and Bakufu in Japan* (1982).

William B. Hauser is professor and chairman of the history department at the University of Rochester. He is the author of *Economic Institutional Change in Tokugawa Japan: Osaka and the Kinai Cotton Trade* (Cambridge, Eng., 1974), among other studies.

Jeffrey P. Mass is professor of history at Stanford University and the author of *Warrior Government in Early Medieval Japan* (New Haven, Conn., 1974), *The Kamakura Bakufu: A Study in Documents* (Stanford, Calif., 1976), and *The Development of Kamakura Rule, 1180-1250* (Stanford, Calif., 1979), among other studies.

Bernard Susser is associate professor at Baika Junior College, Japan, and the author of several articles on Nobunaga and Hideyoshi.

Foreword

The writing of Japanese history has made great strides since World War II. The nature of that progress deserves explanation, for it reveals some important things about international cooperation and cultural exchange.

The first thing to note is that in the West the study of Japanese history was taken up again—one might almost say was begun—at a very strategic time. The Japanese world of scholarship was emerging from a prolonged period of relative isolation. In the face of governmental pressure and patriotic emotion, it had substantially given up work of a broadly comparative or analytic nature. Many historians had retreated into silence; others had sought refuge in the esoteric or in rather barren chronological and political approaches. Their relief on being freed from psychological and political pressures and their new freedom to speculate, to deny, and to doubt made the years around 1950 a period of great ferment and excitement. It was at this moment that Western, and especially American, scholars and students first contacted their counterparts in Japan.

The contact came after Japan had broken with the state ideology of emperor and uniqueness. Historians were now free to view the succession of military regimes that had existed for eight hundred years as something more than an aberration from the proper path of ruler and subject. They could look again, think again, and write for a wider audience. A "history boom" began, one that has yet to run its course. Publications large and small, prestigious and modest, brought the Japanese public a popular history that, in excellence and interest, has few equals and fewer superiors.

On the Western and especially American side, training in the language and culture of Japan that was carried on during the war years under military auspices helped prepare for expanded scholarly contact. Military language programs produced a small cohort of students from which the future specialists emerged in the graduate schools of postwar years. By 1950 they were entering Japan as the students, colleagues, and co-workers of Japanese academics. These future specialists were a new phenomenon. They were committed to professional training and work in a field that had scarcely existed before their time. With the exception of Edwin Reischauer and a handful of others who had begun training before the Pacific War, those who wrote on Japanese history had been gifted amateurs who pursued the subject as an avocation during lulls in diplomatic or other careers. Some of them had lectured after their retirement, but more often they were gentlemen who substituted haiku for Horace as a pastime. The specialist careers for which the new generation prepared, by contrast, were made possible by the awareness of university and foundation leaders of the need for international studies in the postwar world. Sir George Sansom, the greatest of the amateurs, became the first of the professionals as he turned to lecturing in America. But the future belonged to the full-time specialists who began as instructors and assistant professors at the major universities of England, Europe, and especially the United States. It was their hope to give Japanese history full representation in the faculties and curricula of Western institutions of higher learning. At the transition point their efforts frequently built on the work of distinguished Japanese scholars—Asakawa at Yale, Anesaki at Harvard, Tsunoda at Columbia—who had given their best years to begin that process by serving as bridges across the scholarly world of the Pacific.

The new specialists crossed that ocean and entered directly into a scholarly environment they helped create. As cooperation developed, young Japanese scholars spent prolonged periods in residence at major universities in the West, and Western scholars, in turn, joined research seminars in the great historiographical centers of Tokyo and Kyoto. Patterns of influence became increasingly reciprocal, an exchange well symbolized by the long association of John Whitney Hall with Kanai Madoka of the University of Tokyo's Historiographical Institute.

Of the many fields of Japanese history transformed by this sort of cooperation, that of institutional history, the subject of this volume, proved particularly rewarding. In 1940 the Tokugawa shogunate, the last of Japan's Bakufu, was only an old man's life away. Its documents survived in awesome numbers, but they were in the hands of former baronial families too poor to publish them and too proud to share their contents. The war damage diminished the bulk of those collections, and the owners who survived were grateful for public assistance to house and order what remained. New national and regional universities, staffed by historians who realized the potential of what they had at hand, began to benefit from the help of prefectural and local governments anxious to contribute to scholarship and publication that might enhance the name of Okayama, of Tosa, or of Tottori. Documentary compilations, monographs, and popular histories provided a three-tiered coverage that had never been available before. Much of this work is excellent, and the sophistication with which the papers collected here treat the theme of the allocation and location of power in Japan exemplifies the heightening competence in Japanese history.

The theme the editors have chosen goes to the heart of our understanding of Japanese history and society. The multiple overlapping rights that complicated the decline of the imperial court can be compared to the multiple cultural levels that Tsurumi Kazuko has found characteristic of Japan. Viewed in this light, the shift of influence from court to camp, from Kyoto to Bakufu, becomes far more interesting, gradual, and complex than it has previously appeared. And those with an eye to the ironies of more recent history will suspect that a similar process, telescoped into the six short years that followed World War II, accompanied the attenuation of military control under the final Bakufu that was known as Supreme Commander, Allied Powers.

John Whitney Hall has been a prime mover in the progress of cooperative scholarship that has been sketched here. At Michigan's Okayama Center, at the University of Michigan and at Yale University, in the Conference on Modern Japan, in the Joint Committee of Japanese Studies of the American Council of Learned Societies and the Social Science Research Council, in the United States–Japan Conference on Cultural and Educational Exchange, in the Japan–United States Friendship Commission, in the Japan Foundation's American Advisory Committee, and in a hundred other forums, seminars, con-

The Bakufu in Japanese History

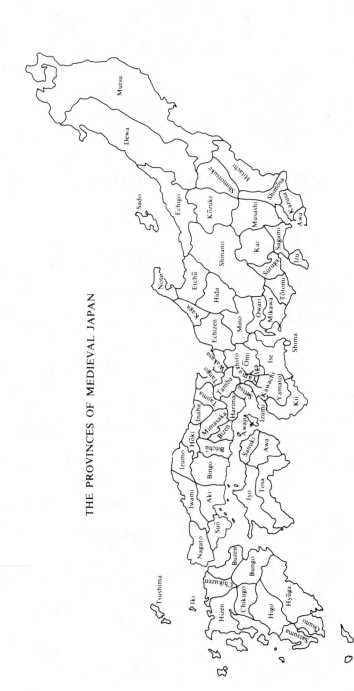

THE PROVINCES OF MEDIEVAL JAPAN

Introduction

JEFFREY P. MASS

This book is the outgrowth of an effort to identify the links connecting the various sub-periods of Japan's medieval and early modern ages. How can this epoch be made comprehensible as a coherent whole? In Japan itself, it has long been known as the "age of military houses," a characterization that is useful but that fails to provide a framework for accessible study. The samurai phenomenon is simply too complex to be dealt with in a single volume. More feasible is to examine some ongoing sub-system or institution. For this purpose, we have chosen the Bakufu model of government, adopted by warriors three times over the course of four centuries. During this period, the condition of warriors changed markedly, moving from an uneasy partnership with courtiers in the earliest stage, to a dominance over them in the middle period, to a rule over the whole of society in the final stage. Yet throughout this progress the Bakufu pattern of organization survived. More than that, it became the archetypal form of government during a long era of incomplete central control.

Though we speak of *bakufu*, it is important to note that the term itself was not integral to the system it came to symbolize. As described in my contribution to the present volume, the word *bakufu* did not mean until much later what modern historians have ascribed to it. Whereas scholars remain wholly committed to it, in other words, contemporaries scarcely used it. Such a limited usage suggests the theme for chapter one—lacunae in Kamakura history that may nevertheless illuminate. Though the metaphor is inexact, it is history, as it were, seen with mirrors.

To distinguish Kamakura from its Kyoto-based predecessor, historians have traditionally juxtaposed warriors and courtiers. Yet, as Andrew Goble's ground-breaking study of the Bakufu's officialdom makes clear, this approach is basically unsound. During the thirteenth century, civilian bureaucrats continued to play a prominent role in Kamakura, even as their outlook was necessarily becoming military. Indeed, Goble might have extended his point to include the later shogunates. The Muromachi regime, located in Kyoto and concerned with courtiers and commerce in addition to warriors, was never able to escape civilian problems; whereas the Tokugawa Bakufu, Japan's ultimate government by warriors, was staffed by men now determined to *become* civilians, at least in their tastes and lifestyles. In any event, in our haste to dichotomize as a way of distinguishing modes of governance, we have tended to forget that all three shogunates exhibited major (if shifting) non-warrior features.

Goble's essay shows us government in action. He identifies the key families that populated Kamakura's bureaus and discusses recruitment, compensation, and tenure. He is also concerned with how Kamakura sought to increase its efficiency. His chapter is a pioneering effort on a subject that has proved daunting even to Japanese scholars.

The Muromachi Bakufu has always seemed more elusive to historians than its Kamakura or Tokugawa counterparts. This is because the realities of power changed more dramatically during the fourteenth to sixteenth centuries than earlier or later, and because there has never been any question of the national scope of the first and last shogunates. The source of Kamakura's claim to countrywide influence was its network of vassals and the perquisites shared by this group, the offices of *shugo* and *jitō*. In the case of the Tokugawa, there was the absence of opposition to the shogun's government from any quarter and the integrative effects of half-time service upon him in his capital (the *sankin kōtai*). But the Muromachi government was different, since Bakufu influence outside the capital seemed to ebb and flow. Thus the historian who asks, "To what extent did the Bakufu rule Japan?" has only to worry about the court-Bakufu axis in the thirteenth century and the dominance of the Tokugawa within the Bakufu-daimyo (*bakuhan*) framework of the seventeenth. For the Muromachi Period, however, there must be considered the lingering authority of traditional Kyoto, the shifting alliance and rivalry with the *shugo*, the rise of the *kokujin*-daimyo, and the existence of *ikki* and other forms of opposition to higher authority. The question about Bakufu rulership thus becomes complex to the point of being almost unapproachable, except for the perception that the Muromachi regime was the weakest of Japan's three shogunates.

The papers by Gay, Harrington, and Arnesen confront this issue of weakness head-on—and from different perspectives offer somewhat divergent conclusions. Gay allows that the Muromachi Bakufu was the hegemonial power within Japan but argues that its authority continued to be shared with the traditional capital elite, the courtier and ecclesiastical institutions. Borrowing from the *kenmon seika* theory of Kuroda Toshio, she maintains that power at the top level could not be unitary. Far from the Bakufu's ruling all of Japan, it was unable to govern alone even in Kyoto. Thus Gay implicitly links the regime more with its Heian-based counterparts—the Fujiwara and the retired emperors, both situated in Kyoto—than with the regionally based government of Kamakura. As an illustration of this, the judicial operations of the Muromachi Bakufu were in large measure concerned with *kenmon* disputes, much as the courts of Kyoto had always been. By contrast, the judicial purview of Kamakura was basically the legal problems of vassals.

Gay, in fact, has expanded on the tendency of recent historians to extend Kyoto's lifespan ever farther. She also revives an older theory—that of Kyoto's enervating influence. Thus we might wonder, as we did in the case of Kamakura, whether the second of Japan's shogunates warrants the label military. Was the Muromachi Bakufu indeed a warrior government? Harrington and Arnesen are quick to reply in the affirmative. As they see it, the Bakufu's purview was no shrunken island, preoccupied with commerce and the problems of *kenmon* peers, in a sea of local warrior autonomy. The Muromachi regime maintained linkages with the provinces on several levels, the most important being its network of *shugo*. Yet this connection, much studied elsewhere, is not the one that our authors emphasize. Harrington is concerned with the development of the regional organs of the Bakufu, a topic hitherto neglected even in Japan. She shows how the Ashikaga leaders tailored their efforts in Kyushu and the Kantō to fit the conditions of those regions but argues that communications were regular and articulation between Kyoto and the two headquarters impressive.

The military flavor of these regional efforts is obvious. Whereas in Kamakura times coercive power readily gave way to the leverage of judicial edicts, under the Ashikaga, with violence no longer limited in duration or localized in the narrow sense, the Bakufu's regional chieftains were first and foremost commanders. This is not to say that the power of the written directive had ceased, for it never did in Japan. But in most matters force was required to back up the exercise of delegated authority. The Bakufu's regional commanders were consequently the fashioners of military alliances and the guardians of local security. At the same time, as Harrington points out, their effectiveness depended on numerous variables, among them the forcefulness of the commanders themselves, the degree of trust they enjoyed with the Bakufu, and the probity and energy with which they sought to smooth over local grievances. Thus even if the central Bakufu in Kyoto was concerned with the jostling movements of the *kenmon* and with elite politics, the regional heads were occupied with the manifold tasks of holding local alliances together. On behalf of the Bakufu, they were judicial administrators, regional policemen, and taxation specialists, all rolled into one.

On the question of whether or not the regional chieftains "held" the provinces for their central patrons, Harrington offers no easy answer. But she does note that the two regional headquarters, like the *shugo*, acquired powers with the passage of time, and that they were most effective when the Bakufu itself was most effective. To argue, as many historians do, that the high point of the Muromachi regime was the era of Yoshimitsu, the third shogun, is to argue as well for a regional dimension to the Bakufu's vigor at this point. Such an advance, according to Harrington, was not limited to the displacement of certain *shugo*, a policy that strengthened the shogun vis-à-vis his great vassals but weakened the Bakufu territorially. The granting of new authority to the regional command structure was designed to offset any potential loss of influence here. A final highlight of the Harrington essay is its explication of the double-tiered *kubō-kanrei* system in the Kantō, a topic never adequately understood by historians in the West. As the power of the *kubō*, who was dominant, tended to become autonomous, the Bakufu shifted its support to the *kanrei*, an authority held hereditarily by the Uesugi. Harrington uses this transfer of support to the deputy regional commander to illustrate the pragmatism of the Bakufu in matters of local control.

Ties to local areas are also of concern to Peter Arnesen in his pioneering essay on the Ashikaga vassal system. This is a subject about which there has always been great confusion. Unlike the Kamakura

Bakufu, which maintained a countrywide network of vassals to whom *shugo* and *jitō* posts were distributed, the Muromachi regime was thought to have concentrated almost exclusively on *shugo*. The reasons for this assumption were the high visibility of *shugo* (contrary to the experience of Kamakura times), the belief that the Ashikaga were obliged to work through the *shugo* to reach warriors lower on the scale, and the fact that *jitō*, now joined by other local titles, came to be submerged under the more general heading of *kokujin*—men of the province. As Arnesen demonstrates, however, the phenomenon of shogunal vassalage did not simply vanish, another casualty of the increasingly truncated power of the Muromachi Bakufu. In fact, the Bakufu maintained ties with local vassals, to the mutual advantage of both. There were thus two hierarchies in operation, one including *shugo* and one not, with local circumstances and other variables determining which was the more important.

Arnesen offers three pieces of evidence to prove that the shogunal tie with non-*shugo* vassals remained viable. The first is that the Bakufu levied imposts on its *gokenin* and continued to do so until well into the sixteenth century. The second concerns the shogun's private guard (*hōkōshū*), drawn from *gokenin* located in selected regions. And the third concentrates on non-guard *gokenin* who maintained close ties with the Bakufu. In recent years research in Japan has focused on the *hōkōshū*, with emphasis on this group's role as a counterweight to the *shugo*. Arnesen believes that such an approach leads to an underestimation of the size and diversity of composition of the Bakufu's provincial vassal corps, and in so doing seriously misjudges the reach of shogunal power. By concentrating on Aki Province in western Japan, Arnesen shows that there were non-guardsmen who were all but immune from the meddling of *shugo* precisely because they were the direct vassals of the shogun. To the extent that this experience had parallels in other provinces, our view of the Bakufu as a limited national organization would warrant review. For Arnesen, indeed, the Muromachi regime was the "true government of Japan," at least up until the Ōnin War. Far from being limited to *kenmon* politics and dealings with *shugo*, the Ashikaga shoguns were vassal overlords with countrywide powers.

Students of the Muromachi Bakufu normally look backward to the model of Kamakura but only rarely look forward to Japan's last shogunate. By contrast, specialists on the Tokugawa seem only to be concerned with what came after. In large part this divergence of perspective derives from the separation between Japan's medieval and early modern epochs. It is difficult, in other words, to see beyond the sixteenth century to yet another regime on the model of its predecessors. The Tokugawa Bakufu may have had *jitō* and *gokenin*, but these bore little resemblance to what were seen as the true holders of those statuses, who came earlier. Only recently have Western historians attempted to bridge Japan's "great divide," hitherto seen as the era when obsolete institutions were totally destroyed and new ones constructed to replace them. In a sense Westerners have started to appreciate what historians in Japan always knew: that the forms and the nomenclature of government constitute important continuities in themselves. In this regard, only a generation (1573-1603) separated the Muromachi and Tokugawa shogunates. Thus, even if the former no longer had the power to control events much past the Ōnin War, the survival of its apparatus meant that a state structure with an identifiable summit was still considered necessary. Until its overthrow by Nobunaga in 1573, the Muromachi Bakufu continued to make decisions and issue decrees affecting certain parts of the country. Yet, already, as we know, new forms of authority were maturing in the provinces. Sovereignty over territory no longer resided exclusively with the occupants of the highest social positions. Because of this disjunction between what was hallowed and what was actual, government in Japan became subject to a more equitable balance between central and local interests. This balance was reflected in the particular shape of the "new unity" that was fashioned at the end of the sixteenth century.

To appreciate the novelty of this so-called *bakuhan* compromise, we need to recall conditions in earlier times. When fighting men went to war for or against the Kamakura Bakufu, it was not for the purpose of seizing territory. Armies did not win or lose parts of Japan, since final authority over land remained anyway in central hands. The hierarchical *shōen* and *shiki* systems, dominated by Kyoto and defended by Kamakura, were simply antithetical to true decentralization; the country's duly constituted governments conjointly ruled Japan. It was only under the Muromachi shoguns that the comprehensiveness of central authority initially came to be questioned. The Ashikaga naturally attempted to arrest this development, and if Harrington and Arnesen are correct, were more successful at this than previously thought. Nevertheless, by the end of the fifteenth century the Muromachi Bakufu could react to, but no longer control, developments in the provinces. As the initiative passed to the new class of magnates called daimyo, new conceptualizations were evolved to rationalize the emergence of principalities (*kokka*) that owed little to higher authority. For the first time, national government was conceived of by locals as the sum total of their own autonomous regimes. Such a condition, inherently unstable, could hardly endure indefinitely. Defensive alliances among daimyo gave way to movements for regional leadership, and ultimately to a push toward national hegemony. Nobunaga, the protector of the shogun, became his destroyer, and then postured to become his successor.

Yet the seeds of some fundamental restructuring were already firmly sown. Japan could be rewelded only up to a point. Under the Heian, Kamakura, and Muromachi regimes, authority was delegated, and perquisites distributed or confirmed, from a central source; participants enjoyed largesse. But now the great men of Japan had won their status principally by their own efforts. Any would-be unifier would need to ally with those who could not be made subservient. The territorial balance, in other words, which had meant little in earlier periods, was now extremely important. Moreover, government needed to be bolstered at two levels—that of the new central administration, and that of the component principalities. This was the only way that the natural tension between them could be defused. Under this arrangement the daimyo would consent to the overlord's rulership as long as it reinforced his own authority. The essays by Susser and Hauser deal with aspects of this new central-local mutuality, which eventually took as its permanent form the shape of another Bakufu.

Until raised by Harold Bolitho, the question most often asked about Japan's other shogunates—the extent to which they governed Japan—seemed almost irrelevant for the Tokugawa. Despite the legacy of autonomous daimyo, the proof of dominant rulership—the multiple attainders, the *sankin kōtai*, the torrent of Bakufu regulations—seemed overwhelming. Yet as Susser and Hauser make clear, what appears to have been rapid and spectacular was in fact obstacle-laden and uncertain. In this context it is no surprise that the model of the Bakufu should have been resurrected, a development that speaks to the larger question of hegemony building in Japan. It might be argued that each of Japan's regimes went through two more or less distinct stages (or upheavals) before power was ultimately secured. Thus, the Taika reforms of 645 were followed by the more definitive

Jinshin War of 672; Hōgen and Heiji were followed by the Taira coup d'état of 1179; the Gempei War by the Fujiwara campaign of 1189; the ouster of Go-Daigo by the Kannō Incident of 1350; Sekigahara by Osaka; and the Meiji Restoration by the Satsuma Rebellion of 1877. In other words, hegemonies, the result of adjustments within elite coalitions, required some traumatic follow-up to finalize the new hierarchy. As is well known, Tokugawa Ieyasu was unusually resourceful in the multi-sided program he developed to aid his own cause. The creation of a new shogunate—time-honored and legitimate—was simply prudent under the circumstances.

The experiences of Nobunaga and Hideyoshi are germane here. Shortly before his death in 1582, Nobunaga was offered the post of shogun, though he did not accept it. Hideyoshi likewise made no move in the direction of a shogunate. Perhaps the format was temporarily discredited, or perhaps it was viewed as potentially confining. After all, the armies of Hideyoshi had spent eight years in the field before he laid claim to a Japan united by his own effort. By comparison, Ieyasu's pretensions to countrywide authority seem almost presumptuous. Sekigahara was but a single battle, and the "uncrowned" heir of Hideyoshi (Hideyori) remained ensconced at Osaka. Thus the resurrection of the Bakufu format made sense: it anticipated an authority that would be national in scope, something that Hideyoshi had earned by 1590 but that Ieyasu could only posture for. Ieyasu, in this regard, reminds us of Takauji: with their major achievements still ahead of them, both men sought the title of shogun.

Susser states in his essay that "daimyo autonomy was the price Hideyoshi and later the Tokugawa had to pay for the right to rule the nation." In this light, he qualifies the long-held assumption that daimyo transfers represented simply an anti-daimyo policy; such moves assisted daimyo more than they hindered them in their efforts to gain control over their own vassals. At the same time, the shape of the country's decentralization was determined largely from above. The pattern of transfers (as well as the host of other initiatives) issued from the overlord; the daimyo now were part of a national system of daimyo, defined and regulated by the suzerain. A new conception of "aggregate Japan" came into being and was eventually made permanent under the Tokugawa *bakuhan* balance.

Two of Ieyasu's most pressing problems were his weakness in central and western Japan and the weakness of many of the daimyo pillars on which the emerging national structure rested. Since the experience of Ieyasu had been exclusively in the east, how was he to extend a physical presence westward? The paper by Hauser shows how seizing control of Osaka was critically important. Because it required a dangerous military campaign, success would permit the dismantling of the Hideyoshi power bloc, as well as the takeover of central Japan's most rapidly expanding commercial center. Hauser goes on to show how Hideyoshi's castle town was converted into a Tokugawa city. Since urbanization had not proceeded very far under the country's previous shogunates, the seizure and transformation of cities—save for Kyoto by the Ashikaga—had been unnecessary. Reflecting the new complexities of the early seventeenth century, Ieyasu's effort was obliged to take account of much that had not existed earlier.

The Bakufu created by Ieyasu and consolidated by his son and grandson (Hidetada and Iemitsu) survived for nearly 275 years. It was Japan's longest shogunate. The story of how the society it ruled changed over time has occupied historians in the West for more than a generation. Yet the "changes behind the facade of seeming permanence"—to use John Whitney Hall's memorable phrase—have in part obscured the fact that a Bakufu format *was* reinstated and that it remained the framework for governance until the nineteenth century. In advance of the Western threat, no internal crisis or development could muster sufficient shock force to seriously endanger the regime. Moreover, like its two predecessors, the Tokugawa Bakufu owed its viability less to energetic leadership than to the sustaining force of institutions. Yet whereas the earlier shogunates had had to contemplate major policy changes as well as to confront enemies, the Tokugawa were more secure; the back-and-forth movement between retrenchment and reform was a factional, not institutional, response to relatively minor problems. Although modern scholars decry the notion of a Tokugawa "encasement," rigidity did set in (after a highly innovative inter-Bakufu era) precisely because the dangers to the regime were not life-threatening.

In the 1850's the arrival of the Western powers interrupted this pattern of inertia. According to Harold Bolitho in his provocative study of Senior Councillor Abe Masahiro, politicians and their policies now potentially made a difference. The Tokugawa might have avoided their downfall had Abe and his colleagues developed programs that were not at cross-purposes. For Bolitho, then, a failure of leadership contributed directly to the collapse of the regime. But why, we might ask, was the Bakufu idea simultaneously discredited? During eight centuries the excesses of the Hōjō, the insufficiencies of the Ashikaga, the neglect of Nobunaga and Hideyoshi, and the severity of the Tokugawa had failed to diminish its acceptability. The difference now was the closure, as it were, to Japan's long era of domestically oriented history. A system of government that balanced central and local power became a liability as Japan struggled to fit into a larger world context. Japan was obliged to see itself as others saw it, and only then became aware of its weakness. Reminiscent of an almost forgotten past, Japan became, in a sense, what it had not been for nearly a millennium—an imperial realm without the fragmentation of the age of shogunates.

The value of the Bakufu format should nonetheless be clear. For fully half of Japan's history, it provided for flexibility in defusing central-local tensions. It represented elasticity in government, the ultimate paradigm for the exercise of incomplete central authority. Within this framework each successive shogunate operated under different requirements as to how and with whom authority needed to be shared. In the case of Kamakura, the division was between the still vigorous courtier government of Kyoto and the fledgling warrior regime in the east. The first Bakufu's limited but crucial role in the governance of Japan was appropriate to an era of outlawry but not one of warfare. Japan's elite fighting class as yet did little fighting.

The transition from warrior to warlord occurred in the next period. Despite this development, Japan's second Bakufu sought to govern largely in unitary fashion. With no rival at its center, it combined in itself the divided judicial responsibilities of Kamakura and Kyoto, impinged upon the provinces through its regional command and twin vassal networks, and developed a national tax system. In the end, however, it never succeeded in inheriting the right to own and administer the country's territory. Indeed, no central authority until the nineteenth century would retrieve this traditional right, which flowed from imperial, not Bakufu, governance.

The Japan of Ieyasu's day comprised a union of principalities. Whereas the Ashikaga coalition could not expand to include the full complement of emerging daimyo, the writ of its Tokugawa successor was comprehensive: to be a daimyo in 1615 was to be part of the new Tokugawa confederation. But to be a daimyo was also to enjoy autonomy, and the task for Ieyasu was thus one of balancing centripetal and centrifugal tendencies rather than of ruling by unchallenged right. Owing to its already demonstrated adaptability, the governmental framework that he adopted for this purpose became Japan's final shogunate.

What Can We Not Know about the Kamakura Bakufu?

All historians seek to retrieve the past using a deck with some cards missing. In the case of the more remote past, the deck becomes slimmer still. For most historians this is simply a reality of their craft: accounts must be based on available records. Yet the surveying of what cannot be known can sometimes deepen understanding. Ways to work around lacunae may be identified and new questions can be posed. In particular, when gaps are unexpected, it is useful to ponder why they are there—and then to build on whatever insights emerge.

Gaps may exist for a variety of reasons, involving more than the mere impoverishment of traces or the fact that certain activities simply went unrecorded. There may have been distortion of the record as well as suppression.[1] Not only must the historian play with a short deck, in other words, but he must play with a potentially stacked short deck. He is obliged to make allowances for what has been lost, to make judgments about what has survived, and to make informed guesses about what has gone unrecorded. The thoughtful scholar is forever adding, subtracting, and refining in order to corroborate the known while acknowledging the unknown. In the case of Japan's Kamakura age (1180-1333), from which only a tiny fragment of the original record remains, historians must be especially resourceful to surmount these difficulties. What, then, are some of the more significant gaps in the record of this era, and what new approaches emerge when we ask why they are there?

Kamakura's Formative Period

More attention has been paid by scholars to the Bakufu's formation and initial character than to any other aspects of its history. This is because the regime's appearance in the 1180's ushered in an era of shogunates that would extend to the nineteenth century. Japan's "age of military houses"—depending on one's reckoning, half or more of Japan's whole history—began here. Because of the scrutiny accorded these events, and since the surviving sources have all been identified and printed, one would not expect problems in ascertaining what is unknowable. Yet, as historians are now aware, the answers to a number of questions depend on sources whose reliability is in doubt. In effect, a good deal of what has been taken for granted must now be reevaluated.

The Word Bakufu

One problem concerns the name of the regime itself. The contributors to this book freely use the word *bakufu*, and so do virtually all specialists on Japan. Yet *bakufu* as a term in regular usage is a product of Tokugawa times, whereas Kamakura Bakufu was coined only in 1887.[2] The ubiquity of both terms, then, is a matter of scholarly preference, not historical proof. This is not to say that the word *bakufu* is not very old. Unlike some terms, which have been given longer histories than they deserve,[3] it dates from the Heian period. Yet its historic meaning developed only very slowly. As we will see in the account that follows, the history of the term is characterized less by its currency over many centuries than by its extreme scarcity during the same period.

The word *bakufu* originated in China, with two usages: as the headquarters of the T'ang emperor's inner palace guards (*konoe fu*, in Japanese), and as the headquarters of a general (shogun) on a military expedition. The oldest surviving reference to a *bakufu* in Japan, that of a mid-tenth-century courtier holding the title of "left captain of the inner palace guards" (*sa konoe taishō*), suggests that the headquarters, in Japanese hands, was less an imperial guards office than the residential compound permitted an imperial guards captain.[4] Since we find no references to a *bakufu* under a shogun,[5] we surmise that, beyond the original meaning, the term's potential had not been grasped by the onset of the Kamakura age.

In the eleventh month of 1190, Minamoto Yoritomo was appointed an imperial guards captain (*u konoe taishō*), and the official chronicle of his regime, the *Azuma kagami*, begins referring to a *bakufu* from that point.[6] Although the *Azuma kagami* is a retrospective account known for fairly frequent distortions,[7] modern scholars have never thought to question a Yoritomo-era *bakufu*. Yet it is precisely this premise that requires qualification. Most significantly, a court diary, the *Sanchōki*, refers to a *bakufu* in 1195—which is not Yoritomo's *bakufu* but rather that of a Kyoto-based guards captain.[8] In other words, during the era of Yoritomo, *bakufu* was not associated either with him exclusively or with Kamakura. Indeed, we may doubt that the word had any significance at all for the system of government he was constructing. The right to establish a *mandokoro*, or chancellery, was the key development of 1190-91; the *bakufu* that accompanied it went mostly unnoticed.[9]

The proof for this conclusion lies in the limited use of the word *bakufu* during this and subsequent generations. Except for the *Azuma kagami*, where it appears fairly frequently, no Yoritomo-era source seems to use the word.[10] More significant, apart from the *Azuma kagami*, no warrior source for the entire Kamakura period uses it, including documents, diaries, laws, biographies, and war tales.[11] Even the *Satamirensho* (1319), a compendium of terms that logically should have given the name of the regime, fails to do so.[12] By contrast, at least one courtier diary, the *Meigetsuki*, cites the *bakufu* in entries of 1226 and 1229,[13] thereby suggesting that *bakufu* was occasionally used by persons accustomed to them—that is, the aristocracy of Kyoto. It was in precisely such a context that the *Sanchōki*, cited above, referred to a non-Kamakura *bakufu*. Similarly, entries in the *Kanchūki*, a courtier diary of the late Kamakura era, speak of non-Kamakura *bakka*—courtiers holding the post of *taishō*—and an emperor's letter of 1319 refers to the *bakufu* of a recently appointed *taishō*, a noble named Saionji Kanesue.[14] Even the *Azuma kagami* demonstrates that the terms *bakufu* and *bakka* were hardly exclusive to Kamakura: in 1238/4/10, it refers to Sanjō Sanechika, another Kyoto aristocrat, as *bakka*.

But what did *bakufu* mean when it was used? All sources agree that the term for the government in Kamakura was not *bakufu* but Kantō, the eastern region in which Kamakura was located.[15] (Kamakura itself, or Kamakura-chū, implied the physical city, not the seat of government.) By contrast, *bakufu* continued to mean what it had always meant—the residence of a *taishō*, or now, of a shogun. The *Azuma kagami* is the only source to use the term consistently, a total of about eighty appearances. Virtually all can be confirmed as referring to the shogun in some personal, rather than governmental, capacity. Thus we see *waka* parties, sutra readings, sumo exhibitions, coming-of-age ceremonies, and gaming of various kinds at the *bakufu*.[16] We also read of Yoritomo's moving to the home of a vassal after a fire destroyed his own *bakufu*, and of a later shogun whose residence was explicitly called a *bakufu*.[17] Even the two usages in the *Meigetsuki* cite visits to the *bakufu* along with (significantly) communiqués "from the Kantō."[18] In the Kamakura age, then, *bakufu* was a term that conveyed nothing abstract. With multiple *bakufu* still possible, the term had hardly developed beyond its original meaning.

The point is an important one. Not only do we wish to know how society referred to the government in Kamakura; we also need to identify what it was that later regimes harked back to. As the foregoing account suggests, these governments did not view themselves as successor *bakufu*. Rather, they were successor shogunates, since the authority attaching to that office became the touchstone of warrior rulership. For this reason, Ashikaga Takauji and Tokugawa Ieyasu sought and secured the title of shogun—and only later were credited (along with Yoritomo) for having established *bakufu*. In the case of the Ashikaga, references to Takauji as shogun appear as early as 1336—two years before he formally assumed that post.[19] Moreover, the *Baishōron*, a mid-century narrative favoring the Ashikaga, begins its account with a history of the office of shogun; whereas *bakufu* appears in a contemporary lexicon in its original Heian meaning,[20] and in the *Taiheiki* in reference to an ancient courtier.[21] The *Masu kagami* and numerous other Muromachi-era sources do not use the word at all,[22] and neither do we find it in the Ashikaga's legislation (the *tsuikahō*), extending to the sixteenth century. Like its Kamakura predecessor, then, the government of the Ashikaga was in no way a *bakufu*. What linked it to the preceding and following regimes was rather the office of shogun.

As central as the tradition of shogunal rule became, it should not be supposed that Yoritomo, the first shogun, deserves credit for this development. Yoritomo resigned the post in 1195 and died in 1199 without ever imagining that he had created either a *bakufu* or a shogunate. As we know, a shogunal succession was soon set into place as part of a Hōjō scheme to create an object for a regency.[23] The interesting point is that whereas the shogunal title meant little to Yoritomo but a great deal to the Hōjō, the name *bakufu* was simply unimportant to both. It remained unimportant for almost the duration of Japan's age of military houses.

This silence on one of Japanese history's best-known phenomena—the sequence of three Bakufu—is striking: the term itself was extraneous to the historical process. Not until almost the end of what we consider the Bakufu era did the word first appear as a synonym for shogunal government, in one of the great leaps, we might say, of the Tokugawa imagination.[24] Yet we should not forget that however much we may now take it for granted, this simple connection was in fact centuries in the making.

The Gempei War and Its Aftermath

Anachronisms of the type represented by the word *bakufu* are in fact common in Japanese history. For example, by inventing the compound Gempei (Genji vs. Heishi, or Minamoto vs. Taira), which might then be applied retrospectively to the fighting of 1180-85, some unknown writer or storyteller greatly simplified a more complex (and actually more significant) phenomenon. At the time, the fighting was referred to as the countrywide (*tenka*) turmoil,[25] or by those who could remember it, as the wars of Jishō and Bunji, after the year periods of that era.[26] The idea that the conflict was a life-and-death struggle between centuries-old rivals appears to be a product of postwar rationalizing, storytelling, or propaganda. In fact, the supposed warrior leagues were no more than combinations of convenience whose reality before Gempei was shadowy, infrequent, and shifting. It is for this reason that no scholar has been able to trace the so-called rise of the Taira and Minamoto very precisely, or comment with any confidence on their composition. What has passed for coherent history is little more than disparate images pulled taut, with unrelated warrior houses portrayed as subject to one or the other of the two clans.[27]

The problem is not merely with the concept of countrywide fighting combinations. There are also difficulties with the Taira and Minamoto leaderships. In the case of the Taira, historians have long emphasized the "meteoric rise" of a single figure, Kiyomori. Accounts were essentially biographical, and Taira organization was assumed but hardly discussed. As the war tales depicted it, the Taira chieftain possessed a vast warrior throng and equally vast estates: his superiority was obvious and overwhelming.[28] As we now know, the Taira grip over men and land was more modest than that, whereas Kiyomori himself remained dependent on the retired emperor's administrative structure virtually until the end.[29] The resulting narrative is leaner, yet closer to capturing the Taira essence. It is also more problematic: the story of the two decades before 1180 can never be told as satisfyingly as when Kiyomori's power was thought to have been all-encompassing. As historians have discovered, it is easier to explain a collapse from Olympian heights owing to "defects of character" than a success that never reached such levels in the first place.[30]

When we turn to the pre-1180 Minamoto we encounter a different kind of problem. Losers in 1160 when their leaders were executed or sent into exile, the Minamoto became all but invisible, at least to latter-day observers. In the absence of sources, all historians have simply hypothesized inaction. Thus the aspirations and activities of the man (Yoritomo) who would shortly become his era's greatest figure are forever lost from view. In 1180 information becomes plentiful, and historians, grateful for the bounty of the *Azuma kagami*, have simply used that narrative to tell the story of the Bakufu's founding. Yet this chronicle, for all its detail, provides no treatment of the pre-1180 background to war and contains little on the court and the Taira during the war. In spite of this silence, prewar tensions have provoked considerable speculation from Japanese historians, though the documentary base on which this treatment rests remains quite thin. We may look at the "before" and "after" of warrior houses and appreciate, from hindsight, a decision to join with Yoritomo. But the countrywide upheaval that fighting men spearheaded in the 1180's remains difficult to square with sources that do not detail intolerably oppressive conditions. Perhaps the lack of evidence of oppression helps explain why the outcome of the fighting was both more and less than we might have expected. Conditions were revolutionary, but not so revolutionary as to lead to some basic top-to-bottom reordering of society. At all events, despite the best efforts of scholars to explain this unprecedented explosion of violence, the sources do not permit a comprehensive examination.

A major problem, as indicated above, is that we know very little of the Taira opposition, either its leadership or its rank-and-file membership. The problem is compounded by the difficulty of distinguishing between main-force Taira armies and persons who assumed the

Taira label in order to enhance their prestige locally. We now know that most of the fighting that took place did not involve large armies but was played out locally among relatives and neighbors, or was otherwise directed against absentee civil landlords or their agents. This helps us see the war as an accumulation of small conflicts, but it also makes more elusive any corporate Taira existence. In fact, the Gempei story cannot be told from the point of view of the losers, and we need to ask why. Is the reason principally that sources are scarce?[31]

Another explanation is possible—and does accord with the data that survive. In this view, the absence of information on the Taira is mostly in the eye of the beholder, a result of misplaced expectations. The Taira can be seen as part of the larger court structure before 1180, and as increasingly estranged from it (as well as from the levers of governance) soon after that date.[32] In other words, the Taira hegemony was so brief that to decry its elusiveness is to exaggerate its importance. This being the case, it is less the "missing" Taira that should concern us than the traditional government of Kyoto: what emerged from the Gempei War was a dual polity embracing Kamakura *and* Kyoto. In this way, sources that are largely mute regarding the Taira can help refocus our inquiry on what was important in the 1180's—the ongoing central system of rule.

A major problem in understanding the Gempei War era is the falsification of the record—or our suspicion of it. Sometimes falsification is blatant—for example, a claim for Yoritomo's initial posting of *shugo* in 1180, when constabulary officers were still being called by another title.[33] In other instances, however, information of a potentially specious or anticipatory nature is not so readily detectable. A case in point is the *Azuma kagami*'s well-known description of a wartime government divided into discrete organs, a development that unfortunately cannot be corroborated.[34] In cases such as these, the historian must judge whether an omission in contemporary sources is more or less persuasive than a presence in a retrospective official account. The issue here is of particular importance, since our assessment of the early Bakufu is ultimately at stake. If we credit the official version, we are admitting an incipient bureaucracy. But if we emphasize Yoritomo's personal rule (as evidenced by his personally signed edicts), we are presenting the case for a patrimonial regime. Whichever, neither can be proved definitively.

The same kind of problem arises concerning other organizational features of the Bakufu. A good example is the well-known institution of *gokenin*. It was long assumed, owing to the *Azuma kagami*'s usage of the term from 1180, that the insignia of vassalage symbolic of the period-long Kamakura system was born simultaneously with the Minamoto movement itself. In this view, when Yoritomo initially sought to win the allegiance of the great warriors of the east, he combined his offer of a confirmation of those warriors' lands and offices with an invitation to join his vassal band and be called *gokenin*. The significance of the second part of this offer was that the word *gokenin* had never been used before and that Yoritomo's fusing of the honorific *go* to the familiar term *kenin* (houseman) must have reflected a plan to organize his fledgling government around the concept of an elite vassalage. Yoritomo's influence would spread outward in direct proportion to the warriors he was able to enroll as *gokenin*.

The *Azuma kagami*'s prolific usage of the term *gokenin* from its very earliest pages seemed to make the modern historian's task easy. Not only were scholars accorded an organizational principle that made obvious sense for an incipient warrior government, but the basis for Japan's early feudalism was also made clear. Here, certainly, the historian and his primary source were in complete harmony. Given this circumstance it required considerable courage for a leading specialist in Japan to question the historicity of the term *gokenin* for the entire Gempei War period. By examining surviving documents from 1180 to 1185, Yasuda Motohisa concluded that the term could not have been contemporaneous; the official account was a distortion.[35] In Yasuda's view, the *gokenin* concept belonged to a period of stabilization in which Yoritomo was seeking to limit, rather than to expand, the number of men eligible for his protection. It was thus an ex post facto rationalizing principle, not a springboard for some dramatic institutional growth. Yet if we grant Yasuda's point, are we not thereby admitting another lacuna? If not by holding out the prospect of some new, elite status, how then did Yoritomo secure his following? Elsewhere, I have attempted to answer this question by stressing the more tangible side of Yoritomo's program, in particular the offer of land and office confirmations as well as the prospect of new holdings.[36] But there is little denying that the earlier thesis emphasizing *gokenin* status remains simpler and much cleaner. The problem, in the end, is how to explain the 1180's without it.

Along with *gokenin*, the two other titles most closely associated with the 1180's are *jitō* and *shugo*. In the case of the former, our major problem centers on demographics: we have no adequate sense of the extent of the *jitō* phenomenon before or after 1185. How accurate is it to speak of a countrywide network soon after Gempei? Our difficulty with *shugo* likewise concerns numbers, though in this instance, not how many, but why, apparently, there were none at all. The authorization to establish a network of *shugo* appears in the *Azuma kagami*'s most famous entry, that of 1185/11/28, which scholars now reject as premature by five years.[37] The upshot of all this redating is to see the Kamakura accomplishment in new perspective. The innovations came not in a rush during the years of the Gempei War but more gradually—one is tempted to say, more logically. Known facts must defer to hypotheses derived in part from lacunae.

The Rise of the Bakufu Regents

As scholars have long been aware, virtually nothing is known of the pre-1180 Hōjō. No new information has turned up, nor is any likely to. Historians surmise that this absence of data means simply the absence of a history: the Hōjō were nonentities before Tokimasa (Yoritomo's father-in-law), their prestigious past a genealogical fraud.[38] Reflecting this lack of roots and a power base, the Hōjō advanced themselves largely by intrigue. The *Azuma kagami*, by emphasizing narrative, reinforces such a view; yet it also skirts questions of responsibility. Themselves guiltless, or so they are portrayed, the Hōjō rose at the expense of other houses who were repeatedly implicated in a succession of conspiracies.[39] One by-product of the *Azuma kagami*'s slanted version of these proceedings is a collective image for the Hōjō in which individual roles tend to be elusive. Thus we do not even know which Hōjō exercised dominant authority in Kamakura during the generation (1205-24) after Tokimasa. Was it his daughter Masako (Yoritomo's widow) or his son Yoshitoki? Some scholars posit a brother-sister tandem, others a stronger voice for one or the other.[40] At any rate, a sanitized narrative leaves unanswered critical questions on the rise of the Hōjō.

To illustrate the point, we need only contrast the *Azuma kagami*'s version of the Hōjō's assumption of the title of regent (*shikken*) with information drawn from other sources. The *Azuma kagami* says simply that Hōjō Tokimasa became *shikken* on 1203/10/9, at the same time that he became a director (*bettō*) of the shogun's chancellery (*mandokoro*). What could be more logical than the first Hōjō also functioning as the first regent? But just as the first shogun became the originator of the shogunal tradition only in retrospect, similar manipulation seems possible here. Specifically, there is no proof that a chancellery existed for the shogun Sanetomo until the latter came to be promoted to high court rank in 1209. Hence no *shikken* title could have been in place before that date, since *shikken* was the alternative name for a chancellery director (*bettō*).⁴¹ Such a discrepancy has broad implications. If Tokimasa was not *shikken* from 1203, how would a delayed regency have affected the process by which the Hōjō constructed their hegemony? It has always been assumed that the regent's title served as a springboard to power, not some later rationalization. At any rate, the problem we are left with is the familiar one: a basic institution with origins long well-known that are now in some doubt.

The Jōkyū War

A dominant theme of historians writing on the Kamakura age is the advance of warrior power at the expense of civilian institutions. Court-Bakufu relations are the most visible expression of this interaction, yet there is much in that story that remains difficult to explain. A case in point is the Jōkyū War of 1221—the era's most important incident affecting relations between the two capitals.

In dealing with this conflict we are reminded of the meagerness of information bearing on the years just before Gempei. The difference is that whereas the social and economic context is lacking for the period before 1180, the political context is what is lacking for 1221. Owing to the *Azuma kagami*'s uncharacteristic reticence for the two years prior to the Jōkyū outbreak, the storm warnings that should have been in the air are nowhere to be seen. Thus, with preparations and prospects on both sides mysterious, evaluating the responses is made more difficult. According to the *Azuma kagami*, word of the war declaration by the retired emperor, Go-Toba, reached Kamakura without warning; yet within a week's time an army of 190,000 men was marching on Kyoto! Limited information makes the efforts of both sides seem miracles of organization.⁴²

If origins tend to be obscure, legacies are often clearer, and so it is with the Jōkyū aftermath. Yet even here some major problems remain. In a famous datum of Japanese history, the *Azuma kagami* informs us that 3,000 estates were confiscated by the victorious Bakufu. Most survey histories duly cite this figure as proof of the dramatic tilt in Kamakura's favor that occurred in 1221. Yet only a tiny fraction of that number can be corroborated, and our sample of new *jitō* posts (the fate for most confiscated estates) is a mere 129.[43] It is on the basis of this smaller total that patterns must be identified, since to rely on the 3,000 figure is to use a number about which we know nothing at all. The enormous discrepancy here underlines once more what is permanently beyond our reach.

Looked at more positively, the 129 transfers constitute our principal source of information on "winners and losers" in the Jōkyū War. Since Kamakura sometimes identified persons being dispossessed, and in any event identified awarded locales, historians have been able to sharpen their understanding of who fought for the court. Though the smallness of the sample remains troubling, the results are nonetheless eye-opening: virtually every dispossession occurred in central and western Japan, with beneficiaries coming exclusively from the east. The basic character of the war thus appears to be defined by a clear east-west dichotomy. In fact, however, this perception is accurate only up to a point. We know that many westerners remained aloof from the fighting and that a substantial number of easterners joined the court. The treachery of the easterners is a major theme in the *Azuma kagami*, quite as we might expect: anti-Hōjō activities are regularly stressed in that chronicle. Yet the new information on rank and file in the west is more significant. The war can now be appreciated as a many-sided opportunity for warriors in diverse relationships with the Bakufu. This insight helps explain why a conflict lasting only a month was followed by a long period of confusion and restabilization.

The foregoing discussion assumes that the Jōkyū settlement centered on warriors—victors taking over from vanquished. This is a corrective of previous interpretations, which emphasized a dramatic curtailment of courtier authority, as if 3,000 proprietorships had changed hands. In fact, an unknown number of estates were transferred, but most of these remained within the orbit of traditional estate holders. Here is an outcome of the Jōkyū War that clearly warrants additional research. There were not only winners and losers among warriors, but winners and losers among the central elite.[44]

At the same time, the Jōkyū War was also the conflict it has always been portrayed as—a struggle between Kyoto and Kamakura. But if we eliminate the 3,000 proprietorships, where is the main axis of change? Certainly, a branch of the Bakufu was established in Kyoto and the defeated ex-emperor was sent into exile. But Kamakura also took steps to resuscitate central authority and to ensure continuity by permitting a new retired sovereign. The dual polity may thus have shifted in favor of the Bakufu, but Kamakura imposed few structural changes and did not rush to claim for itself vast new areas of responsibility. Thus the Jōkyū settlement remains difficult to grasp in precisely the area that always seemed obvious—the relationship between the two capitals. Perhaps this means that the image of a Kamakura rising and a Kyoto falling needs to be shifted to a multi-level view of society in which the most portentous changes were occurring at some remove from the elite decision makers.

Bakufu Governance

Historians have traditionally given much greater attention to the institutionally new Bakufu than to the older imperial court. If Kyoto was their focus of interest for the Heian period, Kamakura assumed this favored position for the period after 1180. Yet more may actually be understood about the Heian system of governance than about its Kamakura counterpart. With the exception of two interrelated activities—the Bakufu's *shugo* and *jitō* policies and its central judicial function—it is surprising how little we know about what we call Kamakura rule.

The Kantō

Kyoto's acknowledgment of Kamakura's governance over the east came in 1183. Yet, for lack of pertinent data, no scholar of the period has been able to explain adequately how this rulership was actually exercised.[45] In contrast to the thousands of judicial records that survive in archives all across Japan, there are few documents for the eastern provinces that are consonant with basic territorial administration. For the Bakufu's own base area, then, we are forced to acknowledge Kamakura's governance without being able really to describe it.

This predicament is admittedly difficult to understand. In an era of otherwise abundant writing, how can there have been effective government in the east without a corresponding written record? The *Azuma kagami* provides scattered hints but hardly solves the problem. It informs us that Yoritomo was formally invested as "proprietor" (*chigyōkokushu*) of nine provinces, a responsibility that traditionally embraced tax collection and security maintenance in the areas concerned.[46] We find no communications between Yoritomo and his nine governors, however, and only fragmentary revenue data. Moreover, four of the nine provinces were outside the Kantō proper, and one—Bungo—was in Kyushu! This raises new questions: did the Bakufu administer these far-flung areas identically with its Kantō proprietorships, and how did Kamakura distinguish between the latter and its larger jurisdictional sphere, the so-called Kantō *gobunkoku*? Ishii Susumu and other scholars have hazarded some answers to the second question, but they have been severely constricted by the meager sources. The particulars have not advanced much beyond the question of which provinces were involved.[47]

As noted above, the essence of Kamakura's governance in Japan was the adjudication of disputes, in particular disputes involving its own vassals. Logically, then, a more comprehensive justice should have prevailed in the Bakufu's own home area. In fact, the traces of such activity are very few. According to the *Azuma kagami*, a magistrate (*bugyōnin*) was dispatched to the *gobunkoku* on 1212/14/22 to judge (*seibai*) the petitions (*shūso*) of the common people (*minshō*). Unfortunately, we are not told why this occurred in 1212, what the new position was intended to replace, or how the unnamed occupant was expected to conduct his business. Thirty years later, the *Azuma kagami* refers to an expanded involvement, with magistrates now assigned to individual provinces to expedite commoner suits (*zōnin soshō*).[48] Though the delay here is noteworthy, nothing is actually explained. Seven years later still, Kamakura ordered functionaries within the provincial governments (*kuni no zōshiki*) to assist in the delivery of summonses.[49] This final item is suggestive because it highlights the true, indirect nature of governance in the east.

On this point, it is necessary to reevaluate the Bakufu's provincial governorships. The provinces best known to us are Sagami and Musashi, the Bakufu's home provinces. As such, Kamakura's leading figures, the Hōjō regent (*shikken*) and cosigner (*rensho*), normally held their governorships. Although consistently identified by these titles,[50] they nevertheless issued no governors' edicts, and did not in other ways emulate their counterparts elsewhere.[51] Even so, the Bakufu clearly dominated in the region of its own capital.[52] Not only was it capable of ruling there quite apart from its governorships, but it was capable of ruling in nearby provinces apart from the governorships of others. In neighboring Hitachi, for example, the Bakufu, though not in control of the governorship, insinuated itself into the resident headquarters by means of the tie of vassalage.[53] Thus Kamakura could exercise hegemony informally, as we see in a pair of judicial edicts from 1239 and 1244. Both were issued in explicit conformity with Bakufu law (Kantō *goshikijō*), but both were also handed down by provincial authorities.[54]

The foregoing account suggests that governance in Hitachi might readily bypass the governor. To that extent a provincial headquarters had been integrated into a regional system. This result was no less than what Kamakura had been seeking since 1180: to break the link connecting eastern officials to absentee civil heads.[55] The summit of a hierarchy would thus have been separated from its operational middle. But Kamakura did not stop there. It received governorships ultimately to eschew them. Valuable as honoraria, they were superseded in practice by officer levels more amenable to control from Kamakura.[56] At least in part, then, Kamakura's inactive governorships become less anomalous in this interpretation. Much remains unclear, of course, since government by influence rather than by command leaves fewer clues: in the east, as elsewhere, Kamakura's written directives went mostly to *shugo* and *jitō*. But the picture, as we saw, is more complex than that. It includes governorships, which were not much used, but also governors' subordinates (*zaichōkanjin*), who became indispensable.

Kamakura Finances

Parallel to the question of how Kamakura administered the east is that of how it supported itself. If Kamakura was dependent on vassals for its political influence, to what extent was it dependent on them economically? Specifically, why did it fail to levy a land tax on the members of its own countrywide band? As is well known, the major reason is that vassals held their land rights on estates generally owned by absentee civil proprietors. This meant that rents (taxes) were directed to Kyoto, not to Kamakura. But there is a second reason, one more specific to the age: the thirteenth century was an era of tax revolt by warriors against their traditional landlords.[57] For the Bakufu to have added to the burden on landholdings would have been to contribute to this unrest—and ultimately to have endangered itself. In such a climate Kamakura devised a substitute system of levies based on an irregular corvée (*onkuji*). We know the form that these dues took (horse and manpower levies, construction materials, and so on) and have substantial data on the division of the responsibility within vassal families.[58] But the frequency and overall burdensomeness of the levies, the process by which vassals were apprised of obligations, the machinery for collecting and storing *onkuji*, and the modes of distribution of received resources are all questions for which answers remain elusive. We know far more of what vassals owed their tenurial lords than of what they owed Kamakura.[59]

A second source of income about which we know even less than we do about *onkuji* is the vast public landholdings of the east that were theoretically subject to Kamakura's taxation. Many scholars have noted that the *mandokoro* was the overall financial organ of the Bakufu, but how did it, or any other agency, collect and distribute the basic land tax that was ostensibly drawn from Kamakura's governor-controlled provinces?[60] It is apropos of the earlier discussion that we are able to gain some notion of Kyoto's exploitation of *its* governor-controlled public lands and yet are not able to do the same for Kamakura's. Since some vassals' holdings were obviously located within such provincial areas, we can only wonder why there are almost no tax records.

A third source of support for the Bakufu was its portfolio of private estates, called Kantō *goryō*. We know that these holdings were widely scattered (that is, they were not based exclusively in the Kantō)[61] and that Kamakura's religious institutions and vassals were granted a liberal range of officerships and perquisites from them.[62] What is much less clear is how extensive these estate holdings were, how they were administered economically, and how the shogun, who was their proprietor, profited from their possession.[63] Kuroda Toshio has averred that the Kamakura Bakufu was fully a member of the estate-owning class known collectively as *kenmon seika*. Yet the designation seems not quite apt, since the term, though contemporaneous, was never applied to Kamakura.[64] In any event, if the Bakufu's administration of the east is poorly documented, the same is true of Kamakura's economy.

But why should this be so? We know that successful governments must safeguard their sources of revenue.[65] Yet in the case of the Kamakura Bakufu, the sources of income seem never to have been molded into anything coherent; Kamakura had no identifiable economic policy.[66] It drew support from a corvée that was irregular, from estate lands that were scattered, and from public fields that were also disparate;[67] and for none of these sources do we have more than the most fragmentary of data. Perhaps this failure to discover a coherent system suggests that our search has been too concentrated, that the economy of Kamakura must be reinterpreted as the economies of its constituencies. In this regard, data abound on the wealth of the Hōjō and on the income of vassals and religious institutions, if not, inexplicably, on that of the shogun.[68] The point, at any rate, is that the Bakufu provided few services requiring a central treasury: the dispensing of justice, the administering of its capital city, and the compensating of its vassalage were all, in their separate ways, largely self-supporting. Thus litigants and city dwellers owed court and residency costs, and traditional central estate holders were obliged to absorb *jitō*. Yet even at that, our explanation is inadequate, for Kamakura did support a bureaucracy with obvious attendant costs.[69] Perhaps the best we can say is that the economy of Kamakura will remain unapproachable if we insist on locating it in some centralized system.

Central and Local Organization

As just indicated, uncertainty over revenues is paralleled by uncertainty over governmental operations. Much of the problem here has in fact little to do with sources. As Satō Shin'ichi has suggested, the Kamakura Bakufu was not organized in the way modern governments are—that is, with discrete agencies responsible for clearly identified activities. Overlapping competencies were standard, with distinctions made by geographical or status criteria rather than by criteria of content.[70] Moreover, though major rationalizing impulses were evident late in the period, the organizational scheme regularly outpaced real change. In other words, the chart of government became more complex, but it remained mostly prescriptive. To cite one example, suits over movables and capital crimes were ultimately accorded places of their own in Kamakura's system. Yet, despite organizational parity with land suits, only a handful of examples survive.[71] This being the case, we must choose between basing our account on Kamakura's own posturings about itself or admitting that the advances were less dramatic than they appear. Practice and principle are of course equally objects of historical inquiry. Yet without some awareness of the gross imbalance between land and non-land matters, the latter, appearing as a new category, might be unduly emphasized. The Kamakura Bakufu's scope of operations, and hence its character as a government, could be misrepresented.

It follows that the only activities about which we do have authoritative knowledge are those so identified by historians a long time ago. The preoccupation with land disputes, so richly documented from beginning to end, holds the first position, followed by the administration of the systems of *shugo* and *jitō*. Yet even in regard to the twin vassal networks, there are naturally questions that remain. This is especially so for the *shugo*, who were far less prominent than the *jitō*. One topic that has not been treated—and that causes us to look once again at provincial governorships—is the extent of interaction between *shugo* and civil governors. Since both shared provincial policing powers (and since *shugo* authority was carved from what had once been exclusively the governor's jurisdiction), conflict between the two should have been constant. Yet compared with the frequency of complaints by estate owners against *shugo*, grievances by governors scarcely exist.[72] Two possible explanations come to mind. In some provinces where the *shugo*'s presence is scarcely mentioned, such as Bizen, the civil governor remained vigorous.[73] By contrast, in Kyushu and elsewhere, the *shugo*'s dominance is unmistakable. This suggests that a vibrant governorship (as in parts of central Japan) might foreclose major inroads by a *shugo*, and conversely, that a shadow governorship was tantamount to a defaulted authority. In both instances, interaction was minimal because the two officers were unequal. Although there are obviously still major problems of interpretation here, some attempt to explain a troubling discrepancy seems necessary. Why do we find abundant evidence of *shugo* incursions against *shōen*, and scant indication of incursions against provincial lands? Where is the confrontation between governor and *shugo* that logically should have been taking place?

Conclusions

Much has been written on Kamakura's judicial system and on *shugo* and *jitō*. Other topics that have received major attention are the establishment of the regime, the Jōkyū and Mongol episodes, warrior inheritance practices, and most recently, the nature of Hōjō rule. Yet fundamental questions such as the character of the Bakufu as an administrative organization, the financial structure of the regime, and Kamakura's governance over the Kantō remain largely untreated. These omissions are due not to oversight but to meager sources. Accordingly, we must ask why the sources are so meager and whether, from those available to us, we have derived an accurate picture of Japan's first warrior government.

The essential correctness of our portrait is explainable by Kamakura's indirect rule. Countrywide, the point of reference is the era's dual polity. That is, the kinds of information that are lacking for Kamakura are in fact often compensated for by records centering on Kyoto. Thus we know a good deal about the flow of taxes to Kyoto from the countryside, and about the linkages between center and periphery that facilitated government from above. Even granting that Kyoto now consulted Kamakura on certain key issues and conveyed as many grievances as it resolved, most of the traditional order remained intact.[74] By contrast, the Bakufu as a government seems curiously limited, its territorial dimension attenuated. Yet Kamakura's role might still be fundamental in its capacity as the country's principal peacemaker. In an era of relative stability, arbitrating disputes was at least as important as policing them, and the resulting judicial authority became the Bakufu's chief contribution to the age. It might even be argued that justice was what now held the society together. What Kamakura gave up in breadth it therefore made up in depth. With its resources taxed to the limit, it eschewed the complementary burdens of government, which remained mostly within the framework of traditional, Kyoto-centered authority. A study of Kamakura and Kyoto in tandem, then, provides a much clearer view of Japan's emerging medieval polity.

The implications of this interpretation are far-reaching. To the degree that Kamakura's gains were less broad-based than previously thought, the same would be true of Kyoto's losses. And in this case, the Kemmu Restoration, following Kamakura's collapse, would be less anomalous than it has always seemed, and the Muromachi Bakufu's slow progress at first that much more comprehensible.[75] At any rate, by seeking to understand why anticipated developments sometimes cannot be corroborated in the sources, we open up new approaches and provide fresh insights. Short of that, we at least take the measure of a field and assist in setting realistic research goals.

The Kamakura Bakufu
and Its Officials

ANDREW GOBLE

If the Kamakura Bakufu had been solely a military command—a "tent government" with a minimal administrative apparatus—we would have little difficulty seeing how it might remain in power for some decades. But though the Bakufu was at first little more than the headquarters of an exile from Kyoto's aristocratic society, it had advanced considerably beyond that level by the end of the twelfth century. We see the beginnings of a more sophisticated administration whose support in society rested on the quality of its judicial operations. As the period progressed, further improvements in judicial procedure and the organs handling suits gave the Bakufu a reputation for efficiency and impartiality.[1]

Granted that the Bakufu relied ultimately on the threat of military force to maintain its preeminence, force could not be employed indiscriminately, given the jurisdictional complexity of early medieval Japan. All segments of society operated within a framework of rights and tenure whose maintenance depended on civil administration. The Hōjō's role in giving the Bakufu an appropriate governing philosophy has long been recognized. What has been less recognized is that putting this philosophy into operation required a stable and experienced body of officials sufficiently distinct from warrior society to be regarded as essentially impartial administrators.

It is well known that in the mid-1180's an influx of scholar-bureaucrats from Kyoto played a critical role in setting up the Bakufu's major administrative organs. It is less well known that the recruitment of officials continued throughout the Kamakura period. A large proportion of the officials came from obscure provincial warrior families and served the Bakufu for the remainder of the period. Such was their competence in all aspects of administration that many of them served both the brief regime of Go-Daigo and the subsequent Muromachi Bakufu.[2]

Not surprisingly, the Kamakura Bakufu's administration changed in size and complexity during the century and a half of its existence. Since officials were an integral part of these changes, a study of their origins and recruitment, the way they were rewarded, and the techniques employed to ensure their competence can tell us much about the Bakufu as a governmental institution.

The Recruitment and Placement of Officials

Even though Yoritomo had established his headquarters in Kamakura by the end of 1180, the eventual success of his undertaking was by no means assured.[3] Undeveloped in its early stage, his administration was concerned with the minimal requirements of controlling the Kantō warrior class and issuing edicts in Yoritomo's name. The latter function was supervised by the *kumonjo*, the Bakufu's first administrative organ.

Recruitment to the *kumonjo* appears to have been haphazard. Despite the fact that the organs of provincial administration in the Kantō came under Yoritomo's sway, there is little evidence that these were a major source of officials. We do have some examples in which provincial headquarters (*kokuga*) officials found their way into service in Kamakura, but by and large the local administration was left intact. Yoritomo worked through it rather than recruited from it.[4] As a result, officials in the early administration came from diverse backgrounds. Some appear to have served Yoritomo while he was in exile, whereas others were co-opted from among the retainers of his vassals.[5] In short, Yoritomo was attempting to build up his own administration independent of any existing organization. His major criteria for recruitment, accordingly, were loyalty and personal dependence. These qualities in the early Bakufu have been noted in the case of Yoritomo's personal staff (*zōshiki*), and it is revealing that even at this early stage efforts to bring members of major warrior families into the Bakufu's administrative organs were eschewed.

By 1184, when it was apparent to Yoritomo that his administration was established, he began to seek the services of professional scholars and bureaucrats from Kyoto. By late 1184 the four most prominent officials of the early Kamakura Bakufu had begun their task of establishing a permanent institution designed to oversee the government of eastern Japan. These four people—Ōe Hiromoto, Miyoshi Yasunobu, Nakahara Chikayoshi, and Nikaidō Yukimasa—all came with impressive credentials. All save Yukimasa had had considerable experience as middle-level administrators in the imperial government or in the households of prominent aristocratic families.[6] Employment in Kamakura gave these men an opportunity to draw on talents that probably would have had few outlets in Kyoto. Yet there were many people in Kyoto like these four. Why were they the particular ones to be chosen?

By and large, all were chosen because of their close links to Yoritomo or to those trusted by him.[7] Yasunobu's mother had been Yoritomo's wet nurse some decades earlier, and while Yoritomo was in exile after 1159 Yasunobu supplied him with thrice-monthly reports on affairs in Kyoto. It was Yasunobu's brother Yasukiyo who brought Prince Mochihito's call for an anti-Taira uprising to Yoritomo in 1180. Chikayoshi's connection appears to have derived from his adoption by Yoritomo's father, Yoshitomo, some decades before. His loyalty to Yoritomo (and his antipathy for the Taira) evidently ran deep.[8] Hiromoto was influenced both by his adoption into Chikayoshi's family and by his service for Kujō Kanezane, an ally of Yoritomo and an enemy of the Taira. Yukimasa's early history is somewhat obscure. It is known that his exiled father married into the Atsuda Shrine family, with which Yoritomo's branch of the Minamoto was intimately connected, so it is likely that this family link, and a mutual antipathy toward Kyoto, gave Yukimasa reason enough for serving Yoritomo.[9] Such powerful, personal links, and the extent to which these people had irrevocably linked their fortunes to that of the Bakufu, largely explain the dedication with which they served the Bakufu even after Yoritomo's death.

Equally important, they recruited their families into Bakufu service. Although the result was not always successful (the sons of Hiromoto caused the Bakufu and the Hōjō much trouble in the first decades of the thirteenth century), these four men and their descendants formed the core of Kamakura Bakufu administration, occupying virtually all top-level administrative posts. The major influx of relatives appears to have begun shortly after Yoritomo's first trip to Kyoto in 1190, as listings of personnel after this date reveal. Family influence is particularly noticeable in the *monchūjo* (board of inquiry), over which the Miyoshi began to establish their hereditary control as early as 1194.[10] In addition, families of hereditary legal scholars such as the Kiyowara and other branches of the Nakahara family begin to appear in our sources at this point in fairly important administrative positions. The Bakufu had thus begun to acquire an hereditary officialdom that had little in common with the warrior society it served. This social isolation could only have reinforced the officials' identification with the Bakufu as an institution.

The *monchūjo*'s highest post, that of *shitsuji*, required specialized skills that members of the warrior class did not possess. This, and the necessity of avoiding overt manipulation of the judicial process, ensured that the hereditary position of the Miyoshi would never be seriously questioned.[11] In the case of the *mandokoro*, or chancellery, the situation was complicated by the fact that until the 1220's its high-level posts reflected the political struggles within the Bakufu.[12] When the Hōjō finally managed to establish their own power independent of the *mandokoro*, the functional head of that agency became a bureaucrat. This headship (also called *shitsuji*) was established in 1218 under the aegis of the Nikaidō family, who had risen with the Hōjō.[13] Significantly, it was given to the branch of the Nikaidō family that had retained its civilian status, the other branch having come to be recognized as a warrior one.[14] By the beginning of Yasutoki's regency in 1224, then, all the Bakufu's administrative organs were in the hands of bureaucratic families that had been in Bakufu service for forty years. The stability these officials had given the Bakufu in a period of unsettled political leadership was now fully institutionalized.

Descendants of the Kyoto group of families served the Bakufu for the remainder of the Kamakura period. Some were appointed officials of the *hyōjōshū* (board of councillors) and *hikitsukeshū* (board of coadjutors) after these organs were established in 1225 and 1249. Most, however, provided the Bakufu with a considerable number of its middle-level officials. Given the family and educational traditions of this group, the Bakufu was able to rely throughout on a core group of literate and experienced administrators. Undoubtedly their presence gave the regime a sense of continuity and collective memory that it might not have been able to achieve by local recruitment.

The Bakufu's dependence on officials originally of Kyoto background and their monopoly of key administrative posts signified a clear stratification within the Bakufu bureaucracy. Yet the Bakufu did not rely on this Kyoto group exclusively. Some officials recruited from the Kantō during the early years continued to serve into the 1230's, though many had been displaced during the late 1180's and 1190's. We have information on only a few of these people, such as Koremune Tadahisa, Sakanoue Akisada, and Sanekage (so obscure that we do not know his family name). Most references associate them with the *mandokoro*, usually dealing with taxation and land registration.[15] Their presence suggests yet another thread of continuity within the Bakufu.

By the mid-1230's this second group of officials, not of Kyoto background, disappears. Since there is no evidence that any of their descendants subsequently served as Bakufu officials, we are confronted with a discontinuity. Yet what we find is a rather large-scale, ongoing recruitment program designed to supply the Bakufu with a greater number of middle-level officials. Although the Bakufu could always rely on the Kyoto group to provide additional officials, the numbers available in any given generation were limited, and the Bakufu seems not to have sought new people from Kyoto.[16] Instead, the majority of this new influx came, like its predecessors, from mostly obscure Kantō warrior families.

The recruitment program may have been related to overall Bakufu expansion accompanying the establishment of the *hyōjōshū* in 1225. The appearance of persons listed as *hikitsukeshū* scribes, and the known age of one of them, provide evidence for this view.[17] Most significantly for the Bakufu, and for the Bakufu relationship with warrior society, the scribes in question cannot be identified as coming from families that had any previous role in the Bakufu's central administration, nor were they Hōjō retainers or associated with other major warrior families. Their status as outsiders thus effectively precluded any significant involvement in Bakufu politics. They could be regarded (as, in fact, they served) as bureaucratic functionaries posing no threat to the Bakufu itself. Moreover, as bureaucratic functionaries, they were probably insulated from the ambitions of warrior society in general.

Many of those recruited during this period founded houses of hereditary officials. Of these families, we have the most information on the Akashi, whose involvement in Bakufu administration can be traced from 1245 through at least 1313.[18] Most references connect the Akashi with judicial administration, though some members also served in the *samurai dokoro* (board of retainers).[19] There is little doubt that they were both competent and trusted, for we find the Akashi given prominent roles in such major programs as setting up the Bakufu's regional headquarters in Kyushu in the wake of the Mongol invasions, and in 1313 being part of the Bakufu's attempt to reinvigorate traditional sources of authority in Kyushu through the shrine-restoration policy.[20] Our sources also enable us to trace some careers over two decades, an indication that even single references to officials from such families do not necessarily signify merely casual association with the Bakufu. Although we have less information on another family, the Osada, we can trace them from 1245 through 1284, and they may have continued in Bakufu service even after that date.[21]

An interesting variation on the policy of recruiting officials from warrior families is the case of the Minayoshi. This family had entered Bakufu, specifically shogunal, service as early as 1222 as *yin-yang* (*ommyō*), or divination, specialists. The second son was recruited as a scribe in the early 1240's, was appointed a *hikitsukeshū* scribe in 1251, and was still active in 1265, when a Bakufu decree directed his descendants to serve hereditarily in that capacity. In fact, we do find that the family served as directed. Individuals appear in sources right until the Bakufu's demise, with at least one of the family being killed in the attendant fighting.[22] Others survived to serve with the Muromachi Bakufu.

Information on several other families, who begin to appear in our sources around 1260, suggests that the Bakufu's recruitment program was an ongoing one. The Shimada first appear in 1261 with appointments as *hikitsukeshū* scribes, and our last Kamakura period reference to them dates from 1325.[23] We have evidence for one Shimada, Yukikane, documenting a career that spanned nearly 35 years.[24] The Saitō family, one of whose members died gloriously defending Rokuhara in 1333,[25] is perhaps the most impressive of the new bureaucratic families.[26] We note individuals serving in Rokuhara, Kamakura, and Kyushu, two of whom worked for the Bakufu for over 30 years.[27] This family served during the final third of the Kamakura period and thus provides our clearest evidence of an ongoing recruitment program. Saitō Yūjō, perhaps its best-known member, was the author of a commentary, the earliest one surviving, on the *Goseibai shikimoku*.[28] Yūjō's commentary, brief as it is, has significance for our present purposes because it suggests that the Bakufu's pool of administrative talent was broader than we might at first have imagined. Ability within the Bakufu's administrative corps was hardly limited to scions of the Kyoto group.

Descendants of the Kyoto group and of locally recruited middle-level officials are not the only types of people for whom we have information. Numerous references to single members of families appear in our sources as well.[29] These people appear frequently as *monchūjo* officials and scribes. They have diverse backgrounds, ranging from families with service originally as shogunal attendants, to less fortunate members of the Kyoto group, to people we would not expect to have any connection whatsoever with the Bakufu. But as with all Bakufu officials, they were usually from social groups on the fringes of Kantō warrior society. A prime example is one Sukemura, born into a family of hereditary cloth dyers in Kazusa Province, who was active in the Bakufu's judicial administration from at least 1241 to 1254.[30] Though continuity of service within the Bakufu was fairly standard, becoming an official did not always mean a lifetime career. Dismissals and resignations sometimes occurred.[31]

At all events, the evidence clearly indicates that the Kamakura Bakufu relied heavily on a core group of hereditary families. Since we do not know the total number of persons who worked for the Bakufu, we cannot claim that all posts were hereditary. But perhaps a majority were. Most important for the Bakufu, these hereditary officials provided Kamakura with a collective memory of techniques and procedures, as well as a degree of loyalty. This loyalty was not directed solely to the Hōjō, but more impersonally to the Bakufu as an institution. Such loyalty, strongly reinforced as it was by the social isolation of officials from groups outside the Bakufu, naturally required economic compensation.

Officials and Their Landholdings

During the Kamakura period the Bakufu's main source of wealth continued to be land and the income from it.[32] Confiscations made Kamakura one of the country's leading proprietors,[33] and Bakufu holdings, known collectively as the Kantō *goryō*, were the source from which it supported itself, made commendations to religious bodies, and rewarded some vassals. The Kantō *goryō* also included

the public lands of whole provinces. Thus we find references to taxation collection and financial inspection,[34] tax ships,[35] the compilation
of provincial land registers,[36] and provinces held by the Hōjō as "al-
lotment" areas (*bunkoku*).[37] The provinces of Musashi, Sagami,
Wakasa, and Echigo figure prominently in our sources, so they may
well have constituted a particular source of Bakufu funds. Overall
management of Kamakura's finances lay in the hands of the *mandokoro*, which was represented in the provinces by local agents (*kuni
zōshiki*).[38] In addition, the Bakufu held various estate positions from
which it might draw income. Certainly many were lucrative enough
for the shogunal retinue to be supported in some style even after the
Hōjō began to appropriate Bakufu lands for themselves.

The question of how the Bakufu supported its officials remains.
Interestingly, Kamakura does not appear to have relied on a system
of office lands. There are some instances of officials being awarded
holdings while they were in office, such as the *jitō* post in Echizen
Province's Ushigahara estate, held successively by Nikaidō Yukihisa
and his son Yukimitsu.[39] But it was much more common for posts
over land to become hereditary, even if the original reward was given
specifically for a term in office or for a particular purpose, as with
Mōri Tokichika.[40] Or, for example, Nakahara Morokazu, appointed
to the *hyōjōshū* in 1225, was awarded a *jitō* post, which he passed to
a son not known to have served the Bakufu, and which was subsequently transmitted in his line.[41] Another post gained by Morokazu
was passed to another line of descendants that rose to high rank in
the Bakufu and that, in common with other bureaucratic families
(described below), gained other holdings independent of their ances-
tor's award.[42] In another case, a holding confiscated in the aftermath
of the Jōkyū War provided support for the *monchūjo* official Gyōnin,
was passed to the *hikitsukeshū* scribe and later *hyōjōshū* member
Satō Naritsura, and was then freely bequeathed by him to his widow
and children.[43] A further example concerns Miyoshi Yasukiyo,
awarded an *azukari dokoro* (custodial office) post in 1186. It subsequently remained in the hands of female descendants before passing
into the hands of the son of one and then out of the family entirely.[44]
In other words, though holdings were granted to officials to support
them while in service, grants were freely alienable by the family even
after the official ceased to serve and irrespective of whether any sons
succeeded him in official service.

The grants noted above were all made soon after the person had entered Bakufu service. That this was a conscious policy of the Bakufu is revealed by other cases. In 1241 the *yin-yang* scholar Fumimoto was granted land rights, income from which was soon supporting his son Minayoshi Fumiyuki, who took his family name from the area in question and entered Bakufu service around that time.[45] Similarly, the Yasutomi family, which began providing scribes around 1260, was awarded a *jitō* post between 1254 and 1265.[46]

Though our evidence is limited, it does appear likely that some who served in Kamakura in nonadministrative capacities were supported by resources deriving from other than personal land rights. For example, a Bakufu decree of 1276 complained that *yin-yang* scholars and physicians were coming to hold warrior lands by being adopted into warrior families. The practice was ordered stopped.[47] The implication of this decree is that learned men were regularly supported by stipend. It also expresses the status distinction between warriors and non-warriors that Bakufu policy maintained.

Although the data on compensation are consistent, they are also unmistakably sparse. For some families, such as the Kiyowara, who provided members for the *hyōjōshū*, I have been unable to find any references at all. But fortunately substantial information survives for the descendants of three early officials, Ōe Hiromoto, Miyoshi Yasunobu, and Nikaidō Yukimasa.

During his forty-year career in the Bakufu, Ōe Hiromoto was awarded (mostly by Yoritomo) at least seventeen holdings in twelve provinces.[48] This was a substantial bloc of land rights, but it is not clear what became of them after his death in 1225. For only five of the total do we have any evidence that Hiromoto's descendants succeeded to them, and in only two cases is it apparent that the recipient subsequently served as a Bakufu official.

Several of Hiromoto's sons did hold important Bakufu posts, but the land rights gained by their lines were not especially extensive. Tadanari, who was dismissed from the *hyōjōshū* in 1247 and whose own descendants later served at Rokuhara, appears to have been granted two holdings apart from those received from his father.[49] The Mōri family, founded by Suemitsu, succeeded to two of Hiromoto's land rights, with Suemitsu holding one of these; the latter received as well an independent tenure in Tōtōmi Province, and a possible second in Higo Province, but all of these were confiscated after Suemitsu's execution in 1247 for anti-Hōjō activity.[50] Suemitsu's son Tsunemitsu was nevertheless confirmed in two holdings (one received from Hiromoto), since he had not been implicated with his father. He and his descendants, who appear to have served at Rokuhara, went on to found one of the most powerful families of the Sengoku period, a noteworthy achievement for a family of onetime scholars.[51] Chikahiro, the Jōkyū War rebel, held tenures independently of his father, and in fact founded the Sagae branch with holdings in Dewa Province.[52] Another line, from a nephew who became an adopted son of Hiromoto, served at Rokuhara and held land rights that cannot be connected to Hiromoto.[53] The fact that one of Hiromoto's daughters was bequeathed tenures in five provinces suggests that the father's holdings were not tied to Bakufu service.[54]

The Nagai branch of the family, descended from Tokihiro, was the last of Hiromoto's sons to arrive in Kamakura. This was in 1218, and he remained in the eastern capital until his death in 1262 at the age of 98. Although he did not receive any lands from Hiromoto, his holdings came to include the *jitō* post of Nagai estate in Dewa Province, and similar posts in Akanabe estate in Mino Province and Hiji *ho* in Bingo Province. Both of the latter were awarded in the early 1220's, but apparently were not Jōkyū War rewards.[55] The Akanabe holding was subsequently rotated among the three branches of the Nagai for the remainder of the period.[56]

These branches received other land rights as well, and the pattern of acquisition is highly revealing. Of the known total of fourteen holdings, only one (apart from Nagai estate) was received by the branch serving in Kamakura, and only in 1272 through the chance dispossession of a Kamakura vassal.[57] In Rokuhara, the line descending from Yasushige provided five *hyōjōshū* officials, while that descending from Yasumochi provided only one (Yasumochi himself). Nevertheless, Yasushige's line is known to have possessed but two holdings plus a residence in Kyoto,[58] whereas Yasumochi's had at least ten holdings plus a residence in Kamakura.[59] The disparities here seem too great to be merely accidental; they suggest an inverse relationship between official service in the Bakufu and the acquisition of land rights.

A similar pattern is discernible in the case of Miyoshi Yasunobu and the families descended from his sons. The only known holding of Yasunobu was the *jitō* post to the productive Kōyasan estate of Ōta in Bingo Province. Yasunobu devised this to two sons, Yasutsugu and Yasutsura,[60] both of whom managed to expand their holdings. The line of Yasutsugu took up residence on Ōta estate and appears to have transformed itself into a warrior family, taking part in punitive expeditions related to the Jōkyū War and being awarded an additional estate post for this service. Yasutsura's line remained in Kamakura, providing *monchūjo* and *hyōjōshū* officials, though it also profited from the Jōkyū War and later acquired at least one other holding.[61]

In contrast to these lines, the Machino line, descended from Yasutoshi, was designated to succeed to Yasunobu's post of *monchūjo shitsuji*. It is significant that the only holding known to have been gained in this period by this family was acquired after the Jōkyū War (and after Yasunobu's death) and was in no way associated with Yasunobu himself.[62] This lack of connection may indicate a degree of disapproval by the Hōjō of its top administrators' enjoying too close a relationship with the inherited holdings of their families. The fact that in 1247 the Machino line was removed after two generations as *shitsuji* in deference to the Ōta line does not negate this view, for the change was the result of political misfortune and not a policy adjustment. Yasunobu's final son, Yukinori, established the Yano family. The only reference to their holdings is a post-Kamakura one referring to rights in Musashi Province. The date of acquisition is unknown, but was almost certainly during the Kamakura period.[63]

A final case study concerns the Nikaidō family. Here we see most clearly the Bakufu's attitude toward rewarding officials in the post-Yoritomo era. An undated register of Nikaidō property rights and a testament of 1241 have sometimes been offered as proof of the rising fortunes of the Nikaidō clan during the Kamakura period. But neither of these documents (nor other papers in the Nikaidō collection as a whole) supports such a claim.[64] All these records refer only to the holdings of one branch of the family, that descending from Yukimasa's son Yukimura. None refers to the land rights of the line descended from Yukimasa's other son, Yukimitsu.

Although Yukimasa himself arrived in Kamakura in 1184, the only holding we can definitely associate with him was a tenure in Echizen Province's Ushigahara estate. His son Yukimitsu succeeded him to that post, but it was subsequently transferred away.[65] For the remainder of the period we have data from non-Nikaidō sources on only six, perhaps seven, tenures being acquired by Yukimitsu's heirs.[66] In marked contrast, Yukimura and his descendants managed to receive 22, possibly 23, rights in land over the same period.[67] This difference might be even more striking if we could discover what happened to the 52 holdings entrusted by the Bakufu to Yukimura in 1224.[68]

Once again, the disparity is too great to attribute to random causes. The total number of offspring in the two lines was approximately the same, and both lines provided the Bakufu with officials at all levels for the entire era. The reasons for the difference are nevertheless apparent. As noted earlier, in 1218 Yukimitsu was appointed to the post of *mandokoro shitsuji*, the same year in which Yukimura was appointed to the *samurai dokoro* and in which one of Yukimura's sons, Motoyuki, received a shogunal decree directing that his line henceforth be a warrior one.[69] All three persons had received rewards after the Wada Rebellion of 1213, but Yukimitsu had been associated with the *mandokoro* from as early as 1194.[70] Thus it was clear from very early on that Yukimitsu's line would serve at the top level of the *mandokoro*. This need not necessarily have meant that Yukimura or his descendants would become warriors, but once having done so they were able to use this status to expand their holdings, a course not open to Yukimitsu or his descendants. Obviously the distinction between warriors and bureaucrats held, even though representatives of both types might provide officials for the Bakufu.

The examples cited above give us some idea of Kamakura's policy toward the land tenures of its officials. As is well known, Yoritomo was extremely generous to those who were loyal to him and whose loyalty he recognized (these were not the same thing). His generosity enabled him to tie officials, as well as others, personally to himself. The post-Yoritomo Bakufu, particularly the post-Jōkyū regime under the Hōjō, adopted a somewhat different policy. Purely administrative officials who succeeded to the top posts in the *mandokoro* and the *monchūjo* were granted tenures that were obviously new benefices. That is, these holdings were not associated with the existing holdings of their respective families. This policy did not mean that other branches were divested of tenures, and neither did it mean that the post-Jōkyū awards were granted only for the life terms of their holders. In this respect, tenure was held in the same way as that of any other recipient of a Bakufu grant. The difference was that officials were not generally permitted to gather a large number of tenures, a clear change from Yoritomo's day. The only apparent exceptions are the military branch of the Nikaidō family and a single branch of the Nagai.[71]

It may be asked whether the volume of holdings is itself a valid indication of income and economic position. Miyoshi Yasunobu, for example, gained only one holding, but it was a very rich one. The only reference to income I have encountered notes that Mōri Toki-chika received 3,100 *kanmon* from three holdings.[72] Perhaps the safest generalization is that though some officials had fewer tenures than others, this did not necessarily mean that they suffered economically. Differences in social status may have narrowed the gap between income and responsibilities, and there may have been hidden perquisites attached to certain positions. Only one point seems certain: officials, particularly in Kamakura, were not permitted to expand their landed holdings to any marked degree.

Bakufu Techniques for Promoting Efficiency

As is well known, the gradual expansion of Kamakura's role in adjudicating disputes brought ever greater pressures on the Bakufu administration.[73] References from 1216, 1233, and 1259—the last two coming after severe countrywide crop failures and famines—allude, for example, to recent upsurges and backlogs in cases.[74] In 1259 the Bakufu directed Rokuhara not to forward cases to Kamakura unless they were of major importance, since it would take "months and years" to process all documents relating to non-vassal suits originating in western Japan. In addition, part of the Bakufu's arbitration technique was to permit the principals in a suit generous time periods for completing their part of the suit procedure. Under the circumstances, a major concern of Kamakura was that litigation be handled as promptly and efficiently as possible.

Throughout the Kamakura period the Bakufu issued complaints about the performance of its officials. Interestingly enough, most of the complaints were concentrated in the period 1238 to 1261, precisely when Kamakura was initiating major organizational changes and introducing a new class of personnel. Perhaps the Bakufu was having "teething troubles," or perhaps Kamakura was under considerable pressure from litigants. In any case, it is useful to look at some of the specific issues.

An increasingly sophisticated judicial procedure resulted in fuller and more complex documents, but it also presented the Bakufu with the problem of trying to strike a balance between officials who followed regulations blindly and those who acted in such a disorganized fashion that the administration of justice was severely compromised.

An attempt to deal with the issue appeared in 1238, in an order that goes to great lengths to elucidate what to us (though not necessarily to bureaucrats) seems common sense:

> If the evidence of a document is clear, then there is no need to pursue further details. If the evidence is not clear, then the testimony of witnesses is to be sought. If the evidence is clear, then is there any need to seek the evidence of witnesses? If both the evidence and the testimony of witnesses are not clear, then an oath is to be sought. If the evidence of witnesses is clear, then an oath is not to be sought.[75]

Another impediment was that officials did not always act on time. In 1241, 1244, and 1248, for example, hearings of the *hyōjōshū* were delayed because the official involved failed to appear, which meant either that there was no one to record the hearings or that the *hyōjō-shū* did not have a quorum.[76] By 1245 the Bakufu was constrained to order that officials who failed to attend a hearing on time and record the proceedings were to be reported.[77] Officials might also be criticized for not sending documents promptly, for labeling them incorrectly, or for making them ambiguous. To correct these problems, ambiguities were ordered removed, relevant documents were to be listed in a register rather than being merely bundled together, copies of documents were to be certified as genuine, and rehearings were to be held every time a case was presented.[78] In 1248 a sweeping condemnation of officials was issued by the regent Tokiyori:

> Officials of the *monchūjo* and other organs have been neglecting attention to their duty and devoting themselves to drinking, banqueting, and pleasure. They do not meet with petitioners. Because they do not inquire scrupulously into the rights and wrongs of evidence, when it comes time to address the *hyōjōshū* an inordinate amount of time is taken up obtaining information normally elicited immediately after a suit has been lodged.[79]

The tone of this complaint suggests genuine concern that the performance and reputation of the Bakufu were being seriously impaired.

Nor were administrators the only ones to be charged with laxity; scribes also were admonished to scrutinize documents presented by defendants and to write up claims only after attempting to verify them. The officials in charge of a case were to read out all documents while the scribes copied them in their presence.[80]

One purely mechanical device used by the Bakufu was deadlines for handling materials. If an official had not taken up a case after being advised of it three times, or if a higher official failed to act on a matter referred to him by a subordinate on three occasions, the matter was to be reported to a superior or to the regent, who would issue orders demanding immediate action. Further procrastination would lead to an interrogation, and when warranted, confiscation of the official's lands.[81]

Another technique involved efficiency reports, which took the form of appraisals of subordinates by superiors. The first reference to these dates from 1261, and in 1273 it was ordered that members of the *hikitsukeshū* be evaluated by their section heads, with all other officials judged by the head of the *mandokoro* or *monchūjo*.[82] A precursor to this system appears to have been in use from at least 1225, when the new regent Yasutoki directed that officials would be rewarded in accordance with the ability they displayed in performing their duties.[83] Presumably a reward system based on merit would not have been possible without evaluations of some type.

The Bakufu also applied a variety of punishments to deal with negligent officials. As early as 1211 we have an instance of an official being suspended for negligence, and in 1244 an official was suspended from his duties for 60 days for failing to report the details of a case to officials subsequently responsible for handling it. A 1241 reference to a blanket pardon for those who had been suspended suggests some level of implementation.[84] On other occasions, however, such as when the ex-regent Tokiyori died and many in Kamakura entered holy orders without permission, suspensions could have been little more than perfunctory: the Bakufu could hardly function if most of its officers were taken off the job.[85]

Still another technique to uphold the quality of administration involved rooting out partiality and corruption. For example, a directive of 1286 ordered that officials with good past records but who were now exhibiting favoritism must be dismissed immediately.[86] Complaints of malfeasance might originate within the Bakufu but could equally well come from litigants. In cases where an official was slandered directly, the Bakufu usually investigated.[87] In other cases, a plaintiff might complain that officials had drawn the wrong conclusions from documents presented to them, as for example when one losing party to a suit insisted that only willful and malicious interpretation of a document (a charge determined to be true) could have resulted in that loss.[88]

Underlying the Bakufu's concern in these matters was an awareness that corruption did exist, sometimes through the exercise of undue influence, sometimes through outright bribes.[89] In an incident of 1226, a warrior member of the *hyōjōshū* actually attempted to direct the outcome of a case by putting in a claim for the lands to be confiscated should that party lose.[90] Episodes such as this one were bound to sully the Bakufu's reputation, and thus by 1235 Kamakura had taken steps to prevent conflicts of interest by stipulating that *hyōjōshū* members must disqualify themselves from hearings involving a broadly defined group of relatives.[91]

The question remains whether any of these regulations worked. In fact, I have encountered for the entire Kamakura period only two instances in which parties to a suit accused jurists of a conflict of interest. In one case, dealing with the Akanabe estate in 1299, a complaint was addressed to the Bakufu charging that during a hearing members of the Nagai family had received the advice and encouragement of relatives who were officials at Rokuhara. It is nevertheless apparent that the accused relatives had not actually heard the case, even though they were present at the trial.[92] In a second incident, involving Ōta estate and the Miyoshi family, a memorandum from the proprietor's side cautioned a representative that his Miyoshi opponent had many relatives in Kamakura's judicial administration.[93] This was true, but decisions had repeatedly gone against the *jitō*. It seems reasonable to conclude that even in disputes involving officials' families, Bakufu verdicts were given in accord with documentary evidence.

The final technique employed by Kamakura was an obligation that officials consent explicitly to the principles of "good government." Usually this requirement entailed having officials (in most instances from the *hyōjōshū*) sign oaths. The only full oath that survives, one signed on the promulgation of the *Goseibai shikimoku* in 1232,[94] enjoined officials to provide rational, impartial, and prompt justice. It served as the foundation for subsequent oaths, which were elicited in 1234, 1261, 1293, 1295, 1308, and 1322, a frequency that suggests the calling of such pledges at least once every generation.[95] Assent was obviously mandatory, since the one recorded instance of refusal brought instant dismissal to the official involved.[96]

Although most of our evidence on consent to such principles involves high-level officials, a late Kamakura source suggests that relatively obscure middle-ranking officials accepted them too. The *Taira Masatsura Isamegusa*, an official's memorial of admonition to the Hōjō leader Sadatoki, is replete with learned historical examples of proper governmental conduct.[97] For our purposes, the significance of this document lies in its being written at all—and by a hereditary official at that.

Conclusions

The Bakufu emerged as a new institution of government but without foreclosing existing institutions; it therefore confronted the necessity of establishing an independent administration. In recruiting officials it sought people who would pose no threat but would contribute to the administration's technical competence and stability. They must be skillful administrators but be subordinate to the Bakufu and loyal to no other groups in society. Pursuing these objectives resulted in a corps of officials with certain characteristics.

First, officials were not drawn from major warrior families. Certainly some warrior families were represented on the *hyōjōshū*, and many, such as the Ashikaga, were socially prominent within Kamakura itself. Yet members of warrior families were only rarely involved in routine administration, and for a compelling reason: whether or not they possessed technical skills such as literacy, involvement in a bureaucracy at a level incompatible with their station in warrior society was not conceivable. An equally valid reason, at least for the Bakufu, was that members of warrior families occupying stations independent of Bakufu service could not be relied on to give unqualified loyalty to the Bakufu as administrators. By contrast, hereditary official families originally recruited from fringe elements of warrior society were irrevocably tied to the Bakufu; apparently they had no other alternatives. For these people service in the Bakufu brought a form of social mobility that they could not have achieved otherwise.

Second, the Bakufu was staffed by administrative specialists. However, because of the extra-bureaucratic criteria—heredity and status—for advancement to the higher administrative positions, the Bakufu had a larger pool of administrative talent than we might have imagined. Individual career patterns of, for example, the Miyoshi and the Saitō were not markedly different up to that point where the Saitō were prevented from rising further. Recruited primarily for administrative purposes, these people generally were not in a position to exercise independent power within the Bakufu, though we can imagine that normal bureaucratic infighting occurred to some extent. The Bakufu officials did not avoid political activity entirely, but their interests were identified with the regime's continued functioning rather than with its leadership. That they were permitted to transfer their talents to subsequent regimes supports the perception that they were administrators above all else.

Third, the Bakufu officials in general do seem to have performed their tasks impartially, regardless of social class or personal connection. Since they did possess rights in land, they were surely aware of the attendant problems. Yet even when officials were directly involved in disputes, the Bakufu was able to ensure that this situation did not impinge on the administrative competence of the Bakufu itself. Conflict-of-interest legislation—itself a surprisingly modern technique for the Bakufu to have employed—was precise on this point. The examples we have all indicate that this legislation was successfully implemented.

Finally, though it is not possible to judge the Bakufu's success solely by the fact that it issued documents or that it had problems in common with other regimes, the sophistication of its procedures and results, particularly judicial decisions, clearly weighs in its favor. A literate and hereditary class of officials contributed to this success by guaranteeing a collective memory and an ongoing knowledge of precedent. It also enabled the regime to continue functioning despite periodic upheavals among the warrior leadership. For though the Kamakura Bakufu was undoubtedly a warrior-led government, with a constituency also mainly of warriors, its functioning and success depended ultimately on its hereditary civil officials.

Muromachi Bakufu Rule in Kyoto: Administrative and Judicial Aspects

SUZANNE GAY

In the summer of 1336, just three years after he had broken away from the Kamakura Bakufu to aid Emperor Go-Daigo, Ashikaga Takauji swept into Kyoto. Disenchanted when Go-Daigo failed to assign the warriors a major role in his new order, Takauji simply seized the reins of power. In the eleventh month of 1336, he established the Muromachi Bakufu, the most characteristic feature of which, in the eyes of modern scholars, was its reliance on powerful warrior leaders called *shugo* for rule of the provinces. Alliances with the *shugo* in time proved unreliable, however, and the Bakufu was gradually forced to retreat to its urban base, Kyoto, the economic, cultural, and ancient political capital of Japan. Thus the Muromachi Bakufu became intimately involved with a complex set of elements from which the Kamakura Bakufu had been shielded: the powerful central proprietors, including aristocratic families as well as large Buddhist temples and Shinto shrines that held rights to a vast amount of land; the imperial court, still the major political authority in the Kyoto area; and the city's commercial sector. By contrast, the Kamakura Bakufu, unrivaled militarily in eastern Japan and a safe distance from the traditional authorities in Kyoto, had been able to function independently, at least within its designated sphere.

The Muromachi Bakufu's establishment in Kyoto traditionally has been interpreted as the completion of a slow process of warrior encroachment on traditional authority begun in Heian times and advanced by the Kamakura Bakufu.[1] But as long as the *shōen* system that supported the established Kyoto authorities as well as most of the warrior class remained strong, especially in central Japan, the warriors could not achieve complete domination. Away from Kyoto the *kokujin*, locally powerful warriors nominally subordinate to the *shugo*, were establishing control over consolidated blocks of land that were quickly becoming their own domains, and the *shōen* system was fast disappearing. In the Kyoto area, however, because of the strength of the proprietary class, the *kokujin* stratum was quite weak, and the *shōen* system survived longer. Economically the *shōen* system defined the medieval order, and until it died the traditional authorities it supported in Kyoto stubbornly refused to capitulate. The warrior class had intruded on the political authority and sources of wealth of the traditional elites, but in Kyoto it failed to displace them entirely. The political order there remained highly variegated, with several groups holding significant power until the sixteenth century, when the *shōen* system gave way completely to landholding by fiefs under the control of daimyo.[2]

The Authority Structure of Medieval Kyoto

Although the Bakufu-*shugo* alliance characterized most of Japan during the Muromachi period, the power structure in Kyoto for the greater part of that period was quite different: the Bakufu, though superior militarily, shared with the traditional proprietary class not only landed and commercial wealth, but also some aspects of the administration of land in the city. Traditional theories, looking ahead to the Sengoku period, tend to downplay the Muromachi Bakufu as a vital institution, stressing instead the independent rise of the warriors in the provinces as central to an understanding of the period.[3] But this is perhaps with an eye too much to the future, for in fact the Muromachi Bakufu's position in Kyoto exemplifies in microcosm the political order characteristic of medieval Japan.

To explain the configuration of established interests in Kyoto, it is useful to borrow the so-called *kenmon* theory as a means of characterizing the medieval period.[4] Historians traditionally have deprived the medieval period of a discrete identity, viewing it instead as simply a long transitional stage between the ancient period of government by aristocrats and the early modern age of government by samurai. The emperor and the aristocracy have been seen as mere remnants of the ancient age, gradually eclipsed and finally overcome by the warriors representing the coming age. Whereas the ancient period has been viewed as the era of the *ritsuryō* system, and the early modern age as the era of the *bakuhan* system, the medieval period has had no similar label. In fact, the notion of a medieval state has been viewed with skepticism, given its comparatively fragmented nature. The *kenmon* theory is an attempt to correct this oversight.

According to the *kenmon* theory, with the rise of the *shōen* system in the eighth century, there began to emerge elite families or family-like authority groups, such as temples, deriving their income from *shōen* lands. These groups, called *kenmon*, had an informal voice in governing matters because of their prestigious status, often codified in defunct offices of the ancient imperial state. But they were essentially private in nature, with a house organization that handled internal and external affairs through the issuance of documents. Rights to land held by a *kenmon* could be divided among various members: the family or temple head, vassals, private soldiers, *shōen* managers, cultivators, and so on. In some cases more than one *kenmon* possessed rights to a single piece of land. For example, the highest-ranking guardian rights might be held by one *kenmon* and the proprietary rights by another. In the late Heian period, the *kenmon* clustered in and around Kyoto began to form interdependent groups that in total constituted the state authority structure of medieval Japan. This political configuration is called the *kenmon* system.

By the end of the twelfth century, *kenmon* could be divided into three general groups, each with a specific function. The first was the *kuge* or aristocratic estate, including the emperor, the retired emperor, prominent members of the imperial family, and members of the nobility. Each of these was a *kenmon* whose function was to serve the state as civil officials, with expertise in customary observances and rituals. The second great *kenmon* estate was the *jige*, the religious establishment, consisting of individual temples and shrines whose function was the spiritual protection of the state. The third was the *buke*, the leading warrior houses, including the Bakufu. Their function was the military defense of the state. Each *kenmon* was a vital component of the system, and no single *kenmon* could rule alone without the support of the others.

By offering advice and applying pressure both formally and behind the scenes, each *kenmon* participated in the medieval governing process. In the course of such maneuvering, one *kenmon* might emerge as dominant, but it would still be dependent on the support of the others. This *kenmon*'s house organization then became the organ for *kenmon* national rule, simultaneously a public and a private entity, exercising actual political control, even while the emperor still held sovereign authority. It is useful to think of the Bakufu in this context—as the means by which warriors made their way into the *kenmon* system hitherto dominated by aristocratic and religious groups.

The establishment of the Muromachi Bakufu represented the continuation of the stable *kenmon* system, now under warrior dominance. Within this structure the Bakufu held a central position because it alone wielded real military and political power, enabling it to defend the interests of all the *kenmon*. The Bakufu represented *kenmon* interests, and the Muromachi *shugo*, whose provincial strength has been the focus of many studies of the period, drew on that influence to build up their local power. For a time the Bakufu, as a *kenmon* power represented by the *shugo*, gave peace and stability to the country. By the Ōnin War, however, the *shugo* no longer functioned simply as extensions of *kenmon* authority. They themselves became or were conquered by daimyo, powerful regional lords who ruled Japan through most of the sixteenth century.

The *kenmon* theory has been applied mainly to the late Heian and Kamakura periods, but it is peculiarly suited to Kyoto until much later. The establishment of the Muromachi Bakufu in Kyoto came about not so much by military conquest as by the step-by-step intrusion into and then domination of the Kyoto-centered *kenmon* power bloc. As the dominant member of that bloc, the Muromachi Bakufu flourished and expanded, inevitably at the expense of the other members, whose support was nevertheless vital to the Bakufu's survival. For this reason, until the mid-sixteenth century the aristocratic and religious *kenmon* continued, if in curtailed fashion, to play a major role in the political and economic life of Kyoto.

The Muromachi Bakufu in Kyoto

Ashikaga Takauji chose Kyoto for his headquarters partly to distance himself from Kamakura. But Kyoto offered other unique advantages: as home of the ancient imperial government, it was a prestigious location; the heavy concentration of religious and aristocratic proprietors there made it an economic and cultural center. Kyoto's thriving economy, by now based on cash and supported by a prosperous and advanced agricultural region, reinforced its importance as the center of domestic and foreign trade.[5] To take advantage of Kyoto's many resources, however, the Bakufu had to move slowly, mindful of the traditional authorities already established there.

Four stages have been defined in the establishment of the Muromachi Bakufu in Kyoto: first, military takeover; second, the establishment and maintenance of order in the city; third, the assumption of judicial authority by the Bakufu; and fourth, the taxation of the commercial sector.[6] This scheme is not flawless, but it does provide a convenient analytical framework that represents the course of events in approximate chronological order. The second and third stages, comprising the two major aspects of administrative control, will be examined here in some detail.[7]

In the first stage, military takeover, Ashikaga Takauji defeated the forces of the southern court, led by Nitta Yoshisada. This campaign, which dragged on for months, is vividly described in *Baishōron*, a chronicle of the Nanbokuchō conflict.

The next day, the twenty-sixth of the fifth month [1336], they departed from Hyōgo and encamped at Nishinomiya. At Minatogawa [Kusunoki] Masashige was defeated. Hearing that a great force was advancing on Kyoto, Emperor Go-Daigo proceeded to Mount Hiei, just as he had done on the evening of the twenty-seventh day of the first month [when Takauji had invaded Kyoto earlier in the same year]. From Tamba together they marched toward Kyoto: Niki Hyōbu Daiyu Yoriaki, Imagawa Suruga no Kami, the armies of Tango and Tajima provinces, each bearing the imperial flag, some thousands of troops. They battled their way into Kyoto. . . . Yoshisada . . . was attacked by a force of several hundred on horseback, but, it was heard, he escaped over Nagasaka. . . . On the night of the twenty-second of the eleventh month [1336], [former] Emperor Go-Daigo declared a reconciliation and came into Kyoto. The Ashikaga troops went forth to meet him on the banks of the Kamo River.[8]

In the course of his conquests, Takauji not only appointed his major followers to *shugo* posts, but also consolidated his hold locally by appointing powerful and wealthy peasants to be Bakufu vassals (*jitō gokenin*) in return for military service. In this way, the area around Kyoto was pacified, and after defeating Nitta's forces, Takauji established the Bakufu in Kyoto. Although the forces of the southern court repeatedly attempted to regain Kyoto, and even succeeded briefly in

1352, military control of the city by the Bakufu can be said to have begun in the eleventh month of 1336.

The Establishment and Maintenance of Order

Following the defeat of Nitta Yoshisada, Takauji began the task of reestablishing order in the city. In the eleventh month of 1336 the Bakufu issued the *Kemmu shikimoku*, a codification of general Bakufu policies and aims. Articles one through six of the code pertain directly to the establishment of order and the revival of commerce in Kyoto.

1. Live in a seemly manner.
2. Stop wild drunken behavior.
3. Stop violent crime.
4. Stop confiscating private homes for one's own use.
5. Return vacated land in Kyoto to its original owners [that is, to those who had fled during the war].
6. Allow credit circles (*mujinsen*) and moneylenders (*dosō*) to practice.[9]

Takauji obviously considered the establishment of order in Kyoto essential not only to ensuring his own security there but also to reviving the city's commercial life. In 1337 the customary guard system was revived, under which Bakufu vassals served rotating night duty (*rinbanya*).[10] At about the same time the Bakufu reopened toll barriers at the roads leading into Kyoto. The primary purpose of the barriers was to control commerce, but undoubtedly they also helped keep order in the city.[11]

In a further step to establish order the Bakufu absorbed into its *samurai dokoro* (board of retainers) low-ranking members of the *kebiishichō*, the old court office of police in Kyoto.[12] This step was also one means of eliminating the *kebiishichō*, and within the first ten years of the Bakufu's establishment, the *samurai dokoro* made a major effort to monopolize policing duties in the city. In 1344, for example, *samurai dokoro* members drove marauding Tōdaiji monks from Nara out of the city.[13] The imperial police office did not immediately disappear, however. In 1346 Iwashimizu Hachimangū, a shrine in the south of Kyoto, complained to the Bakufu that imperial police troops had wounded shrine members, an indication that the office was still alive and well.[14] Although the transition was neither smooth nor immediate, gradually the *samurai dokoro* gained control of police duties, and mention of the *kebiishichō* disappears from documents. When the Nanbokuchō dispute was resolved in 1392, the

Bakufu officially absorbed court functions, including the policing of Kyoto.

For centuries a chronic threat to order in the city had been the agents, both lay and clerical, of Enryakuji, the Buddhist monastery on Mount Hiei. Descending into the city to dun tardy debtors, including both aristocrats and townspeople, they were capable of throwing whole sections of the city into chaos. In 1370 the Bakufu ordered these Hiei agents to stop harassing the people of Kyoto, after even the head priest of Enryakuji had been unable to bring them to heel.[15] This event has been interpreted as an attempt by the Bakufu to deny Hiei's right to deal with debtors on its own, and thus an assertion of Bakufu authority over the administration of the city.[16] Whether the Bakufu really did stop the lawlessness is unclear, but its order to Hiei's monks represents a claim, on paper at least, to a power previously held by Hiei, as well as an attempt to restore order. A similar Bakufu decree of 1386, requiring that Hiei's agents use Bakufu courts to settle debt disputes rather than seizing and confiscating Kyoto homes and persons on their own, is another sign of the Bakufu's determination to establish control over Kyoto.[17]

A perennially ineffective but frequently employed control measure was the proclamation of sumptuary edicts, often to curb waste in times of scarcity. In 1367 and 1369, for example, the Bakufu forbade all manner of luxurious clothing and personal ornamentation, as well as the usual vices, such as gambling; in 1458 expensive hobbies like raising nightingales were forbidden.[18] Many of these laws were aimed at the aristocracy, whose ostentatious display in the face of declining income was frowned on by the Bakufu. Other injunctions proscribed certain items of dress for laymen or for commoners, and they may have been forerunners, if on a very small scale, of the Tokugawa Bakufu's strict codes of dress and behavior for each social class.

In times of unrest such as the Ōnin War, the Bakufu issued numerous regulations against public assembly, in an attempt to minimize the chance of disorder. In 1476, for example, only two troupes of Noh actors, Kanze and Konparu, were given permission to perform, in order to limit the number of public gatherings.[19] By the late Muromachi period the Bakufu was nervous about public assembly even in peacetime. In 1505 street dancing was prohibited because it was too "noisy."[20] The following year the Bakufu banned the summer lantern festival altogether, citing as a reason recent street fights that had resulted in fires.[21]

The Bakufu showed an intense interest in commerce, especially the moneylending establishment, as a potential source of income.[22] In addition, it occasionally legislated measures broadly affecting the economy, and by extension, the welfare of the city as a whole. Rice, both the staple of the diet and the traditional currency, was naturally an object of concern. In 1431 the Bakufu set the price of rice, and then arrested and executed six rice merchants for raising the price during a famine.[23] (This incident occurred during Shogun Yoshinori's "reign of terror," and should not be seen as typical of Bakufu punishment.) During a famine in 1499 the Bakufu erected toll barriers for the express purpose of preventing salt and rice from leaving the city.[24]

The Bakufu also regulated currency as part of its role as the public administrative authority of Kyoto. Especially after the Ōnin War, when the Bakufu was more than ever dependent on Kyoto for its income, attempts to control the currency were frequent. Most of the currency of the Muromachi period was imported from China, and it varied greatly in quality depending on its age. To maintain a balance in the quality of currencies in use, and to put a stop to the arbitrary use of currencies by individual merchants and moneylenders, the Bakufu in the late Muromachi period periodically issued *erizenirei*, laws specifying which currencies were acceptable and in what combinations.[25] Long use meant that the older coins were often worn or broken, and privately minted coins were not universally accepted. When transactions occurred, "bad money" (*akuzeni*, the poorest-quality copper coins) was to be excluded from use and special "bad money" shops (*akuzeniya*) were established to exchange it for better-quality currency. In an *erizenirei* of 1500, the Bakufu decreed that *eirakusen* (Eiraku is the Japanese reading of Yung-lo, the third Ming Emperor—hence, coins from Ming China) would be the standard currency, and that new domestic coins were unacceptable.[26] Merchants were to stop choosing the best coins only and start accepting the major Chinese currencies at the same rate as *eirakusen*. Periodically over the next forty years the Bakufu issued further laws prohibiting the use of "bad money," specifying the exact value of damaged coins, warning of punishment to offenders, and so on.[27] A decree of 1512 even specified the acceptable percentage of each type of currency when a mixture of coins was used. The frequency with which the Bakufu issued laws regulating currency indicates how limited its control really was. But there was no other *kenmon* in Kyoto with the power to exercise even partial control over general matters of commerce. By the early sixteenth century, even in Kyoto the loose stability provided by the *kenmon* order was being stretched to the breaking point.

The edicts and regulations cited above reveal only the general contours of Bakufu policy. The matter of enforcement is not touched on in these Bakufu laws, and only an occasional remark in an individual's diary reveals what, if any, punitive or preventive action was actually taken. The Bakufu had its own troops that could be sent to quell local disturbances, and the *samurai dokoro* served as Kyoto's police, but whether laws were faithfully enforced we do not know. For a fuller view of Bakufu actions in Kyoto, it is necessary to look at judicial affairs in some detail. Here, too, whether verdicts were enforced is impossible to tell, but at least the types of cases submitted to litigation indicate the general intent of Bakufu policy.

The Assumption of Judicial Authority

Under Japanese medieval law, two important concepts dominated the administration of justice: (1) *kendanken*, the right of jurisdiction in criminal matters, including entering property for purposes of pursuit, investigation, judgment, punishment, and property confiscation; and (2) *jungyōken*, the right to enforce Bakufu decisions concerning land.[28] Both rights pertained to land, not persons, but the full exercise of civil judicial authority was impossible without them. The Bakufu's judicial authority over persons, including the right to arrest criminals, was established around 1340, but in Kyoto until about 1380 the imperial police office continued to hold firmly the crucial *kendanken* and *jungyōken* rights to land, severely limiting the Bakufu's ability to pursue and punish criminals.[29] Hence, though the streets of Kyoto were peaceful soon after Takauji's arrival, the Bakufu was not able to wrest complete judicial authority from the imperial police office until much later. As a result, the Bakufu found itself hampered in the administration of justice: even if it had control of the accused, it could not necessarily take investigative or punitive action, such as confiscating land. Furthermore, sources indicate that even after the imperial police office was abolished, *kendanken* and *jungyōken* did not pass automatically to the Bakufu, but in many cases were claimed by the proprietors over their own lands. For example, in a 1413 land dispute between the *samurai dokoro* and Tōji, a major religious proprietor in Kyoto, Tōji insisted that it held the *kendanken* to its own lands and any houses on them.[30] Tōji persisted in this contention for most of the Muromachi period.

In sharp contrast to the Kamakura Bakufu, the Muromachi Bakufu's litigation activities in Kyoto concerned disputes between traditional *kenmon* more often than disputes involving warriors.[31] To cite
some examples, in 1379 the *samurai dokoro* rescinded Hōshōji's
kendanken to some Kyoto lands and returned them to Tōfukuji;[32] in
1399 Tōji complained to the Bakufu of incursions on some of its
lands in Kyoto by an aristocratic family;[33] and in 1404, at Tōji's request, the Bakufu referred to the *samurai dokoro* a dispute between
Tōji and the Yamashina family, an aristocratic house.[34] The concentration of so many *kenmon* in Kyoto explains why litigation under
the Muromachi Bakufu differed so from that under its predecessor,
and at the same time why a significant broadening of Bakufu authority was necessary. The Bakufu form of government no longer applied
only to warriors but extended to the traditional *kenmon* as well. In
short, the Muromachi Bakufu held the most comprehensive mandate
to rule of any institution since the imperial government of ancient
times. The Bakufu's gradual loss of control of the provinces seriously
limited this mandate, but as an institutional development with important ramifications for the Tokugawa Bakufu, the comprehensive
nature of Muromachi rule cannot be ignored. It is in Kyoto that this
development can be seen most clearly.

Notwithstanding its broad mandate, the Bakufu's verdicts and
edicts were sometimes ignored or defied by other *kenmon*. In 1443,
for example, the Bakufu forbade performances by a troupe of actors
at the New Year holiday, presumably in an attempt to keep public
assemblies to a minimum. But the imperial court—whose political
functions and finances were now in Bakufu hands and whose judicial
authority had been weakened accordingly—gave its permission, and
the performances went on as planned.[35] Although the Muromachi
Bakufu was not always able to enforce its laws, it remained the only
institution in late medieval Japan with a regularly functioning and
universally recognized judicial apparatus.[36]

The Muromachi Bakufu's administrative and judicial authority
extended to land taxation. Medieval Kyoto residents did not actually
own the land they lived on in the modern sense, but instead paid a
fixed sum of cash, normally on a semi-annual basis, to the *kenmon* or
overlord of the land. By the fifteenth century this rent-like impost,
called *yajishisen*, was usually based on frontage (*jiguchisen*).[37] In addition, in the Kamakura period the imperial court and aristocratic
families had begun to levy, ostensibly on a temporary basis for special

projects, *munabechisen*, a tax on buildings. In the late fourteenth century the Muromachi Bakufu gained control over both types of tax, both for its own income and as part of its responsibility for functions previously performed by the imperial court. A decree of 1400, for example, exempts Tōji lands in Kyoto from a Bakufu-imposed land tax for the rebuilding of temples and shrines, for court upkeep, and so on.[38] Tōji's ability as a powerful *kenmon* to influence such matters as taxation is also well illustrated by this example. In 1456 the Bakufu levied a general *munabechisen* on the city for palace reconstruction, showing its firm control over taxation in Kyoto.[39]

The Muromachi Bakufu's administrative and judicial control of Kyoto has been described here using documentary examples from the entire period. But this approach fails to convey a sense of change over time in the Bakufu's institutional development.[40] The Bakufu, after all, did not emerge as a mature governing institution from the moment it was established. There was a gradual trend, realized by the middle of the period, toward bureaucratization in judicial matters. By the end of the fourteenth century, as outlined above, the *samurai dokoro* had absorbed the policing and judicial functions of the imperial police office, but gradually the *mandokoro* or chancellery also assumed responsibility for certain aspects of the judicial process. The *mandokoro* dealt with cases involving borrowing and loaning money, pillage, and land disputes; it may have become the Bakufu's receiving office for litigation.[41] This role included performing any document-related functions, earlier the responsibility of the *monchūjo* or records office, which the *mandokoro* had absorbed by the mid-fifteenth century. Along with this change went procedural modifications that streamlined the process of hearing a case and passing judgment on it. The *mandokoro* official who took charge of a case, the *yoriudo*, obtained the necessary signatures and then passed the case for debate to the *honbugyō*, the plaintiff's representative, and the *aibugyō*, the defendant's representative. Whereas the Kamakura Bakufu's procedure had been much more complex, requiring plaintiff and defendant each to submit several rounds of documents, by the mid-fifteenth century the Muromachi system had become bureaucratized: the *honbugyō* and the *aibugyō* debated a case, questioning witnesses or related persons as they saw fit. The final verdict was reached by a council that included the fourteen to twenty *yoriudo* and the *yūhitsu*, secretaries on the board of coadjutors. This so-called *iken* (opinion) system had the status of a shogunal inquiry before the

Ōnin War, but later it became the normal judicial procedure of the Bakufu. By the end of the fifteenth century, the Muromachi legal system had become a bureaucratic process administered by a large number of middle-ranking officials.

This bureaucratization of the Bakufu's judicial process took place slowly, and the system just described existed only from the middle of the Muromachi period. But the potential for bureaucratization was present from the beginning. Recognizing the importance of legal expertise, Takauji had enlisted the services of former Kamakura Bakufu officials like the Nikaidō family to draw up the Kemmu formulary. Similar legal experts were drawn from Ashikaga retainers and collateral lines of the Ashikaga house. They fit the standard profile of bureaucrats: a professional staff of experts with specialized functions whose tenure in office did not depend on who was shogun or deputy shogun (*kanrei*), they made day-to-day decisions on the basis of legal precedent and with the extensive use of written documents.[42] But a closer look shows another, more "feudal" aspect of these officials. They were chosen from a small pool: virtually all were relatives or vassals of the shogun to whom they swore loyalty and from whom they received at least some of their lands or other income. There was no examination system as in China; rather, the positions were hereditary, limited to the same small group of families. Forty percent of the Bakufu laws issued from 1337 to 1466 bear signatures; they include the names of members of only thirteen families, among them the most powerful in the Bakufu.[43] In lieu of military service, these vassal-bureaucrats performed administrative duties for the shogun. Although the coexistence of bureaucratic and feudal aspects may seem contradictory, the two were in some ways complementary. Loyalty to the shogun ensured continuity of membership in officialdom, which was one reason for the remarkable continuity of Bakufu policy. Bureaucratic expertise in turn meant that administrative and judicial affairs were generally conducted in a routine rather than an arbitrary manner.

Restraints on the Bakufu's Control of Kyoto

In spite of an impressive administrative and judicial apparatus, the Muromachi Bakufu's control of Kyoto was far from complete. The most serious limitations came from the religious establishment and the aristocracy. The religious establishment was the more formidable of the two. As spiritual mentor of the rulers and as protector of the state, it held powers of moral suasion and coercion that the Bakufu could not easily challenge. In administrative and economic matters, the religious establishment asserted itself through its proprietary rights to lands and as patron of commercial groups, particularly in the Kyoto area. In the late twelfth century, religious institutions held over 60 percent of the *shōen* land in the country.[44] This figure had declined by the Muromachi period, but in the Kyoto area it was still high. Tōji, Enryakuji, and Gion Shrine, with their vast landed and commercial wealth, were especially dominant in Kyoto. These large temples and shrines defended their interests so aggressively, often with armed force, that they could hardly be ignored. Still less could they be confronted, for an attack by the Bakufu, the military defender of the state, on the religious establishment, the spiritual protector of the same state, would have eroded the recognition the warriors had attained.

In 1345, for example, on the day of an elaborate shogunal ceremony at Tenryūji, the Hiei monks brought their portable shrine into the city in a gesture of defiance, and the warriors assembled there did not attempt to confront them.[45] Carrying a shrine into Kyoto and sometimes leaving it in the streets or even on the grounds of a residence was a favorite tactic of the monks. The portable shrine was believed to house a deity that had the power to bring retribution on anyone violating it. Since people feared offending the deity, it provided a convenient form of defense. The shrine could be handled only in prescribed ways known only to the clergy. The occupant of the land where the shrine had been deposited had to call priests to perform purification ceremonies and make appeasement offerings. The Hiei monks frequently caused disruptions in the city that the Bakufu was hard put to quell. Violence was not always necessary: merely by threatening to send its agents into the city, Enryakuji could influence litigation in its favor. Only in the Sengoku period, when the warriors destroyed the *kenmon* system and asserted themselves as sole rulers, was the religious establishment attacked head on, as epitomized by Oda Nobunaga's destruction of Enryakuji in 1571.

The aristocracy's influence over Kyoto, though less physically imposing than that of the religious establishment, was also an obstacle to Bakufu control. The foremost member of the aristocracy, the emperor, placed subtle restraints on shogunal authority. Although historians have usually emphasized its declining ability to govern, the imperial institution in the medieval period was still a force to be reckoned with. As the agent bestowing legitimacy on the whole *kenmon* system, the emperor was an indispensable part of the political order.[46]

The presence of a kingly authority is generally recognized as essential to the cohesiveness of an otherwise highly decentralized medieval state. It has been suggested that this role of feudal king be assigned to the Ashikaga shoguns instead of to the emperor.[47] The justification for this view is that though the shoguns originally sought legitimacy from the emperor, the emperor gradually lost his value as guarantor of shogunal authority as the Bakufu became one with the court culturally and economically. Instead of turning to the emperor, the Ashikaga house was able to use tally trade relations with Ming China to enhance its political status. In return for paying fealty to the emperor of China, Yoshimitsu, the third shogun, received the designation "king of Japan." By accepting and even flaunting this title, Yoshimitsu took a bold and unprecedented step for a warrior. But this event does not mean that the shogun displaced the emperor as monarch. In medieval Japan foreign relations exercised little direct influence on internal affairs. Domestic political relationships were still determined by the hierarchical system of *kenmon* interests based on the control of land, and not by a monarchy more appropriate to early modern societies. Although the emperor's power was on the wane by the Muromachi period, the emperor was still the titular head of this land control system, based on the ancient imperial state that he nominally governed.

Even more important was the emperor's ideological or religious authority within the medieval polity. With the spread of religious concepts like *shinkoku* (Japan as a land protected by its deities) in the Kamakura period, the emperor acquired an aura of mystery and sanctity. This sacerdotal role made him indispensable to the polity's stability, forcing the conscious recognition of his political importance. Personal ability to rule had nothing to do with this authority. Although weak and only formally a ruler, the emperor was the fountainhead of authority legitimizing a loosely unified rule by *kenmon* groups. Thus it is the emperor, not the shogun, who can best be identified as a feudal king.[48]

The emperor presided over the aristocracy, which continued to hold public offices in the old imperial state even after the establishment of the Muromachi Bakufu. Although these offices had lost their political meaning and were little more than hereditary sinecures by the Muromachi period, they provided the aristocracy with real economic power in the form of income, control of land, and regulation of commerce. In addition, members of the aristocracy still held proprietary rights to vast *shōen* holdings.

In spite of their lingering importance, Kyoto aristocrats were upstaged by the gauche, countrified warriors to a humiliating degree. A well-known incident of the period conveys their discomfiture with the new order. One night in 1342, the *shugo* of Mino Province, Toki Yoritō, returning drunk from a day's revelry, nearly collided with a carriage. From inside came a voice: "Who are you, you ruffian? Dismount." Incensed that anyone would presume to address him in such a way, Yoritō challenged the hidden occupant to a duel, only to be told that the retired emperor would hardly duel with a country bumpkin. Instead of backing down, Yoritō shouted contemptuously, "Did you say the retired emperor (*In*) or a dog (*inu*)?" He then shot an arrow that severed the bridle of the oxen pulling the carriage, forcing the emperor to walk home. In tears the emperor exclaimed that the latter days of the Buddhist law had surely arrived when the gods would not deliver him from such ignominious treatment.[49] Although this incident belongs more to the realm of folklore than to that of historical fact, it illustrates the extent to which the aristocrats felt their position debased by warrior upstarts, many of whom had risen to prominence because of their military prowess only in recent years.

With the coming of the Muromachi Bakufu, the aristocrats' prestige, their importance as civil officials, and their relevance as experts on ritual and custom declined. But as "custodians of the Heian court tradition,"[50] they found their pastimes and tastes emulated by high-ranking warriors residing in the capital. The shoguns from Yoshimitsu onward became patrons of the arts, just as the aristocracy had been for centuries. Although he never attempted to depose the emperor, Yoshimitsu got as close to him as possible, going so far as to become a member of the imperial family by having his wife named mother of the emperor. He also took the highest aristocratic rank, that of *dajō daijin*, and built a palatial residence where for a time he housed the emperor after the imperial palace burned. He even abdicated to affect the lifestyle of a retired emperor, all the while continuing to maintain real control of the Bakufu. The warriors were undeniably attracted to the aristocratic way of life.

This is not to say, however, that warriors in Kyoto merged with the aristocracy in a successful attempt to dominate other *kenmon* culturally as well as politically. There was always a substantive, functional difference between warriors and aristocrats. Since policing, judicial, and military duties required force, or at least the threat of force, responsibility for them fell to the warrior class. The Muromachi Bakufu was particularly distinguishable from other *kenmon* in its judicial role: it was frequently called upon to mediate disputes involving not only warriors but religious and aristocratic *kenmon* as well, especially in Kyoto. This mediating function amounted to a tacit recognition by all *kenmon* of the Bakufu's leadership in the *kenmon* order. Admittedly, there were substantial limitations on the Bakufu in judicial matters, especially in the enforcement of verdicts, but the Bakufu's universally recognized right to adjudicate disputes among all *kenmon* elites clearly distinguished its authority from that of the civil and religious aristocracy in the Muromachi period. This expansion of the earlier Kamakura Bakufu's sphere of authority marks a significant institutional advance in the Bakufu form of governance.

The Muromachi Bakufu ruled for over two hundred years, longer than the Kamakura Bakufu and nearly as long as the Tokugawa Bakufu. Although vivid personalities—like the third and sixth shoguns, Yoshimitsu and Yoshinori—occasionally dominated, the Muromachi Bakufu was for most of the period a government run by professional bureaucrats whose policies were consistent over time, regardless of who was shogun or deputy shogun. The Muromachi Bakufu continued as a governing institution, especially in Kyoto, long after the shogun ceased to be an effective national leader, in part because the Bakufu bureaucracy was able to perform governmental functions quite apart from the shogun's military or landed strength. The Bakufu's relatively long life can also be attributed to the accommodation it reached with aristocratic and religious *kenmon*. These traditional groups continued to exercise limited control over their own spheres. In spite of the challenge they posed to the Bakufu, it was the sole authority with a regularly functioning judicial apparatus, and thus the only institution universally recognized as having the authority to settle disputes between *kenmon*. The *kenmon* system in Kyoto was not forced on an unwilling Bakufu too weak to overthrow the established order and start anew. Rather, the advantages offered by the existing order made accommodating it an acceptable and even favorable arrangement for the Bakufu. The *kenmon* system defined the medieval order and brought a certain loose stability to the age. Not until the *shōen* system of land control broke down completely in the sixteenth century did the *kenmon* order cease to be a useful apparatus for Bakufu rule.

Regional Outposts of Muromachi Bakufu Rule: The Kantō and Kyushu

LORRAINE F. HARRINGTON

The second of Japan's three warrior governments was formed in the 1330's by Ashikaga Takauji, who was chief of a major eastern warrior house and a distant relative of the previous Bakufu's founder. Takauji participated in the overthrow of the Kamakura shogunate as a leading general in Go-Daigo's Imperial Restoration forces but soon thereafter severed his ties with Go-Daigo to establish himself at the head of a new regime. Constructing a new political order is more difficult than overthrowing an outmoded or discredited one, particularly when the society in question is changing rapidly. In fourteenth-century Japan commercial expansion was accelerating, absentee lordship was on the defensive, and the kinship structure of warrior houses was in serious decline. The new regime of the Ashikaga would have to confront these and other problems in order to secure its position.

The military circumstances of the day created additional demands. The existence of two imperial courts battling for supremacy, each serving as a rallying point for dissidents, disorderlies, rebels, and rivals, required that the early Ashikaga shoguns be both generals and administrators. From the outset, then, it was necessary for Takauji to construct a government significantly different from its predecessor. Recent studies have begun to suggest the degree to which the early Ashikaga shoguns, reacting to the vicissitudes of the time, were compelled to innovate for their political survival. Analyses of commercial policies, in particular, and shogunal politics during the tenures of Yoshimitsu and Yoshinori, the third and sixth Ashikaga scions, have modified the image of a period of disorder and weak leadership.[1]

For the most part, however, even these recent studies have focused largely on Bakufu control in central Japan, leaving us with little idea of how the Ashikaga attempted to govern outside this area. Japanese historians have often characterized the Ashikaga political system as a Bakufu-*shugo* system (*bakufu shugo taisei*), distinguishing it from both the Kamakura and the Tokugawa Bakufu by emphasizing the enlarged role of the provincial constables, the *shugo*. Such a characterization is certainly appropriate for central Japan, where *shugo* for the most part were relatives of the shogunal house (Ashikaga *shōgunke ichimon*) or long-standing vassals justifiably described as pillars of Ashikaga rule.[2]

In the nine provinces of distant Kyushu and in the eastern provinces known collectively as the Kantō, however, few *shugo* were close relatives of the Ashikaga. In these regions the Ashikaga were obliged to make concessions to locally powerful military leaders by granting them provincial titles. Here also, however, the shogun appointed special regional officers to act as Bakufu representatives. The role these officers played in the management of the blocs of provinces in their areas must be understood if we are to assess and accurately portray the Ashikaga political system.

It is not entirely surprising that the regional offices—headed by the Kantō *kubō* and *kanrei* in the east and the Chinzei *kanrei* (later, Kyushu *tandai*) in the west—have been virtually ignored by Western studies of the Ashikaga Bakufu, for this is a research theme only recently emphasized by Japanese scholars as well. Studies of Kyushu surpass those on the Kantō, but many documents have been collected and published since the bulk of the early work in either area. These sources reveal several important points about Bakufu administration in the outlying regions. It is obvious, for example, that the regional officers were important links for the Bakufu with warriors there. It is equally obvious, however, that they did not operate consistently as intermediaries for the central government. Like the *shugo*, they acquired powers—and in some cases lost them—as time passed. In fact, the range and depth of their delegated and actual authority varied considerably over time and was not equal between regions.

In a paper of this scope it is not possible to trace in detail each stage in the development of both regional offices. More realistically, we can differentiate general periods and illustrate major changes within the two regions and in the relations between them and the Bakufu. It is no accident, for example, that in both areas the regional offices became noticeably more powerful at the same time that the central Bakufu was increasing in vitality under the *kanrei* Hosokawa Yoriyuki and Shogun Yoshimitsu in the second half of the fourteenth century. Nor is it surprising that the two so-called strong shoguns—Yoshimitsu and Yoshinori—worked to advance Bakufu interests in the regions.

For the purposes of our discussion, the Muromachi Bakufu's first century can be divided into three major periods:

1. The era before and after the so-called Kannō Disturbance (the clash during 1350-52 between elite factions at the center).[3]

2. The late fourteenth century, during which central Bakufu institutions matured and the regional offices greatly extended their functions and geographic range. Marked by exceptionally strong leadership in both regions as well as in Kyoto, the period was one of ascendancy for the Ashikaga system as a whole.

3. The period from 1392, when the country was formally reunified under one imperial dynasty, through the 1430's, near the end of Shogun Yoshinori's tenure. Often recognized as the high point of Ashikaga governance, it encompassed dramatic adjustments in regional control.

Early Ashikaga Representation in the Kantō

One of the earliest innovations in warrior government made by the Ashikaga was the decision to base the Bakufu in Kyoto rather than in Kamakura, the capital of the previous regime. As the preamble to the *Kemmu shikimoku*, the initial set of laws issued by Takauji, reveals, the question of relocating the Bakufu required considerable deliberation.[4] We can only speculate whether the new leaders recognized the potential economic advantages of Kyoto, but no doubt the strategic advantages were immediately clear. A main headquarters in the ancient imperial capital would gain them prestige while allowing them to protect the source of their legitimacy, the northern court emperor Kōmyō, and would situate them in the geographic center of the country.

Once that decision was made, the Ashikaga faced the immediate problem of how to control the volatile eastern provinces, the heart-land of warrior society in the previous age and still the base of powerful military houses. Accordingly, the Ashikaga took care to establish a second base in Kamakura. An Ashikaga family member was stationed there from even before the regime was inaugurated; officials moved back and forth frequently throughout the early years; and for a while during the troublesome Kannō period, the shogun himself ruled directly from the east in order to monitor the region more closely.

The family's initial foothold in Kamakura was established as early as 1333, when Ashikaga Tadayoshi occupied the city at the head of the main support troops for one of Go-Daigo's sons. In late 1335 Tadayoshi moved west to join his brother in competing against Go-Daigo's forces. To ensure that the family's interests would continue to be represented in Kamakura, Tadayoshi left behind Takauji's son and successor, Ashikaga Yoshiakira. Since Yoshiakira was only four years old at the time, a series of relatives and vassals were commissioned to assist him as military commanders.

The first of these was the branch head Shiba Ienaga, a general who had been active in the remote northeastern province of Mutsu.[5] Ienaga's documents reveal that in his capacity as peacekeeping agent and commander of the shogun's troops, he always acknowledged the authority of the Ashikaga.[6] After Ienaga died in 1336, he was succeeded by two other centrally commissioned deputies (*shitsuji* or *kanrei*), reflecting the bifurcated or two-dimensional organization of the Kyoto Bakufu. From approximately 1338 to 1350, members of two prominent Ashikaga vassal families, the Kō and the Uesugi, often served simultaneously as commanders in the east, helping to forge a military balance that would support the fledgling regime. A major victory by one assistant, Kō no Morofuyu, in Hitachi Province in 1344, contributed greatly to the security of the Bakufu.[7]

Because there are large gaps in the evidence from this formative era, the precise sequence of Kamakura deputies is difficult to determine. It is apparent, however, that even though a double-deputy system existed, authority was not neatly divided. Nor were precise succession patterns developed. On more than one occasion deputies returned to Kyoto after service in the Kantō, only to reappear later to resume their posts. In short, in the period before the Kannō era, institutions were in a state of flux, and patterns of authority in both Kyoto and Kamakura were not yet clearly established.

Kyushu Deputies in the Formative Period

The limits of responsibility were not initially well defined for the Bakufu's early representatives in Kyushu either, a problem that troubled the administration of that area for at least a decade. The highest-ranking officer there, unlike in the Kantō, was not a member of the shogunal family, except for one brief and tumultuous interlude in the Kannō era. Assigned to Kyushu were trusted and proven subordinates, branch family members whose skills as military commanders qualified them to lead the Ashikaga effort.

In a sense, the Ashikaga were following long-established precedent by stationing a representative in Kyushu. Because of its proximity to the Asian mainland, it had always played an important role in international exchange—cultural, economic, and at times, military. For many centuries, therefore, an officer of the imperial court had resided in northern Kyushu. Deputies of the Kamakura Bakufu had also been commissioned there to help manage the affairs (most often, the formal complaints) of vassals in the area.

Among the problems faced by the Ashikaga in Kyushu were the absence of any historic ties there, the existence of three powerful families—the Shōni, Ōtomo, and Shimazu—in the region, the perception of a continuing threat of invasion from the continent,[8] and the need to appease and control the area's many smaller-scale warriors. All of these difficulties were exacerbated when a leading representative of the rival southern court army (Go-Daigo's son, Prince Kanenaga) proceeded to Kyushu and made it a major theater of battle.

It was Takauji himself who established the family's initial presence in Kyushu. Early in 1336, after suffering a temporary setback in central Japan, he fled west to cultivate new support. He was in Kyushu only a short time, but while there he managed to entice warriors from as far away as the three southern provinces of Ōsumi, Satsuma, and Hyūga to fight for him.[9] When he departed to retake Kyoto, he left commanders to direct the Ashikaga effort on his behalf.

Foremost among those charged was Isshiki Noriuji, a branch family member who was based in northern Kyushu for nearly twenty years. No appointment document survives specifically designating Noriuji as officer for the region, but as early as 1336/11 a special term, Chinzei *kanrei*, appeared in reference to him.[10] He was therefore distinguished from other Ashikaga representatives in the area—

that is, other relatives sent as generals to specific provinces (*kuni no taishō*) and of course the *shugo*. The title Chinzei *kanrei* also distinguished Noriuji from the regional deputies appointed by the previous Bakufu, who had been called Chinzei *tandai*.

What this unique designation afforded Noriuji in the way of specific authority is nowhere spelled out until later. Only by examining the documents dealing with him can we appreciate his role. First and foremost, he was a military commander charged with subduing Go-Daigo's allies (the southern court loyalists now termed rebels by the Ashikaga) and suppressing the innumerable private skirmishes that were blocking Ashikaga control. In this capacity, the Chinzei *kanrei* differed from his Kamakura-era predecessors, who were arbiters in the courtroom much more frequently than they were commanders on the battlefield.

Judging from the documents that remain, the powers and authority of the *kanrei* were far from complete. One major problem (shared also by the shogun and the eastern regional head) was the lack of a standing army. Troops had to be summoned for specific encounters, rewarded, and then summoned again when next required. Actually, the mobilization and rewarding of troops were basic techniques by which Noriuji built support for the Ashikaga, for they continually reaffirmed the fundamental relationship between lord and vassal.

Noriuji, however, was not the Bakufu's sole military commander in Kyushu, and overlapping jurisdictions greatly hampered his ability to raise forces. For example, the Ashikaga had commissioned another branch member, Hatakeyama Yoshiaki, as a general (*taishō*) in Hyūga Province, probably to ensure extra protection for newly acquired landholdings there.[11] The Bakufu also allowed the Ōtomo, Shimazu, and Shōni considerable authority within their respective base areas.[12] A final problem bearing on recruitment was an insufficient land base from which to allocate rewards. Remarkably, Noriuji even lacked a permanent headquarters on Kyushu for a long time.[13] From the *kanrei*'s point of view, in fact, the situation was intolerable. On at least ten occasions within the first few years of his commission, he asked for permission to return to the capital. Failing that, he begged that his various problems be seriously considered.[14]

In a famous report on the state of Chinzei affairs in 1340, the *kanrei* summarized his dismal working conditions as follows. As he understood his command jurisdiction, he was to have had the highest authority in six of the nine provinces. The three exceptions—Chikuzen, Buzen, and Hizen—had been specifically assigned by the shogun in 1338 to the head of the Shōni family, Yorihisa. Noriuji lamented that in reality his troop requisition orders had had little effect because of the presence of other commanders. Conflicting orders from Ōtomo Ujiyasu, for example, had thwarted his efforts in Hizen and Bungo, and the combined strength of the long-entrenched Shimazu Sadahisa and the newly assigned Hatakeyama Yoshiaki in Satsuma, Ōsumi, and Hyūga had hampered his ability to muster forces there. Lines of command were clear in only one province, Chikugo, and that, Noriuji complained, was an area overrun with southern court adherents.[15]

In the same 1340 report Noriuji provided interesting details regarding his poor economic situation. He had few holdings of his own (*shoryō*) in Chinzei from which to derive personal income. In 1339 the Bakufu had designated four areas to be special office lands (*goryōsho*) for the *kanrei*, including eighty *chō* of paddy in Amauda estate, a particularly fertile area and important water transport site in Buzen Province.[16] According to Noriuji, however, these estates were meager, and all but Amauda were currently embroiled in dispute, making it difficult to use them either for his own support or for reward grants (*onshō*).

The Bakufu appears to have made no response to Noriuji's complaints. Moreover, the Ashikaga seem to have had no clear conception of a rational distribution of power in Kyushu. During these formative years, while Noriuji clamored for formal clarification, the lines of command remained fluid.

Noriuji may have exaggerated the limitations to his powers as a general. An examination by province of his troop calls (*gunsei saisokujō*) and service citations (*gunchūjō*) reveals that, frequent complaints to the contrary, Noriuji was quite active, particularly in Hizen Province, Ōtomo Ujiyasu's involvement there notwithstanding.[17] The *kanrei* often mobilized Hizen vassals, even deploying them on occasion outside their home province. He was also able to extract from them special guard service (*banyaku*) to protect his headquarters at Shōfukuji, around the entrances to the city of Hakata, at various fortresses or temporary campsites, and at other strategic spots, such as barrier gates (*sekisho*).[18]

Noriuji's success in extending his authority early and most markedly in Hizen comes as no great surprise considering the province's history of ties to regional representatives of the central government.

The previous Bakufu's deputies in Kyushu had held the province's *shugo* post concurrently with that of *tandai*.[19] In part as a result of this practice, no single dominant family held sway in Hizen, and by the late 1340's, Noriuji was himself its *shugo*.[20] Several of the regional deputies who succeeded him continued the tradition of holding Hizen.

Noriuji had a more visible control apparatus in Hizen than he did elsewhere. Early on, an officer referred to by title as *samurai dokoro* not only led troops in battle but assisted in the administration of the *kanrei*'s guard service and in general policing functions within the province.[21] Two men appear in documents bearing the title *samurai dokoro* (Satake Shigeyoshi and Omata Dōjō), but the office may not have outlived them.[22] Moreover, no officer seems to have operated in such a capacity in any other province.

Although Noriuji obviously had greater success in Hizen than elsewhere, even there he was constrained at times by his fundamentally weak land base. For example, in 1337 we see him frantically reordering a group of warriors to proceed to the battlefront, even as they were heading instead for Hakata to demand rewards for earlier service.[23] By 1344 the Bakufu had taken steps to relieve Noriuji's plight by granting him the right to commandeer produce for troop provisions from at least ten additional areas (*hyōrōryōsho*). Yet according to Noriuji, these sites were marginal in size and did little to alleviate the larger problem. Woefully he complained that one tiny unit in neighboring Chikuzen Province (Shika shima) was in fact the best of the lot![24]

With such a poor land base, the *kanrei* was obliged to devise other methods to cement relations with Kyushu warriors. He thus frequently reassigned the holdings of enemies, even though rights to such lands were not easily transferred without incident. Sometimes Noriuji could only promise rewards or pledge to report a vassal's loyalty personally to the shogun. In some cases his recommendations included suggestions for appropriate honors; in others his praise was apparently the sole reward.[25] Conversely, as punishment for failures of service the *kanrei* sometimes threatened to discredit a vassal to the Ashikaga, or worse, to confiscate holdings.[26] Finally, to compensate for land shortfalls, Noriuji resorted to encroachments (*ōryō*) on others' holdings, a practice that the Bakufu could scarcely condone.[27]

At long last, in 1346, the Bakufu moved to alleviate the problems the Chinzei *kanrei* had so often complained about. First, an additional area was assigned to Noriuji to increase the total landholdings at his disposal. Second, a permanent headquarters was finally designated. And third, the Bakufu issued an unprecedented statement defining the responsibilities of its regional officer.[28]

These measures seem particularly significant because they coincided with others that together indicate a new emphasis on conditions in all regional outposts. The first and second years of the Jōwa era (1345-46) evidently were a period of general administrative reshuffling. Thus it is no coincidence that the Bakufu dispatched two new assistants to the northeast, assigned a second Isshiki to Kyushu (Noriuji's son, Naouji), increased the landholdings of the Chinzei *kanrei*, and for the first time articulated policy regarding his role.[29]

In the well-known "Memo on Kyushu Affairs" (*Chinzei sata kotogaki*), the Bakufu instructed the *kanrei* on his responsibilities in three main areas:

1. He was to promote the well-being of shrines and temples (presumably this duty implied also protecting landholdings belonging to these traditional powers).

2. In disputes over land rights, he was to act as the Bakufu's investigatory agent. In other kinds of disputes (*zatsumu no koto*), particularly in obvious cases of criminal offense or simple disciplinary problems (*kendan no koto*), the *kanrei* was authorized to deal with the offending parties unless they were Ashikaga vassals (*jitō gokenin*), in which case the Bakufu was to retain final jurisdiction.

3. The *kanrei* was responsible for maintaining foreign defense fortifications (a duty of Bakufu representatives in Kyushu since the days of the Mongol invasions).

It is obvious from this document that in addition to duties of command, the *kanrei* was to carry out administrative duties on behalf of the Bakufu. In fact, he was already operating in an administrative capacity, receiving and relaying central directives, investigating details and forwarding reports, and executing final decisions.[30] In Hizen he had gone well beyond this range of authority by rendering final judgments instead of forwarding them to the Bakufu.[31] Inasmuch as Noriuji had thus ventured to assume authority in an area basic to overlordship—the determining of relationships between vassals and their lands—the Bakufu "Memo" of 1346 may have been more an attempt to restrict than to define the *kanrei*'s area of competence. At any rate, it signified that as far as the Bakufu was concerned, the regional administration was now on a new footing. The role of the *kanrei* had been formalized, though it is not at all clear which of the two Isshiki now in Kyushu was considered the legitimate office-holder.[32]

Even after the arrival of Isshiki Naouji, Noriuji's activities did not diminish. Together father and son endeavored to extend Ashikaga influence by subduing rebel armies while working out a sharing of authority with the other Kyushu powers. The position of the Isshiki was soon dramatically affected, however, by factional splits in the upper echelons of the shogunate. As the Kannō Disturbance unfolded in Kyoto, alliances shifted drastically in Kyushu as well. The Isshiki were defeated militarily in the early 1350's by a revitalized southern court contingent, and it would be nearly twenty years before a Bakufu regional officer could reassert—and then expand—Ashikaga control in the region.

Eastern Japan in the Post-Kannō Period

Tensions within the central elite began to surface in the late 1340's and eventually culminated in the murder of Ashikaga Tadayoshi in 1352, ironically in Kamakura. The shogun himself (Ashikaga Takau-ji) had traveled there a year earlier, and after eliminating his brother, took steps to minimize the resulting dislocation in the Kantō. He replaced many *shugo* and also changed the structure of the Kama-kura office somewhat. Specifically, he declined to designate immediate replacements for the two Kantō deputies, in effect ending the two-man deputy system. Thereafter the position would normally be held by only one person. In the meantime Takauji issued direct orders to eastern warriors.

After the shogun returned to the capital in 1353, the function of the regional office seemed to change also. The exchange of personnel from Kyoto to Kamakura and back became less frequent, and gradually the Kamakura headquarters (*fu*) came to operate less as an adjunct of the central bureaucracy or as a second shogunal base than as a distinct regional organ. This shift was not made explicit at the time, but it begins to be discernible in the documents issued from each official level.[33] The Kamakura *fu* began to operate as an intermediary between the shogun and his Kantō vassals in an increasingly wide range of matters.

The nominal head of the Kamakura office when the period of direct shogunal rule ended was Takauji's third son, Ashikaga Motouji, whose descendants would hold the position of eastern chief (*kubō*) for four successive generations, to the mid-fifteenth century.[34] Motouji was still quite young when Takauji left in 1353, but as he matured he became a forceful leader who made significant strides toward developing the Kamakura *fu* as a regional arm of the Bakufu.

The geographic borders of the Kamakura *fu*'s jurisdiction were fluid during Motouji's tenure as *kubō* (1349-67). The range of Kamakura *fu* activities extended beyond the eight provinces constituting the Kantō proper—Sagami (where Kamakura city was located), Kazusa, Shimōsa, Kōzuke, Shimotsuke, Hitachi, Awa, and Musashi—on occasion into Izu, Kai, Suruga, and less frequently, Shinano.[35] The Bakufu and the Kamakura branch did not divide the country in a strict geographical sense. The Kamakura *fu* officers never became autonomous governors of the region, nor did they provide the Bakufu's sole link with resident warriors. Over time, beginning in this formative period under Motouji, the Bakufu and the Kamakura *fu* established a system of mutual rule.

The *kubō*'s principal subordinate in the Kantō administration was the *kanrei*. At first this position was held by Hatakeyama Kunikiyo, a centrally commissioned Ashikaga branch member, appointed by the shogun to assist Motouji when Motouji was a child. As the *kubō* matured, he assumed decision-making power himself. Moreover, he evidently came to recognize that the stability of the branch headquarters required more than merely strong ties to the central Bakufu. It was necessary to focus attention on the particular political problems of his region. Accordingly, in the early 1360's he drove Hatakeyama out of the Kantō, and in 1363 enticed an eastern leader, Uesugi Noriaki, to replace him.[36]

Noriaki had been Kantō deputy (*kanrei*) once previously, in the pre-Kannō era. The members of his family were becoming a formidable power in the region. As such, they were particularly important vassals of the Ashikaga, as well as a threat to other entrenched eastern powers. To a certain extent, Motouji was taking a risk by inviting Uesugi Noriaki into the Kantō administration, thereby elevating his family above the other Kantō houses. At the same time, it was essential that the Kamakura *fu* have a stable source of support in the area. The bond created between the main branch of the Uesugi and the Kamakura *fu* was mutually beneficial, and it thus persisted for several generations.

Around the same time that Motouji succeeded in enlisting Noriaki as *kanrei*, he also made obvious efforts to attract and control other rising eastern families, including smaller-scale warrior households below the level of *shugo*. In 1361-62 he was successful in summoning local lords (*kokujin*) to his service in the campaign to eliminate Hatakeyama. Augmenting his troops at that time were not only individual *kokujin* but groups or leagues of local leaders (*ikki*).[37] By 1365 he had also attracted an impressive group of powerful *kokujin* as his personal guard (*kinju*).[38]

The techniques Motouji used to cement relationships with his supporters were basically similar to those used by the Chinzei *kanrei* in Kyushu, namely mobilization, recommendation, and reward. The *kubō*, however, had important advantages over his Kyushu counterpart. In addition to the immediate legitimacy and prestige he garnered by virtue of his lineage, that is, his direct descendance from the shogun, Motouji apparently had a more secure land base than the Kyushu deputy. They both had authority to assign holdings taken in battle or otherwise confiscated, but the *kubō* also had at his free disposal parts of Ashikaga estate in Shimotsuke Province.[39] Moreover, the Kamakura *fu* held income-producing support estates (*goryōsho*), to which local representatives were assigned as managers. The yearly dues from these lands were substantial enough to require handling by a special financial bureau (*mandokoro*) in Kamakura. This aspect of the Kantō regional administration closely resembled that of the central Bakufu, where the Kyoto *mandokoro* managed finances, and contrasted sharply with the situation in Kyushu.[40]

Once lands were granted to vassals, they also had to be protected. When problems arose regarding warriors' land rights, the *kubō* sometimes took independent action—for example, on simple matters involving lands he himself had assigned, or when petitions came directly to his headquarters.[41] For the most part, however, the Bakufu held superior authority in land disputes, and Motouji and his subordinates functioned primarily as chief executors of orders from Kyoto.

Centrally issued directives to discipline guilty parties in land disputes or criminal cases were often routed through the *kubō* or *kanrei* and then filtered down through various channels, depending on many circumstances (the province, the nature of the matter, the individuals involved). That there was no set pattern is significant, for it indicates that the sharing of authority in the east was not regularized in this early period.

An Izu Province affair of 1364 offers one glimpse of the chain of command as it was evolving in the Kantō. At stake in this suit was an appointment (*bettō shiki*) at a temple in the province. Orders from the shogun went directly to the Kamakura lord (Kamakura *dono*) to solve the problem. Motouji in turn issued instructions to the *shugo* of the province to secure the petitioner. The *shugo* communicated the order to his agent (probably the deputy *shugo*, or *shugodai*), who handed it over at the locale in question.[42]

On occasion the highest orders came initially from the imperial court. In 1361, for example, a case was delegated by imperial decree (*rinji*) through the shogun to the *kubō*, perhaps because the complaint involved rights within the old provincial office (*kokuga*) of Kōzuke.[43]

The examples above suggest that in its capacity as an intermediary, the Kantō office operated as a sort of supra-*shugo* for the region.[44] The *kubō* and *kanrei* did not always operate through the *shugo*, however. They often commissioned other agents, which in a way gave both the agents and the Kamakura *fu* some leverage over the *shugo*. By the same token, the Bakufu did not always work through its branch office. Sometimes orders went directly to *shugo*, or went simultaneously to both *shugo* and the Kamakura *fu*.[45] Similarly, petitions upward often bypassed the regional headquarters.

In certain matters other than land disputes, the Kantō office began to assume considerable authority. The *kubō* determined appointments to elite positions in several Kantō religious institutions, for example,[46] and was responsible for maintaining a general level of protection to ensure the prosperity of the Tsurugaoka Hachiman Shrine in Kamakura.[47]

By the end of Motouji's tenure, in 1367, the Bakufu's Kantō branch was clearly one of its strongest links to the eastern provinces. The Kamakura chief officer was much more than a military commander; he had an ever-increasing range of administrative functions. Yet, as Itō Kiyoshi has pointed out, it is anachronistic to ascribe to the Kantō branch office from its inception the same range of powers that it later came to wield.[48] The relationship between the Bakufu and Kamakura *fu* evolved, as did the position of the latter within its region. In the broadest terms, what distinguished this period from the pre-Kannō era was the frequency with which the Bakufu used the branch office rather than exercising direct control. What characterized subsequent periods was the widening range of Kamakura *fu* authority.

Setbacks in Kyushu, 1350-1370

During the 1350's and 1360's, the very period when Motouji was working to increase the Bakufu's hold on the Kantō, the Ashikaga lost ground in Kyushu. As the mid-century drive to eliminate Ashikaga Tadayoshi from the Bakufu elite had gained momentum, the latter's adopted heir, Tadafuyu, had also moved farther and farther from the locus of central power. In 1349 he arrived in Kyushu's Higo Province and severely disrupted the military and political situation there by competing for control of local warriors with the Isshiki, the southern court generals, and some of the traditional Kyushu powers.[49]

Tadafuyu had previously been a successful military commander for the Bakufu in central Japan, and on occasion he claimed to be in Kyushu also at the behest of Kyoto. In fact, he seems not to have been dispatched to the region initially for any official purpose. For a brief period during a reconciliation in the capital between his uncle and the shogun, Tadafuyu apparently gained formal status. He was referred to in a chronicle of the period as Chinzei *tandai* (deputy), the term associated with the previous Bakufu's regional appointees.[50] For most of his stay, however, Tadafuyu was in conflict with the Bakufu's official representatives, the Isshiki, at one time attracting enough local support to drive them into the southern court camp against him.

Tadafuyu's opposition to the clique then dominating the Bakufu was obvious from certain stylistic features of his early documents. When dating communications, for example, he blatantly refused to adopt the Bakufu's official name for the era (*nengō*). Specifically, he persisted in using the older reign name of Jōwa until well into the second year of Kannō (1351) in order to show his independence from shogunal control. Those who enlisted as his followers did likewise. Around the time Takauji and Tadayoshi reconciled, Tadafuyu began employing the official *nengō*, but soon thereafter the shogun declared that Tadafuyu was not actually a partner to the rapprochement and ordered troops against him.[51]

Tadafuyu was in Kyushu only three years, but the effects of his presence on the political configuration there were long-lasting. Ultimately, the presence of a member of the shogunal family (even one not in favor with the shogun) split the forces lined up on the Bakufu side. Tadafuyu's lineage obviously conferred on him a degree of prestige and legitimacy. To many local warriors, alliance directly with an Ashikaga lord no doubt seemed pragmatic. At any rate, by the time he left Kyushu, Tadafuyu had attracted a sizable following from many provinces. His backers included some major figures, such as Shōni Yorihisa (whose personal power sphere in northern Kyushu was being directly threatened by the presence of the Chinzei *kanrei*), but the main contingent of his support came from smaller-scale local lords (the *kokujin* class), many of whom were heads of cadet branches in the process of breaking off from their main lines to establish independent bases.

Tadafuyu's rapid success in gaining followers can be attributed to more than his Ashikaga surname. From the moment he arrived he pursued policies that quickly established his credentials as overlord. Most notably, he offered immediate rewards for allegiance. He confirmed (*ando*) his vassals' holdings, for example, and also took it upon himself to make his own *shugo* appointments,[52] thus providing a type of reward the Chinzei *kanrei* had never offered.

Tadafuyu's forcefulness was evident in the style of his orders as well as in their content. In contrast to Chinzei *kanrei* Isshiki Noriuji, who often worded his documents in a way that put him in the role of reporter transmitting orders from a superior authority, Tadafuyu issued commands that were direct and decisive, characteristically acknowledging no higher power. The fact that some of them (such as *kudashibumi* and *uragaki ando*) resembled documents used by the Kamakura Bakufu during what had been the formative era of warrior government no doubt lent them an impressive aura of tradition and authority.[53]

Tadafuyu's short stay in Kyushu was a period of intense activity. Seno Seiichirō has calculated that the total number of Kyushu-related documents notably increased during this time, as all sides were busily trying to stabilize conditions to their advantage.[54] In a very real sense Tadafuyu's success meant failure for the Isshiki and ultimately a severe setback for Ashikaga interests in the nine-province area. The Chinzei *kanrei* family was so weakened that it subsequently suffered major defeats by southern court armies. In 1353 Isshiki Noriuji left Kyushu altogether, and by 1358 Naouji had also departed, effectively ending Isshiki influence in the region. For the next twelve years much of northern Kyushu was dominated by the southern court forces.

The Bakufu sent two other branch family members as deputies, but neither could repair the damage. Shiba Ujitsune was appointed in

1360-61, followed shortly thereafter, in 1365-66, by Shibukawa Yo-shiyuki.[55] Shiba was defeated not long after he arrived, and Shibu-kawa never even made it to the island to take up his appointment. The Ashikaga were not able to reassert their power in the region until significant innovations took place in the central Bakufu administration, and until the arrival in Kyushu of Imagawa Ryōshun in the 1370's.

The Late Fourteenth Century

During the last quarter of the fourteenth century, the Bakufu's regional administrative system matured. The heads of both the eastern and western regions remained in leadership positions for lengthy terms (31 years and 25 years, respectively), during which they extended the authority of their offices both geographically and in range of functions. In the Kantō, after a brief interim of direct rule by the Bakufu, the *kubō* Ujimitsu broadened the administrative (as opposed to military) authority that his father, Motouji, had pioneered. The major component of the eastern branch's strength during this period was the *kanrei* family. In Kyushu the Bakufu deputy Imagawa Ryō-shun made substantial progress toward the twin goals of dominating the three traditionally powerful *shugo* houses and defeating the southern court armies. Through his efforts, the rebel forces were vanquished (eventually leading to a formal unification of the competing courts) and Ashikaga influence in Kyushu reached its zenith.

The Maturity of the Kubō-Kanrei System

When Ashikaga Motouji died in 1367, the emperor suspended all litigation, the Bakufu resumed direct management of Kantō affairs, and Ashikaga Ujimitsu prepared to head the Kamakura branch.[56] Because Ujimitsu was yet a child, the role of *kanrei* became ever more important, a situation that almost mirrored the situation in Kyoto, where the deputy Hosokawa Yoriyuki became the driving force supporting the young Shogun Yoshimitsu. It was a full ten years before the new Kantō *kubō* began issuing documents; until 1378 orders emanating from the Kamakura *fu* were *kanrei* orders, in the *kubō*'s name.[57]

The early years of the new Kantō regime were turbulent. The shogun, *kubō*, and Kantō *kanrei* had all died within a two-year period (1367-68), and this change in top leadership produced a temporary

dislocation. Almost immediately there were uprisings (*ran*). Disturbances continued to punctuate the political history of the east in
Ujimitsu's era, and the Kamakura *fu* was chiefly responsible for their
pacification. Some of the uprisings were initiated in the name of the
opposition southern court, but they reflected more significant political divisions than the simple dynastic split. No single explanation for
the causes of the various *ran* will suffice. The success of the Kamakura
fu in subduing the major outbreaks had clear results, however: the
relative advance of Ashikaga interests vis-à-vis entrenched eastern
rivals, and integral to that, a noticeable increase in the power of the
kanrei Uesugi family. A few examples will illustrate the point.

Close examination of the participants and the political circumstances surrounding two disturbances in 1368—referred to as the
Heiikki and Utsunomiya Ujitsuna uprisings[58]—suggests that these
were not simply timely expressions of opposition to the extension of
the Ashikaga presence (they were not, that is, simply the work of
Kantō magnates in conflict with the new *kubō*). Nor is it adequate to
view them solely as inevitable by-products of the underlying economic and social changes that were dividing warrior households and
transforming eastern society. Certainly such problems contributed to
the disturbances of the age, and they may have prompted some of the
participants in the two instances under consideration here. Yet the
uprisings of 1368 seem to represent most clearly a rising opposition
to the advance of Uesugi family power. The leaders of the Heiikki and
Utsunomiya incidents were former *shugo* who had lost appointments to the Uesugi and their allies.[59] Their defeat in 1368 further
advanced Uesugi interests, and as the century progressed, other successful Kamakura *fu* campaigns garnered additional holdings and
shugo posts for the *kanrei* family.

For example, by putting down the early leader of the famous
Oyama Disturbance, which began in the 1380's, the *kanrei* Uesugi
Norikata added Shimotsuke Province to his family's growing number
of *shugo* posts.[60] The so-called *Oyama no ran* was one of the major
conflicts in the Kantō in the late fourteenth century. It began as a
private dispute (though couched in loftier terms) between members of
two entrenched Kantō families, the Oyama and the Utsunomiya,
who apparently shared the *shugo* appointment for Shimotsuke.[61] The
crisis escalated far beyond the original households and the initial dis-
agreement, however, to become a seventeen-year-long problem for
the Kamakura *fu*. That the Kantō office eventually resolved the affair

was evidence that it enjoyed, through careful alliances, a greater concentration of support than any single opponent or group of opponents.[62] The *kanrei* family played a major part in and profited from the development of these alliances in the east.

It is not possible to provide here a province-by-province account of the spread of Uesugi influence throughout the Kantō. It is important to note, however, that as the main Uesugi branches gathered extensive landholdings, developed private networks of vassals to administer their *shugo* posts, and acquired ever-wider public authority as the *kubō*'s assistants, they became vital allies of the Bakufu, whom the shogun would pragmatically choose to support in the early fifteenth century over his own relative and chief regional officer, the *kubō*. In the course of building their strength, the Uesugi remained dependent on the legitimacy afforded them by their positions as deputies of the *kubō*. Yet in subsequent decades it was precisely because the main branch of the Uesugi (the Yamanouchi) continued to support the Bakufu-Kamakura *fu* system that the system was able to survive.

In the late fourteenth century the *kubō* and *kanrei* were developing together as an executive arm of the Bakufu in the east, and it is not difficult to document the broadening scope of their activities. Evidence of their involvement in regulating commerce is particularly interesting, for it supports from a different geographic perspective the contention made by others with regard to Kyoto and its environs that the Ashikaga Bakufu was attentive to exploiting the commercial sector. In 1382, for example, the Bakufu ordered the Kantō headquarters to tax sake producers in Kamakura, earmarking the proceeds for the upkeep of Engakuji, a Zen temple located there.[63]

In this case the Kamakura *fu* was clearly the executor of a higher order. There is also evidence from this period, however, that the eastern office exercised a degree of independent authority over noncommercial taxes. In 1376 and 1384, for instance, the *fu* allocated province-wide taxes (*munabechisen*) collected by various Kantō *shugo*.[64] Likewise, the *kubō*'s office issued exemptions for a special tax previously not within its jurisdiction. Specifically, it exempted certain Kantō lands from payment of the *yakubutakumai*, an extraordinary levy to support the imperial shrine at Ise. This tax had previously been under the purview of the court or the Bakufu only.[65]

The beneficiaries of the tax allocations and special exemptions in the cases cited above were not the eastern office or the Bakufu, or their vassals, but major religious institutions with which the Ashikaga maintained close relationships: Tsurugaoka Hachiman and Mishima shrines, and the temple Engakuji. The Bakufu and the *fu* were both actively involved in the affairs of the two shrines, but by law all authority over Engakuji was delegated to the *kubō's* office (except for the appointment of the chief priest) because the temple was one of the specially designated eastern Gozan Zen institutions.[66] The Bakufu maintained some connections with Engakuji, as we have seen in the sake tax example above, but the *kubō* was to be the closer supervisor, protecting the temple's physical properties and ensuring its economic prosperity, and thus relieving the Bakufu of these tasks.

Perhaps the area in which Kamakura *fu* authority expanded most notably in the late fourteenth century was that of judicial settlements. Under Kubō Ujimitsu, the eastern headquarters did not merely act as a Bakufu investigatory agent and executor (or policing agent in criminal offenses) but increasingly began to assume the role of arbiter in disputes involving Kantō lands or people. This trend can most easily be recognized from the appearance of the so-called administrative directive (*bugyōnin hōsho*), through which *fu* bureaucrats transmitted judgments. Procedures for settling suits in the Kantō were not regularized to the point where *bugyōnin hōsho* were the only form of document employed; the *kubō* and *kanrei* sometimes issued decisions directly, for example, through *kubō kakikudashi* or *kanrei hōsho*.[67] But as the volume of suits grew, a body of administrators became increasingly active, a trend that accelerated in the Ōei period (1394-1428) under Ujimitsu's successors, Mitsukane and Mochiuji.

Kamakura *fu* authority also expanded geographically. In 1392 the Bakufu granted the eastern office formal jurisdiction over Mutsu and Dewa provinces, and in 1396 Kubō Ujimitsu joined his vassal Yūki Shirakawa Shichirō in southern Mutsu in subduing the final remnants of the Oyama uprising.[68] A few years later, under the next *kubō*, two deputies (Ujimitsu's sons, Ashikaga Mitsunao and Mitsusada) were stationed in areas bordering this trouble spot to serve as permanent *fu* representatives.[69] Their formal authority apparently encompassed both provinces in their entirety, two areas in which the Bakufu had appointed no *shugo*; in practice the deputies' influence seems to have been concentrated in southern Mutsu only. Nevertheless, it represented a direct Ashikaga family involvement in the northeast.

As the fourteenth century came to a close, the Bakufu's power and organizational strength were reaching a peak. The eastern branch office was serving in a progressively wider area and in a greater capacity. The Bakufu retained superior authority in certain matters, particularly the confirmation of its vassals' land rights (*ando ken*)[70] and the appointment of *shugo*,[71] but it increasingly shared power with the Kamakura *fu*. While maintaining more direct control in the central provinces, the Bakufu used the *kubō*'s office as a check on the more distant eastern *shugo*, as a link with local warriors, and as an agent for policing and pacifying, in order to prevent any disruption in the region that might impair the Ashikaga balance. What evolved was a kind of cooperative control, not divided geographically in any strict sense or formally defined.

Advances in Kyushu under Imagawa Ryōshun

The period roughly equivalent to the tenures of Shogun Yoshimitsu and Kubō Ujimitsu was also the time when Ashikaga power reached its greatest extension in Kyushu. The lapses of the 1350's and 1360's following the fall of the Isshiki prompted the new central leadership to post Imagawa Ryōshun to Kyushu in 1371 to reestablish control. By the time this experienced bureaucrat and general was removed from office 25 years later, he had triumphed over the southern court armies and had stretched his influence widely.

Ryōshun, the head of an Ashikaga branch family, was not the first Imagawa to serve the Bakufu in Kyushu. Imagawa generals had been active on the side of the Ashikaga in the early years of the Chinzei *kanrei*.[72] When Ryōshun arrived, he designated additional family members and his most trusted vassals as area commanders, following the pattern of the shogunal house nationally and of his predecessors in Kyushu, the Isshiki.[73]

The new Kyushu officer (soon to be referred to as Kyushu *tandai*) established himself quickly. Within three years he had broken the back of the main southern court (*miyakata*) forces, and after retaking the Dazaifu, turned his attention to the recalcitrants farther south. To increase his chances for success, he invited the help of the traditional powers in Kyushu—the Shōni, Ōtomo, and Shimazu (in the persons of the family heads and *shugo*, Fuyusuke, Chikayo, and Ujihisa). When Shōni Fuyusuke failed to respond to his overture, Ryōshun asked Shimazu Ujihisa to intercede for him, which was successfully done. But Ryōshun had the Shōni leader killed anyway, and by this act greatly diminished the potential for an alliance that might unite the provincial heads under Ashikaga overlordship with Ryōshun as the shogun's personal representative. Shimazu Ujihisa openly opposed Ryōshun from this juncture and remained his major obstacle long after the southern court remnants had died or dispersed.

In a report to the Bakufu in 1375, Ryōshun branded Ujihisa as having gone over to the enemy and recommended that part of his holdings be reassigned to a more trustworthy vassal.[74] From that point Ryōshun seemed to concentrate his efforts on breaking the Shimazu's hold on a sizable portion of southern Kyushu. In short, the fight now moved from the north, where it had been directed against Prince Kanenaga's loyalists, to the south, to weaken a former Ashikaga ally whose loyalty was now in question.

Like his Chinzei *kanrei* predecessors, Ryōshun was first and foremost a military commander. Yet during his long tenure as *tandai*, his role as an administrator and intermediary for the shogun became increasingly important. Furthermore, his official position—and the rewards and services he could render because of it—gave him leverage as he sought alliances on behalf of both the northern court and the anti-Shimazu drive.

Once the Bakufu had decided (in 1376) to enjoin Ryōshun to subdue the Shimazu leaders, Shogun Yoshimitsu shored up Ryōshun's position by appointing him *shugo* of both Ōsumi and Satsuma provinces, thereby divesting Shimazu Ujihisa and Shimazu Korehisa of those posts.[75] Yet, as Ryōshun himself acknowledged in an impassioned letter to the local lords (*kokujin*) of the areas, the titles would be meaningless without active support from them.[76] Ryōshun clearly recognized the political realities of his day: to secure a territory for the Ashikaga, he would have to extend his reach to the lowest level of control. In Ōsumi and Satsuma he communicated directly with local lords, alternately soliciting their loyalty and threatening retaliation for collaboration with the Shimazu.[77] In Hyūga he recruited the locally powerful Tsuchimochi family soon after his arrival. The advantage of this relationship became strikingly evident later: without the support of the Tsuchimochi, the *shugo* of the province (Ōtomo) was rendered ineffective; eventually he relinquished his post.[78]

Ryōshun's position as *tandai* and his status as the shogun's direct representative obviously carried considerable weight. In organizing the region's warriors, he took care to reiterate frequently that he was merely doing the shogun's will, and that the warriors who backed him would be showing their support for the overlord. As he once explained it to the Nejime family of Ōsumi Province, by joining him they would be helping the shogunal house—and would accordingly profit themselves.[79]

In his efforts to cultivate relationships in areas where he had little or no direct control of lands, Ryōshun went beyond merely dealing with individual families. In southern Kyushu, for example, he seems to have been instrumental in the formation of a 61-member league (*ikki*) of local proprietors. A contract signed by the *ikki* in 1377 indicates clearly how significant such a group could be to Ryōshun. While pledging loyalty to the shogun, the group resolved to take land disputes or other conflicts to the *tandai* directly. Only in the event that a grievance might be against Ryōshun himself did the *ikki* reserve the right to petition the Bakufu. Finally, the *ikki* promised to avoid disrupting the social order.[80]

Ryōshun built close relationships with *ikki* in northern Kyushu as well. Even before arriving in Kyushu he contacted a group in Hizen, for example, which he continued to use as his agents in the province.[81] These *ikki* in Kyushu were strikingly different from some of the *kokujin ikki* of central Japan, which had formed out of opposition to higher authority. In Kyushu, by contrast, local interests often coincided with Bakufu interests,[82] with the result that numerous *ikki* came to occupy important positions within the Ashikaga system, rather than standing outside it.[83] Subservient to the regional officers and other generals, but parallel in status to individual vassals (*gokenin*) and the shogun's special corps (*hōkōshū*), these *ikki* functioned as components of a political order far more complex than the standard notion of a Bakufu-*shugo* system would suggest.

The members of *ikki* linked to the Kyushu *tandai* tended not to establish direct ties with the shogun. Rather, they seem to have been given vassal (*gokenin*) status as a group; orders and rewards were often communicated to them as a body (to the *ikki-chū*, for example). In 1373, to cite one instance, Ryōshun authorized the Sonogi *ikki* of Hizen Province to collect half of the proceeds (*hanzeibun*) of a specified area as provisions for service under him.[84]

As vital as it was to Ryōshun's success, attracting local warriors was no easy task. Basically, he faced the same problem that had plagued the earlier Kyushu officers—a weak economic base. By Ryōshun's day, however, the *tandai* had at his disposal a technique not available to the Chinzei *kanrei*—the allocation of *hanzei* (half rights to produce). The authority to grant *hanzei* rights was first recognized by the Bakufu in legislation of 1352 as a temporary expedient for troops in three central provinces. The practice grew, however, and Ryōshun, as a newcomer to Kyushu with few private lands at his disposal, made extensive use of it to advance his position relative to the older families whose holdings were concentrated there.[85]

In general, Imagawa Ryōshun was remarkably skillful at manipulating the political tools available to him to mobilize support throughout Kyushu. During his 25 years as *tandai*, he issued over five hundred documents (many more, doubtless, since that is the number that survives), which stand as tangible evidence of his zeal. In terms of documentary style, many of Ryōshun's papers were "personal," such as letters (*shojō*) or directly issued orders (*kakikudashi*), but their contents often acknowledged his position as intermediary between the central administration and the *shugo*, and between the shogun and the warriors of Kyushu.

In his role as intermediary Ryōshun investigated allegations in land disputes, executed Bakufu decisions, collected taxes for the construction of religious institutions, and made recommendations that land confirmations (*ando*) be granted.[86] He also reported to the Bakufu on the availability of confiscated lands for reassignment, forwarded statements by other agents (such as *shugo*) regarding suits lodged from their provinces, and, an important power, made recommendations for *shugo* appointments.[87]

Ryōshun's power was most complete in the provinces where he also came to hold or control the *shugo* posts. According to Yamaguchi Takamasa's detailed investigations, *shugo* posts in eight of the nine provinces came under Imagawa control at different points during Ryōshun's tenure as *tandai*.[88] Compared to the regional appointees who preceded him, he made remarkable progress as both military commander and Bakufu administrator. He was never able to defeat his long-term enemies, the Shimazu, but he did have considerable success in attracting vassals, even in the south.

In any event, it was Ryōshun's domination of the north of Kyushu that proved most significant for the Bakufu in the long run. Recognizing the growing commercial importance of the north, the Bakufu was able to register gains from trade with Korea largely owing to Ryōshun's efforts. Ryōshun took responsibility for subduing the unruly pirates (*wakō*) troubling the Korean kingdoms, and for exchanging captives and presents, an unofficial form of trade.[89] In a sense Ryōshun functioned as a sort of foreign affairs representative for the

Ashikaga, and he laid the groundwork for future *tandai* who would focus their activities in the north of Kyushu.

By the mid-1390's, indeed, Imagawa Ryōshun had become a considerable power in his own right. His abrupt dismissal in 1395 has correspondingly been much debated. Ryōshun's own explanation was that he was slandered by an envious competitor, Ōuchi Yoshihiro, who had been granted one *shugo* post in Kyushu and was vying for control of foreign relations and trade. In light of subsequent ties between the Bakufu and the Ōuchi, it may be that Ōuchi did influence the decision of Shogun Yoshimitsu to remove Ryōshun from the scene. But other considerations, though not individually compelling, probably had a cumulative impact on the event. For one thing, Ryōshun's main supporter in Kyoto had died shortly before. For another, the unification of the courts in 1392 had in a sense ended his mission. Finally, Ryōshun was by that time quite elderly—seventy, by Kawazoe Shōji's calculations.[90]

Ryōshun's removal at just this juncture is nevertheless curious in light of a directive issued to him shortly before. This instruction of 1395 seemed, in fact, to grant the Kyushu *tandai* an even broader role as officer of the shogun. It praised Ryōshun for his pacification of Kyushu, extended his authority to include the right to bestow and confirm landholdings (*onshō* and *ando*) directly, and assigned him the role of go-between in the recruitment of members for the shogun's personal vassal corps (*hōkōshū*).[91] But the Bakufu simultaneously imposed a significant restriction on Ryōshun's relationship with his troops by stipulating that the issuance of documents recognizing valor (*kanjō*) was the shogun's sole prerogative. In a sense, then, the Bakufu was here firming up guidelines for its Kyushu officer while at the same time attempting to limit his ability to build a personal power sphere. It was attempting to strengthen the institution while weakening the man.

By way of explanation, the Ashikaga political system operated on a theory of shared power. The shogunal family could rule only by allocating to its representatives—*shugo* and regional deputies alike—certain prerogatives within their areas. During the 1390's, however, Yoshimitsu took several measures to tilt this balance more in his own favor. On more than one occasion, he used force to subordinate provincial figures (*shugo*). In the Kantō, as we shall see, he sought to counterbalance the strength of the cadet branch of his own family that held the *kubō* post. In Kyushu he removed Imagawa Ryōshun.

In this sense (and in view of the shogun's other pretensions during this decade),[92] Yoshimitsu's policies were not merely part of a general administrative reshuffling but a direct thrust to tighten central control.

Subsequent steps taken in Kyushu show clearly that the Bakufu was seeking not to break the local alliances the *tandai* had so painstakingly built, but to use them. Soon after Ryōshun's dismissal the shogun sent a personal exhortation to another Imagawa—Ujikane, in Hyūga Province—assuring him that despite the removal of his relative, Ujikane had the Bakufu's backing and should continue to monitor the *kokujin* in his area. On the same day the shogun also sent an order to the *kokujin* of Hyūga urging them to comply.[93] While eliminating Ryōshun's personal influence, Yoshimitsu obviously sought to preserve the former *tandai*'s political connections.

In hindsight it might be argued that the removal of Imagawa Ryōshun did not in the long run tie the area more effectively to the central government. His replacement by another Ashikaga relative who had no connections in Kyushu reduced the Bakufu's overall influence in the region. Certainly none of the *tandai* who followed Ryōshun served as many functions as he, or maintained as effectively ties with forces in the south. Rather rapidly the *tandai*'s activities became limited to the northern provinces. This area remained vital to the Bakufu, but in the fifteenth century, as we shall see, attention was diverted from the political to the economic sphere through a program aimed at commercial profit.

Regional Realignments

In the Kantō adjustments in control patterns were neither as drastic nor as abrupt as in Kyushu, where the dismissal of the regional officer and the redefinition of his office constituted a distinct break. Yet, as the period progressed, changes took place in the east as well, not only in the relationship between the Bakufu and its Kantō branch, but in the manner in which both attempted to maintain control of the area. A realignment of forces gradually occurred, which became dramatically visible by 1438, when armies of the shogun went to battle against the Bakufu's own regional chief, the Kamakura *kubō*.

By relying on chronicles, diaries, and war tales as source materials, treatments of the early fifteenth century have tended to view these events as a sequence of escalating crises brought about by the eccentric inclinations of the leaders of the day—a would-be king (Yoshi-mitsu), a despot (Yoshinori), and a succession of overly, indeed tragi-cally, ambitious *kubō* (Ashikaga Mitsukane and Mochiuji, in office from 1398 to 1438). The publication in recent years of many addi-tional documents has permitted scholars to look beyond the auto-cratic personalities of the rulers to fundamental changes in power relationships. The critical question of the day was how much auton-omy the Bakufu might safely allow its regional commanders when the regime lacked overwhelming military and economic resources.

The Kamakura *fu* was only one of several power centers through-out the country that began to assume more and more authority in order to govern delegated areas. Certain *shugo* had attempted to do likewise, and so had Imagawa Ryōshun in Kyushu. As we have seen, a number of these local agents were disciplined decisively. In the Kantō, however, discipline was a delicate matter because the nominal leader there was a member of the ruling family. Only at great risk to Ashikaga legitimacy and credibility could the shogun reprimand—much less dismiss—the *kubō*.

The Kamakura *fu*'s expanding authority in this period is not diffi-cult to trace. Documents from the latter part of Ujimitsu's tenure through those of his son and grandson, Mitsukane and Mochiuji, show advances in two realms vital for maintaining control and at-tracting greater support: suit settlement and the confirmation of landholdings (*ando*).[94] In 1398, for example, just a few months before he died, the *kubō* Ujimitsu threw out two suits he deemed invalid. One involved a *jitō shiki*; the other, lands held by a reli-gious institution. Both were handled entirely apart from the Kyoto Bakufu.[95]

The eastern officers disposed of Kantō problems independently with increasing frequency during the tenures of Mitsukane and his successor, the fourth *kubō*, Mochiuji, who held his position for thirty years. Although the Bakufu continued to resolve some cases,[96] the trend was now unmistakably toward decision making by the regional head. Nowhere is this trend clearer than in Mochiuji's issuance of land confirmations. From the early days of the first shogunate, confir-mation documents (*andojō*) had epitomized the lord's protection of his vassals' land rights. Mochiuji not only began to confirm such holdings on his own (for example, those of the *kanrei* in 1417), but even guaranteed a family's headship (*sōryō shiki*) on more than one occasion.[97]

The levying of (or conversely, the exemption from) province-wide taxes (*tansen*), normally designated for the upkeep of major shrines and temples, was another key inroad made by the Kamakura *fu*. Long associated with the shogun and *shugo*,[98] the *tansen* now also became a prerogative of the Kantō branch office. To cite one example, the *kubō* directed in 1417 that when the necessary work was completed at a particular temple, the excess *tansen* funds should be allocated to the repair of a certain shrine.[99]

Kamakura *fu* authority was expanding into each of these different realms—*tansen* levies, the confirmation of land rights, and dispute settlement—at the same time that the Bakufu was intensifying its efforts to centralize the polity. The *kubō* thus found himself potentially at odds with the shogun, who began to seek ways to curtail the growing autonomy of his eastern kinsman. The principal strategy evolved for this purpose was to strengthen ties with other eastern magnates.

Even before the end of the fourteenth century, the shogun solicited aid from the main line (Yamanouchi branch) of the Uesugi family to squelch an anti-Bakufu plot that *kubō* Mitsukane, bolstered by recent victories in the northeast, was contemplating joining. Uesugi Norisada played a key role by interceding and restraining the *kubō* in 1399.[100] A year later the Bakufu relied again on Norisada. The problem this time was the former Kyushu *tandai* Imagawa Ryōshun. Dismissed from his Kyushu position a few years earlier, the disgruntled Ryōshun was rumored to be in the Kantō. The shogun alerted Norisada to the potentially disruptive situation.[101]

Norisada subsequently became Kantō *kanrei* and served as an important source and symbol of continuity when both the central and regional Ashikaga family heads (former shogun Yoshimitsu and *kubō* Mitsukane) died in 1408-9. It is important to note that Norisada had not been *kanrei* at the time he began actively helping the Bakufu. His family had held the *kanrei* position for many years, but in 1395 a member of a cadet lineage known as the Inukake Uesugi received the appointment. For two generations thereafter, the Inukake and Yamanouchi branches alternated in the office, suggesting an additional reason for the latter's efforts to curry favor with Kyoto. In 1416 an Inukake branch *kanrei*, Uesugi Zenshū, resigned his position and sought to move against the Kamakura *kubō*. His defeat was a resounding victory for the Yamanouchi,[102] and from this point the Yamanouchi line was clearly the dominant Uesugi family. Its ties to the Bakufu provided the principal basis for its continued influence in the area. Indeed, when the Bakufu ultimately took the field against the *kubō*, it relied on this longtime alliance.[103]

As the bond between the Bakufu and the Yamanouchi Uesugi was strengthening, kinship ties between the Ashikaga lords were weakening. In the decades after the shogunate's founding, the central bureaucracy and its primary regional base had been headed by Ashikaga leaders who were closely related. By contrast, the shogun and *kubō* in the early fifteenth century, Yoshimochi and Mitsukane, were sons of cousins, and the two who clashed in 1438, Yoshinori and Mochiuji, were related even more distantly. As blood ties became thinner, the lord-vassal bonds established with the Yamanouchi Uesugi became more significant, especially as the latter extended its power by broadening its connections with local lords.

During this period the Bakufu created in the Kantō a corps of special support troops called Kyoto *fuchishū* or *fuchisha*. Recruited primarily from powerful northern and northeastern Kantō families sometime before 1423, these troops served as a kind of extraordinary task force for specific military endeavors and in general provided a counterbalance to the *kubō*.[104] The *fuchishū* became especially important in the years following the Zenshū Disturbance. The Bakufu had supported the *kubō* against Zenshū because it could not afford to have its branch office crippled by a regional rebellion. The *kubō* himself became a disruptive element, however, by continuing to make retaliatory strikes long after the short-lived attempt at a coup by the Zenshū forces had failed. Four years after the event, the *kubō* Mochiuji was still chasing Zenshū's offspring and the remnants of his forces.[105] His actions served to stir up the east rather than to pacify it.

What brought the Bakufu and the *kubō* into open conflict was the shogunal succession of 1428. Since Shogun Yoshimochi left no heirs upon his death, the top Bakufu administrators were left to choose a successor. Given his stature as a high-ranking member of the Ashikaga family (albeit not of the main line) as well as his obvious strengths as a regional leader, Mochiuji considered himself an appropriate candidate. The appointment went to Yoshinori, however, and relations between the *kubō* and the Bakufu, already strained, now worsened.

Once again it is important to emphasize the deepening relationship between the Bakufu and the Yamanouchi Uesugi. Control of the Kamakura *fu* and effective power in the region were passing into the Yamanouchi branch's hands. Thus when forces were mounted against the *kubō* in 1438, victory for the Bakufu-*kanrei* side was swift. The shogun mobilized troops from the fringes of the Kantō, especially from the north and northeast. A Yamanouchi Uesugi *kanrei* served as principal mediator at first—and then as principal commander.[106]

Not long after the *kubō*'s defeat and subsequent suicide, some of his vassals began a move to restore his family (and their own) to power, but a second victory by the Bakufu-*kanrei* troops in 1441 (the so-called Yūki *gassen*) secured the region. This was an especially important triumph for the Bakufu, since the head of the regime (the shogun Yoshinori) was assassinated in the same year. The Uesugi eventually supported the return of one of Mochiuji's sons to the post of regional head in the east, which suggests that the presence of an Ashikaga as nominal leader continued to have symbolic importance. It was the Yamanouchi Uesugi family, however, that would dominate the next phase of Kantō history.

When we review the same periods (roughly 1395-1440) in Kyushu, we note the political decline of the Bakufu's regional officers. The deputies appointed after Imagawa Ryōshun were all members of a single Ashikaga branch family, the Shibukawa, for 150 years. A succession of four Shibukawa *tandai* had been appointed by the mid-fifteenth century, but they were not able to preserve the power structure built by Ryōshun.[107] In fact, few sources survive from which to glean details concerning their activities. In contrast to the more than five hundred documents from Imagawa's tenure, a mere fifteen remain from Shibukawa Norinao's, for example, even though he was in office for 45 years.[108] This relatively small number of documents suggests a markedly lower level of political activity, and thus the declining significance of the *tandai* office itself.

The Kyushu *tandai* did appear with some frequency in Korean chronicles of this era, no doubt because of their ongoing participation in trade and foreign relations. The first two Shibukawa (Mitsuyori and his son Yoshitoshi) in particular promoted exchanges with Korea, and on 32 occasions between 1396 and 1428 diplomatic messengers and/or goods passed through Hakata in a route linking Korea, Japan, the Ryūkyūs, and other Pacific island countries.[109] The extent to which commercial relations advanced during this era may be surmised also by the emergence of a group of Hakata merchants whose overseas trade was in the service of the *tandai*.

It is obvious from the stature of the *tandai* in Korean relations that the Shibukawa had succeeded in establishing control over at least part of Hakata. In their attempts to secure a base there, the Shibukawa, like all previous Kyushu officers, faced opposition from the Shōni family, the resident *shugo* of the province (Chikuzen). The Shōni had maintained a reticent and sometimes defiant attitude toward the presence of Bakufu regional deputies in Hakata since the days of the Chinzei *kanrei*. When Shibukawa Mitsuyori arrived to replace Imagawa Ryōshun, their opposition surfaced violently.[110] Mitsuyori received assistance from Bakufu-commissioned generals, but like previous generations of regional officers, he relied mostly on warriors from Hizen Province, summoning them to battle and using them to guard his Hakata headquarters in his absence.[111] The ties which the first Chinzei *kanrei*, Isshiki Noriuji, had nurtured with Hizen thus proved strong and enduring.

Yet, shortly after Shibukawa Mitsuyori handed over his post as *tandai* to his son Yoshitoshi, the Shōni defeated and dispersed his family. In 1423 and 1425 the Shibukawa lost major battles. From that point forward the power of the *tandai* progressively diminished, as did their stature abroad.[112] For its part, the Bakufu evolved countermeasures to maintain control of Kyushu. In particular it enhanced the position of the Ōuchi family, one of the major houses in the Inland Sea area. In earlier generations the Ōuchi had already begun to make inroads against the traditional northern Kyushu families by serving in that region on the Bakufu's behalf and by acquiring rewards. Their involvement there increased after 1428 when the new shogun, Yoshinori, designated portions of Chikuzen (where Hakata was located) to be the Bakufu's "directly controlled lands" (*chokkatsuryō*) and assigned management of these to the Ōuchi, who then forwarded dues (*nengu*) to Kyoto.[113] As direct agent (*daikan*) of the Bakufu, the Ōuchi became the major support for the official area representative, the *tandai* Shibukawa Mitsunao.

By cultivating a special relationship with the Ōuchi, the Bakufu no doubt sought to increase its own strength in the Hakata area and maintain a base there from which to conduct foreign relations. But the power of the Ōuchi was at the same time a potential threat. Probably for that reason, the Ashikaga continued to support the Shibukawa rather than grant the *tandai* post to the Ōuchi. The shogun also took care to secure direct ties with other forces in the area, including his own special vassals (*hōkōshū*). To cite a pertinent example, the shogun attempted to keep close contact with the Asō, a *hōkō* family in the very province in which the Ōuchi were delegated management rights over Bakufu lands.[114]

As this sketch of the post-Ryōshun era in Kyushu illustrates, the Bakufu's approach to central-regional relations may not be analyzed solely from the perspective of the *tandai* family. Various powers were jockeying for a stronger position in northern Kyushu and for greater commercial gain, the *tandai* and Bakufu among them. The *tandai* family itself grew progressively weaker, but as Yanagida Kaimei has aptly noted, the Bakufu retained a role in the development of the political situation,[115] and was able to manipulate or at least capitalize on conflicts among the area's other powers for a while.

By Shogun Yoshinori's day, the conditions under which the Ashikaga had initially formulated an approach to the control of Kyushu had changed enormously. It is not surprising therefore that the role and function of the Bakufu's centrally appointed regional officers had also changed. At first primarily military commanders, the *kanrei* and *tandai* had become administrators, active traders and foreign affairs representatives, and finally, local powers in a single area (eastern Hizen), who retained a measure of prestige, especially abroad.[116]

The Bakufu had never relied on the *kanrei* or *tandai* as its sole link to Kyushu warriors. In the fifteenth century (as in the Kantō) the central government adjusted its regional alignments. In both areas the shogun cultivated the support of entrenched and rising local forces and nurtured overlapping networks of relationships.

Conclusions

In its struggle to establish and maintain hegemony, the Ashikaga Bakufu leadership clearly viewed the Kantō and Kyushu as important to the stability of the regime. Although the Bakufu treated each region differently, the aim in both cases was to prevent the growth of rival power centers. The shogun and the central elite did not rely solely on the Kantō and Kyushu officers to achieve this goal, but the regional deputies did play a major role in neutralizing enemies and suppressing local opposition.

When the two areas are examined together, the contrasts between their regional administrations emerge clearly. In the Kantō the regional head held higher status than in Kyushu, and presided over a more elaborate branch structure, apparently because the eastern provinces had been the base of the previous Bakufu. The *kubō*'s prestige helped legitimize the new regime's occupation of the long-established seat of military power. In Kyushu, far from the center of politics, ability was weighed more heavily than lineage in the appointment of regional officers. Deputies were always kin of the ruling family, but they were not Ashikaga themselves. They were successful generals, charged with establishing a balance of power in a remote area and obstructing potential coalitions of challengers to Ashikaga supremacy. In other words, until the early fifteenth century, when successive *tandai* were appointed from a single family, the Kyushu deputies, unlike the Kantō *kubō*, were not born to their offices but earned them by having victorious careers elsewhere. The Kyushu generals were all adults on their appointment, whereas the *kubō* took their posts as children, symbols of a rule that was guarded by vassals who held the title of *kanrei*.

But contrasts such as these in fact belie a more consistent overall approach to regional government. In both areas the distribution of authority was not rigidly predetermined. Instead, the branch officers advanced when and where they were able, and the Bakufu increased or decreased their jurisdictions as conditions warranted or permitted. Periods of vigorous administration by the branches occurred at times of unity or innovative leadership at the center.

The regional perspective suggests further that Bakufu institutions were not in place until after elite factional conflicts were resolved in the mid-fourteenth century. Only then did the regime come into its own. As the Bakufu firmed up its system of control in central Japan, the branch heads were extending their reach in the east and west, which in turn bolstered the Ashikaga hegemony. At the same time the Bakufu had to remain ever watchful in its alliances to guard against conflicts between the center and periphery. Occasionally regional heads were suppressed or dismissed to obstruct their attempts at building an independent power base.

During the first century of Muromachi Bakufu rule, local power blocs that would coalesce into large-scale units of governance were only beginning to appear. Although the Bakufu's decline in the post-Ōnin era was foreshadowed during this time, its efforts to establish countrywide supremacy were also noteworthy. Ashikaga influence spread farther geographically than prior studies have indicated; certainly, throughout the fourteenth century the Kantō and Kyushu were within its range of concern and influence. Similarly, the special officers appointed in each area were more than mere figureheads. Their control of their regions was often incomplete, but at times the link they provided between Kyoto and distant warriors was vital to the Ashikaga regime.

The Provincial Vassals of the Muromachi Shoguns

PETER J. ARNESEN

To most students of Japan's middle ages, Go-Daigo's Kemmu Restoration seems the preposterous adventure of a quixotic visionary. We know, after all, that Go-Daigo's support was never very strong, and that with Ashikaga Takauji's rebellion in 1335 the emperor's cause was doomed. Yet the hopelessness of Go-Daigo's venture should not blind us to the fact that for some decades the fate of Takauji's own enterprise hung in the balance. Indeed, having risked all in an attempt to establish an Ashikaga shogunate, Takauji and his successors were ultimately forced to give their regime a form that differed markedly from that of its Kamakura predecessor.

Perhaps the most striking feature of the new regime—and certainly the one to which we in the West have devoted the most attention—was the power and authority the Ashikaga shoguns vested in the *shugo*, a group of powerful provincial officials whose closest European counterparts were the medieval counts. To be sure, shoguns had been assigning *shugo* to the various provinces ever since the 1190's. The Kamakura Bakufu, however, had been careful to restrict the *shugo*'s authority to a fairly precisely defined range of official functions, most notably the suppression of major felonies, the mobilization of shogunal vassals for guard service, the collection of certain taxes on behalf of the imperial court, and the pursuit of some judicial investigations. In particular, the shogunate had been extremely reluctant to allow the *shugo* to assume much control over the shogun's own vassals.

During the first few decades of the Muromachi period, however, the *shugo*'s powers expanded enormously. As early as the 1330's, the cooperation of the *shugo* had become essential to maintaining order in the provinces, and by 1346 the *shugo* had been accorded the right to execute Bakufu judicial decrees and to suppress the unlawful harvesting of another's crops. During the 1350's the Bakufu, which had hitherto tried to maintain the Kamakura practice of mobilizing the shogun's vassals directly through his board of retainers (*samurai dokoro*), all but abandoned this task to the *shugo*, and also began allowing the *shugo* to assign to their own followers the confiscated landholdings of traitors. In 1368 the *shugo* acquired the right to partition certain estates between their civil or ecclesiastical proprietors on the one hand, and local warriors on the other, and by the 1390's some *shugo* had complete control over the civil governmental headquarters (*kokuga*) of their provinces.[1]

The net effect of these changes was to afford the *shugo* a far greater degree of control over their provinces and over all the warriors inhabiting them than would ever have been tolerated by the Kamakura shogunate. Indeed, by the end of the fourteenth century a number of *shugo* had created comital dynasties of such enormous power that it has seemed to many historians that the Muromachi Bakufu was as much a coalition of these comital dynasties as it was the shogunal regime of the Ashikaga. At the heart of this view has been the conviction that the *shugo*'s might must have drastically undermined the relationship between shogun and *gokenin*—that is, between the shogun and his direct vassals—that had endured for so much of the Kamakura period.[2]

There can be no doubt that this view is at least partially correct. The *shugo*'s newly acquired authority over military affairs and the bestowal of land rights placed them in an excellent position to assume personal lordship over the land-hungry warriors of late medieval Japan, and we know that by the beginning of the fifteenth century, *shugo* like the Ōuchi and the Yamana were even serving as the ultimate guarantors of the land rights of the shogun's own vassals. Clearly, by infringing upon what had once been among the most important shogunal prerogatives, such *shugo* seriously compromised the bonds between shogun and *gokenin*.[3]

Nevertheless, recent scholarship has shown that these bonds were by no means universally dissolved, and that the relationship between the Ashikaga shoguns and their vassals deserves our attention. There are two important areas in which this relationship is being reexamined. The first is Bakufu finances, where certain imposts levied specifically against the shogun's vassals are now thought to have played an important role in defraying some of the Bakufu's routine expenses. The second is military affairs, where the significance of the so-called *hōkōshū*, or shogunal guard, is becoming more apparent.

Although Bakufu finances have been one of the murkier areas of Muromachi history, it is clear that certain Bakufu expenses were met out of imposts levied against the shogun's vassals. By 1347, for example, the Bakufu had decided to meet the cost of supporting some of its lower-ranking functionaries by levying what amounted to a poll tax of one *kanmon* cash against every shogunal vassal with at least four *chō* of land. (Vassals entitled to serve in the shogunal presence were exempt, however—a point to which we shall return shortly.) It also appears that by the 1340's the *gokenin* were obliged to make annual payments to defray the cost of maintaining shogunal buildings (*shuri kaemono*), and Kuwayama Kōnen has argued that the Bakufu used such *gokenin*-based imposts to defray its routine personnel and maintenance costs well into the sixteenth century.[4]

There was, moreover, still another impost that was extracted from the shogun's vassals. We have long known that an impost of either a fiftieth or a twentieth of a warrior's income was levied throughout the Nanbokuchō War, and recent scholarship has suggested that, first, this impost was levied specifically against the *gokenin*; and second, the impost survived, at a rate that probably stabilized at one-fiftieth of a land's *nengu*, or land rent, well into the fifteenth century.[5] Unfortunately, we cannot tell what the rationale for this *nengu*-based impost was. Though it was clearly distinct from the poll tax that defrayed the Bakufu's personnel costs, more than that is difficult to say. Kishida Hiroshi has argued that such *nengu*-based imposts were levied in lieu of military service, but his evidence is somewhat ambiguous,[6] and it seems equally likely that such imposts were of a more nearly civil character. Thus Go-Daigo's government had once levied an impost of one-twentieth of the *gokenin*'s income, and during the 1340's the shogunal chancellery (*mandokoro*) had demanded at least a portion of the *nengu* from all benefices conferred upon *gokenin* since 1333.[7]

These ambiguities notwithstanding, the Muromachi Bakufu was clearly capable not only of levying imposts against the shogun's vassals, but also of maintaining cadastres that permitted some of these imposts to be based upon the vassal's landed wealth. Indeed, there are indications that these cadastres were being maintained at least as late as 1429,[8] and it is apparent that at least some *gokenin*-based imposts were being levied as late as 1544.[9]

Nor should one assume that the growth of *shugo* power necessarily vitiated the concept of shogunal vassalage that underlay these imposts. True, the *shugo* was responsible for collecting some of them from the very beginning, and by 1460 the Bakufu even was referring to them as "provincial levies" (*koku yaku*)—that is, imposts against the *shugo*, rather than against its vassals.[10] Still, it can be shown that the Kikkawa family of Aki paid such imposts directly into shogunal coffers as late as 1479, and a 1544 decree requiring an assessment in Bizen makes it clear that it was the *gokenin* against whom they were ultimately levied.[11] Thus, even if the *gokenin*'s contribution to Bakufu finances was relatively small—and by the sixteenth century it probably was—the fact that the Bakufu continued to levy imposts against the shogun's vassals implies that the concept of their peculiar relationship to the shogunate must have survived.

But it is the *hōkōshū*, or shogunal guard, that furnishes the most spectacular evidence of a continuing relationship between the shogun and his vassals. The guard was an elite battalion of roughly 300 to 350 men charged with protecting the shogun's person, and entitled to be received into his presence.[12] The battalion's early history is quite obscure, but something of its character can be deduced from three lists of members compiled at various points between 1444 and 1489.[13]

In the first place, guardsmen were drawn from four sorts of families: (1) cadet branches of the Ashikaga; (2) cadet branches of the various *shugo* families; (3) families that were regarded as particularly close retainers of the Ashikaga family; and (4) the families of old Kamakura-period *gokenin*.[14] Furthermore, membership in the five companies (*ban*) that composed the guard was essentially hereditary; most of the men who belonged to any given company in 1487-89 were relatives of the men who had belonged to the same company in 1444-49.[15]

In the second place, command of the guard was vested in captains (*bangashira*) who were closely linked to the shogunal family. Thus the First Company (*ichi-no-ban*) was under the hereditary captaincy of the Awaji-no-kami branch of the Hosokawa; the Second was under the Momonoi; the Third was under the Harima-no-kami branch of the Hatakeyama at some times, the Ueno at others; the Fourth was under Hatakeyama Mochisumi during the 1430's, and later under the Nakatsukasa-no-shō branch of the Hatakeyama; and the Fifth was under the Ōdate. The Hosokawa, Momonoi, Hatakeyama, and Ueno were all cadet branches of the Ashikaga, and the Ōdate were among the most trusted of the Ashikaga's vassals.[16]

Finally, when evidence from the guard registers (*banchō*) is combined with evidence from other sources, it reveals that the guardsmen's landholdings were located almost entirely in western Honshu. No guardsman seems to have held land in any of the provinces from Echigo, Shinano, and Suruga eastward; none can be found holding land in Shikoku; and we know of but one based in Kyushu.[17] Unfortunately, the reason for this rather peculiar distribution of guardsmen's holdings is obscure. The absence of guardsmen's holdings in Kyushu and the Kantō seems easily understood, since by the late fourteenth century the Bakufu had largely abandoned the attempt to govern either of these areas directly.[18] But it is much less clear why there should have been no guardsmen based in Shikoku, or how Kyushu *gokenin* might belong to a shogunal guard force as late as 1395,[19] yet be almost totally absent from the shogunal guard of the 1440's and beyond.

This last point leads directly to the question of the guard's origins. As we have seen, the shogunal guard was an elite force whose members were entitled to be received into the shogun's presence. Now, some sort of elite group of vassals was present from very early in the Muromachi period, for in 1347 the Bakufu had decreed that those vassals who "served in the (shogunal) presence" (*tōsan hōkō no yagara*) were to be exempt from a poll tax levied to support the Bakufu's lower-ranking functionaries. Similarly, a decree of 1372 provided that all such individuals should pay their *tansen* (in this case, a national land tax) directly to the capital, rather than to the *shugo*.[20] Finally, a document of 1395 suggests that by the end of the Nanbokuchō War there were several hundred men who enjoyed this elite status. It records that after Ashikaga Yoshimitsu yielded the shogunate to his son Yoshimochi in 1394/12, roughly one hundred of the men who guarded Yoshimitsu's palace were seconded to guard Yoshimochi's. More than thirty of these men were from distant Kyushu, however, and it seemed pointless to make them journey to the capital any longer. They were therefore to remain in their provinces, but to continue to enjoy the title of men serving in the shogunal palace.[21]

Clearly, if more than a hundred of the men guarding Yoshimitsu's palace could be seconded to guard his son's, there must have been several hundred to begin with. Yoshimitsu was still the major power in Kyoto, and he would scarcely have left himself unguarded in order to protect his successor. Moreover, the men who guarded Yoshimitsu were an especially privileged lot. Their status was something that those being rusticated to Kyushu in 1395 were anxious to preserve, and they were promised that anyone who might prove to have been inadvertently stripped of this status would have it restored to him.[22] Still, the mere fact that in 1395 there was a highly privileged shogunal guard of perhaps two or three hundred men does not prove that that guard was *the* shogunal guard of the later fifteenth century.

There is, however, one further bit of evidence. In a posthumous account of the career of Ōdate Mochifusa (1401-71), it is recorded that when Ashikaga Yoshimitsu had decided to create a five-company military force, he had named Mochifusa's grandfather, Ōdate Uji-nobu, captain of its Fifth Company, and Ujinobu had distinguished himself by leading that company against Yamana Ujikiyo during the Ōei Incident (1399-1400). Inasmuch as the Ōdate are known to have been hereditary captains of the Fifth Company of the shogunal guard by the 1440's, this account—which is plausible enough—suggests that the guard must have been in existence by the end of the 1390's.[23] Moreover, while some evidence implies that the guard may first have been organized as early as the 1360's,[24] it is only with the rustication of Yoshimitsu's Kyushu guardsmen in 1395 that we can really see the guard assuming the form reflected in its membership lists of 1444-49.

Let us return, then, to the document ordering the rustication of Kyushu guardsmen. The same document makes a fairly dramatic concession of shogunal authority to the Kyushu *tandai*, or intendant for Kyushu. Hereafter, the document declares, the shogun's Kyushu *gokenin* are to look not to the shogun to confirm their existing land rights or bestow new ones, but to the shogun's intendant.[25] This provision marks a significant surrender of the shogun's authority over Kyushu, an event that seems obviously connected to the rustication of the Kyushu guardsmen. In other words, the reason that Kyushu vassals can be detected among the shogun's guards in 1395, but are almost entirely absent from the guard registers of the 1440's and beyond, is probably that between 1395 and 1400 the shogun arrived at a number of decisions regarding the prerogatives he intended to enjoy. Among these was a decision about the makeup of the shogunal guard, and another about the shogun's relationship to his vassals in Kyushu. Since the latter decision clearly resulted in a massive delegation of the shogun's authority over Kyushu, the exclusion of his Kyushu vassals from the guard may well have followed more or less automatically.[26]

It therefore seems safe to conclude that the shogunal guard as we know it was established sometime during the second half of the 1390's, at which time it was based in precisely the same geographical area where it was based during the second half of the fifteenth century. A number of puzzling points remain, however, among them the nature of the guard's mission. When the guard became the object of careful study some twenty years ago, its members were seen as performing essentially three functions: they constituted a standing army strong enough to allow the shoguns to maintain their independence in spite of the *shugo*; they served as managers of the shogunal domain (*goryō*); and their landholdings, which were occasionally quite extensive, served as islands of shogunal authority within the provinces of even the most powerful *shugo*.[27] As we shall see, the guardsmen were indeed of considerable importance to the shogunal household, but neither their capacity to serve as a standing army nor the intensity of their devotion to the shogun is as clear as we once thought.

As our awareness of the guard's significance has increased, historians have come to argue that during the Muromachi period the shogun's relationship with the old *gokenin* class was articulated through two parallel hierarchies, the first descending from the shogun to the *shugo*, and only thence to the *gokenin*, the second running directly from the shogun to whatever vassals happened to have been incorporated into the shogunal guard. But even a fairly casual reading of the evidence suggests something more complex. To mention but one issue here, we know that there were extremely powerful *shugo* who could not break the link between shogun and *gokenin* in the matter of confirmation of land rights until well into the fifteenth century.[28] Even in the absence of such evidence, we would still need to make sense of the shogun's apparent decision after 1395 to deal directly with but 300 to 350 of his erstwhile vassals.

In fact, as we shall see, he did nothing of the kind. This point emerges quite clearly from the history of three extremely powerful families from the province of Aki.

The Kobayakawa

The Kobayakawa were descended from Doi Sanehira, a warrior who had rallied to Minamoto Yoritomo at the start of the Gempei War (1180-85) and had—together with his son Tōhira—played an important role in the conquest of western Japan. Sanehira and Tōhira had subsequently been rewarded for their services by being appointed *jitō* over a number of estates in western Honshu, and the estate of Nuta in Aki may have been among these. By 1189, however, Yoritomo's new Bakufu had cut back considerably on some of its wartime *jitō* appointments, and several of the Doi's new holdings had been confiscated from them. While it is impossible to trace the precise history of Nuta during these years, it appears that Tōhira was not able to have his position in that estate confirmed until 1206.[29]

By 1206, however, the Doi family had split into two branches. One branch, headed by Tōhira's son Korehira, had been granted the family's ancestral holdings around Doi village in Sagami and had decided to remain there. The second branch, which was headed by Tōhira's adopted son Kagehira, had assumed the surname Kobayakawa and taken up residence in Nuta. For reasons that are not now clear, no sooner had the Kobayakawa's position in Nuta been confirmed than Tōhira and Kagehira settled the family headship upon Kagehira's son Shigehira and granted him the Honjō and Ajika portions of the estate.[30]

Under Shigehira the Aki Kobayakawa prospered. Despite his close ties to his Sagami kinsmen, Shigehira took no part in the latter's disastrous involvement in Wada Yoshimori's uprising of 1213, instead devoting himself to suppressing piracy in the Inland Sea. When the Jōkyū War broke out in 1221, Shigehira reported the treason of the warriors living in the dual estate of Tsuu-Takehara, which lay just to the west of his own holdings, and thereby won appointment as *jitō* of that estate as well as of Nuta. And though the relative poverty of the position to which he had been appointed in Tsuu-Takehara led him to indulge in a fairly rapacious stewardship, his abuses were ultimately upheld when he was impleaded before the Bakufu.[31] Yet though Shigehira's relationship with Tsuu-Takehara's seigneurs was extremely tense, he was not simply a rude and grasping *jitō*. On the contrary, he was able to develop an excellent relationship with the seigneurial authorities of his original holdings in Nuta, and far from spending his career lurking about in the provinces, he spent a great deal of time in the capital.

Nuta was technically a holding of the Rengeōin, but the estate was effectively controlled by its *ryōke*, the Saionji family of Kyoto. While Shigehira's early relationship with this important noble family is unclear, by 1238 he had persuaded Saionji Kintsune to allow him to reclaim some of the salt marshes of Nuta for cultivation, and by the 1240's he had been appointed the Saionji's overseer (*jōshi*) for the estate. His son Masakage actually served in the Saionji household,[32] and Shigehara may even have helped raise a valuable bird that Saionji Saneuji presented to Emperor Go-Fukakusa in 1254.[33]

But Shigehara's activities were by no means limited to cultivating ties with the Saionji, for he was also a *zaikyōjin* (a *gokenin* who had been permanently stationed in the capital). His responsibilities as a metropolitan vassal are unclear, but he was probably a *kagariya-bushi*, one of the metropolitan guards whom the Bakufu had begun stationing in Kyoto in 1238.[34] In any case, Shigehara is known to have joined with other metropolitan *gokenin* in performing in mounted archery contests at the Ima Hie Shrine in 1253 and 1257.[35]

At Shigehara's death in 1264, then, his family already enjoyed a position of some significance in both the provinces and the capital. Unfortunately, the family was also beginning to show signs of a fragmentation that would cause it considerable trouble later. The Kobayakawa had split into two branches in 1213, when Nuta had been partitioned between Shigehira and his brother Suehira, and Shigehira had fostered yet another branch when he had partitioned his own holdings between his sons Masahira and Masakage in 1258. Thus by the end of Shigehira's career, the Kobayakawa consisted of a Nuta branch, which was headed by Masahira and based in the Honjō section of Nuta; a Shinjō branch, which was headed by Shigehira's grandnephew Sadahira and based in the Shinjō section of the same estate; and a Takehara branch, which was headed by Masakage and based in Tsuu-Takehara.[36]

Although the Shinjō branch of the family was beginning to show signs of restiveness as early as 1258, the Nuta and Takehara still got on quite well, and they seem to have been far more influential than the Shinjō. Both families served the Rokuhara intendancy as metropolitan vassals (*zaikyōjin*), their members were on friendly terms with Bakufu officials, and the Takehara were even granted the estate of Mokake in Bizen for their services in the capital.[37] Given this background, it may seem that the Kobayakawa should have been staunch supporters of the Kamakura Bakufu. But though the family did remain loyal through at least the first stages of the Genkō Uprising (1331-33), neither the Kobayakawa nor the shogun's other Kyoto-based vassals remained loyal once Ashikaga Takauji had thrown in with Go-Daigo in 1333. It is true that Nuta Sadahira, head of the Kobayakawa at the time, was among the Rokuhara forces whose attempt to fall back on the Kantō was cut short at the Banba Pass in 1333/4, but many other *zaikyōjin*, including both the Takehara and Sadahira's own grandfather, seem to have gone over to Takauji almost immediately.[38]

Such widespread treason is unlikely to have had any simple cause, but we know that by the end of the thirteenth century the loyalty of many *gokenin* was being sorely tested by the increasingly despotic behavior of the Hōjō regents. The Takehara, for example, had been unjustly stripped of many of their lands in 1297, and had been struggling to recover them ever since.[39] But whatever the reasons, many former *zaikyōjin* became important retainers of the Ashikaga, and the Kobayakawa were among these.[40] Takehara Sukekage and one of his cousins were members of the retinue accompanying Takauji to the Kamō Shrine in 1334/9, for example,[41] and when Takauji was forced from the capital by imperial forces in early 1336, it was the Kobayakawa, along with Takauji's kinsman Momonoi Yoshimori, who were charged with holding Aki for the Ashikaga.[42] While the Kobayakawa did not thereby become *shugo*—as did the Ōuchi and the Kōtō under similar circumstances—neither did they ever fall under the control of the men who did obtain that office. On the contrary, whereas other Aki families were dominated by their *shugo* as early as the beginning of 1336, both the Nuta and the Takehara continued to serve the Ashikaga more or less directly—albeit under a variety of commanders. With the creation of the shogunal guard, moreover, not only the Nuta and the Takehara, but even the Ura branch of the Nuta, were enrolled as guardsmen.[43]

As guardsmen, the Kobayakawa were presumably among the shogun's most reliable vassals, and one would therefore like to know just what services they rendered, and what benefits they got in return. As we have seen, some scholars have argued that a key function of the guard was to serve as a standing shogunal army. This view has been strongly criticized by Haga Norihiko,[44] however, and the Kobayakawa evidence seems to corroborate his views. Although it is apparent that between 1400 and 1465 the Kobayakawa fought repeatedly at the shogun's behest in Kyushu, Aki, Iyo, and the Home Provinces, there is but one document—and that one dating from 1491—that even hints that they did so as members of a given guard company.[45] In all other cases, they were mobilized independently of their fellow guardsmen and served under non-guard commanders. We had best assume, therefore, that the Kobayakawa's service as guardsmen consisted literally in guarding the shogun.

This is not to deny that the Kobayakawa were extremely useful to the Bakufu. At the beginning of the fifteenth century the Nuta managed a number of shogunal holdings (*goryō*) in Suō for the Ashikaga, and during the 1480's and 1490's they managed other such holdings in Ise and Ōmi.[46] Moreover, both the Nuta and the Takehara seem to have had a hereditary obligation to take part in the New Year's inaugural archery contest (*yumi hajime*), a service that cost the Nuta so much to perform that their Bakufu-backed attempts to recoup their expenses from their branch families met bitter and sustained resistance.[47] Beyond this, during the 1460's Nuta Hirohira served as an intermediary between the Bakufu and the then dangerously autonomous Ōuchi family, and during the 1480's Hirohira's son helped supervise the construction of the Higashiyama Villa.[48]

In return for such services, the Kobayakawa received a variety of benefits. Their lands were confirmed to them by the shogun himself, and they had little difficulty in bringing suits regarding that land before the Bakufu's own courts. By Bakufu law they were exempt from the shogunal imposts levied against ordinary *gokenin*, and they were entitled to render *tansen* (a national tax) directly to the capital rather than to the *shugo*.[49] And by 1463 the *shugo* could not even attempt to punish them for any crimes they might commit; he was allowed only to report them to the Bakufu.[50]

This almost total immunity from the comital authority of the *shugo* is closely related to the development of the Kobayakawa's own local power—an issue that is best approached from the standpoint of taxation. In 1444 the Bakufu reaffirmed the Nuta's right to render their *tansen* directly to the capital, and warned the *shugo* that this privilege extended to all holdings pertaining to any Nuta kinsmen (*ichizoku*).[51] This order did not mean that the various kinsmen were themselves to render their *tansen* to Kyoto, but that the *tansen* would be collected by the Nuta family head (*sōryō*) instead of by the *shugo*. The Nuta's immunity, in other words, did not trickle down to all the

Nuta kinsmen; instead, it allowed the family head to substitute his own authority for that of the *shugo*.[52]

This privilege enhanced the family head's power in at least two ways: it allowed him to extract more income from the land, and it strengthened his lordship over his relatives. Regarding the first point, we know that by 1395 the Takehara were not only collecting Bakufu-assessed *tansen* on their landholdings, but also levying additional *tansen* on their own account.[53] Such income undoubtedly contributed to the family head's wealth and power, but his pretensions to lordship over his kinsmen had greater immediate importance. Families like the Nuta and Takehara were entitled to call out their branch families for Bakufu military service, and to parcel out all manner of other service imposed by the shogunate.[54] From the branch families' point of view, this situation was extremely provoking. Many Nuta branch families had been in existence almost as long as had the Nuta, and had enjoyed direct ties with the Ashikaga as recently as the fourteenth century.[55] For them now to be subjected to the Nuta head's authority was not only to be reduced to a position of rear vassalage with respect to the shogun, but also to be forced to bear what were probably far heavier obligations than they would otherwise have done. We know, for example, that Nuta Hirohira's service as the Bakufu's envoy to Suō in 1461 cost his kinsmen a total of 232 *kanmon* cash plus the use of a fully rigged ship.[56]

As early as 1431 the tensions engendered by the Nuta's lordly pretensions had led a number of Shinjō lineages to band together to resist the authority of Nuta Hirohira's father, Norihira. The Nuta's ability to deal with this rebellion was disrupted by a succession dispute that broke out between Norihira's sons Mochihira and Hirohira in 1433, and that was not finally resolved in Hirohira's favor until 1442. By that time, moreover, the Takehara had been alienated from the Nuta as well, and even some of the Nuta's own branch lineages were beginning to resist the family head.[57] Nevertheless, the Nuta's lordship survived, for once the question of family headship had been resolved, the Bakufu was prepared to back Hirohira's authority over his kinsmen. This backing was not immediately effective—as can be seen from the number of times the recalcitrant branch families had to be admonished—but the confiscation of one especially contumacious kinsman's landholdings during the 1460's seems to have marked the end of overt resistance to Hirohira's overlordship by his Nuta and Shinjō kinsmen.[58]

Despite the enormous value to the Kobayakawa of their close ties to the shogunate, however, the Takehara branch of the family ultimately betrayed the Bakufu. The motives for their treason are obscure, but the Takehara's nasty relationship with the Nuta and close ties with the Ōuchi must surely have been involved.

Although the Takehara had got on reasonably well with the Nuta for roughly the first third of the fifteenth century, by mid-century the relationship between the two houses was dangerously strained. One source of tension was the bitterness engendered when the Bakufu made Takehara Morikage head of the Nuta house as well as the Takehara in 1441, only to restore Nuta Hirohira to his family headship in 1442. A second strain may have arisen from Hirohira's claims of a species of eminent domain over Morikage's holdings in Nashiwa, one of the constituent villages of the Honjō portion of the Nuta estate, and Hirohira may also have been trying to force the Takehara to dismantle the fortifications that the latter had raised in Tsuu-Takehara. Whatever was at issue, by 1455 the relationship between Hirohira and Morikage was so poisonous that the Bakufu was compelled to arrange a truce.[59]

By the time this truce was arranged, however, the Takehara were firmly allied to the Ōuchi of Suō. The Takehara's Ōuchi ties can probably be dated to the late fourteenth century, when the Ōuchi gained authority over Tōsaijō—a section of Aki that lay just to the west of lands that the Takehara had been granted during the 1380's.[60] By 1427 this relationship had been cemented by the Takehara's acquisition of two holdings that lay within the Ōuchi's sphere of influence—Uchinomi, which lay within Tōsaijō itself, and Hatami, which lay on an island under Ōuchi control. Although it is unclear whether it was the Ōuchi that had granted these lands to the Takehara, neither Uchinomi nor Hatami was ever treated as part of the patrimony that the Takehara had received from the Bakufu, and by 1454 the Takehara were rendering service on these lands to the Ōuchi.[61]

The problem with these Ōuchi ties was that by the 1450's the Bakufu, then dominated by the Ōuchi's Hosokawa rivals, was so suspicious of the Ōuchi that conflict between the Takehara's two overlords was inevitable. The first eruption occurred in 1457, when the Bakufu backed the Takeda, then *shugo* of Aki, in an attack upon the Ōuchi's Aki enclaves. The outcome of this conflict is unclear, but we do know that in its aftermath the Bakufu attempted to strengthen the Takeda's position in Aki and weaken the Ōuchi's. Nuta Hirohira's 1461 mission to Suō, for example, was designed to negotiate a partial Ōuchi withdrawal from Tōsaijō.[62] By 1465 the Ōuchi were sufficiently alienated from the shogunate to attack a Bakufu expeditionary force that had been sent to prop up the Hosokawa's authority in Iyo,[63] and during the Ōnin War of 1467-77 the Ōuchi were leading members of the anti-Hosokawa Western Army.

As the relationship between the Ōuchi and the Bakufu deteriorated, the Takehara's loyalty to the shogun began to waver. The earliest concrete indication that we have of their disaffection comes from 1461-62, when Takehara Morikage defied a shogunal order that he resume serving the Bakufu in Kyoto.[64] Since the Takehara's behavior during the Bakufu-Ōuchi skirmishes of 1457-65 remains obscure,[65] it is impossible to determine whether this slippage in loyalty derived from devotion to the Ōuchi; from hatred for the Nuta, whose own loyalty to the shogun is beyond question; or from some other cause. With the outbreak of the Ōnin War, however, such subtleties were of little moment. What mattered was that while the Nuta clave to the shogun, the Takehara threw in with the Ōuchi and proceeded to ravage the Nuta's holdings.[66] Moreover, though the winding down of the war allowed the Takehara to be reconciled with both the shogun and their kinsmen, a pattern had been set that was to persist well into the sixteenth century. On every occasion when the Takehara were faced with a choice between the shogun and the Ōuchi, it was the Ōuchi with whom they aligned.

The case of the Takehara shows clearly that not even the considerable benefits of membership in the shogunal guard could guarantee the loyalty of the guardsmen. This point, which is not really that surprising, is worth pursuing further, but we need first to consider the implications of shogunal vassalage for two families that were not enrolled in the guard—the Mōri and the Kikkawa.

The Mōri

The Mōri were, if anything, even better connected with the Kamakura and the early Muromachi shogunates than were the Kobayakawa. They traced their descent from Mōri Suemitsu, the fourth son of Ōe Hiromoto. Hiromoto had been one of perhaps four or five of the most important figures in the early history of the Kamakura Bakufu, and Suemitsu was one of at least four of his sons—the others being Ōe Chikahiro, Nagai Tokihiro, and Kaitō Tadanari—who came to hold important Bakufu positions in their own right.[67] Indeed, once Ōe Chikahiro had rebelled against the Bakufu and been killed during the Jōkyū War of 1221, it was Mōri Suemitsu that became the most prominent of Hiromoto's descendants. By 1233 he had been appointed to the Bakufu's council (*hyōjōshū*), in 1236 he was sufficiently esteemed by the shogun for the latter to spend the night at Suemitsu's house, and in 1239 Suemitsu's daughter was married to Hōjō Tokiyori, the future shogunal regent.[68]

Even Suemitsu's disastrous adherence to Miura Yasumura during the Hōji Uprising (1247) did not totally destroy his family's position. It is true that Suemitsu, three of his sons, and one grandson were killed in the fighting of 1247/6, that thereafter the Mōri disappear completely from the record of the Bakufu's Kamakura activities, and that the Hōjō's desire to purge the Bakufu of Miura partisans led to the expulsion of Suemitsu's brother Tadanari from the council on 1247/6/11.[69] Nevertheless, Suemitsu's son Tsunemitsu survived and was allowed to retain the family's position as *jitō* of the estates of Sahashi in Echigo and Yoshida in Aki, the combined value of which, as recorded in the fourteenth century, was 3,000 *kanmon* per year.[70]

Despite their fall from grace, moreover, the Mōri remained extremely well connected with the Bakufu. Suemitsu's nephew Nagai Yasuhide had been a member of the council since 1241, had fought for the Hōjō in 1247, and remained a member of the council until his death in 1253; his descendants would continue to sit on the council and on the board of coadjutors (*hikitsukeshū*) until the Bakufu's downfall. Another nephew, Nagai Yasushige, was *shugo* of Bingo and probably a charter member of the Rokuhara council (Rokuhara *hyōjōshū*); moreover, Yasushige's descendants were every bit as successful as Yasuhide's at retaining the positions won by their forebear. A third nephew, Nawa Masamochi, could not duplicate the Nagai's feat of creating a minor dynasty, but did himself sit on the board of coadjutors from 1254 to 1263.[71]

By the end of the Kamakura period, in fact, the Mōri were staging a bit of a comeback. An Ōe family genealogy reproduced in the *Keizu sanyō*—a massive genealogical compilation of the late Tokugawa period—records that Mōri Tokichika, who had become head of the Mōri family in 1270, sat with his Nagai kinsmen on the Rokuhara council.[72] This claim is quite plausible, for we know that Tokichika was in fact a metropolitan vassal (*zaikyōjin*) of some sort, that the Bakufu had granted him a landholding in Kawachi to help meet his expenses, and that he also owned two plots of land in the capital.[73]

In any case, as the Kamakura period came to a close, the Mōri's situation was roughly as follows. Tsunechika, who must have been in his mid- to late seventies by 1333, was serving the Bakufu's Rokuhara intendancy in Kyoto. His grandson Chikahira—who had probably been managing the family's Aki holdings since at least 1323[74]—was living in Aki with his wife and children. The rest of the family was living in Echigo on the estate of Sahashi, which was at the time the Mōri's most important holding. We cannot tell, unfortunately, just how the Mōri responded to the Bakufu's collapse, though it is clear that Mōri Chikahira rallied to Go-Daigo at Funanoe in early 1333. Nor is it apparent how they fared under Go-Daigo's Kemmu regime. Ashikaga Takauji's rebellion of 1335-36 produced a mixed response from the Mōri, with Tokichika and his great-grandson declaring for Takauji and most of the rest of the family for Go-Daigo. By late 1336, however, unity had been restored, and the Mōri were firmly in the Ashikaga camp. Tokichika retired, partitioning his Sahashi holdings among several of his grandsons and great-nephews, the family headship passed to Tsunechika's great-grandson Morochika, and Morochika became both the "godson" (*eboshi-ko*) and the follower of Kō Moroyasu, one of Takauji's most powerful vassals.[75]

Though it is difficult to trace the Mōri's activities between 1336 and 1351, the following points are clear. First, Morochika continued to fight in various Bakufu campaigns under Kō Moroyasu. Second, a substantial part of the Mōri family, including Morochika's father, grandfather, and great-grandfather, abandoned Echigo for Aki.[76] And third, the Mōri were every bit as well connected with the new Bakufu as they had been with the old.

This last point emerges from Satō Shin'ichi's studies of the early bureaucratic structure of the Muromachi Bakufu. As Satō argues, the early Bakufu's most important judicial organ was the board of councillors, or *hyōjōshū*, whose membership around 1344 can be fairly accurately determined. Of the 43 persons thought to have sat on the council in that year, seven—namely Nagai Sadayori, Nagai Tokikazu, Nagai Hirohide, Nagai Takahiro, Nagai Tokiharu, Nagai Munehira, and Mizutani Sadaari—were kinsmen of the Mōri.[77] Furthermore, the fact that during the 1340's Mōri Morochika was able to get Nagai Tokiharu, Nagai Sadayori, and Nakajō Hirofusa (another kinsman) to testify to his great-grandfather's land rights suggests that the relationship among these kinsmen must have been reasonably close.[78]

It may seem, therefore, that the Mōri were destined to have an intimate relationship with the Bakufu, and that they should have been ideal candidates for inclusion in the shogunal guard. In fact, the Mōri were not enrolled in the guard, and one naturally wonders why.[79] The following points are suggestive. First, many of the Mōri's kinsmen were caught on the wrong side of the power struggle between Ashikaga Takauji and his brother Tadayoshi. Thus a list of the warriors who accompanied Tadayoshi when he fled the capital on 1351/7/30 includes the names of Nagai Daizen-taibu (Hirohide), Nagai Chibu-no-shō (Tokiharu), Mizutani Gyōbu-no-shō (Sadaari), Mori (*sic*) Kamon-no-suke (Mōri Shigetsune?), Nakajō Gyōbu-no-shō (Hirofusa), and the lay priest Nuidono-no-suke (Nagai Takahiro?).[80]

Second, Mōri Morochika's father, Chikahira, was clearly in open rebellion against Takauji's *shugo* in Aki by mid-1350. Morochika himself can be seen fighting on behalf of Takauji at least as late as 1350/7, but by 1351/4 he had changed his name to Motoharu and was also in league with the Aki rebels.[81] What inspired this treason is not at all clear. Perhaps the Mōri shared their kinsmen's sympathy for Tadayoshi and threw in with the partisans of Tadayoshi's son Tadafuyu in Aki and Iwami. Or perhaps they seized on the turmoil of 1350-52 to usurp control over some of the lands lying near their own holdings in Yoshida.[82] In any case, by the early 1350's the Mōri had not only lost their Bakufu connections through the purging of their Nagai, Mizutani, and Nakajō kinsmen, but had also sacrificed, by their own rebellion, whatever good will Motoharu (the former Morochika) may have accumulated through his service under Kō Moroyasu.

Nevertheless, the events of the 1350's may not have been enough to bar Motoharu's descendants from the guard, especially since by the 1360's and 1370's Motoharu was once again fighting for the Bakufu, and was serving with some distinction.[83] Still, whatever merit Motoharu was thereby able to accumulate was probably set at naught by the monumental confusion over family headship to which the Mōri succumbed at the end of the fourteenth century. Motoharu left at least five sons—Mōri Hirofusa, Atsumo Motofusa, Ohara Hirouchi, Chūma Tadahiro, and Fukuhara Hiroyo—of whom the eldest, Hirofusa, succeeded to the family headship in 1381. Unfortunately, Hirofusa was killed in battle a few years later, leaving behind but a single son, and that one yet unborn.[84] Motoharu's third son, Ohara Hirouchi, seems thereupon to have begun serving as the head of the Mōri, and he may also have begun serving the Bakufu in Kyoto. But by 1392 Hirouchi was himself dead and had left a minor heir of his own.[85]

Thereafter, the question of who headed the Mōri family is obscure, and it is quite possible that the absence of an acknowledged family head kept the Mōri from being enrolled in the shogunal guard being formed during the late 1390's. At any rate, the Mōri were not enrolled as guardsmen and therefore did not enjoy the same claim to shogunal patronage as the Kobayakawa. Nevertheless, the main line of the Mōri family did maintain direct ties to the Muromachi shogunate, and this relationship had a profound impact on the family's position. In contrast to the *gokenin* of neighboring Suō Province, for example, the Mōri continued to have their land rights confirmed to them by the shogun, rather than by the *shugo*.[86] Similarly, during the fifteenth century the Mōri did not normally fight under the *shugo*'s military command, but were mobilized by direct order of the Bakufu, served under a variety of commanders, and had frequent contact with high Bakufu officials.[87]

Even more interesting is the way in which the Bakufu helped the main line of the Mōri consolidate its authority over its branch families. The evidence here is complex, but the main point emerges from the Bakufu's tax policy—especially concerning the *tansen*—as it was applied to the Mōri. *Tansen* were occasional imposts on land levied to meet such extraordinary expenses as enthronement and abdication ceremonies or refurbishing temples and shrines. Although these taxes had originally been imposed by the imperial court, by the fifteenth century they were imposed by the Bakufu and collected by the *shugo*. Under the standard procedure the Bakufu would first determine that a *tansen* was needed and would order each *shugo* to collect it from his province in accordance with its provincial tax register (*ōtabumi*). The *shugo* would then direct each landholder in his province to render a certain amount of cash by a certain date or suffer the invasion of his holdings by the *shugo*'s agents.[88]

It was entirely possible, however, for a well-connected landholder to obtain the right to pay his *tansen* directly to the capital and thereby to escape the *shugo*'s attentions. We have already seen that members of the shogunal guard were so favored, and it is clear that many of the nation's great religious foundations enjoyed this privilege as well. That the Mōri also enjoyed this privilege is evident from the fact that a 1446 order directing them to pay *tansen* for rebuilding the Inner Shrine at Ise came from the Bakufu rather than from the *shugo*. The order itself, dated 1446/5/3, was addressed to the family head, Mōri Hirofusa, and commanded him to exert additional pressure on those who were withholding their long-overdue *tansen* and to forward his payment immediately. Within a month Hirofusa's agents had drawn up a register apportioning the *tansen* among the six lineages that made up the Mōri family. At that point—if we may extrapolate from the example of the one branch family whose documents survived—the lineages paid their various shares to Hirofusa, and Hirofusa paid the Bakufu.[89]

The Bakufu expected the Mōri head to supervise his kinsmen in other ways as well. He was expected, for example, to mobilize his kinsmen in the event of war, and during the 1440's and 1450's the Bakufu explicitly ordered that the services (*yaku*) incumbent upon the family be rendered through its lineage head. In the event that the branch families defied the head's orders, the Bakufu was prepared to back him up.[90]

Bakufu backing was a mixed blessing, however. At times it served the main line of the Mōri extremely well. When a number of the Mōri branch families rebelled against Mōri Mitsufusa in 1418-19, for example, it was the shogun Yoshimochi's threat to have them punished that brought them to heel.[91] One assumes, moreover, that it was the Bakufu's grant of *tansen* authority to the main line of the Mōri family that allowed Mitsufusa's son Hirofusa to begin collecting *tansen* in his own right as early as 1442.[92] And it is clear that during the 1450's Hirofusa relied heavily upon Bakufu backing to maintain his authority over kinsmen who were once again beginning to defy the family chief's directives.

But reliance upon the Bakufu had its disadvantages, for it subjected the Mōri to all the vagaries of Bakufu politics. During the 1450's and 1460's such politics were very nearly the Mōri's undoing. The full story of the Mōri's difficulties is extremely complex, but its essential points are as follows. At the beginning of the fifteenth century, the Mōri comprised six lineages: the Mōri, Ohara, Saka, Fukuhara, Chūma, and Kawamoto. The question of family headship had been contested among at least three of these lineages between 1385 and perhaps 1406, but by the latter date Mōri Mitsufusa, Motoharu's grandson by his eldest son, had probably been recognized by the Bakufu as head of the entire family, and taken up residence in Kyoto. Nevertheless, the authority of Mitsufusa and of his son Hirofusa had been none to the liking of several other branches of the family, and between 1418 and 1460 these malcontents had repeatedly defied Mitsufusa's and Hirofusa's orders.[93]

The precise reason for the branch families' discontent is not apparent, but at least one of the issues involved was that of service—that is, the obligation of all Mōri branch families to render military service, *tansen*, and a variety of other obligations under the direction of the lineage head. There is some evidence, for example, that between 1434 and 1446 the branch families may have forced Hirofusa to apportion the family's *tansen* obligation in a way that increased his own burden while lessening theirs,[94] and it is quite clear that by the 1450's Hirofusa (who had by then changed his name to Hiromoto) was forced to seek Bakufu assistance in persuading his kinsmen to render their services under his direction.

In 1455 Hiromoto obtained two Bakufu directives—the first commanding that his kinsmen render their services according to his dispositions, and the second commanding Takeda Nobukata to assist Hiromoto in punishing any kinsmen who continued to defy him.[95] Orders of this kind were not uncommon during the fifteenth century; we have already seen that the Kobayakawa obtained similar directives at about the same time. What is interesting about the present case is that the intervention of the powerful shogunal deputy, Hosokawa Katsumoto, was instrumental in enabling Hiromoto to obtain his directives.[96] Katsumoto was by 1455 an extremely influential figure in Bakufu circles, and his patronage was much to be desired. Nevertheless, the decrees that Hiromoto obtained through him not only failed to bring the rest of the Mōri to heel, but may even have contributed to a near disaster that befell Hiromoto some five years later.

The proximate cause of Hiromoto's new difficulties lay in the fact that in 1460 he had finally grown sick enough of his kinsmen's continued defiance to launch an armed attack against them. By thus indulging in a private war, Hiromoto had technically committed an extremely serious crime, albeit one that the Bakufu was frequently prepared to overlook. Hiromoto, however, was severely punished. He was stripped of his family headship in favor of Ohara Korehiro, the very leader of his defiant kinsmen; his hereditary managership (*daikanshiki*) of the village of Irie was granted to Takeda Nobukata; and at least some of the Mōri's holdings were incorporated into the shogunal domain.[97]

Inasmuch as Hiromoto had been implicitly authorized to chastise his recalcitrant kinsmen in 1455, his severe treatment in 1460 demands some explanation. Pertinent here are the facts that the Mōri holdings that were incorporated into the shogunal domain were consigned to the management of Ise Sadachika, that Sadachika entrusted them to Ohara Korehiro in return for a payment of sixty *kanmon* per year, and that Korehiro was enrolled in the shogunal guard.[98] Since Ise Sadachika was head of the shogunal chancellery (*mandokoro*) and Hosokawa Katsumoto's most dangerous Bakufu rival, it seems likely that the Ohara, to whom the Bakufu's 1455 decrees had been a severe blow, must have sought out Sadachika's patronage sometime before 1460, and that Sadachika had then arranged to have Hiromoto's 1460 attack severely punished. Thereafter, Sadachika's position as head of the chancellery had allowed him to cash in on the incorporation of Mōri lands into the shogunal domain, Ohara Korehiro had been the obvious choice to carry out the local-level administration of these lands, and Korehiro's enrollment in the shogunal guard had ensured that his position would be secure.

Hiromoto, in other words, had been undone by the fact that his rivals had obtained the patronage of an exceedingly powerful enemy of Hiromoto's own patron. This turnabout naturally infuriated Hiromoto, but there was little he could do except appeal to the Bakufu to reverse its decision. He continued to serve the Bakufu loyally until his death, as did his son Toyomoto until sometime in 1471. At that point, however, Toyomoto seized upon the upheaval occasioned by the Ōnin War to return suddenly to Aki from a Bakufu campaign in Bingo. Once in Aki, he threw in with the rebellious partisans of Ōuchi Masahiro, recaptured the lands taken from his father in 1460, and served the Ōuchi with such distinction that he was granted enormous new holdings by Ōuchi Masahiro.[99]

The Mōri's treason was ultimately forgiven when the Ōnin War ended, but the close ties that had once bound the Mōri to the Bakufu were never restored. On the contrary, the Mōri began to act with increasing autonomy, and when they felt the need for some sort of external backing, they now looked to the Ōuchi.

The Kikkawa

The Mōri and Kobayakawa were families that enjoyed a minor prominence within the Kamakura Bakufu's Rokuhara intendancy, and that were closely bound to the Ashikaga shoguns from early in the Muromachi period. The Kikkawa were a family of a different sort. Kikkawa Tomokane, the first of his line of whom anything is known, was a petty warrior from Suruga whose most important act was to take part in the destruction of Kajiwara Kagetoki after the latter had fallen out with the Bakufu in late 1199. Tomokane was fatally wounded in this encounter, but before he died he managed to distinguish himself by dispatching Kagetoki's son Kageshige. When the Bakufu divided up Kagetoki's former holdings on 1200/1/25, part of Kagetoki's holdings in the estate of Fukui in Harima were therefore bestowed upon Tomokane's son Tsunekane.[100]

Little more is known of Kikkawa Tsunekane, but his son Tsunemitsu fought for the Bakufu during the Jōkyū War and was rewarded by being appointed *jitō* over the Honjō portion of the estate of Ōasa in Aki. Tsunemitsu apparently succeeded to Tsunekane's holdings of Fukui and Kikkawa in about 1225.[101] Thereafter the Kikkawa made so little impression on the historical record of the Kamakura era that their activities are almost impossible to trace. And though we have a wealth of information concerning the Kikkawa's activities in the Nanbokuchō War of the fourteenth century, this evidence is difficult to interpret because of our lack of information about the various lineages comprising the Kikkawa and because the family's headship between 1268 and 1406 cannot be traced.[102]

By 1406, at any rate, the headship of the Kikkawa had been assumed by a hitherto obscure branch of the family. Kikkawa Tsunemi, the new head, was the grandson of one Kikkawa Tsuneshige and of a redoubtable lady known to us only by her childhood name of Yasa and her religious name of Ryōkai. Tsuneshige himself had been a nearly landless member of his family, but his wife had been the heiress of the warrior Nagayasu Kanesuke of Iwami. Tsuneshige had therefore taken up residence on his wife's holdings in Iwami, and predeceased her early in the fourteenth century.[103]

At the beginning of the Muromachi period, then, Ryōkai and her sons were the sole representatives of what might be called the Iwami branch of the Kikkawa family. The Iwami Kikkawa spent most of the

1330's and 1340's fighting under the Ashikaga's Iwami *shugo*, but by 1350 Ryōkai and Tsunemi's father, Tsunekane, had joined Ashikaga Tadafuyu's rebellion against the Bakufu. In 1349 Ryōkai disinherited her eldest son in favor of Tsunekane, and by 1351 Tsunekane had been confirmed as head of the new and increasingly powerful Iwami branch of the Kikkawa family.[104]

From 1351 until at least 1364 Tsunekane served Ashikaga Tada-fuyu with great distinction, thereby winning appointment not only as *jitō* of the Shinjō portion of the Ōasa estate in Aki but also as *shugo* of Tosa. (There is no evidence of his ever having made the latter appointment effective.) By 1364, however, the tide was beginning to turn against Tadafuyu, and Tsunekane probably joined his maternal kinsman Masuda Kanemi in declaring for the Bakufu in 1364/9.[105] By 1368, in any case, Tsunekane was firmly in the Bakufu camp, had been confirmed in his patrimony by the shogun himself, and had been granted further holdings in the estate of Terahara in Aki. In 1370 Tsunekane was confirmed in the Ōasa Shinjō holdings that had been granted him by Tadafuyu in 1352, and by 1380 his son Tsunemi had been confirmed not only in these Shinjō holdings but in a number of lands within the Aki estates of Terahara and Shijihara.[106]

By the turn of the century, then, the Iwami Kikkawa had exploited the upheavals of the Nanbokuchō War in order to carve out an increasingly large domain in the vicinity of Aki's Ōasa Shinjō, and had managed to get this territory confirmed to them by the Ashikaga shoguns. Moreover, though Tsunemi was not at that point recognized as head of the entire Kikkawa family, his kinsmen seem to have been in considerable disarray, and during the bitter struggle that wracked Aki during Yamana Mitsuuji's attempt to establish himself as *shugo* of the province in 1403-6, Tsunemi was able to persuade Mitsuuji to designate him family head.[107]

Clearly, then, the Kikkawa had none of the close ties to the Bakufu that the Mōri and the Kobayakawa had during the thirteenth and fourteenth centuries. On the contrary, the branch of the Kikkawa that ultimately acquired the family headship had lingered in obscurity until the mid-fourteenth century, and had then won a position of wealth and influence in open defiance of the Bakufu. And though Tsunekane and Tsunemi eventually did serve the Bakufu during the 1370's and 1380's, it was a *shugo*, rather than the shogun, that sanctioned Tsunemi's assumption of the family's headship in 1406.

The Kikkawa continued to maintain far closer ties with the *shugo* of Aki than the Mōri and Kobayakawa ever did. For example, Kikkawa Tsunemi relied upon Takeda Nobumori, then *shugo* of western Aki, to sponsor the reconfirmation of Tsunemi's landholdings in 1415, and Tsunemi's son Tsunenobu even fought for Takeda Nobukata in Wakasa when Nobukata was *shugo* of both Wakasa and Aki in 1441.[108] But the Kikkawa were never the *shugo*'s vassals. The head of the family routinely had his land confirmed to him by the shogun himself, and if the Kikkawa fought occasionally under the Takeda, they fought also under the Ōuchi, Hosokawa, and Kōno. In most of these cases, moreover, it is clear that the Kikkawa were acting under orders from the Bakufu, rather than at the behest of their military commanders.[109]

The Kikkawa's links to the Bakufu are also apparent in an event that occurred in 1455. In that year the Bakufu issued a judgment against Itsukushima Norichika for having defied Bakufu orders that he cease his depredations against the holdings of Koizumi Yukihira. The enforcement of such a judgment was normally entrusted either to the *shugo* of the province involved or to one or two powerful shogunal vassals. In this case the latter course was pursued, and it was Kikkawa Yukitsune who was ordered to put an end to Itsukushima's abuses.[110]

Despite their humble beginnings, moreover, the Kikkawa enjoyed many of the same privileges of shogunal vassalage as did the Mōri and Kobayakawa. Although there is no explicit evidence before 1483 that the Kikkawa rendered their *tansen* directly to the capital, two facts suggest that they had acquired this privilege far earlier. First, when the Kikkawa were issued a duplicate receipt for *tansen* payment in 1459, this receipt was issued by Bakufu envoys rather than the *shugo*'s officials; and second, the Kikkawa were clearly levying *tansen* on their own account as early as 1450.[111]

As a series of events during the late 1450's reveals, the head of the Kikkawa family could also call in the Bakufu to uphold his lordship over his kinsmen. On 1456/2/13 Kikkawa Tsunenobu, who had succeeded Tsunemi as head of the Kikkawa some forty years earlier, died after having partitioned his estate among his successors.[112] For some reason Tsunenobu was then on unpleasant terms with his eldest son, Yukitsune, and so passed the headship of the family to Yukitsune's infant son, the future Mototsune. Because of the child's youth, however, it was in fact Yukitsune who acted as head of the family for the time being, and it was Yukitsune's authority that the Bakufu upheld.

The Bakufu's intervention on Yukitsune's behalf came within a few months of Tsunenobu's death, when Yukitsune impleaded his younger brother Nobutsune for having defied the lineage head and having obtained (Bakufu?) confirmation of those portions of the Kikkawa estate that had been assigned to Nobutsune under their father's will. The precise content of Nobutsune's defiance is not clear from the documents arising directly out of Yukitsune's suit, but a petition lodged by Nobutsune in 1457/6 suggests that it lay in two areas: Nobutsune's having sought outside confirmation of his landholdings, and Nobutsune's having tried to become the vassal of either Hosokawa Katsumoto or Takeda Nobukata (that is, in effect, having attempted to escape the lordship of Yukitsune and his son). Nobutsune maintained that he had merely been following the dying wishes of his father, but the Bakufu was not impressed. Nobutsune's enrollment as a Hosokawa or Takeda vassal was forbidden, the outside confirmation of his lands may possibly have been withdrawn, and both Takeda Nobukata and Kobayakawa Hirohira were ordered to assist Yukitsune's forces in dealing with Nobutsune if he chose to put up a fight.[113]

What this case reveals, in other words, is the Bakufu's insistence that the lordship of one of the shogun's powerful vassals be rigorously preserved, even if that meant intervening to prevent the formation of vassalage ties between a warrior who had escaped that lordship and one of the country's powerful *shugo*. A similar policy seems to be reflected in what happened between the Kikkawa and the Watanuki.

The Watanuki were a minor warrior family, though apparently of *gokenin* status, whose holdings lay in the village of Kawado, near the southeastern frontiers of the Kikkawa's own territories. In a manner now obscure, the Kikkawa established some sort of superior lordship over at least that portion of Kawado that was traditionally regarded as being within the provincial domain, and in 1443 Watanuki Akihisa swore to the Kikkawa that he would always render to them the various military services that were incumbent upon that land.[114] By 1450, however, the Watanuki were defying the Kikkawa, and in 1450/11 and 12 Kobayakawa Hirohira and Takahashi Mitsuyo were ordered by the Bakufu to join forces with Kikkawa Tsunenobu should Watanuki Mitsusuke offer him any resistance.[115]

As of 1450, then, the Bakufu was quite prepared to back up the Kikkawa's lordship over a family that was apparently itself of *goke-*

nin status. The situation was apparently extremely complex, however, for in 1453-54 the Bakufu was intervening to protect the Watanuki against the Kikkawa, and in 1456 Kobayakawa Hirohira had to arrange some sort of compromise in the matter.[116] Nevertheless, for the Kikkawa, as for the Kobayakawa and the Mōri, the Bakufu was a useful prop to local lordship.

It was a prop that had its disadvantages, however, and one whose usefulness declined markedly by about the time of the Ōnin War. Although the disadvantages of reliance upon the Bakufu are less apparent in the Kikkawa's case than in the Mōri's, Kikkawa Yukitsune clearly felt that the Watanuki were faring better before the Bakufu courts in 1456 than they had in 1450 because the shogunal deputy Hosokawa Katsumoto was biased in their favor. Moreover, about 1460 the Bakufu proved completely incapable of resolving a suit between Yukitsune's son Mototsune and one of his relatives over title to Kikkawa lands.[117]

Nevertheless, the Kikkawa did not turn traitor during the Ōnin War—as did the Takehara and the Mōri—but instead served loyally enough to be granted a number of additional landholdings for their services.[118] By the 1470's, however, the Kikkawa clearly were looking to a variety of sources other than the shogunate for the means to increase their power. When the Watanuki were finally brought to accept the Kikkawa's lordship in 1475, for example, they did so because the Kikkawa had launched an armed attack against them and a truce had then been arranged by the Ōuchi, Misumi, Sawa, Fukuya, and Takahashi families.[119] And though it was technically the Bakufu that restored the Kikkawa's ancient holding of Fukui to Kikkawa Mototsune in 1468, it was only by serving Akamatsu Masanori and Urakami Norimune of Harima during the 1480's that Mototsune (who had by then changed his name to Tsunemoto) was able to make this grant good. By that time the Kikkawa seem to have served the Akamatsu and Urakami with far greater devotion than they did the Bakufu.[120]

But the Kikkawa's post-Ōnin activities are ultimately of less interest to us than the fact that the Kikkawa, like the Kobayakawa and the Mōri, maintained a direct relationship with the Ashikaga shogunate until at least the late 1460's or early 1470's. Like the Mōri, moreover, the Kikkawa had failed to be enrolled in the shogunal guard. Since membership in the guard clearly was unnecessary for the maintenance of direct ties between the Ashikaga shoguns and old-line *goke-*

nin families, it behooves us to think a bit more generally about the significance of shogunal vassalage during the Muromachi period.

The Medieval Shoguns and Their Vassals

In reevaluating those views of the Muromachi Bakufu that have emphasized the *shugo* or the shogunal guard, we must recall that both of the first two shogunates were, in part, patrimonial authority structures of the sort that Kuroda Toshio has called *kenmon seika*. In other words, both shogunates were to some degree private household administrations whose chiefs sought to use their own political influence to secure the interests, and thus the loyalty and service, of the household's retainers.[121] This characteristic of the medieval shogunates is particularly clear-cut in the relationship between the Kamakura Bakufu and the *gokenin* of central and western Japan, excluding Kyushu.

Two features of that relationship claim our attention. First, only warriors designated as *gokenin* were of interest to the Bakufu, and only a limited segment of *gokenin*—those appointed *jitō*—were protected to the extent that their holdings were immune from civil jurisdiction.[122] Second, the *gokenin* were normally the only warriors from whom the Bakufu demanded any sort of service. A case in point is the imperial palace guard (*ōban*), for which Minamoto Yoritomo assumed responsibility in the 1180's. Service in the guard had until then been incumbent upon all warriors, and Yoritomo clearly was entitled to mobilize whatever warriors he wished in discharging this authority. In effect, he enjoyed a public right of command over the warriors of the entire country. By 1192, however, Yoritomo was unwilling to levy such service on any but his own *gokenin*. He had made a hitherto public function the exclusive preserve of his private household retainers.[123]

This reliance upon the private resources of the shogunal house is a typical feature of many Bakufu activities and recalls a similar pattern within the great noble and ecclesiastical households of the Heian era. The Bakufu, however, was far more powerful than any of its civilian competitors, and in the long run it assumed a number of characteristics of a fully public government. Although it is difficult to imagine how far this transformation would have gone without the upheavals that attended the creation of a new Bakufu, by the 1390's that regime had in fact assumed most of the governmental prerogatives of the old imperial court. The Muromachi shogunate was very nearly the true government of Japan.[124]

Nevertheless, a perception that the Bakufu was at least partially the private regime of the shogunal household and its retainer corps did survive and was expressed in a variety of ways. That the Bakufu's routine personnel and maintenance costs were met out of imposts levied specifically against the *gokenin* suggests that, in this area at least, men continued to think of the regime as one whose maintenance was the private responsibility of the shogun and his vassals. Likewise, during the Nanbokuchō War it was primarily the old *jitō* and *gokenin* whom the Ashikaga summoned to the fight against Go-Daigo.[125] And the *gokenin* remained the only warriors to whose land rights the Bakufu was prepared to extend its legal protection.

Furthermore, though the enormous power that had been vested in the *shugo* by the early fifteenth century unquestionably allowed some *shugo* to displace the shogun as lords and patrons of much of the *gokenin* class, this displacement was neither automatic nor complete. Even such enormously powerful *shugo* as the Ōuchi had members of the shogunal guard living within their territories, and guardsmen enjoyed considerable immunity from comital authority. As we have seen from the cases of the Mōri and the Kikkawa, even warriors who were not incorporated into the guard might well succeed in maintaining direct ties to the shogun.

Thus the *gokenin*—the direct vassals of the nation's military hegemon—remained a distinct part of the political life of late medieval Japan. There can be little doubt that their direct ties to the Muromachi shoguns had considerable importance both to the Bakufu and to the *gokenin* themselves. From the Bakufu's perspective, the *gokenin*, and particularly those *gokenin* enrolled in the shogunal guard, constituted a body of men who could be called upon to render military service, to enforce legal decisions, to perform in various ceremonies, to supervise Bakufu building projects, to serve on diplomatic missions, or to march in the shogunal retinue. All such services, moreover, must frequently have been rendered at little or no cost to the shogunal treasury.[126] And though the total number of men who were thus available to the Bakufu remains unclear, the guardsmen alone numbered 300 to 350, a figure well in excess of the number of direct vassals maintained by the powerful Ōuchi family around 1550, and one that is 60 to 70 percent of the number maintained by the Later Hōjō.[127]

From the *gokenin*'s perspective, ties to the shogun could be extremely useful in strengthening local power. As we have seen, the Kobayakawa, Mōri, and Kikkawa all benefited from their ties to the shogun in remarkably similar ways. All of them had their lands confirmed by the shogun himself, all were immune from the *shugo*'s authority over taxation, and all were backed by the Bakufu in maintaining the authority of the main line of the family over its cadet lineages.

This last point deserves particular emphasis, for it is closely related to larger questions concerning warrior lordship in fifteenth-century Japan. It has long been known that, in many cases, the enormous political power amassed by the *shugo* during the first half of the Muromachi period disintegrated in the aftermath of the Ōnin War. The explanation usually given is that the *shugo*'s power could not survive the virtual collapse of the Bakufu during the 1470's because it derived from the delegated authority of the Muromachi shoguns, rather than from any reciprocity of interests between the *shugo* and the provincial warriors. By contrast, we are told, the pettier lordships of families like the Mōri and the Kobayakawa were more stable because they were based on a genuine reciprocity of interests between such provincial seigneurs (*kokujin ryōshu*) and the lesser warriors of their domains.[128] As we have seen, however, the Kobayakawa, Mōri, and Kikkawa all had to struggle to maintain their lordship over even their own kinsmen, and they depended heavily upon Bakufu legitimation as a source of power. Only after the collapse of the Bakufu during the 1470's did families like the Mōri and Kobayakawa seek a firmer base of support, and this was surely because the Bakufu could no longer offer any support worth having.

Once the Bakufu began to falter, the *gokenin* were perfectly capable of discovering a community of interest with a great *shugo*. Indeed, the Takehara branch of the Kobayakawa had already developed such close ties with the Ōuchi that they were prepared to throw in with the latter against the Bakufu as early as the 1460's. The Mōri were not driven into the Ōuchi's arms until 1471—and that only after Mōri Hiromoto and his son Toyomoto were roughly handled by the Bakufu's courts—but they served the Ōuchi none the less loyally for the lateness of their conversion. Even the Kikkawa, who remained far less treasonous than the Mōri and the Takehara, were quite willing to serve the Akamatsu in order to win lands in Harima.

Nor is this outcome all that surprising. The *gokenin*'s forebears had originally been won over to Minamoto Yoritomo by the latter's promise to secure their interests in land, and thereafter their families' loyalty to the Kamakura and Muromachi shogunates had depended heavily on the shoguns' continued ability to guarantee those interests. In provinces where the *shugo* became sufficiently powerful to absorb a good deal of the shogun's authority, as did the Ōuchi of Suō, the *gokenin* shifted their primary loyalty to the *shugo* as early as the beginning of the fifteenth century. Even when the *shugo* was quite weak, as he was in Aki, or when a *gokenin* had been enrolled in the shogunal guard, as had the Kobayakawa, the *gokenin*'s loyalty to the shogunate was by no means certain. If a nearby *shugo* offered land or other perquisites to a *gokenin*, as the Ōuchi seem to have done to the Takehara, or if a *gokenin* felt that he had been dealt with unfairly by the Bakufu, as did Mōri Hiromoto and his son, there was every reason to switch one's loyalty from the shogun to a more accommodating overlord.

Nevertheless, we should not assume that the Ōnin War marked the effective end of shogunal vassalage as a meaningful political concept. The collection of *gokenin*-based imposts in Bizen in 1544, for example, suggests that shogunal vassalage had at least some meaning well into the sixteenth century. But the crucial turning point in the *gokenin*'s attitude toward the Bakufu may have come in 1493, when the deposition of the shogun Yoshiki (later known as Yoshitane) by Hosokawa Masamoto effectively destroyed the power of the Ashikaga family. In Aki, at least, the great vassal families can be seen heeding Bakufu decisions, paying Bakufu taxes, and fighting on Bakufu campaigns throughout much of the period between the close of the Ōnin War and the downfall of Yoshiki, but thereafter only the Nuta Kobayakawa seem at all closely tied to the shogunate. By the beginning of the sixteenth century, though the Bakufu was still accorded a certain respect, the *gokenin* of Aki were clearly far less interested in the Bakufu than in the local struggles between the Ōuchi and their various rivals and successors. A new era was beginning, and in it the second of Japan's shogunates was doomed to perish.

The Toyotomi Regime and the Daimyo

BERNARD SUSSER

One major theme in Japanese political history is the tension between central government and local authority: the imperial court in Yamato and the local forces of Izumo and elsewhere; the Heian aristocrats and the rising provincial military class; and the court and the Bakufu in early medieval times are the obvious examples. Giving force to this tension was the ideal of a unified state, an ideal that Toyotomi Hideyoshi expressed when he told Pedro Bautista Blanquez during an audience in 1593, "My armies knew nothing but victory. For the first time in history, all Japan is firmly in one hand—mine."[1]

An analysis of the process of unification in the sixteenth century must begin with the Sengoku daimyo domain, defined by John Whitney Hall as a "composite of separate fiefs held either directly by the daimyo or by his vassals."[2] Some of the Sengoku daimyo had direct, firm control over their vassals, whereas others relied more heavily on the traditional authority of the court or Bakufu to bolster their local authority. In the end, the Sengoku daimyo were never able to establish unified domains; their institutional instability was the major obstacle to unification and peace.

According to Fujiki Hisashi with George Elison, Oda Nobunaga's goal was "nothing less than the overthrow of the disjointed Sengoku pattern of allegiances and the creation of a new order in Japan." They argue that Nobunaga's policies sought to destroy the traditional base of local landholding and to force the daimyo to reorganize their vassalage structure "in a mold approximating the early modern model." They imply that these policies, which were continued by Hideyoshi, led to the Tokugawa-type domain. My own view, based on a close analysis of Nobunaga's "land surveys" (for the most part *sashidashi* or cadastral inquests), is that Nobunaga's main purpose was to prevent the formation of stable daimyo domains that might have competed with his own central authority.[3]

A few days after the fall of Odawara castle (1590/7), which symbolized Hideyoshi's military conquest of the country, Hideyoshi declared that he would "transform Japan."[4] Unlike Nobunaga, he sought to achieve unity and stability by establishing stable daimyo domains under the symbolic authority of the imperial court. Hideyoshi saw that military and political superiority over the daimyo would achieve nothing unless the burgeoning social and economic forces of late medieval times—the local warriors, the farmers, the cities, even foreigners—could be brought under control. But Hideyoshi also realized that policies designed to achieve the former inevitably undermined efforts to achieve the latter: measures that weakened daimyo usually improved the position of local warriors; measures intended to extirpate local warriors or control farmers tended to enhance daimyo power.

The policies of the Toyotomi regime were designed to resolve this dilemma. Hideyoshi's ideological policies served to buttress his authority as national hegemon. His political policies served to establish the daimyo in their domains, keeping them weak with respect to the central government but absolute in their own territories. To lay the foundation for this political structure, he initiated a sweeping transformation of society and strictly regulated trade and commerce. Although Hideyoshi moved against and sometimes destroyed individual daimyo, the major policies of his regime encouraged the formation of strong and stable daimyo domains. These policies were continued by the Tokugawa shoguns.[5]

Ideological Policies

Hideyoshi's political ideology centered on the concept of unity; the theme appears continually in his private correspondence as well as in official edicts. His principal aim was to create an image of himself as the head of the unified nation; this was achieved in part by his policy of accumulating, displaying, and distributing wealth as the visible proof of his power. In Sansom's words, "Magnificence was Hideyoshi's policy as well as his pleasure." His gold tea rooms, his huge palaces and castles built on the sites of former imperial palaces, his splendid entertainments, his lavish distributions of gold, silver, and other valuables, all served to enhance his image as hegemon. His personal letters and the chronicles he commissioned belabor the same themes: his magnificence, munificence, and omnipotence.[6] But behind this seemingly indiscriminate prodigality was a shrewd sense of timing. For example, his presentations of gold and silver were made on three occasions: in 1585, after he had redistributed holdings at the conclusion of the Shikoku and Hokuriku campaigns; on 1589/5/20 at Jūrakudai, before the invasion of the east and north; and just before his death in 1598, when he was trying to enlist the daimyo's support for Hideyori.[7] It must also be noted that Hideyoshi received in turn much gold and other precious gifts.[8]

But Hideyoshi never made the effort to go beyond propaganda and promote a consistent ideology to support his regime and to serve as a theoretical foundation for his policies. He did nothing comparable to Nobunaga's active solicitation of Confucian scholars or to Ieyasu's patronage of Fujiwara Seika and Hayashi Razan. Hideyoshi's letter to the viceroy of the Indies (1591/7/25), often cited as an example of his adherence to Confucianism, is merely a perfunctory recital of platitudes probably concocted by one of the monks in charge of foreign affairs, who gave it the appropriate Chinese idiom.[9] Rather than create a new ideology, Hideyoshi chose to rely on the traditional values and authority of the imperial court, and to a lesser extent on those of Buddhism.

Hideyoshi's government was a combination of the personal and military relationships between him and his vassals, grafted onto the existing imperial court system and reaching its fully developed form on 1588/4/15, when the daimyo swore to obey Hideyoshi as imperial regent (*kampaku*). To make this government effective, Hideyoshi had to reestablish the imperial government as the sole legitimate government in Japan, and at the same time make certain that the emperor and his court did not become independent of his control. He followed Nobunaga in rebuilding palaces for the emperor and making the income of the court and aristocratic families more secure by land grants and cash presents.[10] But he also followed Nobunaga in changing the nature of the court's holdings from public and *shōen* land to fiefs held under his seal. Further, he eliminated other independent sources of income: aristocrats were no longer allowed to levy urban taxes, and much of the income that they had received from guilds was lost as the guilds were abolished. Cut off from politics and restricted in its finances, the court was encouraged to devote itself to peaceful pursuits, which had the happy result of bringing about a revival of the Japanese classics.[11] At the same time Hideyoshi consistently maintained the fiction that he was merely the court's agent; this stance created a symbiotic relationship in which his own prestige accrued to the court, whose increased authority devolved on himself.

Hideyoshi was much gentler toward the Buddhist establishment than his predecessor had been. Aside from the destruction of a few temples like the Negoroji, whose monks had fought actively against him, Hideyoshi achieved his goal of weakening the temples economically and militarily by peaceful means, such as reducing their holdings after conducting a land survey. Their financial resources were further curtailed when Hideyoshi abolished the guilds that had been a source of profit to many temples. The militant temples were disarmed by Hideyoshi's sword hunts; the Honganji in particular was weakened by being moved from place to place before being installed in Kyoto in 1591. Hideyoshi also attempted to regulate the internal affairs of Buddhist temples: he issued a number of edicts and directives forbidding temples to harbor fugitives, thieves, or troublemakers; he demanded the expulsion of women from the compounds; and he encouraged intellectual pursuits by offering rewards to the best scholars.[12]

Hideyoshi actively supported temples throughout his reign by granting them land. He gave permission and assistance in 1584 for the reconstruction of Hieizan, which had been destroyed by Nobunaga in 1571; his edict reads in part: "Truly, the Enryakuji is different from other temples in being the sacred place which protects the peace of the realm as the Guardian of the Imperial Palace. I wish to allow the reconstruction for the sake of peace in the land and for the tranquility of the state."[13] Here Hideyoshi's support for the temple has an obvious political connotation, as did his favors to the Ikkō sect in return for their military help in the campaigns against Shibata and Shimazu. In other instances, such as when he prayed for his mother's recovery from illness, his gifts to temples were motivated by piety or superstition.[14] The building of the Great Buddha image (*daibutsu*) at the Hōkōji seems to have been an attempt to bind up the symbols of religion and state in a visible manifestation of his own magnificence, deliberately competing with the shade of Emperor Shōmu (who had had the Nara *daibutsu* erected in the eighth century); at the same time it provided another excuse to impose heavy levies on the daimyo.[15] In this, as in all of Hideyoshi's ideological policies, practical considerations were never far from the symbolic.

Political Policies

If Hideyoshi was careful to preserve and dominate the symbols of power and authority, he was even more careful to keep in check those who held real military power. Hideyoshi announced his main policies toward his vassals after he had assumed leadership over the Oda vassals by defeating Shibata Katsuie; at that time (1583/8/1) he declared that he would redistribute holdings (*kuniwake*) and demolish castles (*shirowari*) "so that hereafter lawlessness will cease and the provinces will be at peace for 50 years."[16] During the 1580's he redistributed fief holdings on a large scale after each campaign: in 1583/8, after the defeat of Shibata; in 1585/6, after the subjugation of Shikoku and the Hokuriku region; in 1587, after the pacification of Kyushu; and in 1590, after his conquest of the east and north.[17] The old Sengoku daimyo were moved or had their holdings reduced, and new Toyotomi daimyo were created and/or moved in. Transfers were less frequent in the 1590's; by then Hideyoshi had run out of land to grant to his vassals and was looking for excuses to confiscate land: many daimyo were attaindered because of succession disputes or cowardly actions in Korea. Some changes were made after Hideyoshi's nephew and heir, Hidetsugu, and his supporters were purged in 1595, and Gamō Hideyuki's removal from Aizu on 1598/1/10 created a chain reaction of transfers that stretched all the way to Kyushu.[18]

Hideyoshi moved daimyo for three main reasons. First, daimyo were often relocated for strategic reasons, giving loyal vassals control over strategic areas or having them serve as a check on powerful and less trustworthy daimyo in their neighborhood. Second, transfer was a means of rewarding or punishing a daimyo; a larger, more valuable domain was a rich reward, whereas a smaller or poorer one caused great hardship. Third, transfer was an important means of strengthening a daimyo vis-à-vis his vassals, local warriors whose main strength was their close control over their holdings and the farmers who lived there.[19]

When an area was conquered and the holders destroyed or transferred, Hideyoshi commonly destroyed the small castles and forts that had served as the bastions of the local warriors; this policy was called *shirowari* ("demolishing castles"). Hideyoshi first carried out this policy under Nobunaga's orders during the conquest of Harima and continued it throughout his own regime. Sometimes he insisted that only one castle be allowed to stand in a domain, such as Gifu castle, but usually he permitted several local forts to remain as branch castles; thus Nambu Nobunao destroyed only three-fourths of the smaller forts in his domain in the far north, and Uesugi Kagekatsu also retained many as guard castles in Aizu. The immediate purpose of *shirowari* was to destroy the military potential of a conquered area; it was conducted as a mopping-up operation after the conquest of Hokuriku in 1585, Kyushu in 1587, and in the north after the defeat of the Hōjō in 1590.[20] The main result was to reduce the power and independence of the local warriors, forcing them into the castle towns the daimyo were then building, where they were of necessity more dependent on the daimyo.[21]

Hideyoshi's penchant for "fixing boundaries so that no dispute occurs" was a further effort to bring the daimyo under the authority of the central government. When a dispute did occur, Hideyoshi assumed the right to settle it, as in 1583, when he mediated a border dispute in Mino Province between the Inaba, a powerful local daimyo, and the Ikeda, a Toyotomi vassal who had just been granted a holding in Mino. Hideyoshi also ordered, in 1591, that farmers living on land under his direct control or on land held by his vassals could not borrow across fief lines; this measure would prevent land in one domain from coming into the possession of someone in another domain through foreclosure. Instead, Hideyoshi urged his vassals and officials to lend to their own farmers without charging interest, thus protecting the political integrity of the domains against economic pressures.[22]

Hideyoshi continued the Sengoku practice of taking hostages from defeated enemies and untrustworthy vassals. Defeated by Hideyoshi in 1585, Chōsokabe Motochika was ordered to send his natural children to Hideyoshi's headquarters at Osaka; after the conquest of the north in 1590, several daimyo were obliged to send not only their own families but even those of their leading vassals. According to one record the Date had a retinue of over a thousand persons at Hideyoshi's Fushimi castle.[23] The daimyo themselves were required to attend Hideyoshi at his palaces in Osaka, Kyoto, and Nagoya (Kyushu). At first (1589/9) all the daimyo were ordered to build mansions near Hideyoshi's Jūrakudai palace; later they had to move with him to Fushimi. Sometimes the period of attendance was stipulated; for example, three groups of Shimazu hostages alternated every seven months. But usually the obligation was vague and arbitrary, making it more onerous than the Tokugawa's *sankin kōtai*.[24] Keeping the daimyo in attendance and their families as hostages ensured their loyalty and good behavior, and also was a tremendous drain on their purses; the Satake, for example, spent over 300 *mai* of gold per year for expenses incurred while living in Kyoto, and Shimazu Yoshihisa complained of the difficulties at home caused by his imposed residence in the capital.[25]

Hideyoshi made the financial burden of living in Kyoto (or Osaka) easier by granting to some vassals "holdings for maintenance while residing in Kyoto" (*kyō-makanai-ryō*), or as some of the grants stated, "for bearing residence in Kyoto." Life in Kyoto required large amounts of cash or gold, but because of the underdeveloped state of the economy in the provinces, many daimyo could not sell the tax rice they collected for cash in their own domains, nor could they easily ship it to the Kinai; for these reasons, we are told in a chronicle of the Uesugi house, Hideyoshi granted to daimyo a holding in the Kinai, where markets were sufficiently developed to permit them to sell their rice for cash.[26] The accompanying table lists all instances of this type of grant that I have found. The roster is a peculiar one, including near as well as distant daimyo, friends as well as foes (even a vassal of Tokugawa Ieyasu's), but since it includes some doubtful cases and is almost certainly incomplete, there is no point in speculating on the criteria Hideyoshi used to make such grants. It is clear that the possession of such a holding would represent a considerable saving to a daimyo obliged to reside in Kyoto; consequently such grants could be used as a device for manipulating the daimyo's relative economic strength.

The daimyo's attendance at Hideyoshi's court was a symbolic form of service, but it was augmented by two forms of actual service they were obliged to give: providing troops for military campaigns and laborers for construction projects. Hideyoshi's army grew from about 60,000 in 1586 to a huge 280,000 at the time of the invasion of Korea.[27] From the beginning it was a powerful army because Hideyoshi had taken pains to make it a professional army; contemporaries noted that the country samurai of Shikoku and western Japan

Grants of Kyō-makanai-ryō

Date	Daimyo	Domain	Grant location	Source
1584/11/17	Matsuura Shigematsu	Harima(?)	(unknown)	(1)
1586/4/1	Hosokawa Fujitaka	Tango	Yamashiro	(2)
1586/11	Tokugawa Ieyasu	Mikawa[a]	Ōmi	(3)
1587/?	Niwa Nagashige	Kaga	Ōmi	(4)
1587/9/24	Kuroda Yoshitaka	Bizen	Kawachi	(5)
1587/9/28	Asano Nagamasa	Wakasa	Ōmi	(6)
1587/10/14	Shimazu Yoshihisa	Satsuma	(Kinai)[b]	(7)
1588/4/3	Tokugawa Ieyasu	Mikawa[a]	(stipend)	(8)
1588/6/15	Uesugi Kagekatsu	Echigo	Ōmi	(9)
1588/7/5	Shimazu Yoshihisa	Satsuma	Harima	(10)
1588/9/17	Katō Kiyomasa	Higo	Kawachi	(11)
1590/1/8	Ryūzōji Takafusa	Hizen	Higo	(12)
1590/7/27	Nambu Nobunao	Mutsu	(unknown)	(13)
1590/7/28	Tozawa Mitsumori	Dewa	(unknown)	(14)
1590/9	Ikeda Terumasa	Mikawa	Ise	(15)
1591/3/13	Mōri Terumoto	Aki[a]	(unknown)	(16)
1591/3/13	Kobayakawa Takakage	Chikuzen	(unknown)	(17)
1591/4	Tokugawa Ieyasu	Musashi[a]	Ōmi	(18)
1591/9/23	Date Masamune	Mutsu	Ōmi	(19)
1593?/3/6	Maeda Toshinaga	Etchū	Ōmi	(20)
1593/i9	Aoyama Tadanari	Sagami	Ōmi	(21)
1593/i9	Gamō Ujisato	Mutsu	(unknown)	(22)
1594/8/3	Niwa Nagashige	Kaga	Ōmi	(23)
1594/10/17	Shimazu Yoshihiro	Satsuma	Settsu	(24)
1595/7	Ikoma Chikamasa	Sanuki	Sanuki	(25)
1595/8/21	Shimazu Yoshihiro	Satsuma	Harima, Iwami	(26)
1598/7/24	Asano Nagamasa	Kai	Ōmi	(27)

SOURCES: A list of abbreviations used in citing sources appears on page 199. (1) *DNS*, ser. 11, 10: 181. (2) *SJJ*, p. 215. (3) *SJJ*, p. 167. (4) *SJJ*, p. 186. (5) *SJJ*, p. 95; *Hōkō ibun*, ed. Kusaka Hiroshi (Tokyo, 1914), p. 157 (1587/9/24). (6) *DNK, 2: Asano ke monjo* (Tokyo, 1906), p. 539, doc. 319 (1587/9/28); Asao Naohiro, "Toyotomi seiken ron," in *IKNR 9, kinsei 1* (2d ser., 1963): 188. (7) Araki Moriaki, *Taikō kenchi to kokudaka-sei* (*NHK Bukkusu*, no. 93; Tokyo, 1969), pp. 198-99; *SJJ*, p. 122; *DNK, 16: Shimazu ke monjo* (Tokyo, 1966-71), 1: 431, doc. 441 (1587/10/14). (8) Nakamura Kōya, *Ieyasu den* (Tokyo, 1965), chronology, p. 65; *SJJ*, p. 167. (9) *DNK, 12: Uesugi ke monjo* (Tokyo, 1931-63), 2: 217-18, doc. 832 (1588/6/15). (10) *DNK, 16: Shimazu ke monjo*, 1: 431-34, docs. 442-43 (1588/7/15). (11) *Kumamoto ken shiryō, chūsei hen*, ed. Kumamoto ken, 5 vols. (Kumamoto, 1961-67), 5: 150 (1588/9/17). (12) *Nagasaki kenshi, shiryō hen 2*, ed. Nagasaki ken (Tokyo, 1964), pp. 738-39 (1590/1/8). (13) *Morioka shishi, dai-ni bunsatsu, chūsei-ki*, ed. Morioka shi (Morioka, 1949-51), pp. 162-63 (1590/7/27). (14) Mori Kahee, *Tsugaru Nambu no kōsō—Nambu Nobunao* (*Nihon no bushō*, no. 66; Tokyo, 1967), pp. 89-90 (1590/7/28). (15) *SJJ*, p. 28. (16) *DNK, 8: Mōri ke monjo*, 3: 236-38, docs. 956-57 (1591/3/13). (17) *DNK, 11: Kobayakawa ke monjo*, 1: 181-82, doc. 180 (1591/3/13). (18) *Shiga kenshi*, ed. Shiga ken, 6 vols. (Ōtsu, 1928), 3: 441. (19) *SJJ*, p. 140; Nakabe Yoshiko, *Kinsei toshi no seiritsu to kōzō* (Tokyo, 1967), p. 477. (20) *Echinōka sanshūshi*, ed. Tomita Kagechika(?) (rev. ed., Kanezawa, 1933), pp. 643-46; Okumura Tetsu, "Maeda Toshiie kashindan no tenkai," *Chihōshi kenkyū*, 18.3 (1968): 30; Iwasawa Yoshihiko, *Maeda Toshiie* (*Jimbutsu sōsho*, no. 136; Tokyo, 1966), p. 369. (21) *SJJ*, p. 4. (22) Komai Shigekatsu, *Komai nikki* (1593-95), in *Kaitei shiseki shūran*, 32 vols. (reprint, Tokyo, 1967-69), 25: 496, entry for 1593/i9/13; *SJJ*, p. 78. (23) *SJJ*, p. 186. (24) *DNK, 16: Shimazu ke monjo*, 1: 434-36, doc. 444 (1594/10/17). (25) *SJJ*, p. 20; Asao, "Toyotomi seiken ron," p. 188. (26) *DNK, 16: Shimazu ke monjo*, 1: 436-37, doc. 445 (1595/8/21); Takasaka Yoshimi, "Ikeda Terumasa no ni-wari uchidashi nai-kenchi to sono eikyō ni tsuite," *Hyōgo shigaku*, 50 (1968): 85; *SJJ*, p. 122. (27) *DNK, 2: Asano ke monjo*, 545-46, docs. 324-25 (1598/7/24).

[a]The domain extended to other provinces as well.
[b]The location is only approximately known.

made a poor showing by comparison.[28] Originally the army consisted of Hideyoshi's own guards and other contingents, to which was added the retainer corps (*kashindan*) of his own trusted vassal-generals. He made an effort to attach defeated daimyo and local warriors to these vassals as rear vassals (*yoriki*), but the powerful Sengoku daimyo resisted this and remained in an anomalous position.[29] An examination of the rosters for the different campaigns suggests that the nature as well as the composition of groups like the horse guards changed a good deal over time. Very roughly, the army consisted (by the mid-1590's) of a nucleus of Toyotomi warriors, divided into several groups, and the contingents of the daimyo and other vassals, each highly independent, as the events in Korea revealed.[30]

Hideyoshi demanded military service (*gunyaku*) from his vassals as one form of the service they owed him in return for land grants or stipends. Sasaki Junnosuke has seized on this concept of military service as a means of gaining insight into the post-1600 Bakufu-daimyo (*bakuhan*) system and by extension the Toyotomi regime.[31] On examining the grants Hideyoshi gave to his vassals, Sasaki makes two main observations. First, *gunyaku* is not proportional to putative yield (*kokudaka*); that is, one vassal may receive 40,000 *koku* and have to furnish 2,000 men (one man per 20 *koku*), whereas another may receive only 20,000 *koku* and have to furnish 8,000 men (eight men per 20 *koku*). Sasaki contends that the rate of *gunyaku* was determined for each daimyo individually, according to the daimyo's strength relative to Hideyoshi's. Second, the existence of significant portions of a grant that are not subject to military obligation shows that Hideyoshi's power over the daimyo was not absolute.[32] Sasaki concludes that Hideyoshi's hold over his vassals was weak, and that in this respect his regime is more similar to the Sengoku daimyo's than to the Tokugawa shogun's.

There have been many spirited criticisms and modifications of Sasaki's theory. Some scholars emphasize the degree to which Hideyoshi was able to interfere in the internal organization of the daimyo's domain and *kashindan*.[33] Others argue that an examination of the battle levies shows that Hideyoshi's rates of *gunyaku* varied according to the distance from the field of battle but were uniform with respect to individual daimyo.[34] Contemporaries spoke of Hideyoshi's "limitless *gunyaku*": its very arbitrariness was an imposition.[35]

Besides military service Hideyoshi required that the daimyo provide laborers for his numerous construction projects; this obligation was called *buyaku* or *fushin* (corvée). In the early 1580's Maeda Gen'i demanded laborers from both public (that is, Hideyoshi's own lands) and private holdings, including those of warriors and religious institutions, for an irrigation project near Kyoto. There were levies on the daimyo to haul the great stones for Osaka castle; to expedite matters Hideyoshi gave those daimyo temporary grants in the Kinai that supplied provisions for their laborers. The "schedule for the construction of the Great Buddha image" (1588) contains a list of daimyo and the number of men each must send to work on the scheduled date. In 1592 began perhaps the most onerous of the construction levies, that for the construction of Fushimi castle. These levies were burdensome, since the daimyo had to transport and maintain their laborers, but they did give the daimyo occasion to extend their control more directly over the farmers on their domains.[36]

The construction levies, like the military ones, appear to have been imposed arbitrarily, giving support to Sasaki's theory that the Toyotomi regime was not strong enough to unify the obligations of its vassals but was forced to set its demands with regard to the power and position of each individual daimyo. But the apparent irregularity of the statistics does not necessarily mean that the rates were decided ad hoc; the *kokudaka* figures on which the calculations are based are often only guesses, and even if an accurate *kokudaka* figure can be found, there is usually no way to discover what portion of the total was exempt from levies. In a letter to Miyabe Keijun, for example, Hideyoshi notes that Miyabe holds a total of 50,970 *koku*; of this, 10,000 is deductible, so that Miyabe's *gunyaku* obligation of 2,000 men is based on the remaining 40,000 *koku*.[37]

But whether or not Hideyoshi was able to standardize his levies is less important than the fact that these levies constituted a terrific burden on the daimyo, who were obliged to provide for the transportation, upkeep, and equipment of their soldiers and laborers. The Jesuit Organtino Gnecchi-Soldi (1533-1609) noted that daimyo from distant provinces called to Kyoto for construction projects were reduced to opening stalls to sell the products and handicrafts of their domains in order to maintain their coolies. And the demands for soldiers for a new campaign or laborers for a fresh construction project were almost constant; Satake Yoshinobu, for example, was greeted with a demand for laborers to dig the moats at Fushimi castle only four months after he had returned from two years of fighting in Korea.[38] These "limitless demands," as we will see, forced the daimyo to reorganize their financial and tenurial systems, usually strengthening their own position at the expense of their vassals.

Another political policy that provided Hideyoshi with an instrument of control was the cadastral survey (the *taikō kenchi*). The Toyotomi regime conducted cadastral surveys throughout Japan from its inception until Hideyoshi's death in 1598 and beyond.[39] The early surveys were often merely inquests (*sashidashi*), but later large numbers of actual cadastral surveys (*kenchi*) were conducted, either for administrative and fiscal purposes or as a means of stabilizing a territory after a military conquest. Hideyoshi's right to conduct these surveys was based on his "supreme proprietary overlordship" of the entire nation.[40] The theoretical statement of his overlordship appears in the 1587 edict on Christianity: "Grants to vassals of a local holding are temporary; although vassals may be moved from one place to another, farmers may not be moved." Its practical application is stated succinctly in Hideyoshi's letter to Shimazu Yoshihiro (1595/6/3): "The land of Japan is at my disposal." Of course, in practice his authority was not absolute; great numbers of daimyo were confirmed in their original holdings, especially in the frontier areas, and the cadastral survey was not uniformly carried out throughout the realm.[41]

Hideyoshi naturally tried to make his hold over his vassals as secure as possible by basing grants on an actual cadastral survey. Underlying this practice was an effort to make the daimyo's hold over his domain more precarious; now the daimyo could claim only the rights to a specified amount of production rather than absolute rights to an area of land; this change was reflected in a change in terminology from "possession" (*ryōchi*) to "control" (*shihai*).[42] By making grants "on the basis of the survey," Hideyoshi converted the substance of the daimyo's tenure from land to a statistical abstraction. And more specifically, the survey gave numerical quantities of productivity that were used to determine the amount of military service a vassal was obliged to render.[43] But in the end the cadastral survey, like many of the Toyotomi regime's policies, was of more value to the daimyo than to the central government.

Two other purposes of the *taikō kenchi* should be mentioned. First, the survey was also undertaken on lands held by shrines and temples, and by court nobles, in order to bring these holdings under the control of the central government. Many religious institutions had part of their holdings confiscated and the remainder awarded back to them "on the basis of the survey." Hideyoshi tended to be lenient with the temples, whether out of piety or as a matter of policy; many were surveyed but exempted from tax, and others escaped the survey altogether.[44]

Second, cadastral surveys also prepared the way for raising additional revenue for the Toyotomi regime. The more of Japan Hideyoshi conquered, the less new land he had at his disposal to grant to his vassals or to support his own retainers. Consequently, as Asao points out, he conducted repeated cadastral surveys of the land under his direct control (*kurairi*); since each subsequent survey of a given area almost invariably resulted in a higher assessed value of the area's productivity, Hideyoshi could award the "difference" between the new assessed value and the old to a deserving vassal without conquering new territory.[45] In effect, the *taikō kenchi* established nationwide the system of assessing land value in terms of productivity (the *koku-daka-kokumori* system) and making land grants accordingly. This new system formed the basis of land tenure by the warrior class throughout the Tokugawa period.[46]

Social Policies

The principal effect of the Toyotomi social policies was to bring about the separation of warriors and farmers and to distinguish townspeople as a separate status. Evidence from contemporary literature and the accounts of Western missionaries shows that there was in the popular mind of the sixteenth century a distinction between the ruling and the subject classes and a distinction of social function or status among professional warriors, farmers, and merchants.[47] To some extent this social division was an ideal that preceded reality; certainly it appeared in the economically advanced regions first. In less advanced regions such as the Kantō, for example, there was no functional distinction between warriors and farmers. According to the *Hōjō godaiki*, written in the early seventeenth century, "Each district was held jointly by ten or twenty men. The lower samurai worked the land themselves; it was not easy to discern from their customs and manners whether they were warriors or farmers."[48] This pattern persisted in many places right through the Tokugawa period; the best-known example is perhaps the rural samurai of Satsuma.[49]

The term *hyakushō* has been applied to a wide range of statuses in the course of Japanese history, and its meaning in this period is not entirely clear.⁵⁰ Hideyoshi often drafted "farmers" for big military campaigns, calling upon "residents, farmers and others (even more inferior)" to help him in his campaign against Shibata, and promising "a holding, grant or tax exemption" to those who proved their loyalty by taking the head of an enemy; and Hideyoshi was far from being the only one to recruit in this way. On the other hand, there were occasions when he expected warriors to work alongside farmers. When constructing a castle in his newly acquired domain of Nagahama, Hideyoshi did not hesitate to demand that everyone come bringing plows and hoes to work on the project, "including priests, samurai, and vassals."⁵¹

Townspeople were distinguished from farmers and warriors in terms of their social function. The medieval townspeople (*machishū*), who were townspeople by virtue of the place where they lived, now became *kinsei* townspeople (*chōnin*), a distinct social status identifying merchant (function) with town (location).⁵² In general Hideyoshi's social policies had the effect of identifying the ruling class with the warrior status by disarming all but professional warriors and establishing distinctions among warriors, farmers, and townspeople in such matters as dress and place of residence. The status system was developed through a series of edicts, culminating in the edict on change of status issued 1591/8/21. Farmers were forbidden to leave their occupation or their location, or to become townspeople or retainers; warriors were forbidden to change their status or their masters.⁵³

A number of specific measures were taken to implement this status system, including a national census,⁵⁴ the formation of mutually responsible groups,⁵⁵ a ban on slavery,⁵⁶ and others, but these were minor efforts compared to Hideyoshi's series of sword hunts (*katanagari*), begun after the defeat of Shibata in 1583.⁵⁷ The symbolic significance of the confiscation of weapons from non-warriors was as impressive as the policy was pervasive. In less than a century the sword had become the very badge of the samurai; the scholars of the Tokugawa period found it difficult even to conceive of a time when there was no strict distinction between farmers and warriors, eloquent testimony to the success of the measure.⁵⁸

Hideyoshi's early sword hunts, like those of the Kamakura government and Shibata Katsuie before him, were directed primarily against the armed Buddhist temples.⁵⁹ Kōyasan and Nara were periodically stripped of their arsenals from 1584 onward.⁶⁰ Obstreperous farmers, particularly those allied to the temples, were also disarmed, though in at least one case Hideyoshi gave strict orders that their farm implements and animals be returned.[61] All of these confiscations were for military purposes, coming after or in lieu of an actual campaign.

The scope of the sword hunt was broadened with the publication of the famous edict of 1588/7/8, sent to all daimyo and temples in those areas of Japan under Hideyoshi's control. This edict demanded that the daimyo, vassals, and agents (*daikan*) collect all weapons from all the farmers in the nation; the swords thus collected were to be melted down for use as nails and bolts in constructing a gigantic statue of Buddha at the Hōkōji in Kyoto. This pious purpose was doubtless a conscious effort to echo Hōjō Yasutoki's edict (1242) ordering that swords be collected from monks and melted down for the statue of Buddha at Kamakura. The wording of Hideyoshi's edict makes it clear that the confiscation of weapons had other purposes as well: to facilitate the collection of taxes by disarming those who would defy the tax collectors; and to increase productivity by encouraging farmers to "devote themselves exclusively to agriculture."[62]

Hideyoshi's real intentions were not missed by his contemporaries. In 1585 the author of the *Tamon'in nikki* had been delighted when Hideyoshi's officials disarmed the monks of a neighboring temple, declaring with relief that at last the nation was at peace. But he decried the sword hunt edict of 1588, charging that "the real explanation is that this order is to prevent [farmers'] uprisings."[63] The Buddhist diarist was not the only religious to accuse Hideyoshi of hypocrisy. The Jesuit missionary Luis Frois delivered the following indictment:

And all this not from the devotion he has for the idol, but out of mere ostentation and for the greatness of his name in order the better to gain the minds of the populace, who, devoted to this idol, greatly praise this undertaking; and still much more by this and other devices to mask his tyranny and the sordidness of his mind; giving to understand that of the great hoard of gold and silver he is accumulating he does not wish to make use for his own advantage or his own gratification, but for the content and general weal of the people, and for the honor and glory of the gods. And he is astutely planning to possess himself of all the iron in Japan, *having ordered that all the mechanics and common people should leave off wearing swords and carrying any other sort of weapons (with which such people are here always well provided)*, and bring them to a place indicated for the purpose to be converted into the iron work necessary in the temple. Thus the populace is disarmed, and he the more secure in his arbitrary dominion.[64]

In fact, Hideyoshi did have other means of obtaining iron for build-ing the statue, if that had been his sole purpose. And many if not most of the weapons collected were not melted down for the Buddha image but were stored for emergencies; for this reason special care was or-dered for swords with sheaths. Some swords were used to make the "spy-foiling" prongs atop the walls of Osaka and Fushimi castles, and the iron was used in building ships for Hideyoshi's invasion of Korea.[65] Special sword hunts were conducted in Kyushu in 1592 and 1593, primarily to supply weapons to the troops in Korea, despite the fact that those troops were in no need of swords or spears but were begging for guns.[66] Following the conquest of the northern provinces in 1590, a sword hunt was conducted, local castles were destroyed, and a cadastral survey was undertaken in an effort to weaken the power of the local warriors.[67]

Thus all the early sword hunts were conducted primarily for mili-tary purposes: to subdue armed temples or rebellious farmers, to pac-ify a conquered territory, or to arm troops for an overseas war. No specific statement showing that Hideyoshi thought of the sword hunt as a social policy appears until 1589/4/15, when he forbade towns-people as well as farmers to have swords; only vassals could have them. This order changed the policy of the previous year, when Na-tsuka Masaie permitted townspeople to have swords.[68] Hideyoshi ex-pressed himself most clearly on the social aspects of the sword hunt in a letter written to Ishikawa Sadakiyo in 1590. He emphasized the importance of a nationwide sword hunt to disarm the farmers; he forbade slavery and insisted that farmers be bound to their plots. The ideal situation, he wrote, would be one in which "vassals each re-ceived the munificence of their lords and performed their duties, and the farmers tilled the fields."[69] Here vassals as *hōkōnin* (those who served their lords in a military capacity) were equated with vassals as *kyūnin* (recipients of their lord's favor in the form of land grants or stipends); their social status (warriors, and not farmers) was merged with their political status (members of the ruling class). The farmers, on the other hand, were designated cultivators and subjects. This idea was put into practice in the census and the status edict of 1591, both of which provided for the strict separation of vassals, townspeople, and farmers.[70]

It is almost impossible to measure the effectiveness of the sword hunts, since only four instances of quantitative data have survived.[71] But there is some evidence on how the sword hunts were carried out and by whom, which offers at least some hint of their effectiveness. The early sword hunts against the warrior monks of the temples at Kōyasan and in Nara were presumably conducted by Hideyoshi's troops, though an order of 1588/10/4 addressed to both Mukujiki Ōgo (of Kōyasan) and Maeda Gen'i (Hideyoshi's official in charge of religious affairs) suggests that the responsibility may have been shared between the temples' governing authorities and the central government. Maeda Gen'i conducted the sword hunt at the Kuramadera in Yamashiro, and the Toyotomi official Yakuin Zensō ordered the *daikan* of lands under Hideyoshi's direct control in Uji to conduct a search for weapons there; in general, *daikan* confiscated weapons on land under Hideyoshi's direct control.[72] From 1588 Hideyoshi's sword hunt officials took general charge of the project nationwide, even in some daimyo domains. Hideyoshi ordered his officials to carry out his commands "in every village" in a portion of Uesugi Kagekatsu's domain in Shinano, and in a few of the smaller domains in Kyushu he demanded that the daimyo furnish guides for his own officials to ascertain that no weapons were left in the hands of the farmers.[73] There is also some indication that Hideyoshi's officials conducted a sword hunt in Mino, and during the campaign of 1590 and its aftermath Hideyoshi's officials and their vassals were directly involved in the cadastral survey and sword hunt in the domains of the northern daimyo.[74] But in general it appears that Hideyoshi left the daimyo to conduct sword hunts in their own domains by themselves, confining himself to sending letters of congratulation when the confiscation was completed or dispatching his officers to receive the swords collected. There is evidence that the following daimyo conducted sword hunts on their own: Toda in Echizen, Ryūzōji in Hizen, Maeda in Kaga, Mōri in western Honshu, and Shimazu in Satsuma. The Date conducted a search for weapons even before they submitted to Hideyoshi.[75]

In some cases the sword hunt must have been very effective, either because the daimyo was afraid of incurring Hideyoshi's wrath or because he saw that it was in his interest to disarm the obstreperous local warriors. Mizoguchi Hidekatsu was a vassal of Hideyoshi who held 40,000 *koku* in Kaga; only a month after the sword hunt edict was issued, he turned over to Hideyoshi's official a considerable quantity of swords and other military gear. One modern scholar claims that this must be a special case because the number of swords is far greater than one would expect; yet Mizoguchi himself had apparently been afraid that Hideyoshi would think there were too few, as we can infer from the postscript of a letter from Natsuka Masaie consoling Mizoguchi.[76] And Maeda Toshiie apparently conducted a very thorough search for weapons in his domain of Kaga; he sent his vassals to many villages to collect weapons and then summoned the village elders to his castle town of Kanazawa, where he made them give their oath that they were not concealing any.[77]

Some daimyo may have been forced to compromise with local entrenched powers. Sakusa Hyōbujō, the agent who conducted the sword hunt in the holdings of the Izumo Taisha, the famous shrine located in the Mōri domain, was a member of a family that had had long and close relations with the Izumo Taisha; presumably he was at least aware of the needs of the shrine.[78] The Shimazu deliberately defied Hideyoshi's orders. Shimazu Yoshihiro, brother of the daimyo Yoshihisa, was serving as a hostage in Kyoto when he wrote to the elders of the Shimazu family warning that since Satsuma was famous for its long swords, it would be awkward if none of them appeared in the confiscated lot sent to Kyoto. Clearly the Shimazu defied "the spirit, if not the letter" of the decree.[79] A few months later Hideyoshi acknowledged "with exceeding joy" the receipt of 30,000 swords from Satsuma. This was roughly 2,000 swords per (modern) district, one-third less than the number from Enuma district in Kaga (3,313) or Senboku district in Dewa (2,900).[80] Without population data these figures are inconclusive, but they at least support our inference from Yoshihiro's letter. Thus the effectiveness of the sword hunt must have varied widely in different domains. Exceptions permitting commoners to retain weapons were frequent: hunters were allowed to keep their guns, and inhabitants of areas infested with pirates or wild boars could also keep their weapons. Certainly farmers were able to keep some weapons and frequently put them to use in the early years of the Tokugawa period; even so, Hideyoshi's sword hunt had a lasting effect on Japanese society by establishing a rigid status system.[81]

Commercial Policies

Hideyoshi's secretary Ota Gyūichi began his history of the Toyotomi period with a brief section called "Japan's Golden Age." Here he expatiated on Hideyoshi's wealth in precious metals and rare objects; thanks to this wealth and Hideyoshi's benevolence, he wrote, there was not a pauper or beggar in the land. Even allowing for hyperbole, we can see that Hideyoshi's contemporaries realized that his political power depended heavily on his control over the nation's wealth and trade. Hideyoshi hoped to encourage the development of commerce while keeping it under control and deriving profits from it.[82]

An edict of obscure provenance gives us some idea of Hideyoshi's enthusiasm for trade. The first article exempts the area (presumably a town) from all taxes; the third prohibits buying or selling under duress. The second article states: "Whatever one has to sell, one should open a store and carry on trade."[83] To encourage commerce Hideyoshi continued Nobunaga's policy of destroying barriers (*seki*) near and far, whether they were the property of aristocrats, monks, or daimyo.[84] He also improved transportation by constructing dikes, roads, and bridges, and by establishing a network of post-horses.[85] Toward the guilds he was less consistent. At first he reversed Nobunaga's policy and confirmed many guilds that Nobunaga had abolished, presumably in order to conciliate the court and powerful temples (patrons of the guilds) while his own position was still not secure.[86] From 1585 onward we find a number of edicts abolishing guilds in different places, but there is some doubt about how strictly they were enforced; Hideyoshi was still deriving income from some guilds in 1598.[87] Hideyoshi's intention was not to free trade but to replace the traditional forms of control with his own. Thus he maintained some guilds that brought him profit, and often tried to adjust the market by fiat to suit his commercial convenience, as when he regulated shipping rates and hotel rates in Kyushu during the Korean campaign.[88]

Wakita Osamu has suggested that Hideyoshi attempted to create a national market in the Kinai region by judicious location of the land under his direct control (*kurairi*) and in particular by granting to distant daimyo holdings for maintenance while they were residing in Kyoto (*kyō-makanai-ryō*).[89] This theory has attracted a good deal of attention in spite of the fact that the argument for it is based on inference rather than evidence. We have already seen that within the limits of our information, the pattern of *kyō-makanai-ryō* grants is inconsistent with such a theory: near as well as distant daimyo held them, and not all distant daimyo did. Further, produce from distant *kurairi* was often sold locally and not at a central market; in some cases the sale of produce from *kurairi* may have been used to manipulate the market for political rather than economic reasons.[90] This is not to say that a central market did not develop in central Japan, but only that there is no firm evidence that the Toyotomi government planned its development. Likewise there is no evidence that Hideyoshi contemplated devising a system of currency; he minted numerous coins, as did many daimyo, but these coins were presentation pieces or for large-scale transactions, not for circulation. Gold, silver, and copper coins were commonly used in all kinds of transactions, but they were not organized into a national currency system.[91]

Hideyoshi vigorously promoted foreign trade, and even after prohibiting Christianity he made it perfectly clear that he had no objection to trade with Westerners: "Because this is a question of trade and therefore an entirely different matter, trade should be carried on without interruption." But his adherence to the principles of free trade, if vigorous, was only verbal. Despite his promise to "issue orders immediately that trade is to be carried on freely in all articles" (1591), he used his superior political and military strength to corner the market on such imports as raw silk, gold, lead, saltpeter, tin, and Luzon jars.[92] Hideyoshi had some success in promoting seaborne trade by ridding the seas of pirates; only three years after the publication of his edict against piracy in 1588, he could boast to the viceroy of the Indies that "the seas have been rid of the pirate menace."[93] But some modern historians have charged that he was really attempting to suppress private trade—at the time there was little distinction between it and piracy—in order to establish a system of licensed trade (*shūin bōeki* or *kangō bōeki*). Such a system was established by 1592, but it was not a true tally system, since no arrangements had been made with foreign countries; rather it was just a device to distinguish officially approved trade from piracy and private trade.[94]

Conclusions

> But though he had thus brought under his absolute Subjection the whole Island, yet he warily consider'd how to prevent future Inconveniences, and what might happen to his prejudice under his new Acquirements: For several of his Substitute Kings being of Ancient Royal Blood, would not easily submit themselves to an Emperor of so mean an Extract; and that, if any of them should but once appear against him, it might shake his new-laid Foundation, and the whole Fabrick of his Government, the Rest of the Princes being ready to follow their Examples; which might suddenly cause a general Defection, and so his utter Ruine: To prevent all which, he had need to be very circumspect.
>
> Arnoldus Montanus (1670)[95]

On the surface, the policies of the Toyotomi regime may seem to have been directed primarily against the daimyo, to ensure the permanence of its military victories over them. Yet in the end the only possibility for a united Japan lay in the establishment of stable dai-myo domains; daimyo autonomy was the price Hideyoshi and later the Tokugawa had to pay for the right to rule the nation. How did Hideyoshi's apparently anti-daimyo policies actually strengthen dai-myo autonomy while maintaining the dominance of the Toyotomi regime?

One of the most telling powers Hideyoshi had was the authority to move the daimyo from one domain to another. It is commonly said that a transfer of holdings was a device to weaken the daimyo; Ogyū Sorai cited the proverb "Ten years' suffering is the cost of a transfer of fief," and other Tokugawa and modern scholars have agreed.[96] To be sure, a move involved great expense and the loss of traditional ties. But the daimyo himself lost very little by a transfer, other than his family graveyard; the main losers were his vassals, who were cut off from their principal source of strength, their close control over the countryside and the farmers living there. Consequently it was the vassals who staged the uprisings protesting the moves and who put pressure on the daimyo to remain.[97]

But the transfer was the daimyo's great opportunity to cut his vas-sals off from their local bases of power. For this reason Ieyasu did not inform his retainers beforehand of the intended move to the Kantō; when they did learn of the plan, "they were greatly surprised and raised an uproar."[98] An order to move to a new holding was one of the most effective means the Toyotomi regime could employ to strengthen a daimyo vis-à-vis his vassals. And it was not only a way for Hideyoshi to help the daimyo separate the warriors from the farmers, but a means of binding the farmers to the land. In 1598 Hideyoshi specifically ordered Uesugi and Mizoguchi to take all of their vassals with them to their new domains, leaving behind only the farmers registered in the cadastral surveys. Daimyo frequently issued orders of this type, though they were not always completely obeyed.[99]

The Toyotomi regime also encouraged the vassals to gather in the castle towns to serve as the daimyo's officials and standing armies. The Sengoku daimyo had had the same goal; as far back as 1480 Asakura Toshikage enjoined his descendants to "move all high-rank-ing retainers without exception to Ichijōgatani [the Asakura cas-tle]."[100] Daimyo continued to make this effort, often aided by the Toyotomi regime. The policy of destroying local fortifications forced many local warriors into the daimyo's fold; in a few cases Hideyoshi issued specific orders that a daimyo's vassals live in his castle town.

When he established the Tachibana as daimyo in Chikugo, he issued an edict declaring that only the daimyo had the right to levy demands for labor; that no one (referring to the local warriors) could disturb the farmers in the domain; and that the daimyo's vassals could not leave the castle town freely. The Toyotomi regime also banned samurai from certain areas such as the imperial palace in Kyoto and the Hakata market.[101]

When the local warrior was in effect a small daimyo, Hideyoshi would encourage him to become a vassal of a more powerful daimyo in the area; the small daimyo then became Hideyoshi's rear vassal (*yoriki*). This helped the strong daimyo build a stable domain and retainer corps. In some cases the rear vassals' portions were specifically designated in Hideyoshi's grant to the daimyo, at a ratio designed to strengthen the daimyo at the expense of his vassals. There are examples of daimyo grants to vassals that have been countersigned by Hideyoshi, lending the central government's authority to the daimyo. Another method of enhancing a daimyo's position locally was to confer honors on him; for example, Hideyoshi bestowed the Hashiba and Toyotomi names on Mori Tadamasa and saw that he received several court appointments to increase his prestige among the daimyo of eastern Mino and to help enroll the small daimyo there under his banner.[102]

The heavy burdens that Hideyoshi imposed on the daimyo, such as military and construction levies, and the expenses necessitated by his demand that hostages reside in Kyoto, were often passed on by the daimyo to their vassals. This practice gave the daimyo an excuse, backed by the authority of the central government, to attainder those vassals who refused to cooperate or who were unable to meet the demands. The Korean campaigns provide the clearest examples of how daimyo were often strengthened as a result of Hideyoshi's demands. Pressed to supply troops, the daimyo recruited the local warriors, tearing them from their local bases of power in the process. To collect the additional taxes necessary for the war, the daimyo also had to reorganize their internal administrative structures, another process they could turn to their advantage.[103] The Mōri used the central government's military service demands as an excuse to switch their finances to the *kokudaka* system and improve their own position with regard to their vassals. The Ōmura in Kyushu and the Satake in Hitachi were forced to complete the separation of farmers from soldiers and reorganize their retainer corps; the war served as an excuse for them to attainder many vassals, whose lands then came under the daimyo's direct control.[104] Satake Yoshinobu warned his vassals that if they could not meet the military service levies for the Korean expedition, he would "confiscate their holdings, seize the fall crops and take charge of the farmers directly."[105] Hideyoshi ordered the Matsuura, daimyo of Hizen Province, to make sure that only those vassals enrolled as members of the home guard remained behind, and that every other warrior in the domain be sent to Korea; and he encouraged the daimyo to confiscate the land of vassals who showed cowardice on the battlefield. All this suggests that the Korean expeditions might be seen as another device of the Toyotomi regime to assist the daimyo in stabilizing their domains and asserting control over the local warriors within them. At least some of the daimyo recognized the opportunity that Hideyoshi was offering them and took advantage of it by bringing even more troops than Hideyoshi had demanded (as had also happened during the Odawara campaign).[106]

The cadastral survey also served to enhance the power of the daimyo and stabilize their domains; in particular it was a powerful weapon against the vested interests of the local warriors. Just as Hideyoshi made grants "on the basis of the survey" to transform the substance of the daimyo's tenures from land to an abstraction, so did the daimyo make grants to their vassals "on the basis of the survey" to weaken their tenures.[107] Conducting a land survey also served as a good opportunity and excuse for the daimyo to reorganize their corps of retainers, assign their vassals holdings in new areas, or confiscate their lands altogether.[108] Of course, as was the case with Hideyoshi's other policies, the degree to which the cadastral survey was successful depended on the circumstances. Local warriors were often so powerful that the daimyo had to accept their leading position in the countryside and confirm their original holdings; warrior names frequently appear in the cadastral registers as the "cultivators." In Satsuma the units and procedures imposed by the central government's survey officials could not overcome the inertia of local customs, and so the surveys were gradually revised to make them conform to traditional procedures.[109] But on the whole the evidence indicates that the cadastral survey and other Toyotomi policies helped the daimyo substantially in asserting their rule over their domains.

A final point is that the establishment of *kinsei*-type daimyo domains was predicated on the existence of an effective central authority with the right to issue orders to implement policies such as these and the power to compel the daimyo's compliance. In practical terms the policies of the central government usually favored the daimyo over their local opposition, and further, under the Toyotomi governmental system, the daimyo were themselves usually responsible for carrying out these policies within their own domains.[110] For example, when Mōri Terumoto was ordered in 1586 to destroy local fortifications, eliminate the barriers that impeded his own officials, and carry out other measures to strengthen him as a daimyo in preparation for the Korean campaigns, Mōri benefited both from the specific policies he was ordered to undertake and from the fact that he was the one carrying them out. The daimyo were very conscious of the existence of the central authority, even calling on it to settle internal problems within their domains. It is said that Satake Yoshinobu could silence his retainers' objections to having their tenures consolidated just by mentioning Hideyoshi's name.[111]

Even some of the most drastic instances of intervention by the central authorities in a daimyo domain had a way of redounding to the daimyo's benefit. For example, Akita Sanesue, a Sengoku daimyo of Dewa Province, submitted to Hideyoshi and received in return confirmation of his holdings. Fully one-third of the holdings, however, were designated as lands under Hideyoshi's direct control (*kurairi*), which Akita administered as *daikan*. The loss of one-third of one's holdings might seem to be a heavy blow, but in fact the daimyo recouped his loss by confiscating one-third of his vassals' holdings. Further, the daimyo administered his own *kurairi* along with that belonging to Hideyoshi, adopting for his own use the administrative methods required by the central government; this close alliance with the central government was worth the loss of one-third of his holdings for the security it gave him in holding the leading position in northern Dewa.[112]

The Shimazu provide another example of a daimyo strengthened by the authority of the central government. In ordering the Shimazu to confiscate lands belonging to shrines and temples, Hideyoshi advised the daimyo, "If anyone complains, tell them it is by the order of the central government (*kōgi*)."[113] A few years later, in 1595, Hideyoshi ordered Shimazu Yoshihisa to return from Korea and redistribute holdings in his domain. Shimazu took this opportunity to relocate many of his most powerful and independent vassals. As Asakawa notes, "The Shimazu lord could hardly have been reluctant to obey

Osaka Castle and
Tokugawa Authority in Western Japan

WILLIAM B. HAUSER

The death of Hideyoshi in 1598 and his failure to provide an adult male heir resulted in an unstable balance of power among his major administrative and military supporters. Although Hideyoshi established a unity of authority that was unprecedented in Japanese history, he was unable to guarantee that it would remain under Toyotomi control following his demise. His son and heir, Toyotomi Hideyori, was still an infant, and the Toyotomi league that Hideyoshi had created was held together by oaths and agreements, all dependent on his personal authority, which was now but a memory.

The future of Toyotomi authority depended on the capacity of Hideyoshi's house daimyo to maintain a unity of purpose and to preserve a balance among the major military houses, especially the Tokugawa, Maeda, Mōri, and Uesugi. The death of Maeda Toshiie in 1599 left Tokugawa Ieyasu by far the most influential among the daimyo. Sensing the shift in military authority, "nearly half of the daimyo of the Toyotomi league paid homage to Ieyasu and submitted written pledges of allegiance" by the end of the year.[1]

The Toyotomi league split into two camps, one led by Ishida Mitsunari and the other by Tokugawa Ieyasu. At the Battle of Sekigahara, in October 1600, the Tokugawa forces emerged victorious. Within ten days Ieyasu was in Osaka and was the military master of the country.[2] The first obstacle to Tokugawa supremacy was thus eliminated. Others remained, however. Before stability could be ensured Ieyasu had to establish firmly his control over the daimyo; legitimize the position of the Tokugawa house as national leaders; extend Tokugawa authority to western Japan, where Toyotomi support was strongest; and eliminate Hideyori as the legitimate heir to Toyotomi leadership.

Between 1600 and 1615 each of these objectives was pursued. First, lands were confiscated from Tokugawa enemies and redistributed to Tokugawa supporters. Second, in 1603 Ieyasu received from the imperial court the title of shogun, institutionalizing his role as national military hegemon. Third, in 1605 he passed the mantle of leadership to his son Hidetada and established precedents for military leadership and succession within the Tokugawa house. Fourth, in 1614 and 1615 in the battles of Osaka castle he eliminated Hideyori as well as the remnants of Toyotomi support. By the time of Ieyasu's death in 1616, therefore, the Tokugawa Bakufu was firmly established. The hegemon died confident that the future heads of his family would succeed him as the military leaders of all Japan.[3]

Tokugawa power took many forms, not the least of which was the ability to relocate the daimyo at will. Harold Bolitho has noted that in the first half-century of Tokugawa rule, "some 213 daimyo were stripped of land, rank, and title by bakufu attainders."[4] The Bakufu used this power to eliminate or reduce the danger from powerful military rivals and to assert its authority over all daimyo landholdings. The Bakufu also asserted its control over the castles held by its potential rivals by ordering that some be demolished and that the others be repaired or modified only by permission. The size and scale of daimyo fortifications were severely curtailed; meanwhile the Tokugawa required daimyo to assist in the construction of Tokugawa castles, as well as those held by important retainers.[5] Although the *sankin kōtai* system of alternate attendance upon the shogun at Edo castle became the most important and continuous means of controlling the daimyo, the significance of castle management policies in the early years of the Tokugawa period should not be overlooked.[6]

To sustain control the Bakufu had to convince the daimyo of its superior force. One aspect of this process was demanding from the daimyo various forms of service, of which the *sankin kōtai* was the most prominent. Prior to his elevation to the post of shogun, Ieyasu ordered the country's daimyo to provide labor and material for building the city of Edo. Although not yet independent of Toyotomi authority, Ieyasu was changing the focus of vassalage from Hideyori to himself.[7]

In 1611 Ieyasu went still further in institutionalizing his authority. He demanded from the daimyo a pledge of loyalty that included an article requiring them to obey all orders from Edo and citing precedent from the Kamakura Bakufu under Yoritomo. The shogun was defined as a national hegemon, and though the daimyo were granted new authority within their domains, the Tokugawa asserted their dominant position as leader of the military houses. During the battles of Osaka in 1614 and 1615, daimyo from all parts of Japan fought on the Tokugawa side, clearly demonstrating the extent of Tokugawa power.[8]

The assertion of Bakufu control depended on establishing the power of the shogun as legitimated by, but independent of, traditional court offices. The emperor retained symbolic importance, but his role was regulated by the Tokugawa. Court titles were issued to samurai only at the pleasure of the shogun. Once the power of the shogunate was effectively demonstrated, the office of shogun could be sustained after Ieyasu ceased to play an active role.[9]

With the death of Ieyasu in 1616, his son and successor, Hidetada, faced a series of unresolved issues. Primary among them was the need to consolidate and clarify his own role as national hegemon. A variety of mechanisms were useful here, such as the prohibition of Christianity and the associated tight controls over foreign trade.[10] Similarly, Bakufu laws regulating the imperial court and the imperial house helped consolidate shogunal authority over the emperor, as did periodic visits to Kyoto. The establishment of a military stronghold in Osaka likewise had great importance, since it placed a major garrison between the western daimyo and Kyoto, while simultaneously reinforcing control over both cities. The conversion of Osaka into a bastion of Tokugawa strength clearly was one of the keys to Bakufu control over western Japan after 1615.

Osaka under Hideyoshi

The selection of Osaka as the site for a fortified city predated both Hideyoshi and the Tokugawa Bakufu. Located on Osaka Bay and astride major land and water routes from western Japan to Kyoto and the Yamato region, Osaka first appeared during the fourth or fifth century as Naniwa. It was linked at that time to the emerging power of the imperial house within the Yamato area and served as a port for traffic from Japan to Korea and China. Although it was subsequently displaced in importance by other ports along the bay—for example, Sakai and Hyōgo during the ancient and medieval periods—Osaka's location on the bay and on major river systems remained critical to its development.[11]

The history of Osaka as a continuous settlement dates from the late medieval period, when it was chosen as the site for the Ishiyama Honganji, the main temple of the Jōdo Shinshū or True Pure Land sect of Buddhism. Rennyo Shōnin selected the site in 1496, but the construction of the Honganji at Ishiyama did not commence until after the destruction of the Yamashina Honganji—in modern Shiga ken near Kyoto—by rival sects in 1532. A fortified temple town (*jinaimachi*) was built on the site of modern Osaka castle, and the Ishiyama Honganji emerged as the center of Jōdo Shinshū authority.[12]

Jinaimachi like Ishiyama were generally located on major transport routes and were surrounded by walls and moats for protection. They offered a haven for merchants and artisans as well as for their religious inhabitants. Residents owed obligations to the community as guards and were assisted in defending it by farmers from nearby villages.[13] The Honganji *jinaimachi* of Ishiyama developed into a self-governing community with a sizable population of artisans and merchants in addition to its religious population.[14]

The consolidation of authority in the Kinai region by Oda Nobunaga and then Toyotomi Hideyoshi changed all *jinaimachi*, including Ishiyama. In 1568 Nobunaga captured the nearby castle towns of Ikeda, Takatsuki, and Ibaraki, and demanded a 5,000 *kan* contribution from Ishiyama for "arrow money." Severely burdened by this demand, the town was forced to acknowledge Nobunaga's authority in the region. In 1570 Nobunaga began a campaign that over the next decade laid siege to Ishiyama and led to its abandonment and the destruction of the castle in 1580.[15] This conflict broke the authority of the Honganji in the Kinai region and replaced it with the military power of Nobunaga and his successor, Hideyoshi. Renamed Osaka, Ishiyama became part of the domain of Hideyoshi, who controlled both the town and the surrounding area.[16]

After 1583 Osaka entered a major period of castle construction and city expansion. Under Hideyoshi's orders the largest castle in Japan—many times larger than the castle previously built by Nobunaga beside Lake Biwa at Azuchi—was built at Osaka. The construction was carried out by Hideyoshi's retainers, daimyo, and conscript labor. According to reports by the Jesuit Alessandro Valignano in 1583, 20,000 to 30,000 men worked on Osaka castle day and night for three years. When Hideyoshi demanded assistance from daimyo, the labor force increased to 50,000. Artisans assembled from 30 provinces to work on the central keep and castle battlements.[17] The project also required great quantities of building materials. Canals were constructed to bring materials and freight into Osaka efficiently. Vessels loaded with building stones filled the Inland Sea and the rivers leading into Osaka. The Jesuit Luis Frois reported that from his residence, he could see a thousand shiploads of building stones being transported to the castle site daily. As a result of such intense effort, Osaka quickly became a major castle city.[18]

Despite its history as the fortified headquarters of the Honganji, Osaka was completely rebuilt as a city. Hideyoshi used a labor force supplied by daimyo to expand the city's civilian sectors; some 7,000 residences are said to have been built in 40 days. According to the account of Luis Frois, by the end of 1583 houses extended for two leagues around the central keep. Much of the labor used to build the castle and residences of Osaka, including former samurai and farmers, settled in the city, adding to its population and creating new patterns of consumer demand for food, shelter, and recreation. To expand Osaka's population further, Hideyoshi moved many residents of Kyoto, Fushimi, Sakai, Tennōji, and other towns into his new castle city. This population shift reduced economic competition from nearby cities and helped ensure the prosperity of Osaka as a regional market center. When Sakai merchants continued to dominate long-distance trade from the region, Hideyoshi suppressed them and filled in the Sakai canals to reduce the city's freight-handling capacity. The transportation routes developed to bring in materials for Osaka castle were used after the castle's completion to transport other commodities, preserving the link between Osaka and western daimyo domains and contributing to Osaka's emergence as a center of commerce and handicraft industry. When Hideyoshi left Osaka to fight revolts in Negoro and Saga, he left an army in Osaka to protect his new castle city and ensure its prosperity.[19]

After 1585 Hideyoshi relocated many of the daimyo with domains in the provinces surrounding Osaka and kept much of the vacated territory for himself, including most of Settsu Province. He placed close vassals in nearby domains in Settsu, Kawachi, Izumi, Kii, Yamashiro, and Yamato, and consolidated his hold over the whole of the Kinai region. Osaka, in contrast to the Honganji *jinaimachi* at Ishiyama, thus acquired an extensive territorial base to reinforce its dominance of the area. Hideyoshi also consciously linked the daimyo economies to the Osaka market as a mechanism of economic control.[20]

Under Hideyoshi's guiding hand, Osaka emerged rapidly as a trade and population center.[21] Although its actual size cannot be determined with confidence, much of what would become in Tokugawa times the northeast quarter of the city was well developed, and the Higashiyoko, Nishiyoko, and Awa canals were completed by 1600. By the time of Hideyoshi's death in 1598, Osaka was a city of considerable size and importance in the Kinai economy. Equally important, it symbolized the national authority Hideyoshi had consolidated through the wars of unification.[22]

In 1600 Hideyoshi's infant son and heir, Hideyori, received Osaka and a domain of 650,000 *koku*. This bequest was an important element in his claim to succeed his father when he eventually came of age. It was also an issue of considerable concern to Tokugawa Ieyasu, Hideyoshi's successor as military hegemon. Not until Hideyori was eliminated and Osaka brought firmly under the shogun's control could the Tokugawa forget that a rival claimant to national leadership resided close to the imperial capital at Kyoto. The battles of Osaka in 1614 and 1615 eliminated Hideyori but left the castle severely damaged and much of the city burned. Yet this widespread destruction proved essential to the consolidation of Tokugawa authority in western Japan, for when Osaka was rebuilt as a Tokugawa city, little remained of its Toyotomi-period character, though it retained its role as a commercial center.[23]

Following the defeat of the Toyotomi forces, Osaka castle was awarded to Matsudaira Tadaaki, a grandson of Ieyasu and a leader in the victorious campaign. This move brought Osaka under the command of a close Tokugawa vassal, who received control over the city and a domain of 100,000 *koku* in Settsu and Kawachi. A contemporary source noted that when Tadaaki entered Osaka in 1615, roads and bridges were in ruin, the population had fled to safer areas, and the city resembled a deserted village in some remote hinterland.[24] Although this account reflects a degree of poetic license, the city was badly damaged and depopulated. Recognizing its potential importance as a major trade center, Tadaaki set about rebuilding his new castle city. To speed redevelopment he reduced the size of the castle and allowed housing to be constructed within what had been the outermost fortifications. Merchants and artisans (*chōnin*), relocated from Fushimi to help resettle Osaka, built residential districts and canals, which provided a means of transporting construction materials and freight. In the 1620's additional canal projects would facilitate further the movement of goods in the city.[25] During the reconstruction temples, shrines, and cemeteries were relocated from the center of Osaka to its outskirts. This relocation opened up land for *chōnin* settlement, concentrated religious activities in specific areas of the city, and established a first line of defense at the city's outer limits.[26] By isolating the temples and shrines from the central core of the city, it further subordinated the religious character of the former Honganji temple town to military control.

On 1619/7/22 the Bakufu relocated Matsudaira Tadaaki from Osaka to a new domain at Yamato Kōriyama. The Tokugawa Bakufu thus asserted its right to administer the city directly. Tadaaki had rebuilt and reorganized Osaka, dug canals, compiled land registers, established tax rates, and set the stage for Osaka's subsequent prosperity.[27] With Osaka's transformation into a Bakufu-controlled city, there was no longer any need for a garrison at Fushimi. Consequently, the Bakufu relocated the guard to Osaka, took down Fushimi castle, and used some of its materials for the castle at Osaka. The expansion and rebuilding of Osaka castle became a major means of solidifying Bakufu control over the city and a major symbol of the replacement of Toyotomi influence by the Tokugawa presence in western Japan.

Castle Construction during the Tokugawa Period

Even by modern standards, castle construction during the Tokugawa period was a massive undertaking. It required vast quantities of building materials to be transported to the site, large numbers of skilled craftsmen and laborers, and designers and supervisors able to coordinate the many components of the project. Osaka castle, as the principal western outpost signifying the military authority of the Bakufu, was accordingly an enormous structure, reconstructed and enlarged from the remains of the Toyotomi fortress between 1620 and 1629. The building of Osaka castle brought tens of thousands of workers to Osaka, necessitated the improvement of waterborne transport routes to the city, and demanded unprecedented supplies of food, tools, and other daily necessities to sustain the workers. This structure of demand had a profound and lasting impact on Osaka's economic development, for the supply system that emerged played a major role in the development of Osaka as a market and processing center in the Kinai region.[28]

The reconstruction and expansion of Osaka castle from 1620 to 1629 ranks alongside other major building projects in Japan and elsewhere in the early seventeenth century. Although Osaka castle was somewhat smaller than Edo castle, its construction was a major undertaking that continued in three phases for a decade. Phase one, from 1620 to 1623, consisted of constructing the outer walls and the base of the central keep or donjon; phase two, from 1624 to 1626, of constructing the inner walls; and phase three, in 1628 and 1629, of completing the walls, gateways, and various castle buildings. Tōdō Takatora, a 65-year-old man who had previously helped construct Wakayama, Kōriyama, and Yodo castles, as well as the first Osaka castle under Hideyoshi, supervised the construction. Assisting him over the course of the project were 64 daimyo houses. All but three were outside (tozama) daimyo, individuals who became daimyo before becoming Tokugawa vassals, selected in part because of their greater wealth and experience in building castles in their own domains. The other three daimyo participants included the Tokugawa collateral house of Matsudaira from Echizen Fukui, and the vassal (fudai) houses of Honda from Yamato Takatori domain and Ishikawa from Bungo Hita domain.[29] The daimyo participants were largely from the Kinai and western Japan, Ise and Kaga being the two easternmost areas represented (by the Tōdō and the Maeda, respectively). Although some of the great western tozama daimyo, such as the Shimazu of Satsuma, did not participate, many of the larger daimyo did. In effect, the Osaka castle project was a means for the Tokugawa Bakufu to assert its power over the western tozama daimyo, many of whom were of uncertain loyalty.

Some sense of the scale of the project can be discerned from the value of contributions to it. Wakita Osamu has calculated the assessments for the three phases of construction as follows: phase one, 6,688,048 koku from 47 daimyo houses in 1620; phase two, 5,047,624 koku from 58 houses in 1624; and phase three, 4,026,378 koku from 57 houses in 1628. Okamoto Ryōichi offers similar data for the value of daimyo service levies, except that his total for phase two is 5,052,884 *koku*, or 5,260 *koku* greater than Wakita's. The value he gives for the total assessment for constructing Osaka castle is 15,767,311 *koku*, which he translates into 65,247,300,000 yen at the 1970 exchange rate (360 yen to one dollar American), or approximately 181.2 million dollars.[30] More meaningful for purposes of comparison, the cumulative daimyo assessment from 1620 to 1629 for Osaka castle equaled approximately 88 percent of one year's productivity for the entire nation, estimated to have been around 18 million *koku*. Although these figures are only estimates, Osaka castle obviously was a great expense to all concerned.

The range of contributions by individual daimyo varied enormously, depending on the size of daimyo domains and the rate of the levies assessed. Some houses received full assessments, others half assessments; some participated in all three periods of building activity, others in one or two. For example, as Tables 1 and 2 show, the Kuroda of Chikuzen contributed to each phase of the project. In 1620 they provided 1,080 *kan* 47 *monme* silver for wall building. If we assume the price of rice that year was 20 *monme* per *koku*, this levy amounted to approximately 54,000 *koku*, a major expense for a domain assessed at 522,000 *koku*. The Itō house of Hyūga Obi, with a domain assessed at 57,000 *koku*, paid 254 *kan* silver in two installments, or the equivalent of 12,700 *koku*. The Kyōgoku house of Wakasa Obama, with a domain of 92,000 *koku*, contributed over 270 *kan*, the equivalent of 13,500 *koku*; the Tachibana of Chikugo, with a domain of 110,000 *koku*, contributed 1,280 *kan*, or 64,000 *koku*.[31] Why the rates of assessments varied is not clear, but some mechanism presumably existed for determining them.[32] In any case, the levies were a heavy burden on the daimyo treasuries. Assuming daimyo incomes were around 50 percent of the assessed values of their domains, the Itō contribution was around half their expected income, and the Tachibana contribution exceeded the normal *kokudaka*-based income for the year. The Yamanouchi of Tosa contributed 150,000 *koku* to Edo castle and 202,600 *koku* to Osaka castle. These were back-breaking levies, but the Yamanouchi had little choice but to contribute what the Bakufu demanded. When ordered to contribute in 1620, both the Yamanouchi and the Hosokawa requested that their assessments be reduced, but the Bakufu refused to make adjustments, noting that the assessments were military service levies.[33]

Table 1
Daimyo Participants in the Building of Osaka Castle, 1620-1629

Daimyo	Domain	Kokudaka (thousands)	Assessment		
			1620-23	1624-26	1628-29
Maeda Toshitsune	Kaga Kanazawa	1,193.0	Full	Full	Full
Katō Tadahiro	Higo Kumamoto	731.8			
Matsudaira Tadanao	Echizen Fukui	670.0	Full[a]		
Kuroda Nagamasa	Chikuzen Fukuoka	522.0	Half	Half	Half
Hosokawa Tadaoki	Buzen Kokura	399.0	Full	Full	Half
Mōri Hidenari	Nagato Hagi	369.0	Half	Half	Half
Nabeshima Katsushige	Hizen Saga	357.0	Full	Half	Half
Tōdō Takatora	Ise Tsu	323.9	Half	Half	Half
Tanaka Tadamasa	Chikugo Kurume	320.0	—[b]		
Ikeda Mitsumasa	Inaba Tottori	320.0	Full	Full	Half
Ikeda Tadao	Bizen Okayama	315.0	Full	Full	Half
Hachisuka Tadahide	Awa Tokushima	257.0	Full	Full	Full
Horio Tadaharu	Izumo Matsue	235.0		Half	Half
Yamanouchi Tadayoshi	Tosa Kōchi	202.0	Full		
Katō Yoshiaki	Iyo Matsuyama	200.0		Full	
Mori Tadamasa	Mimasaka Tsuyama	186.0	Full	Full	
Ikoma Masatoshi	Sanuki Takamatsu	170.0		Full	Half
Terazawa Hirotaka	Hizen Karatsu	123.0		Half	Half
Tachibana Muneshige	Chikugo Yanagawa	110.0		Half	Half
Date Hidemune	Iyo Uwajima	100.0	Full	Half	Half
Kyōgoku Tadataka	Wakasa Obama	92.0	Full	Full	Half
Arima Toyouji	Tamba Fukuchiyama	80.0			Half
Kyōgoku Takatomo	Tamba Miyanotsu	78.0	Full	Full	Half
Nakagawa Hisamori	Bungo Takeda	70.4		Half	Half
Hitotsuyanagi Naomori	Ise Kambe	70.0	Full	Half	Half
Ikeda Nagayuki	Bitchū Matsuyama	65.0	Full	Half	Half
Ikeda Terunobu	Harima Yamazaki	63.0	Full	Half	Half
Matsuura Takanobu	Hizen Hirado	63.0		Half	Half
Ishikawa Tadafusa	Bungo Hita	60.0	Half	Half	Half
Katō Yasuoki	Iyo Ōzu	60.0		Full	Half
Itō Sukenori	Hyūga Obi	57.0	Half	Half	Half
Yoshida Shigehisa	Iwami Hamada	54.0		Half	Half
Tokunaga Masashige	Mino Takasugi	53.7		Half	
Arima Naoyoshi	Hyūga Nobeoka	50.0		Full	Full

SOURCE: Okamoto Ryōichi, Ōsakajō (Tokyo, 1970), pp. 146-48.
[a]Reduced to 260,000 in 1623.
[b]Extinct, 1621.

Table 1 continued

Daimyo	Domain	Kokudaka (thousands)	Assessment 1620-23	Assessment 1624-26	Assessment 1628-29
Inaba Tsunemichi	Bungo Usuki	50.0		Full	Half
Yamazaki Ieharu	Bitchū Nariwa	50.0	Full	Half	Half
Matsukura Shigemasa	Hizen Shimabara	50.0		Full	Full
Koide Yoshihide	Tajima Izushi	50.0		Full	Half
Inaba Toshimichi	Tamba Fukuchiyama	49.0		Half	Half
Kamei Koremasa	Iwami Tsuwano	43.0	Full		
Oda Nobutsune	Tamba Kaibara	36.0	Half	Full	Full
Ikeda Masatsuna	Harima Akō	35.0	Full	Full	Full
Kyōgoku Takamitsu	Tamba Tanabe	35.0		Full	Half
Sugihara Nagafusa	Tajima Toyooka	35.0		Half	Half
Honda Masatake	Yamato Takatori	30.0		Half	Full
Togawa Tatsuyasu	Bitchū Niwase	30.0		Half	
Oda Nobuyoshi	Yamato Uda	30.0			
Koide Yoshimi	Tamba Sonobe	30.0		Half	Half
Akizuki Shigeharu	Hyūga Takanabe	30.0		Full	Half
Kinoshita Nobutoshi	Bungo Hinode	30.0		Half	Half
Shimazu Tadaoki	Hyūga Sadowara	30.0	Full	Full	Full
Katagiri Takatoshi	Yamato Tatsuta	28.0		Full	
Ōmura Yoshinori	Hizen Ōmura	27.9		Full	Full
Endō Yoshishige	Mino Hachiman	27.0		Half	Half
Kuwayama Sadaharu	Yamato Taniyama	26.0		Full	Half
Ikeda Teruoki	Harima Sayō	25.0		Full	Full
Wakebe Mitsunobu	Ōmi Ōmizo	20.0		Full	Half
Mōri Takamasa	Bungo Saeki	20.0		Half	Half
Ichihashi Nagamasa	Ōmi Ninjoji	17.4		Full	Half
Kuwayama Kazunao	Yamato Shinjō	16.0		Half	Full
Kurushima Michiharu	Bungo Mori	12.5		Full	Half
Hijikata Takeuji	Ise Komono	12.0		Full	Full
Oda Nagatsune	Mino Nomura	10.0		Half	Half
Tachibana Shigetsugu	Echigo Miike	10.0		Half	Half
Hiraoka Yoriyasu	Mino Tokuno	10.0		Half	Full
65 daimyo houses[c]		8,924.6[d]	48[e]	58[e]	57[e]

[c]Corrected from Okamoto's 64, which excludes Tokunaga Masashige, who was unable to meet his service obligation and lost his domain.

[d]Corrected from Okamoto's 9,050,600.

[e]Total number of assessments.

Table 2
Osaka Castle Wall Building Assignments by Length in *Ken*

Daimyo	Domain	Kokudaka (thousands)	Wall building assignments (*ken*)			
			1620[a]	1624[b]	1628[c]	Total
Maeda Toshitsune*	Kaga Kanazawa	1,193.0	1,044	562	305	1,911
Katō Tadahiro	Higo Kumamoto	731.8	310[d]			310
Matsudaira Tadanao	Echizen Fukui	670.0	398			398
Kuroda Nagamasa*	Chikuzen Fukuoka	522.0	62	70	84	216
Hosokawa Tadaoki*	Buzen Kokura	399.0	131	41	39	211
Mōri Hidenari	Nagato Hagi	369.0	115	63	52	230
Nabeshima Katsushige	Hizen Saga	357.0	144	21	94	259
Tōdō Takatora	Ise Tsu	323.9	134	106	113[e]	353
Tanaka Tadamasa	Chikugo Kurume	320.0	36[f]			36
Ikeda Mitsumasa	Inaba Tottori	320.0	160	59	38	257
Ikeda Tadao	Bizen Okayama	315.0	165	94	102	361
Hachisuka Tadahide	Awa Tokushima	257.0		29	77	106
Horio Tadaharu	Izumo Matsue	235.0	103	25	29	157
Arima Toyouji	Tamba Fukuchiyama	80.0	30[g]			
	Chikugo Kurume	210.0			87	117
Yamanouchi Tadayoshi	Tosa Kōchi	202.0	68			68
Katō Yoshiaki	Iyo Matsuyama	200.0	51	14		65
Mori Tadamasa*	Mimasaka Tsuyama	186.0	97	41	31	169
Ikoma Masatoshi*	Sanuki Takamatsu	170.0	37	90	33	160
Terazawa Hirotaka	Hizen Karatsu	123.0	34	31	11	76
Tachibana Muneshige	Chikugo Yanagawa	110.0		16	16	32
Date Hidemune	Iyo Uwajima	100.0	25	16	14	55
Kyōgoku Tadataka	Wakasa Obama	92.0	114	41	10	165
Kyōgoku Takatomo*	Tamba Miyanotsu	78.0	65	30	11	106
Nakagawa Hisamori	Bungo Takeda	70.4	24	7	12	43
Hitotsuyanagi Naomori	Ise Kambe	65.0	22	20	9	51
Ikeda Nagayuki	Bitchū Matsuyama	65.0	7	20	11	38
Ikeda Terunobu	Harima Yamazaki	63.0	9	16	5	30
Matsuura Takanobu	Hizen Hirado	63.0	20	21	13	54
Ishikawa Tadafusa	Bungo Hita	60.0	16	9	13	38
Katō Yasuoki	Iyo Ōzu	60.0	28	12		40
Itō Sukenori	Hyūga Obi	57.0	23	16	8	47
Yoshida Shigehisa	Iwami Hamada	54.0		6	20	26

SOURCE: Ono Kiyoshi, *Ōsakajō shi* (1899; reprinted, Tokyo, 1973), table 5, pp. 290-98. Ono's data are in *ken*, *shaku*, *sun*, and *bu*, with each unit added separately and no cumulative totals across units. One *ken* equals 1.82 meters. Ono's *ken/shaku* units have been converted to *ken* + percent of *ken*, e.g., 6 *ken* 9 *shaku* = 7.5 *ken*. Smaller units are ignored.

NOTE: Totals do not necessarily agree with those provided by Ono. All figures for wall building assignments are rounded to the nearest whole *ken*. Asterisks indicate that daimyo succession occurred between 1620 and 1629.

[a] 1620 construction included the outermost walls (Sannomaru) and the west, north, and east walls of the second enclosure (Ninomaru). Ono's table includes separate listings for the outer and second enclosure, which have been blended into single figures.

[b] 1624 construction included the innermost walls (Honmaru and Yamazatomaru). The 459.67 *ken* of the Yamazato enclosure was all assigned to the Maeda.

Table 2 continued

Daimyo	Domain	Kokudaka (thousands)	Wall building assignments (ken)			
			1620[a]	1624[b]	1628[c]	Total
okunaga Masashige	Mino Takasugi	53.7		18		18
rima Naoyoshi*	Hyūga Nobeoka	50.0	20	9	15	44
naba Tsunemichi*	Bungo Usuki	50.0	18	10	9	36
amazaki Ieharu	Bitchū Nariwa	50.0	6	11	5	22
Matsukura Shigemasa	Hizen Shimabara	50.0		28	14	42
oide Yoshihide	Tajima Izushi	50.0		26		26
naba Toshimichi	Tamba Fukuchiyama	45.0		20	8	28
amei Koremasa	Iwami Tsuwano	43.0	10			10
da Nobutsune	Tamba Kaibara	36.0	4	6	10	20
keda Masatsuna	Harima Akō	35.0	12	13	9	34
yōgoku Takamitsu	Tamba Tanabe	35.0		15	7	22
ugihara Nagafusa	Tajima Toyooka	35.0	9	5	7	21
Honda Masatake	Yamato Takatori	30.0	9	9	14	32
ogawa Tatsuyasu*	Bitchū Niwase	30.0	5	11	7	23
da Nobuyoshi	Yamato Uda	30.0	3	4		7
oide Yoshimi	Tamba Sonobe	30.0		11	4	15
kizuki Shigeharu	Hyūga Takanabe	30.0	18	3	7	28
inoshita Nobutoshi	Bungo Hinode	30.0	12	2	5	19
himazu Tadaoki	Hyūga Sadowara	30.0	12	11	12	35
atagiri Takatoshi	Yamato Tatsuta	28.0	10	11	8	29
mura Yoshinori	Hizen Ōmura	27.9	15	11	10	36
ndō Yoshishige	Mino Hachiman	27.0		6	10	16
uwayama Sadaharu	Yamato Taniyama	26.0	4	17	5	26
keda Teruoki	Harima Sayō	25.0		6	4	10
akebe Mitsunobu	Ōmi Ōmizo	20.0		7	10	17
Mōri Takamasa	Bungo Saeki	20.0	13	3	4	20
hihashi Nagamasa	Ōmi Ninjoji	17.4		10		10
uwayama Kazunao	Yamato Shinjō	16.0		4	4	8
urushima Michiharu	Bungo Mori	12.5	9	9	2	20
ijikata Takeuji	Ise Komono	12.0	6	5	3	14
da Nagatsune	Mino Nomura	10.0		6	1	7
achibana Shigetsugu	Echigo Miike	10.0		6	5	11
iraoka Yoriyasu	Mino Tokuno	10.0		4	3	7
5 daimyo houses[h]		9,125.6	3,667	1,793	1,439	6,898

1628 construction included the south walls of the second enclosure (Ninomaru) and the Tamazukuri gate. The data ve been blended into single figures.

The 1620 data for Katō Tadahiro include his 1622 assignment for the base of the *donjon* (Tenshudai) within the nmaru innermost enclosure.

The 1628 data for Tōdō Takatora include a 54 ken segment of the Tamazukuri gate built in 1629. This was the final ll section of the castle.

Extinct, 1621.

Domain changed, 1621.

Original total of 64 excludes Tokunaga Masashige, whose domain was confiscated when he was unable to meet his vice obligations.

A detailed contemporary account of the Kuroda house contributions illustrates the kinds of cash outlays that were required. Specific costs listed in the records include wages, material, and transport, among others. The bulk of the cost for building stones and gravel was labor for quarrying and transporting these materials. Other labor costs included payments to domain officials, samurai, servants and farmers from the domain, and day laborers hired at the site. Those brought to Osaka from the Kuroda domain had to be housed, fed, and transported to Osaka as well as paid for their work. The domain constructed a dormitory for them near the castle and gave them a daily food allowance while they were in Osaka. The Kuroda contributions were a major expense: Okamoto estimates that they amounted to approximately one-fifth of the annual income that the daimyo received from his domain.[34] If we assume that tax levies in the Kuroda domain were around 50 percent of assessed productivity, this figure would be consistent with the value of the outlay estimated above.

The records of other houses also provide details on expenses. The Kyōgoku house of Obama domain transported building stones to Osaka from Iimoriyama and employed laborers to lay them in the walls. While they used both day laborers and domain vassals, the daily wages accounted for 34 percent of total outlays. The Yamanouchi house of Tosa transported over 500 men to Osaka in 1620 and also hired laborers at the site. The daimyo complained that the two to three thousand day laborers hired at the work site were far less reliable than domain workers, and that hired workers slowed progress on the Tosa portions of the project.[35] Another approach to fulfilling obligations to the castle project was subcontracting construction assignments to *chōnin*. The Hosokawa contracted with Shioya Tozaemon and four others to build a bridge, offering cash in payment for the work. The Kyōgoku also contracted with local builders for part of their obligations and with Kiya Gorōbei to transport building stones from the remains of Fushimi castle to Osaka. Many daimyo employed *chōnin* as labor contractors to hire and supervise bands of day laborers, thus avoiding direct involvement in selecting workers from outside their domains.[36]

The size of the obligations undertaken by the daimyo can be understood by the number of man-days of labor they contributed. According to Wakita Osamu, the Kuroda in 1620 paid out wages for 21,964 man-days worked by only one of four groups of laborers they employed. The Yamanouchi used two to three thousand workers daily in 1620/9. Wakita estimates that if construction continued from the third through the ninth months—around two hundred work days— then approximately ten thousand laborers worked each day for the Kuroda, Kyōgoku, and others assigned to build Osaka castle. He estimates that by 1628, when the walls were completed, over one million man-days had been expended on the project. This figure seems high, but Hosokawa records from 1636 indicate that when Edo castle was being built, some 102,530 workers were employed on the project. Edo castle was even larger than Osaka castle, and the capital outlays demanded from the daimyo for both were very extensive.[37]

The experience of the Nabeshima illustrates the repeated demands made by the Bakufu on daimyo resources. The Nabeshima assisted at Fushimi castle in 1602, Nagoya in 1603, and Edo in 1605. They worked on Suruga castle in 1608, Nagoya castle in 1609-10, Edo castle in 1614 and 1619, Osaka castle from 1620 to 1628, and Edo castle again in 1635-36. On top of all this they were also active in the battles of Osaka castle in 1614 and 1615, and in suppressing the Shimabara Rebellion in 1637. The Bakufu demanded extraordinary expenditures from the Nabeshima between 1603 and 1637, resulting in a large debt for the domain. By 1620 the Nabeshima owed 2,600 *kan* silver, equal to approximately 130,000 *koku* of rice at 20 *monme* per *koku*. The Nabeshima debt rose and fell from one year to the next, but for a domain with an assessed value of 357,000 *koku* and an average income of 240,000 *koku*, it was impossible to pay back debts of this size out of normal domain income. Even the 5 percent interest on the debt was a major drain on the domain treasury.[38]

The Nabeshima experience was by no means unique. All daimyo were called on for contributions to major building projects, and the wealthier daimyo were called on most often. The Mōri of Chōshu sent two thousand men to work on Edo castle in 1606. Date Masamune worked on Edo castle in 1607, 1611, 1620, and 1629, as well as on Takada castle in 1614. He was deeply in debt to Kyoto moneylenders before his building projects were completed. The Yamanouchi of Tosa were required to contribute to Edo castle in 1605 and 1614, Sumpu castle in 1607, Nagoya castle in 1610, and Kizu castle in 1614, as well as to Osaka castle in 1615, 1620, and 1625. By the 1620's many of the larger *tozama* daimyo were accordingly deeply in debt.[39] Bakufu service obligations thus not only confirmed the superior power of the Tokugawa, but also severely compromised the economic status of many domains and tied them to the Kinai area, where they borrowed much of the necessary capital.

As Table 1 shows, the Bakufu made repeated building assessments on large and small daimyo alike, from the Maeda of Kaga Kanazawa at 1,193,000 *koku* to the Hiraoka of Mino Tokuno at 10,000 *koku*. Some daimyo, like the Maeda, were required to make full contributions in each period of construction. Others, like the Kuroda of Chikuzen Fukuoka, were assessed half shares in all three periods. No excuses were tolerated for failure to pay military levies like those for castle construction. Tokunaga Masashige of Mino Takasugi, assessed a half share in the second phase of construction, was unable to comply due to illness and a succession of bad harvests. Consequently, the Tokunaga domain was confiscated and the daimyo exiled.[40] Some smaller houses contributed in only two of the three periods, but domain size does not appear to correlate either with the levy of a full or half share, or with the demand that contributions be made in one, two, or all three periods of construction.

The wall building assignments shown in Table 2 indicate the scale of involvement of each daimyo house. Appropriately enough, Maeda Toshitsune of Kaga Kanazawa, who held the largest domain, was assigned by far the largest contribution. According to Table 1 he was also one of only four daimyo assigned a full levy for each phase of the project, the others being Hachisuka Tadahide of Awa Tokushima, Ikeda Masatsuna of Harima Akō, and Shimazu Tadaoki of Hyūga Sadowara. The Maeda levy was thus heavier relative to domain size than that demanded from most other daimyo. On examination, the data in Tables 1 and 2 appear inconsistent. Table 1 lists a full contribution for the Hachisuka for 1620-23, for example, but Table 2 shows no assignment for them for 1620. Similarly, Table 1 shows Ikeda Mitsumasa and Ikeda Tadao with the same assessment shares for each period, whereas Table 2 shows Ikeda Tadao, holder of the smaller of the two domains, with larger wall-building assignments in each period. Two explanations for these inconsistencies come to mind. First, one or both sources may be in error or incomplete, or Okamoto may be incorrect in his assumption that a consistent mechanism was used for all daimyo levies, based on domain size. Second, the costs of constructing a wall section of a given length varied dramatically. Since walls varied in height from 11 to almost 25 meters, the quantity of building stones and man-hours required for each segment cannot be effectively estimated by wall length alone. Thus both tables offer insights into the burdens imposed on the daimyo by castle building obligations, but neither can be directly translated into a value in *koku* or *kan* silver with any reliability.

Neither size nor distance from Osaka appears to have played any role in the process by which the 65 daimyo were selected to participate in the construction of Osaka castle. Their domains were widely distributed in the Kinai, western Honshu, Kyushu, and Shikoku. All daimyo owed military service to the Tokugawa. All were required to meet their obligations, whether or not they imposed a severe burden on domain resources. The contributions required for Osaka castle thus served to reinforce the superior position of the Bakufu over the western daimyo and to dispel any sense that distance from Edo reduced the obligations of military service or subordination to Tokugawa authority. The massive size of the project, the large assessments and contributions demanded for it, and the inability of any daimyo to evade participation made the building of Osaka castle a symbolic act that reflected the unification of national military power under the Tokugawa Bakufu. It simultaneously reinforced Bakufu power in the Kinai region.

The daimyo were not the only participants in the building of Osaka castle. The Bakufu itself took responsibility for building the Tokugawa family residence in the castle, the central keep, and various gates. As shogun, both Hidetada and Iemitsu were directly involved in various aspects of the project. Both visited the site during the construction to supervise progress and to reward those whose services were especially meritorious. When Hidetada visited Kyoto in 1619, for example, he also spent time in Osaka, examining the castle and discussing with Tōdō Takatora the plans for reconstruction and expansion.[41] Hidetada came to inspect the city on 1619/9/7, shortly after it came under the direct administration of the Bakufu. He visited again on 1623/7/6 and stayed seven days, inspecting progress on Osaka castle before returning to Kyoto. When Iemitsu visited the city in 1623/8/19, he had succeeded his father as shogun. He remained for four days, inspecting the castle and other facilities in the immediate Osaka area. As a result of his visit, additional work was ordered on the castle walls to enhance their defensive capacity. Hidetada visited again in 1626/7 and was followed by Iemitsu two months later. In 1633 the Osaka city magistrate Kugai Masatoshi was called to a shogunal audience in Edo and asked about conditions in the city by Iemitsu; the following year Iemitsu visited both Kyoto and Osaka, where he stayed for three days of inspections, sight-seeing, and entertainment. The repeated visits by Hidetada and Iemitsu reflect the importance of Osaka to Tokugawa efforts to consolidate their authority in the Kinai region and western Japan.[42] Moreover, Osaka castle provided occasion to demonstrate the succession from Hidetada to Iemitsu, thus reinforcing the suzerainty of the Tokugawa house. In 1620 Hidetada had ordered the daimyo from 32 provinces west of Ise and Etchū to assist with the castle; in 1624 and 1628 it was Iemitsu who issued similar orders for the second and third phases of construction.[43]

By 1630 the walls, shogun's residence, turrets (*yagura*), gates, storehouses, central keep, and other facilities were all completed. Specialists oversaw each part of the project. Kobori Seiichi supervised the turrets, the Tamon gates, the residence, and the central keep. The Osaka city magistrates Shimada Naotoki and Kugai Masatoshi took charge of procuring building materials. Tominaga Masayoshi and Yokochi Yoshitsugu supervised storehouse construction. The famous archer Yoshida Motosada and the firearms expert Yonemura Kuzunaga managed construction of the narrow turret gates, great gates, and fences.[44]

The castle was immense. The inner enclosure, including the central enclosure (Honmaru) and Yamazato enclosure, had walls 1,134 meters (623 *ken*) in length and covered an area of 46,340 square meters (14,000 *tsubo*). The Honmaru was on the highest ground within the castle, and its walls varied in height from 24.57 meters to 13.65 meters. It was surrounded by a moat, partly dry and partly filled with water, which varied in width from 28 meters to 74.6 meters. In the midst of the inner enclosure, presiding over the entire castle, was the central keep, five stories high. The wall surrounding the inner enclosure was planned by Tōdō Takatora, and 57 daimyo from 32 provinces assisted in building it.[45]

Construction tasks were often divided among many daimyo. In 1624/1, when the second phase of construction began on the Sakura gate, portions of the project were assigned to Ikeda Tadao, Ikeda Terukiyo, and Ikeda Terutomo. The walls linking the Sakura gate to the Hime gate were assigned to Ikeda Mitsumasa, Tōdō Takatora, Ikoma Takamatsu, Mōri Takamasa, and 26 other daimyo; those linking the Sakura gate to the Honmaru to the east, to 36 daimyo. Some daimyo were assigned large portions of specific elements of the castle, whereas others were given responsibility for a piece of wall here, a section of moat there, and perhaps a portion of a gateway. The practice of parceling tasks out among daimyo required that individual domains maintain several separate working groups to accomplish their various tasks simultaneously, and that the efforts of many separate daimyo be closely coordinated.[46]

The shogun's residence reflected the splendor, wealth, and power of the Bakufu. An earlier residence built on the site had been deemed unsatisfactory by Hidetada in 1623. It was accordingly taken down, and a more luxurious building designed and built in its place. Located in the southern portion of the Honmaru enclosure, the new residence contained 66 rooms in 11,916 square meters (3,600 *tsubo*). Like other important residences built at this time, it included decorated ceilings and beams, painted paper and wooden doors, and paintings on gold leaf by artists of the Kano school.[47]

Surrounding the inner walls was the second enclosure (Ninomaru). Its walls varied from 11 to 22.75 meters high, and they were surrounded by a water-filled moat. The moat ranged from 51 meters to 138 meters wide, thus providing a major barrier to any assault on the walls. Two periods of construction were required to complete the Ninomaru and its moat. The west, north, and eastern sides, 5,252.7 meters in length, were begun in 1620, and the southern side, 2,453 meters in length, was completed in 1628. Forty-eight daimyo from 31 provinces were involved in the project. Here, as elsewhere, specific segments of the walls were assigned to individual daimyo, and Bakufu officials supervised the work to ensure proper coordination. Some of the workers who participated did not return to their domains until the entire eight-year project was completed. Throughout the construction effort, emissaries from Hidetada and Iemitsu inspected progress on the castle and issued rewards for meritorious service.[48]

Conclusions

Osaka castle was the primary stronghold of the Tokugawa Bakufu in western Japan. Repeated visits by the shogun and retired shogun symbolized the extension of Tokugawa authority over the entire country. The new Osaka castle and the shogunal representative in Kyoto at Nijō castle manifested the displacement of Toyotomi influence. The capacity and willingness of the Tokugawa Bakufu to use military force against any challenger were demonstrated to all those obliged to participate in the castle project. The castle's size, its cost, and the financial drain on those who helped construct it laid bare the inferiority of potential rivals to the Tokugawa Bakufu. Osaka, Kyoto, and the Kansai region were firmly under Tokugawa control. Any challenge to the unified authority of the Bakufu was no longer realistic.

The construction of Osaka castle accomplished several specific purposes. First, it demonstrated the Bakufu's ability to levy service obligations on the western daimyo, especially those in the Kinai region, the traditional focus of imperial authority and of Toyotomi Hideyoshi's power, as opposed to the Kantō region, where Tokugawa dominance was already firmly established. Second, it forced the western daimyo to participate in creating the stronghold that would be the major barrier to any challenge to Tokugawa control over the emperor from the western domains. Third, it assisted the process of consolidating Bakufu control over Kyoto, for the repeated visits to Osaka by Hidetada and Iemitsu during construction were all associated with visits to Kyoto. Osaka was linked to Kyoto as a Tokugawa-controlled city, and the Kinai was tied to the Tokugawa power base in Edo and the Kantō region. Fourth, by building a castle which was even larger and better defended than the previous Toyotomi stronghold at Osaka, the Tokugawa showed that they had not merely replaced Hideyoshi as hegemon but surpassed him as a source of central authority and military control.

Osaka castle was by no means the only evidence of this expanded authority. The exclusion edicts of 1633 and 1638, the revisions in the laws for military houses (*buke shohatto*) in 1635, the inclusion of all daimyo in the alternate attendance system (*sankin kōtai*) in 1642, and the transfer of daimyo and use of attainders to confiscate domains were all used by Iemitsu to assert his authority as shogun.[49] Yet the construction of Osaka castle clearly was a means of both intimidating and impoverishing the daimyo of western Japan. It symbolized in new and imposing fashion the national role of the Bakufu and its now unassailable military dominance.

senior councillor (*rōjū*), and only twenty-six when he leapfrogged over his colleagues, all of whom were very much his senior, to become *rōjū shuseki*. Nevertheless, his willing assumption of, and remorseless grip upon, high Bakufu office cannot have been free from strain. Abe's death at the tragically early age of thirty-eight, accompanied by all the signs of physical exhaustion—chest pains, pallor, loss of weight—is a poignant reminder that his political career, impressive though it was, was purchased at a terrible cost.[4]

It could also be argued that Abe Masahiro was something more than the last great politician thrown up by the old order, that he was in a sense the precursor of something new. True, when he died in 1857 his only tangible bequest to the new Japan was a design for a national banner—a scarlet solar disk on a white field—to be displayed by all Japanese vessels.[5] Otherwise, he left the country's diplomatic and military problems almost completely unsolved. Yet at the same time he left behind him in many quarters a regret for promise unfulfilled, for if Japan's problems were of a totally different order from those his predecessors had faced, then Abe had shown himself ready to entertain unfamiliar solutions to them. His receptivity to new ideas, and his willingness to, as he put it, "govern along new lines,"[6] have impressed some of the most unlikely scholars. Inoue Kiyoshi, for example, no admirer of the Tokugawa Bakufu, nor of the privileged daimyo class to which Abe Masahiro belonged, sees him as a talented man, one with sufficient wit to grasp Japan's new situation and to consider what new initiatives might be needed.[7] Indeed, Abe Masahiro, to judge from the accounts of his life, was the last Bakufu leader to preserve—by his honesty and transparent reforming zeal—the illusion that the government he served was capable of leading Japan out of the diplomatic and military thicket in which it had become entangled. Certainly scholars are in general agreement that what had been during his lifetime an amicable series of relationships between Bakufu and court, Bakufu and daimyo, Bakufu and people, was irretrievably lost with his death. Within a month Tokugawa Nariaki, the former daimyo of Mito, with whom Abe had collaborated for many years, resigned his official post within the Bakufu and moved into overt opposition; within fourteen months, he and several other "able daimyo" who had been so very much in Abe's confidence were publicly humiliated, either bundled into retirement or house arrest, or chillingly rebuked; within eighteen months the court in Kyoto, whose eager servant Abe had so clearly been, had been bullied into mutinous silence. Whatever magic Abe possessed, it did not survive him.

There can be little doubt that Abe Masahiro's policies during his years as senior councillor, from 1843 to 1857, and more particularly during his years as chief senior councillor, from 1845 to 1855, were often innovatory. Sometimes, of course, they were not, for naturally he shared at least some of the predilections of his class. His condemnation of immorality, like his wish to curb extravagance, both public and private, could have come from any one of his predecessors over the past two hundred years.[8] Yet undeniably the overall thrust of his actions in government would have been considered quite unthinkable at any previous time in Tokugawa history.

Under Abe, for example, the Bakufu developed a totally new diplomacy. For most of the Tokugawa period relations with foreign countries had been of the most limited kind, tied entirely to trade and carried on only at Nagasaki, in the case of the Chinese and Dutch, or through Tsushima, in the case of the Koreans. Occasional requests from other countries, such as Russia, to break into the charmed circle were invariably rebuffed. All of this changed in 1854, however, when Abe's government negotiated the Treaty of Kanagawa, allowing the United States access to port facilities and provisions in Shimoda and Hakodate, and countenancing the exchange of diplomatic representatives. Similar treaties with Russia, Great Britain, and the Netherlands were soon to follow.

He could also have claimed, for that matter, to be the architect of the Bakufu's new defense policy, in which he displayed an interest at least as early as 1845, when he took charge of coastal defense,[9] a move resulting two years later in strengthened defenses for Edo Bay, Sagami, Awa, and Kazusa. It must also be added that reform was urgently needed, because the Bakufu had largely neglected coastal defense since the early seventeenth century. Nor was this all. The events of 1853 were to produce still more dramatic initiatives and more positive results, as Abe's government began to order Western-style steamships, sailing ships, cannon, and muskets. In that year the Dutch received orders for a steam corvette, 56 sailing corvettes, two steamships, a bronze carronade, and 3,000 percussion-capped army muskets.[10] This may not sound so very innovative, but in the context of late Tokugawa Japan—where, for example, Western cannon were denounced as cowardly weapons, used only by those without the stomach for swordplay *à la Japonais*—it most certainly was.

Equally novel was Abe's decision to free the Japanese daimyo from one of late Tokugawa Japan's more irksome seventeenth-century survivals. This was the Bakufu's prohibition against large sea-going (as opposed to coastal) vessels, introduced early in the seventeenth century, and finally lifted in 1853, to enable the Japanese to defend themselves against what was generally thought to be the greatest threat their country had ever faced. In fact, under Abe the Bakufu went still further, encouraging the Japanese to build ships of their own, not just buy them from abroad, and Abe saw to it that the Bakufu gave the lead—whether with steam (ordering blast furnace parts from Holland so that Japan might begin the construction of steamships) or sail (building Japan's first schooner in 1856).[11] Equally, he gave a fresh impetus to the study of foreign technology, and of the foreign languages needed to absorb it. He managed this in two ways. First, he founded, in swift succession, a number of academic institutions for the study of Western languages and technology, beginning with the Nagasaki Naval Academy, which opened its doors in 1855 to students from Bakufu and *han* wishing to learn the skills of shipbuilding, design, navigation, and warfare. To help him he procured a 500-ton steamship (the Soembing, renamed Kankō Maru) from Holland, and employed 22 of its crew, including the captain, as instructors. The Nagasaki academy was followed by a similar institution in Edo, founded in 1857, and by the Kōbusho, a military academy also in Edo.[12] There was, too, the Yōgaku-sho (renamed Bansho Shirabesho in 1856), initially a Bakufu research institute where people studied alien subjects in alien tongues, and which proved so successful that in 1857 it began to teach as well, numbering among its students a great many of the intellectual leaders of late Tokugawa and early Meiji Japan.[13] It seems likely, in fact, that had Abe lived longer his government would have taken this process still further by sending students overseas for training, something he was considering shortly before he died.[14] Abe's second way of advancing the study of foreign technology was to surround himself with men who had knowledge of it. There was Egawa Hidetatsu, for example, a student of Western gunnery appointed to a high position in the Finance Bureau despite the spirited opposition of other officials. Kawaji Toshiakira, with similar skills, was similarly promoted. Katsu Kaishū, another gunnery student, was chosen to be one of the first students at the Nagasaki Naval Academy after he had come to Abe's notice.[15] Takashima Shūhan, the Nagasaki importer who had run afoul of the government in 1842, was released from captivity in 1853 at Abe's insistence, and set to work building the Bakufu's gun emplacements at Shinagawa. Later he became gunnery instructor at the Edo Military Academy.[16] Even

Yoshida Shōin, whose career was more checkered still, though not exactly an Abe protégé, owed the senior councillor his life. When Shōin was in prison awaiting execution for his attempt to stow away on Perry's ship in 1853, Abe ordered his release. He did no less for Sakuma Shōzan, also imprisoned for having written rather intemperately in Yoshida Shōin's defense.[17]

All of this activity represents a significant degree of openness in a country that had been, until then, extremely insular. But Abe went further, refurbishing not only Japan's diplomacy, defense, and military and technical education, but reaching into the very recesses of the Tokugawa system of government. This had, in the past, been maintained strictly as the preserve of the main branch of the Tokugawa house; neither the imperial court (silent since the beginning of the seventeenth century) nor the daimyo (most of whom were kept at arm's length) were given any permanent part in it. Abe Masahiro changed this policy. No sooner did the Kyoto court show its concern over increasing foreign contact in 1846 than the Bakufu, under Abe's direction, began to keep it abreast of diplomatic developments, whether receiving imperial emissaries in Edo, or sending Bakufu messengers to Kyoto to discuss the foreign policy issues of the day.[18] Ultimately, too, Abe came to use imperial authority in a way unknown since the very inception of the Bakufu. In late 1854 Abe prevailed upon the court to issue its first direct order to the Japanese people in almost 250 years. The order, understandably a controversial one, required temples to surrender their bells, that they might be cast into guns, and to cast no new bronze images.[19]

With the daimyo Abe Masahiro was prepared as no previous Tokugawa official had ever been to consult them and ask for advice. As early as 1849 he solicited the opinion of those daimyo with coastal domains, asking them whether the old *uchiharai-rei* (under which foreign vessels were to be fired on at sight) should be revived.[20] Then, after Perry's first voyage in 1853, he had a translation of Millard Fillmore's letter shown to all daimyo, and asked them for their opinion on the issues raised. Should Japan open to the foreigners, or stay closed? Should she opt for war or peace?[21] This, it might be thought, was innovative enough, but Abe was prepared to go still further in his search for consensus. In 1854 he was considering what might be done about giving Japan a kind of parliament, where those Japanese with special skills—whether in Confucian learning, *rangaku*, or military matters—might meet to discuss issues of common concern.[22]

A parliament was not to be achieved in the lifetime of the Tokugawa Bakufu. But Abe Masahiro did widen the circle of his confidential advisers to an extent never before seen in the Bakufu. He achieved this simply through his friends—a group of influential daimyo who, though taking no formal part in national politics, were nevertheless highly interested in it, and who provided Abe with lines of communication to the daimyo community at large. There was, for example, Matsudaira Yoshinaga, the daimyo of Echizen, with whom Abe was in frequent and cordial correspondence. Abe's second wife, indeed, was Yoshinaga's adopted daughter, and when the senior councillor died, Yoshinaga's own personal physician was at his bedside. For Abe, Yoshinaga's personal influence with the daimyo of the Ōrōka would have made him a valuable ally.[23] Then there was Shimazu Nariakira, the daimyo of Satsuma, and arguably Abe Masahiro's closest ally. It was Abe Masahiro who intervened in a squalid succession dispute in Satsuma, forcing the current daimyo to resign and installing Nariakira in his place. As a leading member of the Ōbiroma, the new Satsuma daimyo would surely have been a welcome ally, and indeed in 1854, after concluding the treaty with Perry, Abe made use of him to persuade his fellows that the Bakufu had taken the best course. Katsu Kaishū, who knew both men, described the arrangement by which Abe and Shimazu were to secure the opening of Japan. "Lord Ise [Abe] would take care of internal reform, while Lord Satsuma [Shimazu] would be responsible for harmony with Kyoto and unity among the daimyo."[24]

But Abe's most notable personal link was with the formidable Tokugawa Nariaki, the irascible former daimyo of Mito, one of the three Tokugawa branch houses. Their relations began rather badly in 1844, when Abe, noting seven areas of concern over the state of affairs in the Mito domain, forced Nariaki to resign and enter house arrest in the Mito residence at Komagome. By the end of the year, however, after Abe freed Nariaki from house arrest, the relationship began to improve. Thereafter Abe became kinder and kinder—allowing Nariaki to be consulted on the conduct of Mito affairs in 1848, giving him control of Mito government the following year, making him a government consultant (*seimu sanyo*) in 1853, and putting him in charge of projected Bakufu military reforms in 1854.[25] Realizing, too, that the way to a man's heart is through his son, the senior councillor lavished considerable attention upon Tokugawa Yoshinobu. As Nariaki's seventh son, Yoshinobu would have had little chance of preferment, but with Abe's assistance the young man became heir to the Hitotsubashi Tokugawa line in 1847, and by 1856, almost certainly with Abe's blessing, he had established himself as the logical successor to Iesada, the ailing thirteenth shogun.[26] Not unnaturally, this barrage of favors went hand-in-hand with more cordial relations. By 1853 Abe was constantly seeking Nariaki's opinion on policy issues, by personal letter, by messenger, and not infrequently in face-to-face meetings, for many of which the chief senior councillor would make the three-mile journey from the castle to Nariaki's residence at Komagome.[27] The former Mito daimyo, for his part, responded unstintingly, heaping upon Abe and his government the benefits of years of accumulated wisdom and experience. By the end relations between the two men had become so cordial that Nariaki felt moved to present the dying Abe with a bottle of tonic wine, a special product of the Mito area.[28]

It seems quite clear, therefore, that Abe Masahiro was groping towards a new kind of Japan, one far better equipped to meet the demands of the nineteenth century. But I use the word "seems" advisedly, for I do not for a moment think it is true. Abe Masahiro's Bakufu did preside over substantial changes in defense and diplomacy, just as it encouraged daimyo, and for that matter the imperial court, to make known their opinions on matters of national concern, but these achievements were not nearly as modern as they might seem. The modernity of Abe's defense and diplomatic policies, on the one hand, was both accidental and reluctant, the product of forces over which he had no control. The modernity of his style of government, on the other hand, was illusory, and the real makers of the new Japan, when they came to build a nation in the 1870's, were to reject it without compunction.

Certainly it is true, as I have noted, that Abe expressed interest in defense matters. Under the circumstances he could hardly have done otherwise. From the beginning of the nineteenth century a stream of Japanese commentators had urged that more thought be given to protecting Japan from foreign attack. Koga Kiyosato had written on this subject in 1809, and his theme was to be taken up by both Tokugawa Nariaki and Egawa Hidetatsu in 1837, and by Takashima Shūhan in 1840.[29] Increasingly those warnings were bolstered by events. Right through the 1840's British, French, and American ships were sailing in Japanese waters—stopping off at the Ryukyus to ask for trade, for example, or taking on food and fuel at Nagasaki, or even, as in 1837 and 1846, arriving at Uraga to return castaways and, ever so delicately, ask for trade. Abe's initial reaction to such signs was traditional in the extreme; like Mizuno Tadakuni, his predecessor in Bakufu office, he ordered a report on fortifications in the Izu area by the mouth of Edo Bay.[30] Like many other governments, however, Abe's preferred reassurance to accuracy: when Ōkubo Tadatoyo and Hitotsuyanagi Naokata, the two Bakufu officials in charge of defense installations at Uraga, on the Izu peninsula, complained of inadequate resources, they were quietly replaced.[31] A direct query—in itself without precedent in Tokugawa history—from the imperial court on the state of Japan's defenses galvanized Abe into a brief spasm of activity in late 1846 and 1847, resulting in a commendation from the shogun together with gifts of clothing, a saddle, and stirrups the following year,[32] but one may doubt how effective it all was. Like the official commendation and gifts he had awarded himself, Abe's activities here, too, seem to have been largely cosmetic. When Perry arrived at Uraga in the summer of 1853, the old *uchiharai-rei*, revived four years earlier, required that he be driven off immediately, but this was frankly impossible. Between them, the sixteen batteries guarding the mouth of Edo Bay could muster no more than 124 cannon capable of firing anything heavier than a three-pound shot, and of these only eight had an aperture greater than six inches.[33]

This level of defense was ludicrously inadequate, as Abe well knew. Asano Naganori, the Bakufu's chief official at Uraga, had told him as much the previous year, but Abe's reaction to this disagreeable news was precisely what it had been with Asano's predecessors six years earlier: the warning was ignored, and Asano was quietly transferred.[34] Abe's negligence did not stop there, however, for he had also, astonishingly enough, failed to draw up any contingency plans. Only after Perry's initial visit had exposed the weakness of Edo's first (and only) line of defense did the Bakufu begin to consider a second. This time it was decided to build a series of eleven offshore batteries much closer to Edo. Within three weeks of Perry's departure for Hong Kong, officials had begun to take soundings to determine the most appropriate locations; within another month Shinagawa had been settled upon. The preparation of estimates took a further three weeks, and then finally, ten weeks after Perry's departure, construction began. Abe was working with unwonted haste to close the stable door, but with no more than his usual efficiency. Of the eleven batteries planned, only six were ever built. Those six ultimately cost ten times as much as the original eleven, and not one was ready in time to inhibit the signing of the Treaty of Kanagawa the following year.[35] Small wonder, with this sort of record, that Abe was savagely lampooned in a document which, addressing him in a variety of uncomplimentary terms (*chikushōme, chikushōyarōme, garigari-yarōme*), drew attention to the lamentable state of Japan's defenses, and went on to suggest, both unflatteringly and indelicately, that eating sweet potatoes, a well-known avenue to flatulence, might be more effective in repelling foreign overtures.[36]

Abe's diplomacy was no more effective than his defense policy, and here again there was no excuse. There had been ample warning that sooner or later some kind of diplomatic approach would be made, whether by the British or by the Americans. Certainly the Dutch had said so often enough—in general terms in 1844, and then in increasingly ominous detail. In 1850 they reported that the initiative would come from the United States; in 1852, while Perry was organizing his expedition, they alerted the Bakufu again.[37] Some Japanese, at least, paid attention: the official record of Perry's activities in Japan notes that the fleet was met at Uraga by a Bakufu official who "asked if the ships came from America, and seemed to have expected them."[38] Yet nothing in the reaction of Japan's chief administrator suggests any such expectation. On hearing the news of Perry's arrival, Abe immediately made the three-mile journey to Tokugawa Nariaki's residence in Komagome to ask what he should do. Only after the Dutch predictions had come true did he begin to consider that it might be worthwhile to discuss world affairs with the trading community at Nagasaki.[39] He really had no policy to deal with this long-foreseen event— which is why, of course, he then took the Japanese daimyo into his confidence, and asked them whether Japan should open or stay closed, fight or make peace. He honestly did not know, and the history of Japan's negotiations with Perry, and then with Harris, makes it quite clear that he did not know. Asked by his friends what line he would take, Abe's normal reply tended to be that most palatable to his questioner. To Matsudaira Yoshinaga, who wanted war, Abe too seemed to be about to give Perry "a firm reply" that would in all probability lead to war. To Shimazu Nariakira, who wanted peace and trade, Abe also seemed to want peace and trade. What Japan got, however, at the end of the negotiations, was exactly what the Americans wanted. Perry's success was the clearest of all tributes to Abe's total lack of diplomatic and military preparation.[40]

Similarly, Abe's policy of government by consensus, despite its apparent modernity, was a disastrous mistake. In a sense it is understandable that Abe should have been receptive to the ideas of others. After all, he seems to have had very few of his own. But consultation, whether with the imperial court, the daimyo at large, or his own particular friends, does not seem to have served him terribly well. Take for example the response to the Bakufu's request for daimyo opinion on the issue of opening the country. Of those replies remaining to us, two favored accepting the American demands; two more favored accepting them for a while; three favored allowing the United States to trade, subject to certain other restrictions; one suggested allowing trade for a short time, while preparing to attack; three advocated treating the foreigners politely for a longer time, and then, once an adequate defense had been prepared, expelling them; four supported prolonged negotiations, preparing an adequate defense the while, and then refusing; eleven urged fighting on Perry's return; three were undecided.[41] Clearly it was impossible to derive a mandate from this response—and so Bakufu policy drifted. On other occasions, when a policy did emerge—as in 1849, when daimyo with coastal domains almost unanimously favored reviving the old *uchiharai* law—that policy was too unrealistic to be acted upon, and so once again matters were allowed to drift.[42] Nor, for that matter, was the Bakufu guaranteed any more authority or popularity from the process of consultation. Choosing between conflicting forms of advice always meant that someone's advice would be rejected, and that someone would therefore be alienated.

In fact, by his policy of consultation, Abe managed to do the Tokugawa Bakufu a great deal of harm. At its best, the process was time-wasting, helping to defer decisions that should have been taken quickly. At its worst, it invited a degree of interference in Bakufu policy-making that was paralyzing in its effect. The court, for example, now concerned as never before in Bakufu policy decisions, proved to be simply one more implacable element to be placated. Thereafter, the Emperor Kōmei and his courtiers—not one of whom knew anything of the world beyond the Kamo River—proved a consistent burden to all Bakumatsu politicians, irrespective of their political views. It was court interference, for example, that was to commit the Bakufu to its ludicrous promise to drive the foreigners away in 1863.

Abe Masahiro, in fact, always seemed to tie himself to those whose views were at variance with his own, insofar as we know what those were. He was, we are informed, resigned to the prospect of opening the country. The court, we know well, was bitterly opposed to it. But so were Abe Masahiro's political allies. Tokugawa Nariaki, it will be remembered, was supposed to bring the Tokugawa branch families in to support Abe Masahiro's policies. This can only have been difficult, since Nariaki was famous for his vehement insistence that Japan be kept closed. Matsudaira Yoshinaga, who was supposed to plead Abe's policy to the daimyo of the Ōrōka, was totally opposed to that policy, urging war in 1854 and abusing Abe for permitting the burial, on sacred Japanese soil, of an American who happened to die at Kanagawa. Date Munenari, another close friend, was an equally vehement exclusionist. Shimazu Nariakira, whose task it was to win over the court and the Ōbiroma daimyo to opening the country, was not totally certain that that was what he wanted, and was far more prepared, in 1853, to back Tokugawa Nariaki, exclusionist or no.[43] Just how these men helped Abe Masahiro, despite the extent to which he took them all into his and the government's confidence, is not really clear.

This policy of consultation, then, had severe defects, and nowhere can these be seen more clearly than in the case of Tokugawa Nariaki, the man whom Abe appointed government adviser (*seimu sanyo*) in 1853. Nariaki was undoubtedly a born adviser, giving the benefit of his experience and wisdom to Bakufu officials, to the shogun himself, and even to the court, in a long series of letters, memorials, and position papers starting in the 1830's. Shortly after his release from house arrest in late 1844, he began his relationship with Abe Masahiro, peppering the senior councillor remorselessly for the next thirteen years with advice on all subjects, but most particularly on matters of defense, foreign affairs, and the government of his former domain at Mito. He was an indefatigable adviser, as he was also an indefatigable demander of information, secret or not, and, once in office, an indefatigable threatener to resign.

It must be noted, in all candor, that much of Nariaki's advice was unhelpful. I do not know what would have happened had Japan gone to war with the United States in 1854, but I doubt that Japanese swords and pikes would have won the day, as Nariaki imagined. Nor do I know what useful purpose would have been served had the two hapless Japanese negotiators of 1854 been ordered to commit *seppuku*, as Nariaki wanted.[44] Much of his advice was also, frankly, paranoid. He was suspicious of the Dutch and Chinese communities at Nagasaki and argued that they should be expelled. He was opposed to a visit from Korean ambassadors in 1847, on the ground that wily Frenchmen or Englishmen could easily don disguises and pass themselves off as members of the official retinue, thereby gaining access to many of Japan's secrets. On two occasions in 1854, during negotiations with the Russians, he urged Abe Masahiro to have them all massacred.[45]

It is therefore a matter for some congratulation that Abe took so little of Tokugawa Nariaki's advice. Nothing could have led to pandemonium more quickly. But the fact remains that Nariaki, in a position after 1853 that entitled and even obliged him to give advice, was not the kind of man to see that advice casually ignored. He had never been firmly allied to Abe Masahiro. As early as 1847, at a time when Abe had been showing Nariaki nothing but goodwill, the Mito politician was quite willing to countenance getting rid of him. By 1854 he was, as Hashimoto Sanai observed, intriguing feverishly against Abe to get his own way. He therefore cannot have been a comfortable ally. Just what good he did Abe Masahiro (tonic wine notwithstanding)—or for that matter, Japan—is highly questionable. But there is no gainsaying Nariaki's influence, whether with the daimyo, within the lower ranks of Bakufu officialdom, or even within the cabinet itself, for he had a large part in the dismissal of two senior councillors in 1855.[46]

In a way, Tokugawa Nariaki personified the defects of government by consultation. He personally agreed with hardly any government decisions after 1853—and with precious few before that; he was never reconciled to them—as in 1854, when he demanded that the Treaty of Kanagawa be renegotiated, this time on terms more favorable to the Japanese[47]—and he did not scruple to work actively against those decisions with which he disagreed. The other daimyo of Abe Masahiro's inner circle were no more supportive than Nariaki, although perhaps more self-effacing. Opposed when he should have expected support, blocked when possible, lobbied and intrigued against, Abe must surely have come to regret his policy of consultation. The politics of consensus are no doubt all very well, save for what happens on those issues where no consensus is possible. In Japan, from 1853 to Abe's death in 1857, the result was paralysis.

The same point can be made about the decentralization of military power, countenanced in 1853 by the relaxation of the Bakufu's traditional prohibitions against building large ships and acquiring new arms. Setting the daimyo free to do both for the first time in more than two hundred years was in a way a natural consequence of involving them in the making of foreign policy. Perhaps, too, it was no more than sensible—although in that case sadly belated. But it certainly does not argue either for Abe's foresight or for his common sense that he should at no stage have given any thought to the two major problems attending this policy reversal.

The first of these concerned just who was to coordinate the national defense of a nation that was really nothing of the sort, but instead a collection of semi-autonomous, and increasingly fractious, principalities. It is an obvious question, but undeniably an unpleasant one, and we have already seen what Abe Masahiro's attitude to such issues was. But did he really expect that the many, many daimyo who disagreed with his diplomacy would accept his military leadership? The second problem was just as obvious, and rather less palatable. If these semi-autonomous principalities were to be free to arm themselves, what could guarantee that those arms would be used against the foreigners, and not against the Bakufu itself? The issue was hardly new: Mizuno Tadakuni and Tokugawa Nariaki had debated it at some length more than a decade before.[48] Abe, indeed, was aware of the possibility, for he spoke to Matsudaira Yoshinaga in 1855 of those who believed that "there is now a greater danger of internal rebellion than of foreign attack."[49] But though aware of the danger, he did nothing about it, and so presided over the birth of an arms race that would, just ten years after his death, bring the Bakufu down. Even his educational policy contributed to this result, since the first intake of the Nagasaki Naval Academy included samurai from domains like Satsuma, Chōshū, Saga, Fukuoka, and Kumamoto, who were taught at Bakufu expense skills that many of them were soon to use against it.[50]

Whatever it was, Abe's policy of consultation and cooperation was not modern. It was, in fact, a deliberate retreat from centralized authority and responsibility, and as such, an indulgence Japan could not afford. Of course, Tokugawa Nariaki could urge it when it suited him—speaking of "public discussion" of Perry's demands—but it is quite certain that the only ideas that interested him were his own, and further, that he himself believed public discussion a waste of time. "Lord Ise [Abe] stupidly claims that there should be consultation on foreign affairs," he wrote in a secret memorial to the shogun in 1846, "but while these consultations take place over a long period of time, we shall find the Ryukyus and Ezo, and finally Japan itself, taken away from us."[51] There can be no doubt about whose ideas he thought should prevail. Nor can there be any doubt that Abe's other confidants, though more than happy to be consulted, were already moving to enhance their own political influence. His friends, the "able daimyo," were very much more than his creatures. All were arming themselves, and all were making surreptitious overtures to the imperial court: Matsudaira Yoshinaga in 1855, with an unprecedented request that the protection of the court in this period of grave danger be entrusted to him; Shimazu Nariakira and Yamauchi Toyoshige, with requests that in this time of crisis they be allowed to donate large sums of money to it.[52] Nothing could be more reminiscent of the chaotic scramble for power after Toyotomi Hideyoshi's death in 1598. The five *tairō* then were ambitious men who could scent their opportunity; so, too, were Abe Masahiro's friends. Did he not see, or did he not mind?

It has been said in Abe's defense that he had no alternative. The Bakufu was far too poor to defend Japan, so it had to call upon the daimyo for their cooperation. Calling on the daimyo, or the court, for cooperation (no longer freely given) could not be done without also giving them a voice in the way that cooperation was used, and what direction it took. Abe therefore—so the argument goes—had no alternative but to take the court and the daimyo into his confidence, and to free the latter to buy the arms and ships with which they could defend themselves.

Such an excuse is plausible enough, except for the fact that Abe had a whole series of alternatives open to him; the first, of course, was the fairly simple alternative of not making rods for his own back. In 1844 Tokugawa Nariaki was very far from the eminence he later attained; he was, in fact, under house arrest, and control of his domain, where opposition to him was very strong, had been taken away from him. Throughout the rest of the 1840's, while he was gradually and painfully reestablishing his position, his only support came from Abe Masahiro. In the opinion of Fujita Tōkō, it was only Abe's "cordial support" that stood between Nariaki's faction and disaster in the dark days of 1848. "All we can do," wrote Fujita in that year, "is depend on Lord Fukuyama's wish to change things for the better."[53] And he was right. Abe supported Nariaki first against the three Mito branch houses (which had been entrusted with control of the Mito domain), and then against the incumbent daimyo, Tokugawa Yoshia-tsu.[54] The same applied to Shimazu Nariakira, since it was Abe Ma-sahiro's support during the Satsuma succession dispute of 1848-50 that established Nariakira as daimyo.[55] The Emperor Kōmei and his courtiers, too, were a rod Abe had helped fashion for himself. In 1846, when the court first declared its open interest in foreign affairs and defense, Abe had three courses open to him. He could have forced the emperor to retire; this had been done before during the Tokugawa period. He could have purged the emperor's advisers—since the emperor himself was only fifteen years old at the time—as would happen in the late 1850's and again in the early 1860's. The third alternative was to do nothing, and this is the one he chose. In so doing he tacitly acknowledged the right of the court to give advice in an area of which it was ignorant, and for which it would never have to accept one jot of responsibility.

There was another set of alternatives open to Abe Masahiro. He could have used what was left of Bakufu authority to silence his critics, and to compel their obedience. The obvious question is, what authority? And to this the equally obvious answer must be, precisely that authority which was used after Abe's death by Ii Naosuke, the man who replaced him as leader of the government. In what was to become known as the Ansei Purge, Ii Naosuke broke the logjam that had kept Abe Masahiro's government immobile. He did it by means freely available to Abe—that is, simply by overruling the court, and by forcing his critics into retirement and silence. It was done quickly, and it was done effectively. But it was not done painlessly. It earned Ii Naosuke himself a violent death, at the hands of Mito assassins, and it also earned him, in history books from that day to this, a reputation as the blackest of reactionaries.

Yet curiously enough, as far as Japan was concerned, Ii Naosuke and his purge, and the concept of authoritarian government behind it, represented the real wave of the future. When the new government finally came to power in 1868, it left no doubt about its own position on such matters as foreign policy, defense, and consultation. These followed the Ii Naosuke pattern, not the Abe Masahiro pattern. There was to be no argument in 1868 about opening the country. That was settled quickly, and those refusing to accept this decision were dealt with promptly and ruthlessly. On defense the early Meiji years saw a direct and crushing reversal of all Abe's policies: in 1869 it was announced that domains were no longer free to buy their own ships; in the same year a similar restriction was imposed on the employment of foreign advisers and instructors; in 1870 a series of reductions in domain military forces was ordered. At the same time the domains were to lose commercial freedoms that Abe had left untouched: their monopolies were prohibited in 1869, and in 1870 they were deprived of the right to borrow money overseas.

As far as government by consultation went, Katsu Kaishū complained early in the Meiji period that the Tokugawa Bakufu had simply been replaced by the Satsuma Bakufu,[56] and in many respects he was correct. The consultative council (*kōgisho*), established as a sop to regional feeling, was abolished after only one session because it raised "many unnecessary matters" and got on Ōkubo's nerves.[57] This again was the attitude of an Ii Naosuke, not an Abe Masahiro. By mid-1869 only three of Japan's 260 daimyo had positions of any prominence in national life, and none of these was to last very long.[58] Consultation, the representation of local interests, and respect for the integrity of daimyo domains were obviously passé, and ironically Abe Masahiro, who had encouraged such things himself, had also encouraged the very forces that were to turn their backs so conclusively on his politics just ten years after his death. The sort of Japan he had been prepared to accept, they were not, and history has given them the best of it.

Afterword

WILLIAM B. HAUSER

The purpose of this book has been to examine the Bakufu as an institutional structure of authority in medieval and early modern Japan. As evolving systems of military power, the Bakufu of the Kamakura, Muromachi, and Tokugawa periods reflected the need for new forms of centralized control, the evolution of new mechanisms for balancing central and regional authority, and most important, the limitations imposed on central authority by competing sources of governance in Japanese society. Sources of competition included the emperor and the court aristocracy, the remnants of the imperial government, the *shōen* system, the great temples and shrines, the *shugo* and *jitō*, and the *kokujin* and early modern daimyo. As political institutions the Bakufu represented new sources of central power. Over the course of the Kamakura, Muromachi, and Tokugawa periods, the nature of their authority, the range of their influence, and the balance between the Bakufu and holders of competitive or local power shifted and were redefined. As political institutions the Bakufu were dynamic, not static. Power shifted, authority was often ambiguous, and it is the ebb and flow of central authority that enhances the importance of the Bakufu as a source of political power in medieval and early modern Japan.

Each of the foregoing papers approaches the problem of the Bakufu from a different perspective. The distinctive approach taken in the Mass paper reflects an awareness that many of the issues raised about subsequent periods cannot be effectively confronted for the Kamakura Bakufu. The difficulty stems from the limited role played by Kamakura relative to its successors, as well as from the limitations of the documentation. That we know so little of Kamakura rule rightly raises the question of the extent to which the Bakufu displaced the imperial government and the Kyoto aristocracy as a source of national authority. Yet we do know that Kamakura played a major role in adjudicating land disputes and that its role as peacemaker and arbiter was central to its function. This role was the foundation of its national authority, which was broadened through the mechanism of the *shugo* and *jitō* offices. Yet the overall extent of Kamakura authority cannot be known. The Mass contribution helps to define the boundaries of our knowledge and to clarify the areas in which future work is likely to prove most productive.

The Goble paper contributes greatly to our understanding of how the Bakufu worked as a government institution. The existence of a stable core of literate, experienced civilian bureaucrats permitted a level of continuity and consistency in administrative procedures that the warriors alone could not have achieved. This continuity reinforced the ties between Kamakura and Kyoto, for the imperial capital served as the initial source of procedures, personnel, and concepts of good government. The judicial functions of the Bakufu required the development of bureaucratic procedures, and from Goble we learn how experienced civilian officials made this possible. The Bakufu's efforts to ensure promptness and efficiency, and to avoid overt conflicts of interest, illustrate the rationalization of governance, even at this early stage. Justice and good government required administrative specialists, and Goble has identified an important class of hereditary officials who contributed to the success of Kamakura rule.

Suzanne Gay takes a different approach in her analysis of the Muromachi Bakufu in Kyoto. Here the emphasis is on the integration of the Bakufu into the governing of the capital and its relations with traditional sources of elite power, the *kenmon*. Although the Bakufu increased its power at the expense of the other elites, it needed their support to preserve its position. Exhibiting both feudal and bureaucratic features, the Bakufu expanded its judicial functions to include adjudicating disputes between aristocratic and religious *kenmon* as well as between warriors. The sphere of Bakufu involvement broadened with the increasing interaction between the Bakufu and the traditional sources of elite power.

In the Harrington and Arnesen papers we find that the Muromachi Bakufu's capacity to govern outside of Kyoto depended on both military force and new institutions. Harrington shows how Ashikaga Takauji required a new structure for his Bakufu as well as regional subordinates who were both generals and administrators. The existence of powerful provincial military houses obliged the Bakufu continually to adjust ties with its supporters. By examining administration in the Kantō and Kyushu during successive periods of the Muromachi era, Harrington shows how the Ashikaga maintained national influence and prevented power from being concentrated elsewhere, though they were unable to control the political situation totally. The Bakufu placed powerful subordinates in the Kantō and Kyushu to preserve central authority, sharing with them both military and administrative powers, even though the Kantō *kubō* and *kanrei* and the Chinzei *kanrei* and Kyushu *tandai* were not easily controlled. As it became increasingly difficult to maintain control from the center, local authority was shifted from the relatives who had exercised it during the early Muromachi period to powerful military subordinates. Local alliances and direct relations with locally powerful military houses were essential if the Bakufu was to control its own representatives in the Kantō and Kyushu.

The Arnesen paper complements Harrington's analysis. Whereas Harrington focuses on the increasing need to allow regional autonomy and the difficulties in keeping it under control, Arnesen examines the ties remaining between the Ashikaga shoguns and their provincial vassals, which were critical to curbing local power. He shows how, despite the expansion of *shugo* authority, the Bakufu was able to make levies against the *gokenin*, incorporate them into the shogunal guard, and preserve relations with non-guard vassals while offering them a degree of immunity from the *shugo* in return. Thus shogunal power prevented the unlimited expansion of *shugo* authority, even in regions quite distant from Kyoto, like Aki. The *gokenin* maintained a distinct role in the political life of medieval Japan, and their direct ties to the shogun were important to them and to the national authority of the Muromachi Bakufu. The Bakufu proved able to manipulate local forces in order to extend and preserve its authority. Although its success varied considerably over time, it was by no means at the mercy of its regional representatives or the *shugo* until the Ōnin War in the later fifteenth century.

The local autonomy that emerged and expanded during the Muromachi era was well established by the end of the sixteenth century. Local military leaders—the daimyo—created their own legitimacy through military power. Hideyoshi and the Tokugawa faced the necessity of stabilizing this local autonomy and integrating it into a national system of control. Too much local autonomy could threaten centralized authority, but unstable local autonomy might lead to military conflict and destabilize both the region and the country as a whole. As noted by Susser, many of Hideyoshi's policies were designed to strengthen the daimyo and enhance their power over their vassals. This strategy not only placed the daimyo under the control of the central government, but also helped ensure the continuity of their local power by reducing the opportunities for local opposition. Hideyoshi claimed the right to settle boundary disputes over land, eliminating a major source of local conflict. He relocated daimyo, often enhancing their authority as well as his own in the process. He kept hostages and imposed onerous service obligations on his subordinates. Through cadastral surveys he redefined the character of landholding and asserted his overlordship over all territory. Finally, he changed the social class structure by distinguishing warriors from farmers and merchants. Local stability contributed to national stability and to the development of new structures for national control. Yet Hideyoshi failed to solidify a new system, and it was left to the Tokugawa to fully install the mechanisms necessary to ensure the continuity of national authority under a Bakufu.

My own paper is designed to show how castle control, construction projects, and service obligations were utilized to affirm Tokugawa authority over the western daimyo. As noted by Mass in the Introduction, as of 1600 the Tokugawa claim to national power rested on a flimsy foundation. The victory at Sekigahara was not sufficient to guarantee Tokugawa suzerainty, and the military alliances that made that victory possible needed to be stabilized to provide continuity from one generation to the next. Establishing the Bakufu, taking the title of shogun, and asserting the right to the proprietary control exercised by Hideyoshi were each an essential step, but it was still necessary to eliminate Hideyori as Hideyoshi's successor, create effective controls over the daimyo, and demonstrate Tokugawa authority in the Kinai and western Japan. The *sankin kōtai*, as well as controls on foreign trade and Christianity, helped to limit the autonomy of the daimyo, but military and construction obligations were also important. Thus the various castle projects in the early years of the seventeenth century had major significance: they reinforced the military superiority of the Tokugawa, helped subordinate the daimyo as vassals of the shogun, and in the case of Osaka castle, created a major Tokugawa power base in western Japan.

The Tokugawa Bakufu proved more durable than any of its predecessors. The *bakuhan* system with its clearly defined areas of Bakufu and daimyo power, and with its control mechanisms to prevent the development of competition in Kyoto or the domains, enjoyed remarkable stability for much of the Tokugawa period. This is not to suggest that Japan was a static society—that nothing changed behind the facade of political stability—but that an effective accommodation was reached between central and local authority. Urbanization, social and economic changes, and cultural developments all point to a dynamic society in transformation, but the basic structure of the *bakuhan* system was preserved into the mid-nineteenth century. Over the course of the Tokugawa era the Bakufu encountered a series of crises, attempted reforms to resolve them, and each time managed to muddle through without ever addressing or even recognizing the fundamental issues that brought the crises about. Despite the limited fiscal base of samurai authority, despite societal changes that challenged the philosophical justifications for the social system, despite intellectual assaults on the political order, the system survived. Until the coming of the West, none of the crises were great enough to challenge the established institutional structure.

By the last years of the Tokugawa Bakufu, however, there were severe constraints on policy choices. As the Bolitho paper shows, Bakufu authority had withered. Those in a position to reaffirm it, like Abe Masahiro, were unable or unwilling to stand up to a newly assertive imperial court, restive daimyo, and demands by foreign barbarians for diplomatic recognition and trade rights. The last decades of the Tokugawa period were a time of trial. Those who aggressively pressed the interests of the Tokugawa did so at great risk, and few Bakufu leaders were so foolhardy. Whether due to institutional atrophy, inadequate leadership, or a failure of will, the Tokugawa Bakufu proved unable to deal with either the troubles at home or the dangers from abroad. The Bakufu form of military-bureaucratic government proved unable to contend with the pressures associated with the opening of Japan to the modern world. As a result, it was swept aside and replaced by a new form of centralized authority in the conflict and reforms of the Meiji Restoration.

As a form—or better, as forms—of political and military power, the Bakufu provide a key to understanding the nature of governing authority in pre-modern Japan. John Whitney Hall's *Government and Local Power in Japan, 500 to 1700* (1966) established a new pattern for studies of Japanese institutional history. This classic work provides important precedents for the work presented here. Professor Hall was the first to articulate in English many of the themes discussed here, and he raised many questions that others have since attempted to answer. Among these themes, one of the most important is the role of bureaucratic procedure versus arbitrary power. As evident in the above discussions, legal codes, bureaucratic officials, and rational decision-making were features of each of the three Bakufu. The Kamakura Bakufu used the services of educated, professional officials or bureaucrats to regularize administrative and judicial processes. The transference of power from aristocratic to military hands was gradual and did not eliminate rational procedures and precedent from government. At both the national and local levels, control was, within obvious limits, systematic. Insofar as possible, it was also consistent. Bureaucratic elements were included in the Bakufu from the Kamakura through the Tokugawa era.

Another major theme is the balance between central authority and local power, which was one of the most important problems faced by each of the Bakufu. It is interesting to note how relations between the Bakufu and their vassals changed over time as local autonomy increased and new mechanisms were required to keep it in check. The Harrington paper, in particular, shows that the difficulties of preserving influence over the regional representatives of the Muromachi Bakufu were a major impediment to the creation of stable central authority. Relatives were untrustworthy and could use their family status to challenge the shogun. The autonomy granted to non-family regional representatives was difficult to limit from Kyoto, and alternative ties to powerful local figures were necessary to preserve central influence. Whereas the Muromachi Bakufu was unable to create a consistent mechanism to deal with this problem, we see Hideyoshi and the Tokugawa Bakufu developing more comprehensive and lasting procedures to prevent local autonomy from getting out of hand. Local autonomy was not inconsistent with enhanced central authority, but the model developed by the Tokugawa to ensure their dominance included elements that went well beyond anything envisioned by their predecessors. The Tokugawa Bakufu held more central authority and conceded more local power than the Kamakura or Muromachi Bakufu; yet it managed to create a more stable and enduring balance than its predecessors had done, and to exercise controls over the daimyo that effectively subordinated them. Each Bakufu departed from the models offered by its predecessors. Although each confronted a different political context, one can only wonder how much was learned from the limitations of the political order just replaced.

As political institutions the Bakufu were transformed by the changing character of control over the land, as fiefs replaced *shōen* and as the ties between the Bakufu and its vassals changed. A fundamental shift occurred under Oda Nobunaga and Toyotomi Hideyoshi following the displacement of the *shōen* system and the creation of daimyo domains. Whereas vassalage was personal and direct, the bureaucratization of authority depersonalized power relationships. Local authority and local control were fundamentally altered as ties to the center intruded more forcefully into the autonomy accorded to the daimyo within their domains. Enhanced power at the center is apparent in the sword hunts and land surveys under Nobunaga and Hideyoshi, the relocations and attainders of the Tokugawa, and the service obligations demanded by them all. Early modern daimyo were both autonomous and dependent, free to administer their own domains and expected to adhere to Tokugawa models, independent of fixed tax obligations to the Bakufu and subject to potentially onerous levies and service obligations. As both central and local authorities increased their capacity to eliminate potential rivals, they also faced new limitations imposed by their dependence on each other.

Within the *bakuhan* system of the Tokugawa period, neither the Bakufu nor the Han faced as much competition as had their Kamakura and Muromachi predecessors. The emperor, the aristocrats, the great temples and shrines—all of the so-called "multiple successors to the throne"—had been displaced by the Bakufu and daimyo. Yet the bureaucratization of authority was so advanced that none of the symbolic wielders of autonomous power were able to exercise it arbitrarily—or as arbitrarily as their forebears. Power was now tied to responsibility and was to be exercised within the confines of newly defined norms of rational governance. The rule of law, the force of precedent, each served to limit the options available to those in authority. The destabilization of the Bakufu that resulted from the foreign intrusions of the 1850's and 1860's reflected its inability to adjust quickly to new challenges or to respond flexibly to new sources of competition from the imperial court and the daimyo. The weakness of the

Bakufu went far deeper than the limitations of individual policy makers. By the time an effective response was forthcoming, it was too little and too late.

Military authority was transformed and refined from the Kamakura through the Muromachi and Tokugawa Bakufu. New concepts of state emerged, and more sophisticated and comprehensive structures became identified with local and national power. Different conceptions of government and local power evolved from the medieval to the early modern period. More officials, more records, and more comprehensive political and social controls transformed the character of political authority in Japan. By examining the Bakufu in Japanese history, we enhance our understanding of both the continuities and differences that defined central and local authority in the Kamakura, Muromachi, and Tokugawa eras.

Reference Matter

Notes

The following abbreviations are used in the Notes:

AK   *Azuma kagami*. Ed. Nagahara Keiji and Kishi Shōzō. 6 vols. Tokyo, 1976-79. (Edition cited by Goble: Tokyo, 1968.)

CHS   *Chūsei hōsei shiryōshū*. Ed. Sato Shin'ichi and Ikeuchi Yoshisuke. 4 vols. Tokyo, 1955-78.

DNK   *Dai Nihon komonjo*. Ed. Tōkyō daigaku shiryō hensanjo. Tokyo, 1901-.

        Iewake 1: Kōyasan monjo. 8 vols.

        Iewake 2: Asano ke monjo.

        Iewake 3: Date ke monjo. 10 vols.

        Iewake 8: Mōri ke monjo. 4 vols.

        Iewake 9: Kikkawa ke monjo. 3 vols.

        Iewake 11: Kobayakawa ke monjo. 2 vols.

        Iewake 12: Uesugi ke monjo. 3 vols.

        Iewake 13: Aso monjo. 3 vols.

        Iewake 16: Shimazu ke monjo. 3 vols.

DNS   *Dai Nihon shiryō*. Ed. Tōkyō daigaku shiryō hensanjo. Tokyo, 1902-.

IKNR   *Iwanami kōza, Nihon rekishi*.

        1st series. 18 vols. Tokyo, 1933-35.

        2d series. 23 vols. Tokyo, 1962-64.

        3d series. 26 vols. Tokyo, 1975-77.

KBSS   *Kamakura bakufu saikyojō shū*. Ed. Seno Seiichirō. 2 vols. Tokyo, 1970-71.

KI   *Kamakura ibun*. Ed. Takeuchi Rizō. Tokyo, 1971-.

KKS   *Kanagawa kenshi, shiryō hen, kodai-chūsei*. Ed. Kanagawa ken. Yokohama, 1971-.

NBI   *Nanbokuchō ibun*. Ed. Seno Seiichirō. Tokyo, 1980-.

SJJ   *Sengoku jimmei jiten*. Ed. Takayanagi Mitsutoshi and Matsudaira Toshikazu. Rev. ed., Tokyo, 1973.

TKR   *Taikō kenchi ron*. Ed. Miyagawa Mitsuru. 3 vols. Tokyo, 1959-63.

Mass, *"What Can We Not Know about the Kamakura Bakufu?"*

I am indebted to seven people for assistance with this essay: my students Lorraine Harrington, Joan Piggott, Andrew Goble, Bruce Batten, and Thomas Keirstead, and my colleagues Peter Arnesen and William Hauser.

1. For a discussion see Jeffrey P. Mass, "Translation and Pre-1600 History," *Journal of Japanese Studies*, 6.1 (1980): 61-88.

2. See the entry "Kamakura Bakufu" in the new *Kokushi daijiten*, vol. 3 (Tokyo, 1983).

3. Mass, "Translation and Pre-1600 History"; and Jeffrey P. Mass, "The Early Bakufu and Feudalism," in Mass, ed., *Court and Bakufu in Japan: Essays in Kamakura History* (New Haven, Conn., 1982).

4. In *Honchō monzui*, 955/9/17, *Shintei zōho Kokushi taikei*, 29.2: 115. For the sake of brevity in these notes, publication information on primary sources is omitted. For diaries, chronicles, and other narrative sources, see Endō Motoo and Shimomura Fujio, *Kokushi bunken kaisetsu* (Tokyo, 1957-65), 2 vols. For document collections, see Jeffrey P. Mass, *The Kamakura Bakufu: A Study in Documents* (Stanford, Calif., 1976).

5. We do, however, find a reference to a famous eleventh-century general, Minamoto Yoriyoshi, as *bakka*, a related term; see *Mutsu waki*, in *Gunsho ruijū, gassen bu* (1941 ed.), 20: 23. *Bakka* refers to a person, not a place.

6. The guards captaincy was awarded on 1190/11/24 (*AK*), and several references to a *bakufu* follow: *AK*, 1191/3/3, 3/4, 4/3, 6/7. See note 10 below.

7. A typical misrepresentation is *AK*'s very earliest reference to a *bakufu* in its entry of 1189/6/5. This was a year and a half before Yoritomo was appointed to the requisite office of *taishō*.

8. Sanjō Nagakane, *Sanchōki*, entries for 1195/8/29, 9/6, 9/9, 9/17, *Shiryō taisei*, 37: 271-72. The holder, Fujiwara Yoshitsune (referred to in *ibid.*, 1196/11/4, as *utaishō*, the same title formerly held by Yoritomo), was the son of Kujō Kanezane, the author of *Gyokuyō*, the most famous diary of the era. This latter work does not cite a *bakufu* in reference to Yoshitsune (though neither does it in reference to Yoritomo). The *Sanchōki* (1195-1206) was the diary of a Kujō supporter.

9. From early in 1191 the edicts issued by Yoritomo began as follows: "The chancellery of the former *utaishō* orders. . . ." For a discussion of the *mandokoro*'s significance, see Jeffrey P. Mass, *The Development of Kamakura Rule, 1180-1250: A History with Documents* (Stanford, Calif., 1979), pp. 7, 67-70, 75-80.

10. There are at least eighteen appearances of the word *bakufu* in the *Azuma kagami* (a noncontemporaneous account) before 1199. In the diary *Gyokuyō* I have located a single reference to Yoritomo as "former *bakka*" (an equivalent of "former *utaishō*") amid a profusion of references to "Lord Yoritomo" (Yoritomo-*kyō*) and "former *utaishō*." See *Gyokuyō*, 1191/4/26. The term *bakka* (*baku* plus *ka* = "under") appears variously to refer to Yoritomo; see, e.g., *AK*, 1190/11/24, 1191/1/23, 1192/7/24; *Hōjō kudaiki*, 1199/1/13, *Zoku Gunsho ruijū*, 29.1: 397; *Kujō ke monjo*, c. 1293-95 Kujō

Konoe ryōryū shidai, *KI*, 24: 39, doc. 18314; *Kemmu shikimoku* preamble; and *Baishōron*, in *Gunsho ruijū, gassen bu*, 23: 157.

11. The warrior sources consulted are as follows: a majority of the voluminous petitions and edicts to and from Kamakura; the entire body of Kamakura laws; the diaries *Kenji sannenki* and *Einin sannenki*; the biographical and personnel lists *Shōgun shikken shidai, Hōjō kudaiki, Kantō hyōjōden*, and *Buke nendaiki*.

12. The excellent translation by Carl Steenstrup uses *bakufu* throughout, though the word does not appear in the original; see "Sata Mirensho," *Monumenta Nipponica*, 35.4 (1980): 405-35. This, in fact, is the hub of our dilemma—whether or not to rely on a concept created by historians.

13. *Meigetsuki*, 1226/10/13, 1229/10/6. But other diaries, such as *Sankaiki* (coverage to 1194) and *Myōkaiki* (1243-75), seem not to use it. Neither do the chronicles *Hyakurenshō* (coverage to 1259) and *Rokudai shōjiki* (coverage to c. 1223).

14. For the meaning of *bakka* see note 10 above. *Kanchūki*, 1275/12/2, 1275/12/3, 1279/1/11, 1279/2/4, 1279/10/25, *Shiryō taisei*, vol. 34; c. 1319 Go-Fushimi-in onshōsoku, in *Shinkan eiga*, comp. Teikoku gakushi-in, 1: 221-22, doc. 129.

15. Every source, warrior and courtier, uses "Kantō" in this meaning. See, e.g., the list in note 11 above, plus *Gyokuyō, Meigetsuki, Hyakurenshō*, and *Baishōron*. Frequently, we find usages of the term *buke*, not in its later meaning of "military houses," but rather to designate the authority of Kamakura or its branch in Kyoto, Rokuhara. See, e.g., Mass, *Development of Kamakura Rule*, doc. 37 and *KI*, 22: 337, doc. 17215, 23: 178-79, doc. 17763, 23: 209, doc. 17819, and 24: 110-11, doc. 18467.

16. In sequence, see, e.g., *AK*, 1210/9/13, 1227/1/8, 1227/2/15, 1194/2/2, 1250/4/4.

17. *AK*, 1191/3/4, 1260/4/26.

18. See note 13 above.

19. See *KKS*, 3: 55-56, docs. 3297, 3299, 3304.

20. That is, in reference to the office of *taishō*; see Kitabatake Chikafusa, *Shokugenshō*, in *Gunsho ruijū, kanshiki bu*, 4: 652.

21. *Taiheiki*, book 12, *Nihon koten bungaku taikei*, 34: 393.

22. E.g., in such diaries of the era as *Kaei sankaiki* (1367-1425), *Saitō Chikamoto nikki* (1465-67), and *Saitō Mototsune nikki* (1440-56); and in the guidebooks *Bummei ittōki* (fifteenth century) and *Shōdan chiyō* (fifteenth century).

23. For this subject see Mass, "The Early Bakufu and Feudalism," in Mass, ed., *Court and Bakufu in Japan*.

24. The *Buke myōmokushō*, compiled around the beginning of the nineteenth century by Hanawa Hokiichi (compiler also of the *Gunsho ruijū*), makes this equation explicit. But did it evolve earlier?

25. See this reference in a document of 1184: Mass, *Kamakura Bakufu*, doc. 1.

26. For example, a document of 1238 (*ibid.*, doc. 99) refers to the "treachery of Jishō" (Jishō *rangyaku*), whereas a document of 1258 (*ibid.*, doc. 70) refers to the "war of Bunji" (Bunji *no ran*).

27. See Yasuda Motohisa, *Bushidan* (Tokyo, 1964), pp. 13-141, for a corrective of the view stressing constantly expanding lord-vassal networks under the Taira and Minamoto.

28. For the Taira episode as biography, see George Sansom, *A History of Japan to 1334* (Stanford, Calif., 1958), chap. 13.

29. The best writing on the Taira has come from Ishimoda Shō and Takeuchi Rizō. In particular, Ishimoda, *Kodai makki seijishi josetsu* (Tokyo, 1964), pp. 382-403, 470-87; and Takeuchi, "Heishi seiken seiritsu no shojōken," *Nihon rekishi*, 163 (1962): 2-12; Takeuchi, "Heishi seiken to insei," *IKNR 5, chūsei 1* (2d ser., 1962): 57-85; and Takeuchi, "Heishi seiken ron," *Nihon rekishi*, 200 (1965): 41-48.

30. For the Taira episode in recent perspective, see Jeffrey P. Mass, *Warrior Government in Early Medieval Japan* (New Haven, Conn., 1974), chap. 1.

31. By far the most valiant effort to examine Taira policy during the Gempei War has been by Ishimoda Shō: "Kamakura bakufu ikkoku jitō shiki no seiritsu," in Ishimoda Shō and Satō Shin'ichi, eds., *Chūsei no hō to kokka* (Tokyo, 1960), pp. 36ff; "Heishi seiken no sōkan shiki setchi," *Rekishi hyōron*, 107 (1959): 7-14; and *Kodai makki seijishi josetsu*, pp. 403ff.

32. Kiyomori's death came early in 1181, and the Taira were in flight from the capital by mid-1183.

33. The contemporaneous title was *sōtsuibushi*; see Yasuda Motohisa, *Shugo to jitō* (Tokyo, 1964), pp. 22-42.

34. The three organs, *samurai dokoro*, *monchūjo*, and *kumonjo*, are cited in almost every textbook. For a critique, see Mass, *Development of Kamakura Rule*, chap. 3.

35. Yasuda Motohisa, "Gokenin-sei seiritsu ni kansuru isshiki ron," *Gakushūin daigaku bungakubu kenkyū nempō*, 16 (1969): 81-110.

36. For a full discussion of the *gokenin* question, see Mass, "The Early Bakufu and Feudalism."

37. Mass, *Warrior Government*, chap. 4.

38. For an analysis of the Hōjō genealogy, see Okutomi Takayaki, *Kamakura Hōjō shi no kisoteki kenkyū* (Tokyo, 1980), pp. 3-10.

39. An expert treatment of the political rise of the Hōjō is H. Paul Varley's "The Hōjō Family and Succession to Power," in Mass, ed., *Court and Bakufu in Japan*, chap. 7.

40. For example, the 1979 NHK television drama of Masako's life depicted her as the innocent victim of her brother's scheming, whereas Kenneth Butler sees her nearly as an autocrat; Butler, "Woman of Power Behind the Kamakura Bakufu: Hōjō Masako," in Japan Culture Institute, ed., *Great Historical Figures of Japan* (Tokyo, 1978), chap. 9. The story is complicated by the absence of any Kamakura-era documents bearing her name, despite the existence of retrospective references to such records. For instance, a document of 1274 (*KI*, 15: 297, doc. 11673) refers to a Masako edict ("ni-i ke onkudashibumi") of 1223/9/13, which upon inspection bears the single signature of her brother (*KI*, 5: 224, doc. 3154).

41. For details see Mass, *Development of Kamakura Rule*, pp. 77-79.

42. *Ibid.*, pp. 16-35.

43. Tanaka Minoru, "Jōkyū no rango no shinjitō buninchi," *Shigaku zasshi*, 79.12 (1970): 50-53. A few more have probably been discovered since Tanaka published his findings.

44. For the Jōkyū settlement see Mass, *Development of Kamakura Rule*, pp. 34-58.

45. The difficulties loom large in Ishii Susumu, *Nihon chūsei kokkashi no kenkyū* (Tokyo, 1970), pp. 224-44. Professor Satō's claim of a full administrative authority (*gyōseiken*) over the east is now considered unsustainable; see Satō Shin'ichi, *Kamakura bakufu soshō seido no kenkyū* (Tokyo, 1943), chap. 1. Satō himself has substantially diluted it in "Juei ninen jūgatsu no senshi ni tsuite," *Rekishi hyōron*, 107 (1959).

46. *AK*, 1186/3/13, lists the nine provinces and notes that taxes in arrears, owing to the disrupted times, were to be excused, though payments were henceforth to be made in full. Other entries make clear that the preparation of field registers (*ōtabumi*) was undertaken as part of the overall process, though nothing on actual mechanics is included; see *AK*, 1199/11/30, 1200/12/28, 1210/3/14, 1211/12/27.

47. Ishii, *Nihon chūsei*, pp. 224-44.

48. *AK*, 1241/6/11.

49. *Shimpen tsuika*, 1248/3/20, *CHS*, 1: 163-64, no. 262.

50. These were the titles (Sagami *no kami*, Musashi *no kami*) affixed to the thousands of Bakufu edicts issued under their names. Similarly, Sōshū and Bushū (equivalent terms) appear frequently in the *Azuma kagami* and other narratives.

51. See, e.g., the governors' edicts from Kawachi (1203), Awa (1214), Sanuki (1221), Harima (1223), and Shinano (1309), in Mass, *Development of Kamakura Rule*, docs. 3, 9, 17, 45, 48.

52. For details see Okutomi Takayuki, "Musashi-Sagami ni okeru Hōjō shi tokusō," *Nihon rekishi*, 280 (1971): 32-43.

53. Yukie Mamiya, "Shoki Kamakura seiken to kokuga zaichō kiko ni tsuite—Hitachi no kuni o chūshin to shite," *Shisō*, 16 (1975): 112-36; and Ishii, *Nihon chūsei*, p. 233.

54. Mass, *Development of Kamakura Rule*, docs. 82-83.

55. The rise of the Bakufu can be explained largely in these terms; Mass, *Warrior Government*, chap. 3.

56. Yoritomo, for example, tended to distribute titles to his own kinsmen; after his death this dispersal of titles was broadened somewhat to include the Hōjō. See Varley, "The Hōjō Family and Succession to Power," pp. 149ff. The point, however, is that it is rare to find any indication of real activity by a governor despite occasional prescriptive references to responsibility for "provincial affairs" (*kokumu*); see, e.g., *AK*, 1190/2/11, and note 46 above.

57. Information on this subject is voluminous; see, e.g., Mass, *Kamakura Bakufu*, docs. 91-99; and Mass, "Jitō Land Possession in the Thirteenth Century," in John W. Hall and Jeffrey P. Mass, eds., *Medieval Japan: Essays in Institutional History* (New Haven, Conn., 1974), chap. 7.

58. Information here comes almost wholly from the testamentary records of vassals, which commonly enjoined secondary heirs to pay their *onkuji* shares through the principal heir. See, e.g., *KI*, 11: 290, doc. 8268.

59. A recent study is the first to look at these *onkuji* directly: Yasuda Motohisa, "Kantō onkuji kō," in Gokenin-sei kenkyūkai, ed., *Gokenin-sei no kenkyū* (Tokyo, 1981), pp. 437-61.

60. According to *AK*, 1200/12/28, the provincial registers of paddy fields (*ōtabumi*) were placed under the authority of that organ. In *AK*, 1211/12/27, orders were given by two *mandokoro* members for registers to be prepared in Musashi, Suruga, and Echigo provinces. For further details, see Andrew Goble's essay in this volume.

61. An inventory just published shows 180 such holdings spread across 43 provinces. Nearly two-thirds of the total were in central and western Japan, and only a handful were in fact located in the Kantō proper. See Kakehi Masahiro, "Kantō goryō kō," *Shigaku zasshi*, 93.4 (1984): 30-31.

62. In 1288, for example, a one-half (*hanbun*) *jitō shiki* from Ōmi Province and a one-half custodianship (*azukari dokoro shiki*) from Suō Province were commended by the Bakufu to Kamakura's Tsurugaoka Shrine. See *Kamakura shishi, shiryō hen*, 1: 7, doc. 11.

63. Several fresh (though still preliminary) looks at the Kantō *goryō* have recently appeared. In addition to Kakehi above (note 61), see Ishii Susumu, "Kantō goryō kenkyū nōto," *Kanazawa bunko kenkyū*, 267 (1981): 1-13; and Ishii, "Kantō goryō oboegaki," *Kanagawa kenshi kenkyū*, 50 (1983): 1-13. Older studies are unsatisfactory, e.g., Maki Kenji, *Nihon hōken seido seiritsu shi* (Tokyo, 1935), pp. 149-55; and Watanabe Sumio, "Kōbu kenryoku to shōensei," in *IKNR* 5, *chūsei* 1 (2d ser., 1962): 208-12.

64. A vassal will of 1191, for example, admonishes the heir not to subordinate his inheritance to any *kenmon seika*. The meaning here—and elsewhere—obviously excludes the Bakufu; see *KI*, 1: 388, doc. 514.

65. The Muromachi Bakufu gave continuous attention to this problem, a fact we have been reminded of by numerous scholars; see John W. Hall and Toyoda Takeshi, eds., *Japan in the Muromachi Age* (Berkeley, Calif., 1977). By contrast, the economic concerns of the Kamakura regime have gone almost unnoticed.

66. What passed as policy were admonitions of thrift and promptness in discharging financial obligations; see the numerous pronouncements to this effect in *CHS*, vol. 1. The sophisticated "estate planning" techniques being refined by warriors had no parallel at the level of the Bakufu. For these techniques in their formative Heian phase, see Jeffrey P. Mass, "Patterns of Provincial Inheritance in Late Heian Japan," *Journal of Japanese Studies*, 9.1 (1983): 67-95.

67. The last were disparate in the sense that Kamakura's governor-controlled provinces were not concentrated in a bloc in the Kantō. Several of the original nine (*AK*, 1186/3/13) changed over time, with the total number becoming smaller.

68. Current knowledge on the Hōjō is summarized in Okutomi, *Kamakura Hōjō shi no kisoteki kenkyū*; for the vassalage, Mass, *Warrior Government*, chaps. 7-8, is introductory; and for the eastern capital's religious establishment, the volumes of the *Kamakura shishi* are authoritative.

69. For details, see the essay by Andrew Goble in this volume.

70. Satō, *Kamakura bakufu soshō seido*, pp. 55-61. For a brief discus-

sion, see H. Paul Varley, *Imperial Restoration in Medieval Japan* (New York, 1971), pp. 41-42.

71. Satō admits as much in *Kamakura bakufu soshō seido*, pp. 121-34; and Satō, *Komonjogaku nyūmon* (Tokyo, 1971), p. 201.

72. For a sampling of *shugo* violations against *shōen*, see Mass, *Kamakura Bakufu*, docs. 140-55; and Mass, *Development of Kamakura Rule*, docs. 21-25. By contrast, virtually the only references to *shugo* in conflict with governors are general admonitions from Kamakura against overinvolvement in provincial affairs (*kokumu*); e.g., Mass, *Kamakura Bakufu*, docs. 138-39. An exception is a petition by the governor of the remote island province of Tsushima against the *shugo*'s unlawful intrusions upon provincial services (*kokuyaku*); referred to in *KI*, 21: 286-87, doc. 16300.

73. Fairly numerous governors' edicts survive for Bizen during Kamakura times; see the Kinzanji document collection in *Okayama ken komonjo shū*, ed. Fujii Shun and Mizuno Kyōichirō, vol. 2. Professor Hall also argues for a minimal advance by the *shugo* of Bizen: John W. Hall, *Government and Local Power in Japan, 500 to 1700: A Study Based on Bizen Province* (Princeton, N.J., 1966), pp. 179ff.

74. A description of this is only beginning to appear in English. See, e.g., the essays by Kiley, Piggott, and Arnesen in Mass, ed., *Court and Bakufu in Japan*; Ishii Susumu, "The Decline of the Kamakura Bakufu," in *Cambridge History of Japan*, forthcoming; and the Ph.D. dissertation, in progress, by Andrew Goble.

75. For this progress, see the essay by Suzanne Gay in this volume.

Goble, "The Kamakura Bakufu and Its Officials"

1. See Jeffrey P. Mass, *The Development of Kamakura Rule, 1180-1250: A History with Documents* (Stanford, Calif., 1979), chaps. 3-5, pp. 61-153.

2. Satō Shin'ichi, "Muromachi bakufu sōsetsuki no kansei taikei," in Ishimoda Shō and Satō Shin'ichi, eds., *Chūsei no hō to kokka* (Tokyo, 1960), pp. 449-511.

3. See Jeffrey P. Mass, *Warrior Government in Early Medieval Japan* (New Haven, Conn., 1974).

4. Mezaki Noriie, "Kamakura bakufu sōsetsuki no shiryō ni tsuite," *Miura kobunka*, 15 (1975): 6.

5. *Ibid.*, pp. 3-11; Fukuda Toyohiko, "Yoritomo no zōshiki ni tsuite," *Shigaku zasshi*, 78.3 (1969): 15-16, citing, among others, Hōjō Tokimasa's retainer, Echigo no suke Takanari.

6. Mezaki, "Kamakura bakufu," p. 13.

7. The following discussion draws on *ibid.*, pp. 8-13.

8. These associations are not beyond dispute. See Seno Seiichirō, *Chinzei gokenin no kenkyū* (Tokyo, 1975), p. 52; and the undated genealogy of heads of the Taira patron shrine, the Itsukushima Shrine in Aki Province, in Itsukushima kannushi keizu utsushi, *Hiroshima kenshi, kodai-chūsei shiryō hen*, ed. Hiroshima ken, 5 vols. (Hiroshima, 1974-80), 3: 415-19. On the other hand, there is a traditional suggestion that Chikayoshi was Yoritomo's illegitimate son; Mezaki, "Kamakura bakufu," p. 8.

9. For the importance of the Atsuda Shrine connection, see Uwayokote Masataka, "Insei ki no Genji," in *Gokeninsei no kenkyū*, ed. Gokeninsei kenkyūkai (Tokyo, 1981), pp. 153-92.

10. *Azuma kagami* (Tokyo, 1968; hereafter *AK*), 1194/10/1, notes that Yasunobu's son Yukitomo was to take over Yasunobu's task of recording judicial proceedings, since Yasunobu was busy with other matters.

11. From 1284 to 1293, when the Hōjō retainer (*miuchinin*) Taira Yoritsuna dominated the Bakufu, the *monchūjo shitsuji* post was held by the *hyōjōshū* member Settsu Chikamune, a direct descendant of the *hyōjōshū* founding member Nakahara Morokazu.

12. Mass, *Development of Kamakura Rule*, pp. 67-80.

13. It is commonly believed that this post was created on 1218/12/20, when it is first mentioned in the *Azuma kagami*. But a document from the middle of that year makes it clear that the *AK* reference is to the office's existence rather than to its creation. See 1218/7/21 Bakufu mandokoro shitsuji hōsho, *KI*, 4, doc. 2386.

14. The warrior/bureaucrat division within the initial *hyōjōshū* should thus be modified to four/seven; cf. Andrew Goble, "The Hōjō and Consultative Government," in Jeffrey P. Mass, ed., *Court and Bakufu in Japan: Essays in Kamakura History* (New Haven, Conn., 1982), p. 175 and n. 14.

15. Tadahisa, *AK*, 1184/4/3, 1184/8/28, 1185/5/8, 1205/3/12, 1211/7/11, 1233/4/16; Akisada, *AK*, 1204/4/1, 1233/4/16, 1238/5/11; Sanekage, *AK*, 1194/12/2, 1231/3/19; for officials through the 1190's, see Mezaki, "Kamakura bakufu," pp. 6-7.

16. An exception to this was Nakahara Morokazu, brought from Kyoto by Yasutoki after the latter's period as Rokuhara *tandai*.

17. Full lists of *hikitsukeshū* scribes appear in the *AK*: 1251/6/5, 1251/6/20, 1252/4/30, 1253/12/22, 1254/12/1, 1257/(3)/2, 1261/3/20. The death of one Masamune at age 54 is noted in *AK*, 1256/1/16.

18. *AK*, 1245/10/6; 1313/2/20 Chinzei saikyojō, *KBSS*, 2, doc. 43. Since one Akashi was a signatory to the *Kemmu shikimoku* in 1336, there is little doubt that the family served until the end of the Kamakura period. See Kenneth A. Grossberg and Kanamoto Nobuhisa, eds. and trans., *The Laws of the Muromachi Bakufu: Kemmu Shikimoku (1336) and Muromachi Bakufu Tsuika hō* (Tokyo, 1981), p. 22.

19. *Einin sannenki*, in *Zoku shiryō taisei*, 10 (Tokyo, 1967), entries for 2/10 and (2)/12.

20. 1284/9/10 Hōjō Hisatoki shojō, *KI*, 20, doc. 15302; 1284/11/25 Kantō migyōsho, *KI*, 20, doc. 15363, for Akashi Yukimune. For an excellent study of the Bakufu's shrine restoration policy, which involved a major attempt to shore up its position by supporting traditional sources of authority in Kyushu, see Murai Shōsuke, "Mōko shūrai to Chinzei tandai no seiritsu," *Shigaku zasshi*, 87.4 (1978): 1-43; and Murai, "Shōwa no jinryō kōgyō o megutte," *Rekishigaku kenkyū*, 459 (1978): 17-22, 35.

21. *AK*, 1245/10/28; (1273?)/12/8 Yūki Tomohira shojō, *KI*, 15, doc. 11595; *CHS*, 1, no. 562.

22. See note 45 below, and *AK*, 1265/5/23; *Kenji sannenki*, *Zoku shiryō taisei*, 10, entry for 8/29; 1285/12/24 Kantō migyōsho, *CHS*, 1, no. 373;

Einin sannenki, entry for 2/13; 1318/4/28 Kantō saikyojō, *KBSS*, 1, doc. 305; 1333/5/9 Ōmi no kuni Bambashuku Rengeji kakōchō, *Shinkō Gunsho ruijū, zatsu bu*, vol. 22 (Tokyo, 1932).

23. *AK*, 1261/3/20; 1325/6/12 Kantō saikyojō, *KBSS*, 1, doc. 305.

24. Yukikane first appears as a lower-level official associated with Bakufu attempts to restrain the priest Nichiren; 1273/11/14 Yukikane tō rensho hōsho utsushi, *KI*, 15, doc. 11464. He later was active in judicial matters; 1290 Kantō hyōjō kotogaki, *CHS*, 1, nos. 367-68; 1307/5 Taira Tsunemoto mōshijō an, *KKS*, 2, doc. 1588.

25. Helen McCullough, trans., *The Taiheiki* (New York, 1959), pp. 253-54. Yet others died fleeing Kyoto. See 1333/5/9 Ōmi no kuni Bambashuku Rengeji kakōchō, *Shinkō Gunsho ruijū, zatsu bu*, vol. 22 (Tokyo, 1932).

26. This family, descended from Motonari, is not to be confused with another family of the same name (Saitō Nagasada's line), which provided Kamakura with *hyōjōshū* and *hikitsukeshū* members through at least 1266.

27. For Mototsura, who served in Kamakura, 1300/3/3 Kantō saikyojō, *KBSS*, 1, doc. 224, and 1332/12/23 Kantō saikyojō, *KBSS*, 1, doc. 326. For Motoaki in Rokuhara, 1299/6/1 Rokuhara bugyōnin rensho hōsho, *KI*, 26, doc. 20134, and 1325/8 Kanazawa Sadaaki shojō, *KKS*, 2, doc. 2440. For Kyushu, Chinzei hikitsuke ki, *Dazaifu, Dazaifu Tenmangū shiryō*, ed. Takeuchi Rizō (Dazaifu, 1964-), 10: 234ff.

28. Yūjō first appears in 1275/7/23 Yūjō shojō, *Kii no kuni Ategawa no shō shiryō*, ed. Nakamura ken, 2 (Tokyo, 1978), doc. 213; see also 1312/6/4 Tamba no kuni Miyata no shō zasshō gonjō jō an, *ibid.*, 2: 7-10. For the commentary, 1290 Goseibai shikimoku uragaki, see *CHS*, 4, pp. 1-21.

29. E.g., Echizen Shirō Tsuneari, *AK*, 1253/12/22, 1254/12/1; or Takamizu Ukon Saburō, *AK*, 1265/6/11.

30. *AK*, 1241/6/16, 1251/6/5, 1254/12/1, 1254/12/17. On the last occasion he was asked to provide the shogun with information on traditional techniques of cloth dyeing.

31. E.g., Tametada, who resigned as a *hikitsukeshū* scribe; *AK*, 1265/6/11. Since Tametada's name does not appear on the 1261/3/20 list, his service as a scribe must have lasted at most four years.

32. Most recently, see Ishii Susumu's attempt to identify some of the Bakufu's lands in "Kantō goryō kenkyū nōto," *Kanazawa Bunko kenkyū*, 267 (1981): 1-13; and "Kantō goryō oboegaki," *Kanagawa kenshi kenkyū*, 50 (1983): 1-13. See also Kakehi Masahiro, "Kantō goryō kō," *Shigaku zasshi*, 93.4 (1984): 1-44.

33. For two early lists, dated 1186/2 and 1190/4/19, see *KI*, 1, docs. 60, 439.

34. See, e.g., *AK*, 1195/9/19, 1233/4/16.

35. *AK*, 1263/8/27, notes that 61 boats carrying tax rice from Kyushu were washed away by great waves in Izu Bay near Kamakura during a violent storm.

36. For a list of extant registers, see *Nihonshi jiten*, ed. Takayanagi Mitsutoshi and Takeuchi Rizō (Tokyo, 1974), p. 1094. It is evident that the compilation of registers was an ongoing, period-long activity. See 1299/1/27 Kantō saikyojō, *KBSS*, 1, doc. 218, which refers to attempts to compile registers

during the Kōan era (1278-87); and 1328/11 Kumedadera zasshō Kaijitsu mōshijō an, *Senshū Kumedadera monjo*, ed. Toda Yoshimi (Kishiwada, 1973), doc. 44, which notes that in the early 1250's the Bakufu had sought registers from western Japan, that is, from half the country.

37. For Wakasa see *KI*, 15, doc. 11838; for Echigo, *KI*, 22, doc. 17128. See also Satō Shin'ichi, *Nihon no chūsei kokka* (Tokyo, 1983), pp. 186-87.

38. *AK*, 1194/11/26; 1249/6/3 Kantō migyōsho, *KI*, 10, doc. 7082; 1290/2/18 Kantō migyōsho, *CHS*, 1, no. 628. For *kuni zōshiki*, 1295/10/1 Bakufu mandokoro shitsuji Nikaidō Yukifuji tō rensho denbata chūmon, *KI*, 25, doc. 18909.

39. 1222/4/5 Kantō gechijō, *KBSS*, 1, doc. 24; Jeffrey P. Mass, *The Kamakura Bakufu: A Study in Documents* (Stanford, Calif., 1976), doc. 116; and 1243/7/19 Kantō gechijō, *KBSS*, 1, doc. 72; Mass, *Kamakura Bakufu*, doc. 88.

40. See undated Mōri Motoharu jippitsu kotogaki an, *DNK, 8: Mōri ke monjo* (Tokyo, 1920-28), 1, doc. 15, noting a grant to Tokichika in Kawachi Province while he served on the *hyōjōshū* in Kyoto.

41. 1250/11 Kujō Michiie shobunjō; 1260/8/27 Chikakazu yuzurijō; 1261/9/3 shōgunke mandokoro kudashibumi; 1263/2/17 Nakahara uji yuzurijō; 1269/12/19 Kantō gechijō; 1332/12/14 Fujiwara Shigechika yuzurijō; 1345/5/27 Ashikaga Tadayoshi sodehan kudashibumi. For these, see *Gifu kenshi, shiryō hen, kodai-chūsei shiryō*, ed. Gifu ken, 4 (Gifu, 1972): 1059-63. The 1260 and 1263 documents have been missed in *KI*.

42. 1308/2/7 Kantō saikyojō, *KBSS*, 1, doc. 250; 1334/3/21 Go-Daigo tennō rinji, *NBI, Kyūshū hen*, 1, doc. 21; 1334/5/3 Go-Daigo tennō rinji, *Saitama kenshi, shiryō 5, chūsei 1, komonjo 1*, ed. Saitama ken (Urawa, 1982), doc. 275; 1335/10/14 Daijōkan fu, *DNS*, ser. 6, 2: 615; 1341/8/7 Settsu Chikahide yuzurijō, *DNS*, ser. 6, 6: 881-89.

43. Undated, but probably early fourteenth century, Kaga no kuni Karumi gō chigyō shidai, *KKS*, 2, doc. 2730.

44. 1312/7/23 Kantō saikyojō, *KBSS*, 1, doc. 252; Ishii, "Kantō goryō kenkyū nōto," p. 6.

45. *AK*, 1241/7/26, notes that Fumimoto was granted Minayoshi gō in Kazusa Province.

46. Seno, *Chinzei gokenin no kenkyū*, p. 249, citing *KI*, 13, doc. 9322; *KI*, 21, doc. 16380.

47. 1276/7/7 Kantō hyōjō kotogaki, *KI*, 16, doc. 12397.

48. Seven holdings have been identified for Ise Province, three in Suō, two in Higo, and one each in Sagami, Mino, Musashi, Echigo, and Harima. In addition, holdings in Inaba, Bizen, and Bingo provinces are referred to, though not identified, in *Shirakawa fudoki, Essa shiryō*, comp. Takahashi Yoshihiko, 2 (Niigata, 1926): 172. *AK*, 1186/2/7, 1187/(4)/29, 1188/12/2, 1190/4/19; 1191/3/22 Yashiro no shō sōkumon shiki buninjō an, *KI*, 1, doc. 524; 1192/6/3 Saki no utaishō ke mandokoro kudashibumi, *KI*, 2, doc. 594; *AK*, 1194/8/8, 1213/5/7; 1233/(7)/13 Kantō saikyojō, *KBSS*, 1, doc. 153; *Gifu kenshi, tsūshi hen, chūsei*, ed. Gifu ken (Gifu, 1969), p. 272.

49. 1226/9/17 Ōe Tadanari kishinjō, *KI*, 5, doc. 3526, refers to an unnamed estate in Ōmi Province. Amino Yoshihiko, "Owari no kuni no shōen

kōryō to jitō gokenin," in *Gokeninsei no kenkyū*, p. 28 and notes 182-83, mentions a holding in Owari Province's Kaitō district.

50. 1227/2/15 Kantō migyōsho, *Ōita ken shiryō*, ed. Ōitaken shiryō kan-kōkai, 30 (Ōita, 1960-): 438-39; 1247/6/23 Shōgun sodehan kudashibumi, *KI*, 9, doc. 6845; Ishii, "Kantō goryō kenkyū nōto," p. 6; Yūyama Manabu, "Sagami no kuni Aikō gun no shōen," in *Chihōshi kenkyū*, 144 (1976): 16-17. The award of two of these estate posts to the Adachi family provides a sidelight to that family's subsequent rise within the Bakufu. See also H. Paul Varley, "The Hōjō Family and Succession to Power," in Mass, ed., *Court and Bakufu in Japan*, pp. 164-66.

51. *Essa shiryō*, 2: 5, 19-20; 1270/5/5 Mōri Tsunemitsu yuzurijō, *KI*, 14, doc. 10647; 1311/8/22 Ōe saki no Tango no kami jiryō kishinjō utsushi, *Niigata kenshi, shiryō hen 4, chūsei 2*, comp. Niigata ken (Niigata, 1983), doc. 2291; 1330/3/5 Mōri Tokichika yuzurijō, *DNK, 8: Mōri ke monjo*, 1, doc. 3.

52. *Yamagata kenshi*, comp. Yamagata ken (Yamagata, 1920), 1: 216-17; *Yamagata shishi*, comp. Yamagata shi shishi hensan iinkai (Yamagata, 1971), 1: 540.

53. *Hyōgo kenshi*, 2: 262.

54. *Essa shiryō*, 2: 172.

55. The Nagai *jitō* post is referred to initially only in 1226: *Yonezawa shishi*, comp. Yonezawa shi (Tokyo, reprint, 1973), pp. 29-30; *Yamagata shishi*, 1: 540. The first mention of the Akanabe post is 1223/8 Tōdaiji bettō Seihō kudashibumi, *KI*, 5, doc. 3143; a confiscation from a violent *gokenin* is noted in *Hachiman jinja kiroku*, 1 (Kyoto, 1923): 582. For Tokihiro's age, see *Hagi han batsu etsu roku*, ed. Yamaguchi ken monjo kan, 1 (Yamaguchi, 1967): 161. For an excellent study of the Nagai, see Koizumi Yoshiaki, "Gokenin Nagai shi ni tsuite," in Takahashi Ryūzō sensei kiju kinenkai, ed., *Kokiroku no kenkyū* (Tokyo, 1970), pp. 707-65.

56. See the table of *jitō* and the family genealogy in Koizumi Yoshiaki, "Jitō uke ni kansuru ichi kōsatsu," *Nihon rekishi*, 298 (1973): 17-18.

57. 1319/11/8 Ama Jōshin yuzurijō, *Gifu kenshi, shiryō hen, kodai-chūsei shiryō*, 4, doc. 429; 1347/4/7 Ashikaga Tadayoshi saikyojō, *Yamagata kenshi, kodai·chūsei shiryō hen*, comp. Yamagata ken (Yamagata, 1977), 1: 947-48. The latter document lists other holdings, which may well have been Kamakura period acquisitions.

58. 1285/12 Tajima no kuni ōtabumi, *KI*, 21, doc. 15774; *Rokuhara shugo shidai*, entry for 1297/7/27; 1325/9 Kenzen shotai Bingo no kuni Hiji ho monjo mokuroku, *Hiroshima kenshi*, 5 (Hiroshima, 1980): 772-73, citing two no longer extant Yasushige documents of 1251/2/9 and 1255/7/9.

59. 1273/8/12 Nagai Yasumochi ukebumi, *Hiroshima kenshi*, 5: 151 (this document has been missed in *KI*); 1285/12 Tajima no kuni ōtabumi, *KI*, 21, doc. 15774; 1300/5/23 Rokuhara saikyojō, *KBSS*, 2, Rokuhara doc. 31; 1329/12/22 Nagai Yorihide yuzurijō, *DNK, 8: Mōri ke monjo*, 4, doc. 1372; 1330/12/25 Ama Shōin yuzurijō, *ibid.*, 4, docs. 1373, 1374; 1337/12/21 Ashikaga Tadayoshi ando kudashibumi, *Ehime kenshi shiryō hen, kodai-chūsei*, comp. Ehime kenshi hensan iinkai (Matsuyama, 1983), doc. 663.

60. 1196/10/22 Saki no utaishō ke mandokoro kudashibumi, *KI*, 2, doc.

867; 1207/8/6 Miyoshi Zenshin yuzurijō an, *KI*, 3, doc. 1695; 1217/8/2 Miyoshi Yasunobu [*sic* Zenshin] yuzurijō, *KI*, 4, doc. 2329. Two edicts, both dated 1226/9/16, confirm these transfers: Kantō gechijō, *KI*, 5, docs. 3156, 3157.

61. 1223/11 Bingo Ōta no shō jitō Ōta Yasutsugu dō Yasutsura rensho chinjō an, *KI*, 5, doc. 3180; undated, but post-dating 1246/3/7, Ōta no shō Akaya gō sata shidai an, *DNK, 1: Kōyasan monjo* (Tokyo, 1968), 8, doc. 1713; *KI*, 9, doc. 6293; 1329/3 Kantō migyōsho, *Shinano shiryō*, ed. Shinano shiryō kankōkai, 5 (Nagano, 1954): 70-76.

62. See the Kantō judicial edict written sometime between 1288 and 1293/8, *KI*, 24, doc. 18310. Also, land was granted to a member of the Machino family in Kyushu in the second half of the thirteenth century. See Monchūjo Machino shi kafu, mss., 1887, Tōkyō daigaku shiryō hensanjo.

63. See 1335/11/9 Tachibana Yukisada uchiwatashi jō an, *Gumma kenshi, shiryō hen 5, chūsei 1*, comp. Gumma ken (Maebashi, 1978), p. 200. A major problem here is that no full genealogy of the Miyoshi family survives. Who, for example, is the Miyoshi Yasunao directed to exchange lands with Adachi Yoshikage in the 1249/10/30 Shōgun sodehan kudashibumi, *KI*, 10, doc. 7128? For the most comprehensive genealogy of the Miyoshi who served the Bakufu, see *Shinshū Onomichi shishi*, comp. Onomichi shi (Onomichi, 1971), 1: 217-18.

64. 1240/10/14 Nikaidō Motoyuki yuzurijō, *KI*, 8, doc. 5627; undated Nikaidō shi shoryō shōmon mokuroku, *KI*, 14, doc. 11143 [*sic* 11043]; Mass, *Development of Kamakura Rule*, pp. 89-90. The Nikaidō document collection is in manuscript copy in two volumes in the Shiryō Hensanjo of Tokyo University. Many of the documents have been published in *Satsuma no kuni Ata gun shiryō*, comp. Kagoshima kenritsu toshokan (Kagoshima, 1967).

65. See note 39 above. Additionally, Yukimitsu was entrusted with sixteen holdings in Wakasa Province that had been confiscated from Wakasa Tadasue in 1203. They were returned to Tadasue in 1205.

66. *KI*, 13, doc. 9422; *KI*, 20, doc. 15700; *KI*, 24, doc. 18386; *Gifu kenshi, tsūshi hen, chūsei*, p. 312; 1335/9/2 Daijōkan fu, transcribed in Inamoto Noriaki, "Ise no kuni ni okeru Hōjō shi ichimon ryō," *Fubito*, 38 (1981): 1-10; 1336/4/2 Yūki Munehiro yuzurijō utsushi, *Yamagata kenshi, kodai-chūsei shiryō*, 1: 895-96.

67. 1240/10/14 Nikaidō Motoyuki yuzurijō, *KI*, 8, doc. 5627; 1247/6/23 Shōgun sodehan kudashibumi, *KI*, 9, doc. 6846; 1249/8/9 Kantō migyōsho, *KI*, 10, doc. 7105; 1278/12/27 Kantō saikyojō, *KBSS*, 1, doc. 144; 1285/12 Tajima no kuni ōtabumi, *KI*, 21, doc. 15774; 1295/7/29 Nikaidō Yukifuji kishinjō, *KI*, 25, doc. 18880; 1304/5/26 Kantō gechijō, *Satsuma no kuni Ata gun shiryō*, doc. 33; 1335/1/25 Go-Daigo tennō rinji, *DNS*, ser. 6, 2: 251-52; 1335/10/26 Rikuoku kokusen an, *Fukushima kenshi, kodai-chūsei shiryō*, comp. Fukushima ken (Fukushima, 1966), pp. 376-77; 1340/6/29 Kitabatake Chikafusa sodehan senshu shojō, *ibid.*, pp. 507-8; *Gifu kenshi, tsūshi hen, chūsei*, p. 312; Amino Yoshihiko, "Hitachi no kuni ni okeru shōen kōryō no shacha," *Kairo*, 24 (1972): 10-14.

68. *AK*, 1224/7/19, notes that Yukimura was entrusted with these hold-

ings—despite his connections to the traitorous Iga—because he enjoyed the confidence of Hōjō Masako. One of them, Wakasa Province's Hyūga *ura*, found its way into Yukimitsu's line, but there is little information on the other 51. See also note 65 above.

69. *AK*, 1218/7/22, 1218/12/26.

70. For the awards, *AK*, 1213/5/7. *AK*, 1194/3/9, notes Yukimitsu's appointment as a *mandokoro* official. Yukimura appears only sporadically in *AK* until his 1205/12/24 appointment as commissioner for Kazusa Province.

71. The extent to which close family links maintained under the *sōryō* (family head) system may have lessened the impact of tenurial disparities deserves consideration, for there is no doubt that official families, like warrior ones, did adopt this system.

72. See note 40 above.

73. See Mass, *Development of Kamakura Rule*, pp. 90ff.

74. *AK*, 1216/12/1, 1233/11/2; 1259/6/18 Kantō migyōsho, *KI*, 11, doc. 8388.

75. 1238/8/5 Kantō migyōsho, *KI*, 7, doc. 5293. See also 1243/5/7 Kantō migyōsho, *KI*, 9, doc. 6813.

76. *AK*, 1241/5/10, 1244/6/7, 1248/2/18.

77. *AK*, 1245/5/3.

78. See 1241/3/20 Kantō migyōsho, *KI*, 8, doc. 5785; 1241/6/15 Kantō migyōsho, *KI*, 8, doc. 5887.

79. *AK*, 1248/11/23.

80. *CHS*, 1, no. 351.

81. 1244/10/12 Kantō hyōjō kotogaki, *CHS*, 1, no. 453; *AK*, 1258/5/10.

82. See *CHS*, 1, nos. 352, 354, 453, 547.

83. *AK*, 1225/9/20.

84. *AK*, 1211/7/11, 1211/12/1; 1244/2/6 Kantō hyōjō kotogaki, *CHS*, 1, no. 215; *AK*, 1241/8/10.

85. *AK*, 1263/11/22, 1263/11/23, 1263/12/10.

86. 1286/12 Kantō hyōjō kotogaki, *CHS*, 1, no. 604.

87. *AK*, 1245/12/25.

88. 1328/11 Kumedadera zasshō Kaijitsu mōshijō an, *Senshū Kumedadera monjo*, doc. 44. For another complaint, see 1309/6 Takeo sha daigūji Fujiwara Kunikado mōshijō, *Dazaifu, Dazaifu Tenmangū shiryō*, 9: 314-17.

89. Amino Yoshihiko, *Mōko shūrai* (Tokyo, 1974), p. 319; 1286(?) Kantō hyōjō kotogaki, *CHS*, 1, no. 608. I have encountered no actual cases mentioning bribes to judicial officials, though in 1293 officials were required to sign an oath vowing that they would not take bribes; 1293/5/25 Kantō hyōjō kotogaki, *CHS*, 1, no. 635. For a former Kamakura official's rejection of a gift from a successful plaintiff, see 1339/11/16 Settsu Chikahide shojō, *NBI, Kyūshū hen*, 2, doc. 1429.

90. *AK*, 1226/10/9, 1226/10/12.

91. 1235/(6)/21 hyōjōsho taiza bungen sadame, *CHS*, 1, no. 72. The relations were parents, grandparents, stepparents, step-grandparents, children and grandchildren, stepchildren and step-grandchildren, brothers, sisters, sons-in-law, fathers-in-law, siblings' fathers-in-law(?), paternal uncles, neph-

ews and nieces, fathers and brothers of retainers, brothers-in-law, wives, and those for whom one had officiated at a coming-of-age ceremony. This order was revised in 1240 to exclude reference to stepparents, stepchildren, and step-grandchildren; *CHS*, 1, no. 140.

92. 1299/6 Raishin teichū gonjō jō toshiro, *KI*, 26, doc. 20151.

93. 1329/3/13 Zasshō Hisashiro Ryōshin shojō, *DNK, 1: Kōyasan monjo*, 1, doc. 129.

94. For the oath, *CHS*, 1, pp. 29-30. For an excellent English translation, see Carl Steenstrup, "Sata Mirensho," *Monumenta Nipponica*, 35.4 (1980): 435.

95. See *AK*, 1234/7/6, an oath of shogunal and *monchūjo* officials; 1261/2/30 Kantō shinsei jōjō, *CHS*, 1, no. 350; 1293/5/25 Kantō hyōjō kotogaki, *CHS*, 1, no. 635, a *hyōjōshū* and *hikitsukeshū* oath; *Hōjō kudaiki, Zoku Gunsho ruijū*, 29 (Tokyo, 1925), *jō*, entries for 1295/8/25, 1308/7, and 1322/8/10.

96. See *AK*, 1261/3/20, for the dismissal of Nikaidō Yukihisa, a member of the *hyōjōshū*. The reason for his refusal is not given. Apparently no further punishment was meted out, for he was able to bequeath his lands to his daughters; 1266/6/10 Nikaidō Yukihisa yuzurijō, *KI*, 13, docs. 9541, 9542.

97. Text in *KKS*, 2, doc. 1636. For a brief discussion of authorship, content, and significance, see Kawazoe Shōji, *Kamakura bunka* (Tokyo, 1978), pp. 179-84.

Gay, "Muromachi Bakufu Rule in Kyoto"

Most of the material for this paper can be found in chapters 1 and 2 of my dissertation, "The Muromachi Bakufu in Medieval Kyoto" (Ph.D. dissertation, Yale University, 1982).

1. See, for example, John W. Hall, *Government and Local Power in Japan, 500 to 1700: A Study Based on Bizen Province* (Princeton, N.J., 1966), p. 196; John W. Hall, *Japan from Pre-history to Modern Times* (New York, 1970), p. 105.

2. This process is described in Peter J. Arnesen, *The Medieval Japanese Daimyo: The Ōuchi's Rule of Suo and Nagato* (New Haven, Conn., 1979), pp. 5-21.

3. The rise of the warriors is a basic theme of Nagahara Keiji, *Daimyō ryōgokusei* (Tokyo, 1967).

4. The discussion that follows is a condensation of the pertinent points of Kuroda Toshio's *kenmon taisei* theory as set forth in his "Chūsei no kokka to tennō," in *IKNR 6, chūsei 2* (2d ser., 1962): 261-301.

5. Hayashiya Tatsusaburō with George Elison, "Kyoto in the Muromachi Age," in John W. Hall and Toyoda Takeshi, eds., *Japan in the Muromachi Age* (Berkeley, Calif., 1977), p. 18.

6. Satō Shin'ichi, "Muromachi bakufu ron," in *IKNR 7, chūsei 3* (2d ser., 1963): 35.

7. See Prescott B. Wintersteen, Jr., "The Early Muromachi Bakufu in Kyoto," in John W. Hall and Jeffrey P. Mass, eds., *Medieval Japan: Essays in Institutional History* (New Haven, Conn., 1974), pp. 201-9, for an account

of some policies aimed at furthering Bakufu control of Kyoto up to the end of the fourteenth century.

8. Kami Hiroshi and Yashiro Kazuo, eds., *Baishōron* (Tokyo, 1975), pp. 125-29. The imperial flag refers to the flag of the imperial troops, given to them by the Emperor Kōmyōin as a symbol of legitimation. Nagasaka is a road in northwest Kyoto leading to Tamba Province.

9. *CHS*, 2: 4-5, nos. 1-6. For an English translation of the *Kemmu shikimoku* and supplementary Bakufu laws (*tsuikahō*), see Kenneth A. Grossberg and Kanamoto Nobuhisa, eds. and trans., *The Laws of the Muromachi Bakufu: Kemmu Shikimoku (1336) and Muromachi Bakufu tsuika hō* (Tokyo, 1981).

10. Satō, "Muromachi bakufu ron," p. 35.

11. *Ibid.*

12. *Ibid.*, p. 39.

13. *Moromoriki*, 1344/8/15, *Shiryō Kyōto no rekishi*, ed. Kyoto shi, 3 (Tokyo, 1979): 242, doc. 3.

14. *Entairyaku*, 1346/8/11, *Shiryō Kyōto no rekishi*, 3: 260, doc. 1.

15. *CHS*, 2: 45-46, no. 105.

16. Satō, "Muromachi bakufu ron," p. 36.

17. *CHS*, 2: 59, no. 145.

18. *Muromachi Bakufu tsuikahō*, 1367/12/29 and 1369/12/29, *Shiryō Kyōto no rekishi*, 3: 303, docs. 34-35; *Zokushigushō*, 1458/1/13, *Shiryō Kyōto no rekishi*, 3: 306, doc. 46.

19. *Chikanaga kōki*, 1476/3/6, *Shiryō Kyōto no rekishi*, 3: 305-6, doc. 45.

20. *Sanetaka kōki*, 1505/7/18, *Shiryō Kyōto no rekishi*, 3: 367, doc. 26.

21. *Sanetaka kōki*, 1506/7/11 and 1506/7/16, *Shiryō Kyōto no rekishi*, 3: 367-68, docs. 27-28.

22. Chapter 3 of my dissertation, "The Muromachi Bakufu in Medieval Kyoto," describes in detail the Bakufu's relations with the moneylending establishment.

23. *Kanmon gyoki*, 1431/7/6, and *Mansai jugō nikki*, 1431/7/8, *Shiryō Kyōto no rekishi*, 3: 284-85, docs. 28-29.

24. *CHS*, 2: 248, no. 231.

25. For a discussion of *erizeni* and a convenient summary of related scholarship, see Takizawa Takeo, "Erizeni," in Nagahara Keiji et al., eds., *Chūseishi handobukku* (Tokyo, 1973), pp. 67-69.

26. *CHS*, 2: 105-6, no. 320.

27. *CHS*, 2: 109, no. 334; 110, no. 335; 111-14, nos. 344-48; 117-18, nos. 360-62; 119-20, nos. 372-74; 123-24, nos. 385-89; 141-42, nos. 489-90.

28. Definitions of *kendanken* and *jungyōken* are drawn from Jeffrey P. Mass, *The Kamakura Bakufu: A Study in Documents* (Stanford, Calif., 1976), pp. 199, 200.

29. Haga Norihiko, "Muromachi bakufu samurai dokoro kō," in Ogawa Makoto, ed., *Muromachi seiken* (Tokyo, 1975), pp. 46-52.

30. *Tōji hyakugō monjo*, 1413/8/8, *Shiryō Kyōto no rekishi*, 3: 256, doc. 45.

31. Jeffrey P. Mass, in *The Development of Kamakura Rule, 1180-1250: A History with Documents* (Stanford, Calif., 1979), describes through the extensive citation of documents the Kamakura Bakufu's central concern of balancing the interests of the rising warriors with those of the traditional *kenmon*. In Kyoto, by contrast, numerous cases were brought before the Muromachi Bakufu that involved only traditional *kenmon*, and no warriors at all.

32. *CHS*, 2: 187, doc. 69.

33. *Tōji hyakugō monjo*, 1399/8, *Shiryō Kyōto no rekishi*, 3: 254, doc. 38.

34. *Tōji hyakugō monjo*, 1404/5/30 and 1404/7/26, *Shiryō Kyōto no rekishi*, 3: 261, doc. 3.

35. *CHS*, 2: 217, doc. 154.

36. The impression that the dispensing of justice rather than, say, sheer force, was the main way the Bakufu governed is shaped largely by the fact that the tools of research, *komonjo* (old documents of an official nature), deal almost entirely with litigation.

37. For a discussion of urban taxation, see Wakita Haruko with Susan B. Hanley, "Dimensions of Development: Cities in Fifteenth and Sixteenth Century Japan," in John W. Hall, Nagahara Keiji, and Kozo Yamamura, eds., *Japan Before Tokugawa* (Princeton, N.J., 1981), pp. 302-9.

38. *Tōji monjo*, 1400/4/8, *Shiryō Kyōto no rekishi*, 3: 266-67, doc. 10.

39. *Saitō Mototsune nikki*, 1456/4/2, *Shiryō Kyōto no rekishi*, 3: 269, doc. 18.

40. For details of the Bakufu's administrative organization, see Kenneth A. Grossberg, *Japan's Renaissance: The Politics of the Muromachi Bakufu* (Cambridge, Mass., 1981), pp. 87-105. Grossberg's account gives a chronological sense of administrative developments in the Bakufu, including changes over time in the relative strength of the shogun, *kanrei*, and other high officials.

41. Kuwayama Kōnen, "Chūki ni okeru Muromachi bakufu mandokoro no kōsei to kinō," in *Nihon shakai keizaishi kenkyū, chūsei*, ed. Hōgetsu Keigo Sensei kanreki kinenkai (Tokyo, 1967), pp. 124-30.

42. Some of the ideas presented here were included in Suzanne Gay, "Hereditary Bureaucrats in the Muromachi Bakufu," a paper in the panel "Kinship and Power in the East Asian Bureaucratic State," Association for Asian Studies, New England Conference annual meeting, Wesleyan University, Middletown, Conn., Oct. 17, 1981.

43. *CHS*, 2: 11-93, docs. 1-267; Ishii Susumu, ed., *Chūsei seiji shakai shisō* (Tokyo, 1972), pp. 155-76.

44. Kuroda Toshio, "Chūsei jisha seiryokuron," in *IKNR 6, chūsei 2* (3d ser., 1975): 247.

45. Atsuta Kō, "Basara no bunka," in *Kyōto no rekishi*, ed. Kyōto shi, 2 (Tokyo, 1971): 529, citing *Sanmon gōsoki* and *Gukanki*, entries for 1345/5.

46. "Emperor" here refers to three aspects of imperial authority: the emperor as high priest, the person of the emperor as the living representative of the ruling stratum (that is, all *kenmon*), and the imperial house as one *ken-*

mon, possessing lands and controlling various commercial groups. For most of the medieval period the imperial house was actually controlled by the *in* (the retired emperor), not by the reigning emperor. The first and second characteristics of imperial authority are primarily public, the third private. See Kuroda Toshio, "Chūsei tennōsei no kihonteki seikaku," in Kuroda, *Genjitsu no naka no rekishigaku* (Tokyo, 1977), pp. 163-64.

47. Nagahara Keiji, "Chūsei kokkashi no ichi mondai," *Shisō*, 475 (1964): 42-51; Satō, "Muromachi bakufu ron," pp. 43-45; Grossberg, *Japan's Renaissance*, p. 36.

48. Kuroda compares this aspect of imperial authority to that of the pope in medieval Europe; "Chūsei tennōsei," p. 165.

49. Atsuta, "Basara no bunka," pp. 531-32, citing *Taiheiki*, 1342/9/3.

50. H. Paul Varley, "Ashikaga Yoshimitsu and the World of Kitayama: Social Change and Shogunal Patronage in Early Muromachi Japan," in Hall and Toyoda, eds., *Japan in the Muromachi Age*, p. 184.

Harrington, "Regional Outposts of Muromachi Bakufu Rule"

1. See, e.g., Prescott B. Wintersteen, Jr., "The Early Muromachi Bakufu in Kyoto," in John W. Hall and Jeffrey P. Mass, eds., *Medieval Japan: Essays in Institutional History* (New Haven, Conn., 1974), pp. 201-9; Satō Shin'ichi, with John W. Hall, "The Ashikaga Shogun and the Muromachi Bakufu Administration," in John W. Hall and Toyoda Takeshi, eds., *Japan in the Muromachi Age* (Berkeley, Calif., 1977), pp. 45-52; Kuwayama Kōnen, with John W. Hall, "The Bugyōnin System: A Closer Look," in *ibid.*, pp. 53-63; and Kenneth A. Grossberg, *Japan's Renaissance: The Politics of the Muromachi Bakufu* (Cambridge, Mass., 1981).

2. Haga Norihiko, "Muromachi bakufu ron," in *Nihonshi no mondaiten*, ed. Nihon rekishi gakkai (Tokyo, 1965), p. 102.

3. Rivalry between Ashikaga Tadayoshi and Kō no Moronao (respectively, the shogun's brother and his closest vassal) led to major dislocations within the central Bakufu and had serious repercussions locally. For a discussion of the division of authority between Takauji and Tadayoshi, see Satō, with Hall, "Ashikaga Shogun and Muromachi Bakufu," p. 48.

4. The body of Ashikaga Bakufu legislation—the *Kemmu shikimoku* and the more than five hundred supplementary laws (*tsuikahō*)—has recently appeared in translation. See Kenneth A. Grossberg and Kanamoto Nobuhisa, eds. and trans., *The Laws of the Muromachi Bakufu: Kemmu Shikimoku (1336) and Muromachi Bakufu Tsuika hō* (Tokyo, 1981). An authoritative Japanese edition, and the one on which this translation is based, is *CHS*, vol. 2 (Tokyo, 1969).

5. Because his command jurisdiction extended into Mutsu, Ienaga has been referred to as deputy of both the Kantō and Ōshū regions. See Endō Iwao, "Ōshū kanrei oboegaki—Toku ni seiritsu o meguru mondai seiri," *Rekishi*, 38 (1969): 26; and Koyō Hiroshi, "Kantō fu shōron—Bakufu to no kankei o chūshin ni shite," in *Nihon chūsei no seiji to bunka*, ed. Toyoda Takeshi Sensei koki kinenkai (Tokyo, 1980), p. 241. The term applied to later

eastern deputies, *kanrei*, was apparently not used in reference to Shiba; his public titles were "general" *(taishō)* and "provincial governor of Mutsu" *(Mutsu no kami)*. Endō, "Ōshū kanrei oboegaki," p. 41, n. 3.

6. See, e.g., 1336/12/23 Kamakura fu shitsuji (Shiba Ienaga) hōsho, *KKS*, vol. 3, pt. 1: p. 60, doc. 3314; 1336/7/12 Kamakura fu shitsuji hōsho, 49-50, doc. 3279; 1336/10/28 Kamakura fu shitsuji hōsho utsushi, 55, doc. 3299. Shiba Ienaga's documents have been arranged and analyzed by Endō in "Ōshū kanrei oboegaki." They all appear in *KKS*, 3, 1: 45-69.

7. Morofuyu defeated Kitabatake Chikafusa, the leading general of the rival southern court forces. For a discussion of the two-man *shitsuji* system in the Kantō, see Itō Kiyoshi, 'Shoki Kamakura fu shōron," *Bunka*, 32.4 (1969): 105; and the more recent work by Koyō, especially "Kantō kanrei bunin enkaku shōko—Sono ichi," *Hōsei shiron*, 5 (1978): 1-18. A more detailed discussion of the activities of the Kō and Uesugi deputies in this early period appears in my dissertation: "Regional Administration under the Ashikaga Bakufu: Power and Politics Outside the Central Provinces," Stanford University, 1983.

8. On more than one occasion before the mid-fourteenth century, the Bakufu assigned Kyushu generals various duties related to foreign defense, such as keeping defense walls in repair and so on. Overall responsibility for foreign defense was assigned to the chief regional officer, at least from 1346. See 1346/12/7 Chinzei sata kotogaki narabi ni Ashikaga Tadayoshi migyōsho an, *Dazaifu, Dazaifu Tenmangū shiryō, chūsei hen* (hereafter *Dazaifu, chūsei*), ed. Takeuchi Rizō (Kyūshū bunka sōgō kenkyūjo), 7 (Fukuoka, 1957-58): 1133.

9. See, e.g., 1336/3/26 Ashikaga Takauji gunsei saisokujō, *NBI*, 1: 169, doc. 519.

10. 1336/11 Koyama Ikkyō mōshijō an, *NBI*, 1: 247-48, doc. 798. Kawazoe Shōji has identified this as the earliest use of the term. See Kawazoe, " 'Chinzei kanrei' kō," pt. 1, *Nihon rekishi*, 205 (1965): 6. The *Hokuhi senshi*, a chronicle of the period compiled some time later, referred to Noriuji as Chinzei sōkanrei *(kanrei*-in-chief) at the time of Takauji's return to Kyushu. The relevant passage is quoted in *Dazaifu, Dazaifu Tenmangū shiryō*, ed. Takeuchi Rizō, 11 (Fukuoka, 1979): 71-73.

11. Yamaguchi Takamasa, "Zenki Muromachi bakufu ni yoru Hyūga no kuni 'ryōkoku' ka," *Nihon rekishi*, 329 (1975): 42-44. It was not unusual, of course, for the Ashikaga to appoint special generals to provinces where the *shugo* post was not held by a related house. The *shugo* of Hyūga initially was Shimazu Sadahisa.

12. See, e.g., 1339/12/12 Ashikaga Takauji gohan migyōsho an, *Hennen Ōtomo shiryō*, ed. Takita Manabu, 2 (Kyoto, 1946): 350, doc. 609.

13. The *kanrei* established a temporary base at a temple (Shōfukuji) in Hakata, but he traveled often to distant encampments, occupying and vacating fortresses in rapid succession.

14. 1340/2/5 Isshiki Dōyū shojō, *NBI*, 2: 55, doc. 1475. (Dōyū was Noriuji's name after he became a lay priest.)

15. 1340/2 Isshiki Noriuji chūshinjō, *Hennen Ōtomo shiryō*, 2: 156-58, doc. 618.

16. These and other Chinzei *kanrei* support lands are discussed in Yamaguchi Takamasa, " 'Chinzei ryōsho,' Buzen no kuni Amauda no shō to Andōshi," *Nihon rekishi*, 314 (1974): esp. 43-44, n. 1.

17. All documents relating to Isshiki Noriuji have been categorized and analyzed according to both content and province by Kawazoe Shōji. His seminal articles were written in 1965, and therefore require some updating to add documents which have appeared since then. The basic point regarding Noriuji's power in Hizen remains valid, however. See Kawazoe, " 'Chinzei kanrei' kō," pt. 1, pp. 2-14; and pt. 2, *Nihon rekishi*, 206 (1965): 29-53.

18. See, e.g., 1338/10/17 Isshiki Dōyū gunsei saisokujō an, *NBI*, 1: 384, doc. 1266. Guard duty was not served at regular intervals or shared on anything approaching an equal basis, but some aspects of the service were systematic. Length of duty, for example, seems to have been set at either one day and night, or for periods of twenty or thirty days. Certification that duties had been fulfilled was given in the form of a signature by Noriuji or his subordinates on a ratification request (*chūshinjō*) submitted to his office (*onbugyōsho*) by the vassal in question. Many such examples may be found in the document collections of prominent Hizen warrior houses, such as Fukabori and Ryūzōji, all of which appear in *Saga ken shiryō shūsei*, ed. Saga kenshi hensan iinkai (Saga, 1955-).

19. Hattori Hideo, "Kyūshū tandai (Chinzei kanrei) no Hizen no kuni shugoshiki kenpo ni tsuite—Nanbokuchōki ikō," *Harukanaru chūsei*, 2 (1972): 22; *Nihonshi jiten*, ed. Takayanagi Mitsutoshi and Takeuchi Rizō (Tokyo, 1974), p. 1094.

20. Hattori, "Kyūshū tandai," p. 24; and Yamaguchi Takamasa, "Nanbokuchōki no Hizen no kuni shugo ni tsuite," *Kadai shigaku*, 15 (1967): 26, n. 2, and 18-22. Hattori and Yamaguchi differ about when Noriuji began operating as *shugo*. Hattori posits the early 1340's; Yamaguchi suggests that Noriuji and Ōtomo Ujiyasu shared or divided the post for a while before control passed to the Chinzei *kanrei*.

21. See, e.g., 1336/9/24 Satake Shigeyoshira rensho hōsho, *NBI*, 1: 233, doc. 752; and 1338/3/17 Omata Dōjō shigyōjō, *NBI*, 1: 347, doc. 1149.

22. Satake and Omata seem to have operated simultaneously for a while, and then Omata continued for several more years and extended his range of functions. For a discussion of the role of the *samurai dokoro* in Noriuji's early control of Hizen Province, see Kawazoe, " 'Chinzei kanrei' kō," pt. 1, pp. 8-10.

23. 1337/7/11 Isshiki Dōyū kakikudashi, *NBI*, 1: 300, doc. 986.

24. See 1344/11/17 Ashikaga Tadayoshi gechijō, *DNS*, ser. 6, 8: 509. There is some question whether Noriuji had actually been granted authority over the Shika shima area, or had simply assumed it. This document canceled Noriuji's rights. The case is also discussed in Kawazoe, " 'Chinzei kanrei' kō," pt. 2, p. 34.

25. 1337/12/24 Isshiki Dōyū kakikudashi an, *NBI*, 1: 332, doc. 1105; 1346/5/26 Isshiki Dōyū kakikudashi, *NBI*, 2: 311, doc. 2202; 1336/9/10 Isshiki Dōyū gunsei saisokujō, *NBI*, 1: 227, doc. 741.

26. 1337/2/7 Isshiki Dōyū gunsei saisokujō, *NBI*, 1: 260, doc. 840.

27. As we have seen in note 24 above.

28. 1346/8/11 Ashikaga Takauji migyōsho an, *Aokata monjo*, ed. Seno Seiichirō, 2 (Tokyo, 1976): 33, doc. 285, and 1346/8/11 Kō no Moronao shigyōjo an, *ibid.*, 2: 34, doc. 287. The site chosen for the *kanrei*'s residence was Okinohama (Chikuzen Province). Unfortunately, there is no evidence to indicate whether Noriuji ever established himself in the new location.

29. 1346/8/11 Ashikaga Takauji migyōsho an, *NBI*, 2: 319-20, doc. 2227; 1346/12/7 Chinzei sata kotogaki narabi ni Ashikaga Tadayoshi migyōsho, *Dazaifu, chūsei*, 7: 1133.

30. Accordingly, he characteristically ended documents in such circumstances with the set phrase (*kakitome*) "yotte shittatsu kudan no gotoshi," acknowledging at least superficially some superior authority, even when the order apparently originated with him.

31. 1337/9/3 Isshiki Dōyū kakikudashi an, *NBI*, 1: 312, doc. 1032. See also Kawazoe, " 'Chinzei kanrei' kō," pt. 1, pp. 12-13.

32. Identical orders from the shogun to both Noriuji and Naouji on the same day suggest the possibility that the Bakufu considered both *kanrei*. (?)/4/10 Ashikaga Takauji gonaisho, *DNS*, ser. 6, 19: 20. This question is also addressed in Kawazoe, " 'Chinzei kanrei' kō," pt. 2, p. 53, n. 23.

33. This shift in function has prompted one scholar to use distinguishing labels when discussing the eastern office in the pre- and post-Kannō eras. Koyō Hiroshi suggests referring to the former as the Kamakura headquarters (Kamakura *fu*), and to the latter as the Kantō headquarters (Kantō *fu*), a regional organ. See Koyō, "Kantō fu shōron," in *Nihon chūsei no seiji to bunka*, p. 257, n. 2. The discussion below draws from that article and from several analyses by Itō Kiyoshi, especially "Kamakura fu oboegaki—bakufu tōji kikan kara no 'jiritsu' katei no kisoteki bunseki o chūshin to shite," *Rekishi*, 42 (1972): esp. 17-22; and "Muromachiki no kokka to Tōgoku," *Rekishigaku kenkyū, bessatsu tokushū, 1979 nendo rekishigaku kenkyūkai taikai hōkoku* (1979), esp. pp. 63-64.

34. Motouji had been chief Ashikaga representative in the Kantō since 1349. His official coming-of-age ceremony was conveniently celebrated the day before Ashikaga Tadayoshi was killed in Kamakura on 1352/2/26. *Nanbokuchō hennenshi*, ed. Yūra Tetsuji, 1 (Tokyo, 1964): 634.

35. Contemporary references to the Kantō as a geographic unit allude to as few as eight and as many as eleven provinces. See, e.g., Tan'ei shojō, *KKS*, 3, 1: 260, doc. 3810. On Shinano Province, see also Tanabe Hisako, "Nanbokuchō zenki Muromachi bakufu ni okeru Shinano no kuni kankatsuken no suii," *Nihon rekishi*, 286 (1972): 64-77; and Fujieda Fumitada, "Muromachi shoki Shinano no kuni tōkatsu o meguru Kyō-Kamakura no tairitsu," *Nihon rekishi*, 266 (1970): 71-81. Both of these articles have updated earlier research by Satō Shin'ichi, who was the first to revise the long-held contention that the province was under Bakufu control throughout the Nanbukuchō period. Both Fujieda and Tanabe illustrate that control actually shifted back and forth, and Tanabe has refined the dates of the shift on the basis of newly introduced evidence.

36. Motouji's famous letter to Noriaki, dated 1363/3/24, is in *KKS*, 3, 1: 462, doc. 4445.

37. See 1361/11/26 Kantō kubō (Ashikaga Motouji) migyōsho an, and

on the same day, Kantō kubō migyōsho, *KKS*, 3, 1: 444, docs. 4386, 4387; and 1362/2/21 Kantō kubō migyōsho utsushi, *KKS*, 3, 1: 446, doc. 4392.

38. 1365/10/8 Kantō kubō (Ashikaga Motouji) kinju rensho hōgajō, *KKS*, 3, 1: 498-99, doc. 4556. Listed in this document as making contributions in the *kubō*'s honor are members of many rising families. Itō Kiyoshi has made the important observation that while Motouji was building support among such local lords, the Bakufu at the same time issued fewer documents directly to eastern *kokujin* by the end of the Jōji era (1362-68). Itō, "Muromachiki no kokka to Tōgoku," p. 64.

39. See, e.g., 1362/4/29 Kantō kubō shoryō ateokonaijo, *KKS*, 3, 1: 454, doc. 4412, or 1362/2/22 Kantō kubō genpojō, *KKS*, 3, 1: 447, doc. 4394.

40. See, e.g., 1363/4/25 Kamakura fu mandokoro shitsuji hōsho, *KKS*, 3, 1: 464, doc. 4450.

41. See, e.g., 1363/5/28 Kantō kubō shoryō ateokonaijō utsushi, and 1363/6/2 Kantō kubō migyōsho utsushi, *KKS*, 3, 1: 471, docs. 4459, 4460; and 1366/9/16 Kantō kubō migyōsho, and migyōsho an, *KKS*, 3, 1: 503-4, docs. 4575, 4576.

42. See the following, all in *KKS*, 3, 1: 1364/12/13 Shōgun (Ashikaga Yoshiakira) shojō an, 489, doc. 4524; 1364/12/25 Kantō kubō (Ashikaga Motouji) migyōsho an, 489, doc. 4527; 1364?/12/28 Izu no shugo Takasaka kasanete jungyōjō an, 490, doc. 4528; and 1365/1/19 saemon no jō Mitsu uchiwatashijō an, 492, doc. 4536.

43. 1361/10/3 Shōgun (Ashikaga Yoshiakira) migyōsho, *KKS*, 3, 1: 445, doc. 4384.

44. Itō makes this suggestion also, in "Kamakura fu oboegaki," p. 22.

45. See the two documents labeled 1354?/6/24 Shōgun (Ashikaga Takauji) migyōsho utsushi: *KKS*, 3, 1: 405-6, doc. 4258 (to Motouji's assistant, Hatakeyama Kunikiyo), and 406, doc. 4259 (to Sagami Province *shugo* Kawagoe Naoshige).

46. See, e.g., 1364/12/2 Kantō kubō (Ashikaga Motouji) bettō shiki buninjō, *KKS*, 3, 1: 488, doc. 4521 (for Myōōin in Kamakura). Tanabe has pointed out, interestingly, that the Bakufu resumed authority for this appointment after the *kubō*'s death in 1367/4. See 1367/9/20 Shōgun (Ashikaga Yoshiakira) bettō shiki buninjō, *KKS*, 3, 1: 517, doc. 4609; and Tanabe, "Nanbokuchō zenki Muromachi bakufu," p. 77.

47. See 1362/12/27 Kantō kubō kinzei utsushi, *KKS*, 3, 1: 458, doc. 4431. The Kyoto Bakufu was also directly involved with this important shrine. The two headquarters cooperated in the promotion of its welfare.

48. Itō, "Kamakura fu oboegaki," p. 22.

49. A call for support shortly after he arrived was perhaps Tadafuyu's earliest document, dated 1349/9/16, in *Seisei shōgun no miya*, ed. Fujita Akira (Tokyo, 1976 reprint of 1915 edition), p. 612, doc. 84, cited in Seno Seiichirō, "Ashikaga Tadafuyu," in Kasaharu Kazuo, ed., *Muromachi bakufu: Sono jitsuryokushatachi* (Tokyo, 1965), p. 149.

50. *Entairyaku*, 1351/3/3, as quoted in *Dazaifu, Dazaifu Tenmangū shiryō*, 11: 344-45.

51. 1351(Jōwa 7)/2/21 Ashikaga Tadafuyu kanjō an, *Dazaifu, Dazaifu Tenmangū shiryō*, 11: 341; 1351(Jōwa 7)/5 Yasutomi Yasushige mōshijō,

Saga ken shiryō shūsei, 4: 287-88, doc. 58; 1351(Kannō 2)/6/10 Ashikaga Tadafuyu kanjō, *Dazaifu, Dazaifu Tenmangū shiryō*, 11: 364-65; 1351 (Kannō 2)/9/24 Ashikaga Takauji migyōsho, *ibid.*, pp. 377-78.

52. See, e.g., 1349/11/19 Ashikaga Tadafuyu andojō, *Hennen Ōtomo shiryō*, 2: 489, doc. 825; and 1350/11/22 Ashikaga Tadafuyu andojō, *ibid.*, 513, doc. 877.

53. *Uragaki andojō*, confirmation documents with Tadafuyu's consent written on the reverse side of requests for confirmation, were similar to Kamakura period *gedai andojō*, where confirmation was written in the document's margin. The petitions were initiated by individual warriors. See, e.g., 1350/11/15 Ashikaga Tadafuyu andojō, *Dazaifu, Dazaifu Tenmangū shiryō*, 11: 317. For further discussion, see Yamaguchi (Chūsei bukai), "Kannō seihen to Kyūshū," *Kyūshū shigaku*, 43 (1970): 8-13; and Kawazoe Shōji, " 'Chinzei tandai' Ashikaga Tadafuyu–Kyūshū ni okeru Kannō seihen," in Kawazoe, ed., *Kyūshū chūseishi kenkyū*, 2 (Tokyo, 1980): 236-37, n. 26.

54. Seno Seiichirō, "Kyūshū chihō ni okeru Nanbokuchō jidai monjo no sūryōteki bunseki," *Nihon rekishi*, 312 (1974): 78-79.

55. See 1360/3/14 Ashikaga Yoshiakira gohan migyōsho, *Ōita ken shiryō*, ed. Ōita ken kyōiku iinkai, 26 (Beppu, 1974): 200, doc. 301; and 1366/1/23 Ashikaga Yoshiakira gohan migyōsho, *ibid.*, 202-3, doc. 308.

56. 1367/5/4 Go-Kogon tennō rinji an, *KKS*, 3, 1: 513, doc. 4599; Tanabe, "Nanbokuchō zenki Muromachi bakufu," pp. 73 and 77, n. 45.

57. See, e.g., 1368/16/23 Kantō kanrei (Uesugi Noriaki) hōsho, *KKS*, 3, 1: 521, doc. 4620; and 1378/5/26 Kantō kubō (Ashikaga Ujimitsu) migyōsho, *KKS*, 3, 1: 594, doc. 4807.

58. For convenient, recent summaries of these incidents, see *Kanagawa kenshi, tsūshi hen*, ed. Kanagawa ken kenminbu kenshi henshūshitsu (Yokohama, 1981), pp. 791-93.

59. One of the leaders of the Heiikki was Kawagoe Naoshige, former *shugo* of Sagami Province, who had lost his post to a member of the Miura family just at the point when Uesugi Noriaki was called in as *kanrei*. Utsunomiya Ujitsuna lost two *shugo* posts (Kōzuke and Echigo) to Noriaki at the same time. See *Kanagawa kenshi, tsūshi hen*, p. 792; 1354/6/24 Shōgun (Ashikaga Takauji) migyōsho utsushi, *KKS*, 3, 1: 405, doc. 4258; 1354/8/12 Kawagoe Naoshige shigyōjō utsushi, *KKS*, 3, 1: 406-7, doc. 4262; and Shimizu Shōji, "Nanbokuchōki no Utsunomiyashi–Utsunomiya Ujitsuna o chūshin ni," *Shigaku zasshi*, 85.7 (1976): 15-26.

60. The *shugo* posts of the Uesugi clan numbered as many as six in the late 1380's. Shimizu, "Nanbokuchōki no Utsunomiyashi," p. 25; Itō, "Kamakura fu oboegaki," p. 31; *Nihonshi jiten*, p. 1109.

61. Kantō *kanrei* orders to collect province-wide taxes (*munabechisen*) went on one occasion to both, suggesting that they shared control (probably on some geographical basis). 1377/11/17 Kantō kanrei (Uesugi Noriharu) hōsho, *KKS*, 3, 1: 584-85, docs. 4790, 4791.

62. For further details, see *Kanagawa kenshi, tsūshi hen*, pp. 795-97; 1380?/6/1 Kantō kubō (Ashikaga Ujimitsu) migyōsho, *KKS*, 3, 1: 603, docs. 4843-45; and Shimizu, "Nanbokuchōki no Utsunomiyashi," pp. 24-25.

63. See 1382/5/7 Shōgun (Ashikaga Yoshimitsu) migyōsho, *KKS*, 3, 1: 616-17, doc. 4895; and [1382]/5/7 Muromachi bakufu kanrei (Shiba Yoshimasa) soejō, *KKS*, 3, 1: 617, doc. 4896.

64. 1376/9/24 Kantō kanrei (Uesugi Noriharu) hōsho, *KKS*, 3, 1: 576, doc. 4763. During the previous *kubō*'s tenure, the *fu* had merely collected this type of tax for the Bakufu.

65. See 1385/6/1 Kantō fu bugyōnin rensho hōsho, *KKS*, 3, 1: 658, doc. 4988; and 1391/12/25 Kantō kubō (Ashikaga Ujimitsu) migyōsho, *KKS*, 3, 1: 710, doc. 5086. In the first instance the *fu* upheld an exemption already in effect; in 1391 it issued its own exemption. One scholar thus marks the latter date as the earliest exercise of independent authority in this context. See Itō, "Kamakura fu oboegaki," p. 30.

66. Tsuikahō, no. 125, *CHS*, 2: 54, translated in Grossberg and Kanamoto, eds., *Laws of the Muromachi Bakufu*, p. 75. The Gozan Zen temples represent a rare category of affairs for which the Bakufu attempted to formalize a division of authority.

67. Tanabe Hisako makes this point also in "Kamakura fu ni okeru shomu sataken no hensen," *Shiron*, 29 (1975): 5. For an example of the type of administrative directive (usually cosigned) that appears, see 1378/9/6 Kamakura fu bugyōnin rensho hōsho, *KKS*, 3, 1: 596, doc. 4812.

68. See 1392/1/11 Kantō kubō (Ashikaga Ujimitsu) migyōsho, *KKS*, 3, 1: 711, doc. 5089; and 1395/6 Kamada Shigemoto chakutōjō utsushi, *KKS*, 3, 1: 741, doc. 5165.

69. Also called *kubō* and *gosho* because they were members of the Ashikaga family, they were dispatched from Kamakura to Sasagawa and Inamura, respectively. Until the publication of the *Fukushima kenshi* in the late 1960's, Mitsusada was often misidentified as Sasagawa *gosho*, who later sided with the Bakufu against the Kantō *kubō*. This confusion is understandable, in view of the fact that nearly contemporary chronicles diverge on the identification of the two. Watanabe Yosuke resolved the matter in favor of Mitsusada as Sasagawa *gosho*, and his interpretation remained standard until the editors of the *Fukushima kenshi* reversed the identification on the basis of documentary analysis and by comparing signatures (*kaō*). See Watanabe, *Kantō chūshin Ashikaga jidai no kenkyū* (Tokyo, 1971 reprint), pp. 183-85; and *Fukushima kenshi, tsūshi hen*, ed. Fukushima ken (Fukushima, 1969), pp. 713-39.

70. See, e.g., 1397/12/3 Kantō kubō (Ashikaga Ujimitsu) kyojō, *KKS*, 3, 1: 752-53, doc. 5201; and Itō, "Kamakura fu oboegaki," p. 22.

71. Itō has recently challenged this commonly held view, but the evidence seems inconclusive as yet; Itō, "Muromachiki no kokka to Tōgoku," p. 64.

72. See, e.g., 1336/4/13 Ashikaga Tadayoshi gunsei saisokujō an, *NBI*, 1: 183, doc. 575.

73. See, e.g., 1376/7/13 Imagawa Ryōshun shojō, *Imagawa Ryōshun kankei hennen shiryō*, ed. Kawazoe Shōji, 2 vols. (Fukuoka, 1960-61), 1: 105-6, doc. 392; Kawazoe Shōji, *Imagawa Ryōshun* (Tokyo, 1964), p. 92; Toyama Mikio, *Chūsei no Kyūshū* (Tokyo, 1978), p. 144; and Yamaguchi Takamasa, "Nanbokuchōki no Chikugo no kuni shugo ni tsuite," pt. 2, *Nihon rekishi*, 251 (1969): 26-27.

74. 1375?/9/11 Imagawa Ryōshun ukebumi, *Imagawa Ryōshun kankei hennen shiryō,* 1: 90, doc. 330.

75. 1376/8/12 Shōgunke (Ashikaga Yoshimitsu) migyōsho an, *Imagawa Ryōshun kankei hennen shiryō,* 1: 109, doc. 12.

76. 1376?/5/25 Imagawa Ryōshun shojō an, *Imagawa Ryōshun kankei hennen shiryō,* 1: 102, doc. 377, addressed to the *kokujin* of Ōsumi. Probably a similar document was sent to Satsuma warriors.

77. 1377?/12/13 Imagawa Ryōshun shojō an, *Imagawa Ryōshun kankei hennen shiryō,* 1: 125-26, doc. 478.

78. ?/2/18 Imagawa Ryōshun shojō, *Imagawa Ryōshun kankei hennen shiryō,* 1: 115, doc. 436.

79. 1377?/9/14 Imagawa Ryōshun shojō, *Imagawa Ryōshun kankei hennen shiryō,* 1: 122, doc. 467.

80. 1377/10/28 Ikki jinzui keiyakujō an, *Nejime monjo,* ed. Kawazoe Shōji *(Kyūshū shiryō sōsho,* 14), 1 (Fukuoka, 1955): 171-76, doc. 501.

81. Murai Shōsuke, "Imagawa Ryōshun to Kami-Matsura ikki," *Nihon rekishi,* 388 (1976): 29; and 1383/12/11 Imagawa Ryōshun kakikudashi an, *Imagawa Ryōshun kankei hennen shiryō,* 2: 181, doc. 684, cited in *ibid.* As we have seen, the Kantō *kubō* also used *ikki* in this manner, commissioning them as troops to quell local disturbances.

82. In southern Kyushu, for example, Ryōshun was able to exploit anti-Shimazu rivalries by timely alliances with the *kokujin.*

83. Fukuda Toyohiko, "Kokujin ikki no ichi sokumen—Sono jōbu kenryoku to no kankei o chūshin ni," *Shigaku zasshi,* 76.1 (1967): 78.

84. 1373/3/9 Shami soregashi kakikudashi an, *Saga ken shiryō shūsei,* 4: 205-6. Fukuda identified the author of this document as Imagawa Ryōshun; Fukuda, "Kokujin ikki no ichi sokumen," pp. 65, 72.

85. Tsuikahō, no. 56, *CHS,* 2: 29, translated in Grossberg and Kanamoto, eds., *Laws of the Muromachi Bakufu,* p. 48. For a discussion of *hanzei* laws and practices in Kyushu, see Masaki Kisaburō, "Kyūshū ni okeru hanzei no igi—Nanbokuchō nairanki ni okeru," *Kyūshū shigaku,* 44-45 (1971): 2-18.

86. See, e.g., 1375/9/12 Shōgunke (Ashikaga Yoshimitsu) migyōsho an, *Imagawa Ryōshun kankei hennen shiryō,* 1: 90, doc. 331; ?/9/16 Imagawa Ryōshun ukebumi utsushi, *ibid.,* 91, doc. 335; and ?/3/28 Imagawa Ryōshun kyojō, *ibid.,* 79, doc. 292.

87. 1375/8/28 Imagawa Ryōshun kakikudashi, *Imagawa Ryōshun kankei hennen shiryō,* 1: 89, doc. 327; 1374/10/7 Imagawa Ryōshun shojō utsushi, *ibid.,* 68-69, doc. 259; ?/9/11 Imagawa Ryōshun ukebumi, *ibid.,* 90, doc. 330; and 1375/4/5 Imagawa Ryōshun kyojō an, *ibid.,* 79, doc. 294.

88. *Shugo* posts under Ryōshun's control were held at times apparently by family members under him. See the following, all by Yamaguchi Takamasa: "Nanbokuchōki no Buzen no kuni shugo ni tsuite," *Tōkyō daigaku shiryō hensanjo hō,* 13 (1978): 12-13; "Nanbokuchōki no Chikuzen no kuni shugo ni tsuite," *Kokushigaku,* 95 (1975): 25; "Nanbokuchōki no Chikugo no kuni shugo ni tsuite," pt. 2, p. 16; "Nanbokuchōki no Hizen no kuni shugo ni tsuite," pp. 27-37; "Nanbokuchō kōki Imagawa shi no Higo no kuni shihai ni tsuite," *Kadai shigaku,* 19 (1971): 19-21; "Zenki Muromachi

bakufu ni yoru Hyūga no kuni 'ryōkoku' ka," p. 57, n. 17; "Nanbokuchōki no Ōsumi no kuni shugo ni tsuite," pt. 2, *Kyūshū shigaku*, 36 (1966): 14, and pt. 3, *ibid.*, 41 (1967): 14-16; "Nanbokuchōki no Satsuma no kuni shugo ni tsuite," *Shigaku zasshi*, 76.6 (1967): 64-65.

89. Kawazoe, *Imagawa Ryōshun*, pp. 160-69.

90. *Ibid.*, pp. 23-24, 214-15.

91. 1395 Kyōto fushinjōjō kotogaki, *Nejime monjo*, 3: 84-85, doc. 613.

92. Yoshimitsu became Dajōdaijin on 1394/12/17, according to the 1395 directive (*ibid.*).

93. 1376?/8/3 Ashikaga Yoshimitsu naisho an, *Nejime monjo*, 2: 129-30, docs. 435, 436.

94. See also Itō, "Kamakura fu oboegaki," pp. 26-32; Itō, "Muromachiki no kokka to Tōgoku," pp. 65-66; and Tanabe, "Kamakura fu ni okeru shomu sataken no hensen," pp. 5-8.

95. 1398/3/10 Kantō kubō (Ashikaga Ujimitsu) migyōsho, *KKS*, 3, 1: 753, doc. 5203; and 1398/14/28 Kantō kubō migyōsho, *ibid.*, 756, doc. 5210.

96. 1427/5/13 Kantō kanrei (Uesugi Norizane) ke bugyōnin rensho hōsho, *KKS*, 3, 1: 948, doc. 5788.

97. See, e.g., 1417/15/25 Kantō kubō (Ashikaga Mochiuji) shoryō andojō, *KKS*, 3, 1: 873, doc. 5530; and 1428/12/29 Kantō kubō shoryō sōryō shiki andojō, *ibid.*, 956, doc. 5819.

98. See, e.g., Momose Kesao, "Tansen kō," *Nihon shakai keizai shigaku, chūsei hen* (Tokyo, 1967), pp. 1-34; Kuwayama Kōnen, "Muromachi bakufu keizai no kōzō," pp. 210-15; and Peter J. Arnesen, *The Medieval Japanese Daimyo: The Ōuchi's Rule of Suo and Nagato* (New Haven, Conn., 1979), esp. pp. 159-69.

99. 1417/11/27 Kantō kubō (Ashikaga Mochiuji) migyōsho an, *KKS*, 3, 1: 880, doc. 5551; Itō, "Kamakura fu oboegaki," p. 30.

100. 1399/12/29 Saki no shōgun (Ashikaga Yoshimitsu) gonaisho, *KKS*, 3, 1: 771, doc. 5258; and 1400/6/15 Kantō kubō ganmon, *ibid.*, 772-73, doc. 5264.

101. 1400/1/18 Saki no shōgun (Ashikaga Yoshimitsu) gonaisho, *KKS*, 3, 1: 771, doc. 5259. Imagawa was said to have acted as a go-between to link *kubō* Mitsukane to the anti-Yoshimitsu movement.

102. The Zenshū Disturbance has been the focus of many studies. Watanabe Yosuke's treatment of the progression of events remains standard. Readers are referred to his work and to the following for details and differing analyses: Watanabe, *Kantō chūshin Ashikaga jidai*, pp. 217-37; Nagahara Keiji, *Gekokujō no jidai*, Chūō kōron *Nihon no rekishi*, 10 (Tokyo, 1974); Shibatsuji Shunroku, "Uesugi Zenshū no ran to Tōgoku josei," *Rekishi techo*, 5.2 (1977): 12-16; and for the most recent updating of facts and interpretations, *KKS, tsūshi hen*, pp. 825-34.

103. The question of the competition between the rival branches of the Uesugi family is an aspect of Kamakura *fu* history that has been underemphasized. It offers a particularly important perspective from which to analyze not only the shifts in Bakufu-Kamakura *fu* relations, but also the patterns of shifting allegiances within the eastern region.

104. Perhaps the earliest documentary reference to the special Kyoto supporters is in 1423/9/24 Shōgun (Ashikaga Yoshimochi) migyōsho an utsushi, *KKS*, 3, 1: 921, doc. 5687.

105. See, e.g., 1420/7/20 Kantō kubō (Ashikaga Mochiuji) migyōsho, *KKS*, 3, 1: 898, doc. 5619.

106. See, e.g., 1438/8/8 Muromachi bakufu kanrei (Hosokawa Mochiyuki) hōsho an, *KKS*, 3, 1: 992, doc. 5936.

107. In order of service, the first four Shibukawa *tandai* were Mitsuyori, Yoshitoshi, Mitsunao, and Norinao.

108. Kawazoe Shōji, "Kyūshū tandai no suimetsu katei," *Kyūshū bunkashi kenkyūjo kiyō*, 23 (1978): 106-8.

109. Kawazoe Shōji, "Kyūshū tandai to Nissen kōshō," in *Sainan chiikishi kenkyū*, ed. Sainan chiikishi kenkyūkai, 1 (Tokyo, 1977): 3.

110. Kawazoe Shōji, "Shibukawa Mitsuyori no Hakata shihai oyobi Chikuzen, Hizen keiei," in *Zoku shōensei to buke shakai*, ed. Takeuchi Rizō hakushi koki kinenkai (Tokyo, 1978), pp. 344-45.

111. See, e.g., 1404/1 Shibukawa Mitsuyori shojō, *Saga ken shiryō shūsei*, 4: 316-17, doc. 100; and 1412/11/21 Fukabori Tokizumi Hakata banyaku kinshi chūshinjō, *ibid.*, 234, doc. 371.

112. Kawazoe, "Kyūshū tandai to Nissen kōshō," p. 29.

113. ?/7/2 Shibukawa Mitsunao shojō, *DNK*, 13: *Aso monjo*, 1 (Tokyo, 1979): 698, doc. 257; and Yanagida Kaimei, "Muromachi bakufu kenryoku no kita Kyūshū shihai—jūgo seiki zenpan no Chikuzen no kuni o chūshin ni," *Kyūshū shigaku* (1976), p. 42.

114. 1438/9/10 Ashikaga Yoshinori sodehan gonaisho utsushi, *Asō monjo* (*Kyūshū shiryō sōsho*, 39), ed. Kyūshū shiryō kankōkai (Fukuoka, 1966), p. 19, doc. 43, cited in Yanagida, "Muromachi bakufu kenryoku no kita Kyūshū shihai," p. 50.

115. Yanagida, "Muromachi bakufu kenryoku no kita Kyūshū shihai," pp. 37-38.

116. In a Korean document of 1455/7, for example, the Kyushu *tandai* Shibukawa Norinao was described as a member of the king's (shogun's) family who not only headed the Kyushu army but was the conduit for shogunal communiqués and generally divided control of Japan, west and east, with the "Kamakura dono" (Kantō *kubō*). The passage is quoted and discussed in Kawazoe, "Kyūshū tandai no suimetsu katei," p. 111.

Arnesen, *"The Provincial Vassals of the Muromachi Shoguns"*

1. For convenient treatments of the points raised in this paragraph, see Ogawa Makoto, "Nanbokuchō nairan," in *IKNR* 6, *chūsei* 2 (3d ser., 1975): 86-101, 108-9; Haga Norihiko, "Muromachi bakufu samurai dokoro kō," *Hakusan shigaku*, 10 (1964), and *Chūsei no mado*, 13 (1963), as reprinted in *Muromachi seiken*, ed. Ogawa Makoto (*Ronshū Nihon rekishi*, 5; Tokyo, 1975): 39-40; Tanuma Mutsumi, "Muromachi bakufu, shugo, kokujin," *IKNR* 7, *chūsei* 3 (3d ser., 1976): 22-26; and Peter J. Arnesen, *Medieval Japanese Daimyo: The Ōuchi Family's Rule of Suō and Nagato* (New Haven, Conn., 1979), pp. 93–115.

2. See, e.g., Satō Shin'ichi, *Bakufu ron* (*Shin Nihonshi kōza*, 33; Tokyo, 1949).

3. Arnesen, *Daimyo*, chap. 5.

4. Kuwayama Kōnen, "Muromachi bakufu keizai no kōzō," in *Nihon keizaishi taikei 2, chūsei*, ed. Nagahara Keiji (Tokyo, 1965): 215-17, citing Tsuikahō, nos. 43, 45, *CHS*, 2: 24-25, and *DNK*, 12: *Uesugi ke monjo* (Tokyo, 1931), 1: 206-10. Kuwayama's thesis is also corroborated by a document in Kishida Hiroshi, "Shugo Yamana-shi no Bingo-no-kuni shihai no tenkai to chigyōsei," in *Nihon chūseishi ronshū*, ed. Fukuo kyōju taikan kinen jigyōkai (Tokyo, 1972), pp. 120-21 (where one must, however, reinterpret the meaning of the term *ōban*); and by Tsuikahō, no. 491, *CHS*, 2: 142-43.

5. The imposts of a fiftieth and a twentieth are known to us from a long-familiar passage in the *Hosokawa Yoriyuki ki*, but Kuwayama was the first to argue that these imposts were levied against the *gokenin* (see "Muromachi bakufu keizai," pp. 215-16). This hypothesis has since been strengthened by Kishida, "Shugo Yamana-shi," pp. 120-24, and Tanuma, "Muromachi bakufu, shugo, kokujin," pp. 21-22; and the old interpretation of the *Yoriyuki ki* passage reflected in H. Paul Varley's *The Ōnin War* (New York, 1967), p. 51, must now be rejected.

6. Kishida, "Shugo Yamana-shi," pp. 116-24; and Kishida, "Muromachi bakufu taisei no kōzō: Shu to shite tōkaku jidai fuka-futan kankei wo tōshite mita," in *Nihonshi wo manabu 2, chūsei*, ed. Nagahara Keiji (Tokyo, 1975): 178.

7. Satō Shin'ichi, "Muromachi bakufu ron," in *IKNR 7, chūsei 3* (2d ser., 1963): 40-41; *DNK, 9: Kikkawa ke monjo* (Tokyo, 1923-25), 2: 210-11, doc. 1041; Sankō shiryō, no. 35, *CHS*, 2: 168.

8. Tsuikahō, nos. 152, 195, *CHS*, 2: 61-62, 70-71; cited in Satō, "Muromachi bakufu ron," p. 41.

9. Tsuikahō, nos. 491-92, *CHS*, 2: 142-43; see also *DNK, 12: Uesugi ke monjo*, 1: 206-10, docs. 203-8.

10. Kuwayama, "Muromachi bakufu keizai," pp. 217-18.

11. *DNK, 9: Kikkawa ke monjo*, 1: 253-54, doc. 298; and Tsuikahō, no. 491, *CHS*, 2: 142-43.

12. The outstanding treatments are Satō, "Muromachi bakufu ron," pp. 20-25; Fukuda Toyohiko, "Muromachi bakufu no 'hōkōshū': Gobanchō no sakusei nendai wo chūshin to shite," *Nihon rekishi*, 274 (1971): 46-65; and Fukuda, "Muromachi bakufu 'hōkōshū' no kenkyū: Sono jin'in kōsei to chiiki-teki bunpu," *Hokkaidō-Musashi joshi tanki daigaku kiyō*, 3 (1971), as reprinted in *Muromachi seiken*, pp. 220-49.

13. These are contained in (1) *Bun'an nenchū gobanchō*, (2) *Eikyō irai gobanchō*, and (3) *Chōkyō gannen kugatsu jūninichi Jōtokuin-tonosama Kōshū godōza tōji zaichin-shū chakutō*, in *Gunsho ruijū*, ed. Hanawa Hokinoichi, 39 vols. (Tokyo, 1929-34), 29: 156-74, 181-90. Fukuda has dated these (in "Muromachi bakufu no 'hōkōshū,' " pp. 47-54) to 1444-49, 1450-55, and 1487-89, respectively.

14. I am here following Gomi Fumihiko's modifications of the categories set forth by Fukuda in "Muromachi bakufu 'hōkōshū' no kenkyū," pp. 221-

31. For details, see Gomi Fumihiko, "Zaikyōjin to sono ichi," *Shigaku zasshi*, 83.8 (1974): 1-5.

15. See the table of guardsmen in Fukuda, "Muromachi bakufu 'hōkō-shū' no kenkyū," and Fukuda's accompanying discussion.

16. Fukuda, "Muromachi bakufu no 'hōkōshū,' " pp. 55-56; and Fukuda, "Muromachi bakufu 'hōkōshū' no kenkyū," pp. 221-24 and 235, n. 16.

17. Fukuda, "Muromachi bakufu 'hōkōshū' no kenkyū," pp. 231-33, as corrected by Kawazoe Shōji's discussion of the Asō family in his "Muromachi bakufu 'hōkōshū' Chikuzen-no-kuni Asō-shi ni tsuite," *Kyūshū shigaku*, 57 (1975): 1-33.

18. Fukuda, "Muromachi bakufu 'hōkōshū' no kenkyū," pp. 232-33. On the Bakufu's delegation of control over Kyushu and the Kantō, see the paper by Lorraine F. Harrington in this volume.

19. This point emerges from a Nejime family document quoted in *CHS*, 2: 191-93. Note that my own interpretation differs somewhat from that offered in Satō, "Muromachi bakufu ron," pp. 21-23.

20. Tsuikahō, nos. 43, 112, *CHS*, 2: 24-25, 48-49.

21. *CHS*, 2: 191-92.

22. *Ibid.*, pp. 192-93.

23. Miura Hiroyuki, "Ashikaga jidai ni okeru jōryū bushi no kōshi sei-katsu: Ōdate Mochifusa gyōjō no kenkyū," *Shirin*, 16.1 (1931): 32-34; Satō, "Muromachi bakufu ron," pp. 22-23; Gomi, "Zaikyōjin," p. 17; and Kawai Masaharu, *Chūsei buke shakai no kenkyū* (Tokyo, 1973), pp. 247-48. Note that Gomi's emendations vitiate Fukuda's criticism of Satō in "Muromachi bakufu no 'hōkōshū,' " pp. 62-63, n. 24.

24. Gomi, "Zaikyōjin," pp. 17-20. However, this analysis must be read against that in Fukuda Toyohiko and Satō Ken'ichi, "Muromachi bakufu shōgun kenryoku ni kansuru ichi kōsatsu: Shōgun kinjū wo chūsin to shite," *Nihon rekishi*, 228 (1967): 37-53, and 229 (1967): 48-56.

25. *CHS*, 2: 192.

26. I am thus largely in agreement with Satō, "Muromachi bakufu ron," pp. 21-23, though I do not share his belief in the existence of a *zaikoku hōkōshū* (provincial shogunal guard).

27. *Ibid.*, pp. 20-25.

28. See Kishida Hiroshi's discussion of the Kyōgoku in "Shugo shihai no tenkai to chigyōsei no henshitsu," *Shigaku zasshi*, 82.11 (1973): 6-11.

29. Kawai Masaharu, "Kobayakawa shi no hatten to Seto Naikai: Saigoku daimyō no keisei," in *Seto Naikai chiiki no shakaishi-teki kenkyū*, ed. Uozumi Sōgorō (Kyoto, 1952), as revised and reissued in Kawai's *Chūsei buke shakai no kenkyū*, pp. 361-62.

30. *DNK, 11: Kobayakawa ke monjo* (Tokyo, 1927), 1: 90-99, doc. 115; Kawai, "Kobayakawa shi no hatten," pp. 362-63. Nuta seems to have consisted of three sections at the beginning of the Kamakura period—Ajika, Honjō, and Shinjō. Shigehira received the first two of these in 1206, and his brother received the third in 1213.

31. *DNK, 11: Kobayakawa ke monjo*, 1: 90-99, doc. 115; 543-56, docs. 1-3, 5-7.

32. *Ibid.*, 1: 90-99, doc. 115; 547-48, doc. 4.

33. Ishii Susumu, *Chūsei bushidan (Nihon no rekishi*, 12; Tokyo, 1974), pp. 264-66.

34. Shigehira's *zaikyōjin* status emerges from *DNK*, 11: *Kobayakawa ke monjo*, 1: 583, doc. 12. On the *zaikyōjin* and the *kagariya-bushi*, see Gomi, "Zaikyōjin"; and *Kyōto no rekishi 2, chūsei no meian*, ed. Kyōto shi (Kyōto, 1971), pp. 421-27.

35. *Tsunetoshi-kyō ki*, 1257/5/11, in *Hiroshima kenshi, kodai-chūsei shiryō hen*, ed. Hiroshima ken, 5 vols. (Hiroshima, 1974-80), 1: 441 (cited in Gomi, "Zaikyōjin," p. 6); and Shinshutsu Itsukushima monjo, no. 112, *Hiroshima kenshi*, 3: 354.

36. *DNK, 11: Kobayakawa ke monjo*, 1: 35-37, 90-99, docs. 52-53, 115. The partitioning of property and family were actually even more involved than this, and the main branches had not yet assumed the names I give them above, but these complexities need not concern us here.

37. *Ibid.*, 1: 18, 37-39, 583, docs. 29, 54, 55, 12, and 2: 160-63, doc. 285; *Kanchū ki*, 1280/5/9, *Hiroshima kenshi*, 1: 453-54 (cited in Gomi, "Zaikyōjin," p. 6); and *Kanazawa bunko komonjo*, 1: 348 (so cited in Gomi, "Zaikyōjin," p. 6, but unavailable to me).

38. *DNK, 11: Kobayakawa ke monjo*, 1: 1-2, 41, docs. 2, 58, and 2: 191-92, doc. 337. On the *zaikyōjin*'s treason, see Gomi, "Zaikyōjin."

39. *DNK, 11: Kobayakawa ke monjo*, 2: 160-65, docs. 285-86.

40. Gomi, "Zaikyōjin."

41. *DNK, 11: Kobayakawa ke monjo*, 2: 168-71, doc. 294.

42. *Baishōron*, as quoted in *Hiroshima kenshi*, 1: 483; *DNK, 11: Kobayakawa ke monjo*, 2: 165-66, doc. 288.

43. See *DNK, 11: Kobayakawa ke monjo*, 1: 42, 591, 593, and 2: 166-68, 172, 174-76, 278-80, 321-29, 514-21 (Kobayakawa ke monjo, doc. 59, Kobayakawa ke shōmon, docs. 24, 27, 289, 292, 298, 302, 304, 305, 307, 435, 438, 516-24, 526-33, and Kikkawa Kachū narabi ni jisha monjo, docs. 14-20, 22-24) and the Guard Registers cited in note 13 above.

44. Haga, "Muromachi bakufu samurai dokoro kō," pp. 25-55.

45. The single document is *DNK, 11: Kobayakawa ke monjo*, 2: 122, doc. 225.

46. *DNK, 11: Kobayakawa ke monjo*, 1: 20, 30, docs. 32, 33, 47; and 2: 99-100, 125, docs. 218, 229.

47. *Ibid.*, 1: 24-25, doc. 39; and 2: 27-28, 40-41, 43, 190, 336, docs. 103, 104, 120, 121, 126, 355, 545.

48. *Ibid.*, 1: 82-83, 86, docs. 108, 110; and 2: 45, 46, 75, docs. 129, 130, 180. See also Kawai, *Chūsei buke shakai no kenkyū*, pp. 253-55.

49. Tsuikahō, nos. 43, 112, *CHS*, 2: 24-25, 58-59. See also *DNK, 11: Kobayakawa ke monjo*, 2: 18-19, 202, docs. 91, 352.

50. Tsuikahō, no. 266, *CHS*, 2: 92-93.

51. *DNK, 11: Kobayakawa ke monjo*, 2: 18-19, doc. 91.

52. While the Kobayakawa evidence on this point is fairly obscure, that relating to the Mōri and Masuda is quite clear; see Kishida Hiroshi, "Nanbokuchō-Muromachi ki zaichi ryōshu no sō-sho kankei: Shoshi bunryō zuden tansen no chōshū keitai wo tōshite mita," in *Shigaku kenkyū gojū shū-*

nen kinen ronsō, Nihon hen, ed. Hiroshima shigaku kenkyūkai (Okayama, 1980), pp. 155-79. See the treatment of the Mōri below.

53. *Hiroshima kenshi,* 4: 340, doc. 17, as cited and discussed in Kishida, "Shugo shihai," pp. 20-22.

54. See the sources cited in notes 47 and 48 above.

55. See *DNK, 11: Kobayakawa ke monjo,* 1: 70-77, 89-99, docs. 93-102, 113-15.

56. *Ibid.,* 1: 82-83, doc. 108.

57. *Ibid.,* 1: 9-13, 21-23, 61-63, 78-81, 83-85, and 2: 2-4, 12, 14, 16-17, 198-201, 290-91 (Kobayakawa ke monjo, docs. 15-21, 34-37, 81-82, 104-6, 109, and Kobayakawa ke shōmon, docs. 58, 60-61, 75, 80, 86-88, 351, 460.

58. See the sources cited in note 47 above, and *DNK, 11: Kobayakawa ke monjo,* 2: 55-56, doc. 143.

59. *DNK, 11: Kobayakawa ke monjo,* 1: 23, 61-62, docs. 37, 81; and 2: 29-37, 198-201, docs. 106-15, 351.

60. The Ōuchi's position in Aki is discussed in Matsuoka Hisato, "Ōuchi-shi no Aki-no-kuni shihai," *Hiroshima Daigaku Bungaku-bu kiyō,* 25.1 (1965): 67-87. The Takehara's early link with the Ōuchi is revealed by the fact that Takehara Hirokage, who was head of the family by 1398, wrote his name with characters that indicate he must have been the "godson" (*eboshi-ko*) of Ōuchi Yoshihiro.

61. *DNK, 11: Kobayakawa ke monjo,* 1: 51-54, 58-61, 64-66, docs. 72-75, 78-80, 84-86; and 2: 181-82, doc. 317.

62. The events of the 1457 war must be pieced together from *DNK, 8: Mōri ke monjo* (Tokyo, 1920-24), 1: 90-91, 97-99, docs. 87, 88, 97; and *DNK, 9: Kikkawa ke monjo,* 1: 27-28, 35, docs. 45-46, 56. On Hirohira's 1461 mission, see *DNK, 11: Kobayakawa ke monjo,* 2: 41-42, 45, docs. 123, 129.

63. *DNK, 8: Mōri ke monjo,* 1: 95-96, 100-101, 138-39, docs. 93-95, 101, 118, 157, and 4: 255, doc. 1342; *DNK, 9: Kikkawa ke monjo,* 1: 29, 263, 266, 286-87, docs. 47, 48, 310, 313, 316; and *DNK, 11: Kobayakawa ke monjo,* 2: 51-55, docs. 136-41.

64. *DNK, 11: Kobayakawa ke monjo,* 2: 46-47, docs. 131-32.

65. I suspect that Kobayakawa ke shōmon, doc. 134 (*ibid.,* 2: 48), reflects a 1460 attack by the Takehara on the Ōuchi's enemies in Aki, but I cannot yet prove it.

66. *DNK, 11: Kobayakawa ke monjo,* 1: 6, 28-29, 63, 67-68, 102, docs. 10, 44-46, 83, 88-90, 119; and 2: 55-75, 79-94, 216-28, 230-34, 574-75, docs. 143-47, 150, 151, 153-57, 159-63, 166-79, 188, 189, 191, 193, 194, 196-210, 376-89, 392, 394-97, 591.

67. The careers of Ōe Hiromoto's sons may be traced in the *Azuma kagami* passages cited in *(Zendoku) Azuma kagami,* 6 vols., ed. Kishi Shōzō and Nagahara Keiji (Tokyo, 1976-79), 6: 152, 192, 214, 238.

68. *AK,* 1221/5/19, 1221/5/21, 1221/6/12, 1221/6/14, 1233/11/3, 1236/11/22, 1239/11/2.

69. *AK,* 1247/6/4, 1247/6/5, 1247/6/11, 1247/6/22.

70. *DNK, 8: Mōri ke monjo,* 1: 2, 18-34, docs. 2, 15.

71. On the Nagai, see Koizumi Yoshiaki, "Gokenin Nagai-shi ni tsuite,"

in *Kokiroku no kenkyū*, ed. Takahashi Ryūzō Sensei shuki kinenshū kankō-kai (Tokyo, 1970), pp. 707-65; and Satō Shin'ichi, *(Zōtei) Kamakura bakufu shugo seido no kenkyū* (Tokyo, 1971), pp. 168-70. Nawa Masamochi's career emerges from the *Kantō Hyōjōshū den*, in *Gunsho ruijū*, 4: 302-10.

72. *Keizu sanyō*, 18 vols. (Tokyo, 1973-77), 13: 156.

73. *DNK, 8: Mōri ke monjo*, 1: 8-16, 18-34, docs. 13, 15.

74. This can be deduced from the fact that Chikahira's eldest son was born in 1323 to a woman whose family's lands lay near the Mōri's own holdings in Yoshida; *ibid.*, 1: 18-34, doc. 15.

75. *Ibid.*

76. *Ibid.*

77. Satō Shin'ichi, "Muromachi bakufu kaisōki no kansei taikei," in *Chūsei no hō to kokka*, ed. Ishimoda Shō and Satō Shin'ichi (Tokyo, 1960), pp. 453-86. I am here assuming that Nagai Kunai-no-gon-no-taifu and Nagai Chibu-no-shō, whom Satō leaves unidentified, are the Nagai Tokikazu and Nagai Tokiharu who are so designated in *Sonpi bunmyaku*, 4 vols. (*Kokushi taikei*, 58-60.2; Tokyo, 1957-62), 4: 101. On the other individuals referred to above, see *Sonpi bunmyaku*, 4: 97-107.

78. *DNK, 8: Mōri ke monjo*, 1: 18-34, doc. 15.

79. There are Mōri listed in the 1444-49 and 1450-55 guard registers, but they were clearly not members of the Aki Mōri.

80. *Kannō ninen hinami ki*, 1351/7/30, *Zoku gunsho ruijū*, 29.2, ed. Hanawa Hokinoichi (Tokyo, 1903), pp. 371-72.

81. *DNK, 8: Mōri ke monjo*, 1: 18-35, docs. 15, 17; *DNK, 9: Kikkawa ke monjo*, 1: 18-19, doc. 30, and 2: 220-23, 321-23, docs. 1052, 1053, 1159; *DNK, 11: Kobayakawa ke monjo*, 2: 357-58, doc. 570; *Taiheiki* 28, as quoted in *Hiroshima kenshi*, 1: 504-5.

82. See *Hagi han batsuetsuroku, 58: Naitō Jirōzaemon*, doc. 77, in *Hagi han batsuetsuroku*, ed. Yamaguchi ken monjokan, 4 vols. (Yamaguchi, 1967), 2: 433. All citations of the *Hagi han batsuetsuroku* will be to document numbers and pages of this Yamaguchi ken monjokan edition.

83. *DNK, 8: Mōri ke monjo*, 1: 3-16, 18-34, docs. 5, 7-13, 15.

84. *Keizu sanyō*, 13: 157-59; and *DNK, 8: Mōri ke monjo*, 1: 37-38, 58-59, docs. 19-21, 46.

85. *DNK, 8: Mōri ke monjo*, 4: 248-52, docs. 1331-36; and *Hagi han batsuetsuroku, 8: Fukuhara Tsushima*, 1: 157, doc. 57.

86. *DNK, 8: Mōri ke monjo*, 1: 63-64, 100, docs. 54, 100.

87. *Ibid.*, 1: 61-68, 70-71, 73, 84-87, 94-96, 100-108, 111-14, docs. 49-52, 55-57, 60, 62, 66, 69, 79, 81, 82, 94, 95, 101, 103-11, 113-16, 118, 119; and 4: 260-62, docs. 1353-56.

88. Kobayashi Hiroshi, "Muromachi jidai no shugo funyūken ni tsuite," *Hokudai shigaku*, 11 (1966), as reprinted in *Muromachi seiken*, pp. 197-219.

89. *DNK, 8: Mōri ke monjo*, 1: 74-76, docs. 71-72; *Hiroshima kenshi*, 5: 199-200, doc. 17. Cited and discussed in Kishida, "Nanbokuchō-Muromachi ki zaichi ryōshu," pp. 156-60.

90. *DNK, 8: Mōri ke monjo*, 1: 86-88, 106-7, 111-14, 121-22, docs. 82-84, 112, 119, 131.

91. *Ibid.*, 1: 111-14, doc. 119.

92. *Ibid.*, 1: 69-70, doc. 65, as discussed in Kishida, "Shugo shihai," pp. 14-19.

93. See the sources cited in note 90 above, and *Hagi han batsuetsuroku, 8: Fukuhara Tsushima*, 1: 138-39, docs. 2-4.

94. Cf. *DNK, 8: Mōri ke monjo*, 59-60, 74-76, docs. 47, 72.

95. *Ibid.*, 1: 86-87, doc. 82.

96. *Ibid.*, 1: 87-88, docs. 83-84.

97. *Ibid.*, 1: 106-7, 111-14, 121-22, docs. 112, 119, 131, and 4: 252-53, doc. 1338; *Hiroshima kenshi*, 5: 538, doc. 65.

98. *Ibid.*; *DNK, 8: Mōri ke monjo*, 1: 126, doc. 138; *Gunsho ruijū*, 29: 186.

99. *DNK, 8: Mōri ke monjo*, 1: 119-20, 128-35, docs. 127-29, 141-45, 149, 150.

100. *AK*, 1200/1/20, 1200/1/23, 1200/1/25; *Kikkawa ke keifu*, in *Gunsho keizu-bu shū*, ed. Hanawa Hokinoichi, 7 vols. (Tokyo, 1973), 5: 280; *DNK, 9: Kikkawa ke monjo*, 1: 1-2, doc. 1, and 2: 163-64, doc. 989.

101. *AK*, 1221/6/14; *Kikkawa ke keifu*, in *Gunsho keizu-bu shū*, 5: 280-81; *DNK, 9: Kikkawa ke monjo*, 1: 2, doc. 2, and 2: 210-11, doc. 1041.

102. Although there are a number of genealogies purporting to show how the Kikkawa family headship was transmitted, none is really credible.

103. On Ryōkai's inheritance, see *DNK, 9: Kikkawa ke monjo*, 2: 276-95, docs. 1120-31.

104. *Ibid.*, 1: 15-16, doc. 27, and 2: 176-77, 179-83, 185-87, 203-4, 229-45, docs. 1001, 1005-7, 1013, 1014, 1034, 1057-74, 1077.

105. *Ibid.*, 1: 18-19, 195-96, 198-99, docs. 30, 31, 219, 220, 224, 226, and 2: 179, 183-85, 187-92, 245, 298-300, docs. 1004, 1008-12, 1015-23, 1078, 1134-36. The original Tokugawa-period compiler of these documents mistakenly labeled a number of them as pertaining to Kikkawa Tsuneaki, but it is clear that they in fact pertain to Tsunekane. On the Masuda, see Matsuoka Hisato, "Nanbokuchō-Muromachi ki Iwami-no-kuni to Ōuchi-shi," *Hiroshima daigaku bungaku-bu kiyō (Tōyō)*, 32.1 (1973): 2.

106. *DNK, 9: Kikkawa ke monjo*, 1: 22, 196-97, 199-201, 206, docs. 35, 221-23, 227, 228, 235. Again, the original compiler mislabeled a number of these documents.

107. *Ibid.*, 1: 22-23, 209-13, 216-18, docs. 36, 241-47, 254-56. Kobayashi Hiroshi's heroic attempt to sort all this out is not very convincing; see his "Nanbokuchō-Muromachi ki ni okeru Aki-no-kuni Kikkawa-shi no dōkō ni tsuite: Muromachi bakufu no gokenin-sei," *Hokudai shigaku*, 13 (1971): 26-29.

108. *DNK, 9: Kikkawa ke monjo*, 1: 26, 213-15, docs. 42, 249-51.

109. *Ibid.*, 1: 23-27, 29, 215, 222-34, 266, 277-78, 286-87, docs. 37-41, 43, 44, 47, 48, 251, 260, 262-74, 313, 325, 326, 336.

110. *Ibid.*, 1: 240-41, doc. 283.

111. *Ibid.*, 1: 239-40, 254-55, docs. 282, 299, 300; and 3: 6, doc. 7. See also Kishida, "Shugo shihai," pp. 22-23.

112. *DNK, 9: Kikkawa ke monjo*, 1: 244-47, docs. 286-88; *Keizu sanyō*, 2: 374.

113. *DNK, 9: Kikkawa ke monjo*, 1: 244-47, docs. 286-88.

114. *DNK, 9: Kikkawa ke monjo*, 1: 232-33, doc. 272.

115. *Ibid.*, 1: 233-34, docs. 274, 275.

116. *Hagi han batsuetsuroku, 126: Watanuki Sahyōe,* 3: 700, docs. 12, 13; *ibid., 121: Sufu Kichihyōe,* 3: 564, doc. 119; *DNK, 9: Kikkawa ke monjo,* 1: 236-39, docs. 279-81.

117. *DNK, 9: Kikkawa ke monjo,* 1: 39, 288-91, docs. 63, 337-40; and 2: 578-80, docs. 1354, 1355.

118. The land grants appear in *ibid.*, 1: 250, 252-53, docs. 292, 296.

119. *Ibid.*, 1: 294-95, doc. 342; and 2: 271-73, docs. 1116, 1117.

120. *Ibid.*, 1: 32-34, 255-62, 267-69, 271-72, 280-84, 295-98, docs. 54, 55, 301-9, 315-17, 319, 328-33, 343-45; and 2: 575-78, docs. 1352-53.

121. Kuroda Toshio, "Chūsei no kokka to tennō," in *IKNR 6, chūsei 2* (2d ser., 1962): 261-301.

122. See Jeffrey P. Mass, *The Development of Kamakura Rule, 1180-1250: A History with Documents* (Stanford, Calif., 1979), chaps. 4, 5.

123. Gomi Yoshio, "Kamakura gokenin no ban'yaku kinshi ni tsuite," *Shigaku zasshi,* 63.9-10 (1954), as reprinted in *Kamakura seiken,* ed. Kurokawa Takaaki and Kitazume Masao, *Ronshū Nihon rekishi,* 4 (Tokyo, 1976), p. 179.

124. I therefore cannot agree with Suzanne Gay's characterization of the Muromachi shogunate as but one of a constellation of *kenmon seika* (see Chapter 3 above).

125. Indeed, Satō has argued (in "Muromachi bakufu ron," pp. 12-15) that there was only very limited recruitment of new warriors into *gokenin* ranks.

126. We have seen in the case of the Kobayakawa, for example, that the Nuta's service as envoys and in ceremonial archery contests was paid for by the Nuta's kinsmen, rather than by the Bakufu.

127. See Matsuoka Hisato with Peter J. Arnesen, "The Sengoku Daimyo of Western Japan: The Case of the Ōuchi," in John W. Hall, Nagahara Keiji, and Kozo Yamamura, eds., *Japan Before Tokugawa: Political Consolidation and Economic Growth, 1500-1650* (Princeton, N.J., 1981), p. 90; and Nagahara Keiji with Kozo Yamamura, "The Sengoku Daimyo and the Kandaka System," in *ibid.,* p. 50.

128. See, e.g., Miyagawa Mitsuru with Cornelius J. Kiley, "From Shōen to Chigyō: Proprietary Lordship and the Structure of Local Power," in John W. Hall and Toyoda Takeshi, eds., *Japan in the Muromachi Age* (Berkeley, Calif., 1977), pp. 89-105.

Susser, "The Toyotomi Regime and the Daimyo"

This paper is based on research conducted in Japan during 1967-69. I am grateful to Miyagawa Mitsuru, Asao Naohiro, Matsuo Hisashi, Takagi Shosaku, and the many other scholars, students, librarians, and others who were so generous in giving me help; my thanks also to John Whitney Hall and William B. Hauser for their encouragement.

1. Thomas Uyttenbroeck, O.F.M., *Early Franciscans in Japan* (Himeji, 1959), pp. 7-8; see also Michael Cooper, *They Came to Japan* (Berkeley, Calif., 1965), p. 111.

2. John W. Hall, *Government and Local Power in Japan, 500 to 1700: A Study Based on Bizen Province* (Princeton, N.J., 1966), p. 247. See also John W. Hall, "Foundations of the Modern Japanese Daimyo," in Hall and Marius B. Jansen, eds., *Studies in the Institutional History of Early Modern Japan* (Princeton, N.J., 1968), pp. 69ff; Matsuoka Hisato with Peter J. Arnesen, "The Sengoku Daimyo of Western Japan," in John W. Hall, Nagahara Keiji, and Kozo Yamamura, eds., *Japan Before Tokugawa: Political Consolidation and Economic Growth, 1500-1650* (Princeton, N.J., 1981), pp. 64-100; Peter J. Arnesen, *The Medieval Japanese Daimyo* (New Haven, Conn., 1979); Bernard Susser, "The Cadastral Surveys of the *Sengoku Daimyō*," *Baika tanki daigaku kenkyū kiyō*, 26 (1977): 35-36.

3. Fujiki Hisashi with George Elison, "The Political Posture of Oda Nobunaga," in Hall et al., eds., *Japan Before Tokugawa*, pp. 149-93, quotations from pp. 186 and 188; Bernard Susser, "The Policies of the Oda Regime," *Baika tanki daigaku kenkyū kiyō*, 28 (1979): 1-16.

4. Letter of Ogasawara Sadayoshi, 1590/8/3, cited in Kawata Sadao, "Tokugawa Ieyasu no Kantō tenpu ni kansuru shomondai," *Shoryōbu kiyō*, 14 (1962): 76.

5. In developing the thesis stated here I have relied heavily on the work of Japanese historians, though to my knowledge no Japanese scholar has stated this thesis so explicitly. Recently, a number of important works dealing with the Toyotomi period have appeared in English. They include Adriana Boscaro's translation of Hideyoshi's private correspondence, *101 Letters of Hideyoshi* (Tokyo, 1975); Beatrice M. Bodart's "Tea and Counsel: The Political Role of Sen Rikyū," *Monumenta Nipponica*, 32.1 (1977): 49-74; several essays in Hall et al., eds., *Japan Before Tokugawa*; George Elison's articles in Elison and Bardwell L. Smith, eds., *Warlords, Artists, and Commoners* (Honolulu, 1981); Wakita Osamu's "The Emergence of the State in Sixteenth-Century Japan," *Journal of Japanese Studies*, 8.2 (1982): 343-67; my study "The Structure of the Toyotomi Regime," *Baika tanki daigaku kenkyū kiyō*, 31 (1982): 1-23; and Mary Elizabeth Berry's *Hideyoshi* (Cambridge, Mass., 1982), the first modern book-length treatment of this period in English.

Three of the studies listed above deal with subjects discussed in the present article. John W. Hall's "Hideyoshi's Domestic Policies" displays the author's continuing interest in the question of legitimacy. Concerning the relationship between the Toyotomi regime and the daimyo, Hall stresses that "the daimyo had to give away some of his potential autonomy in order to safeguard his own authority within his domain. For the daimyo under Hideyoshi, ultimate legitimation and protection came from the investiture they received from him." (*Japan Before Tokugawa*, p. 203.) Hall is well aware of the role Hideyoshi's policies played in the formation of daimyo domains, but his article surveys the main issues without analyzing specific policies in detail or citing the evidence for his conclusions.

George Elison's "Hideyoshi, the Bountiful Minister" is also concerned with the question of legitimacy, in particular Hideyoshi's efforts to gain legitimacy for himself. Elison makes extensive use of contemporary chronicles to document Hideyoshi's relationships with the Bakufu and court but has little to say about the regime's policies toward the daimyo.

Mary Elizabeth Berry's *Hideyoshi*, though welcome as the first modern full-length study of this period, is in many ways a disappointment. It is based on very few primary sources and neglects a large number of important secondary works. As a biography, it lacks character analysis and psychological insight; as a study of the Toyotomi regime, it lacks details on finances, military organization, and other vital subjects. Concerning the effect of Hideyoshi's policies on the daimyo, Berry states that "in conviction as in disposition, Hideyoshi shared the daimyo's perception of the importance of the domain" (p. 165; see also pp. 101, 161). For Berry, Hideyoshi's concern for the "survival of the domains" is a "conservative" policy (p. 164; see also pp. 5, 161, 166). She ignores the consensus of Japanese and Western scholarship, which emphasizes the fragility of Sengoku daimyo authority, and instead portrays the Sengoku domain as a "strong and independent unit of government," a "constant of the warring-states world" that Hideyoshi "preserved" (pp. 34, 126; see also pp. 121, 151, 159, 169). She attributes Hideyoshi's "curious" decision to retain the daimyo domains to his friendship with and admiration for many daimyo (p. 166; pp. 162-63). She does mention the effect the Toyotomi policies had in stabilizing daimyo domains (pp. 105, 110, 129, 154), but she makes little effort to analyze it in detail or offer evidence supporting her assertions.

The thesis presented in this article must be considered tentative until all the extant documents are collected, edited, and published. As Berry points out, there is no collection of Hideyoshi's papers comparable to the magnificent editions of Nobunaga's documents by Okuno Takahiro and Ieyasu's papers by Nakamura Kōya. The most complete edition of Toyotomi documents is still *Hōkō ibun*, ed. Kusaka Hiroshi (Tokyo, 1914). Consequently, the evidence cited here is drawn from diverse published materials; some documents are quoted from secondary monographs. In each case I have provided the date of the document so that the references will be useful when a standard edition of the Toyotomi papers finally appears.

6. George Sansom, *A History of Japan, 1334-1615* (Stanford, Calif., 1961), p. 341; Fujikawa Asako, *Cha-no-yu and Hideyoshi* (Tokyo, 1957), pp. 68ff; Cooper, *They Came to Japan*, pp. 136-38; R. A. B. Ponsonby-Fane, *Kyoto, the Old Capital of Japan, 794-1869* (Kyoto, 1956), pp. 231ff; Sakurai Narihiro, *Toyotomi Hideyoshi no ijō, Osakajō hen* (Tokyo, 1970), pp. 30, 33; Yamana Takahiro, "Taikō Hideyoshi no takagari," *Kokugakuin zasshi*, 70.10 (1969): 53ff; Hayashiya Tatsusaburō, *Tenka ittō* (*Nihon no rekishi*, no. 12; Tokyo, 1966), pp. 336ff; Kuwata Tadachika, *Toyotomi Hideyoshi* (Tokyo, 1965), pp. 86ff; Asao Naohiro, "Toyotomi Hideyoshi," in Okada Akio, ed., *Nobunaga to Hideyoshi* (*Jimbutsu Nihon no rekishi*, no. 7; Tokyo, 1965), pp. 70, 113ff.

7. Delmer M. Brown, *Money Economy in Medieval Japan* (Far Eastern Association Monograph no. 1; New Haven, Conn., 1951), p. 81; Iwasawa Yoshihiko, *Maeda Toshiie* (*Jimbutsu sōsho*, no. 136; Tokyo, 1966), pp. 151ff, 259-60; Sansom, *History of Japan*, p. 342; Okuno Takahiro, *Nobunaga to Hideyoshi* (Tokyo, 1955), p. 58; Kuwata, *Toyotomi Hideyoshi*, p. 148; Oze Hoan, *Taikōki* (c. 1617), ed. Kuwata Tadachika (Tokyo, 1971), book 22, pp. 601ff.

8. Brown, *Money Economy*, pp. 80-81; Iwasawa, *Maeda Toshiie*, p. 211;

C. R. Boxer, *The Christian Century in Japan, 1549-1650* (Berkeley, Calif., 1951), p. 112.

9. *Shiryō ni yoru Nihon no ayumi, kinsei hen*, ed. Ōkubo Toshiaki, Kodama Kōta, Yauchi Kenji, and Inoue Mitsusada (Tokyo, 1964), pp. 56-57 (1591/7/25); Okuno, *Nobunaga to Hideyoshi*, pp. 61-62.

10. *DNS*, ser. 11, 13: 297 (1585/2/17); Matsuyoshi Sadao, "Katsura gosho no zōei to Toyotomi Hideyoshi," *Keizai to keizaigaku*, 17 (1966): 157ff; Ponsonby-Fane, *Kyoto*, pp. 245-50; *Kyōto no rekishi*, comp. Kyoto shi, 10 vols. (Tokyo, 1969-76), 4: 286ff; Ōmura Yūko, *Tenshōki* (c. 1580-90), in *Taikō shiryōshū*, ed. Kuwata Tadachika (*Sengoku shiryō sōsho*, no. 1; Tokyo, 1965), book 7, pp. 111-12; Kodama Kōta et al., *Azuchi Momoyama jidai*, rev. ed. (*Zusetsu Nihon bunkashi taikei*, no. 8; Tokyo, 1966), pp. 88-90; Hall, *Government and Local Power*, p. 288; Okuno Takahiro, *Oda Nobunaga monjo no kenkyū*, 2 vols. (Tokyo, 1969-70), 2: 137, doc. 585a (1585/11/21). Kobata Atsushi, "The Production and Uses of Gold and Silver in Sixteenth- and Seventeenth-Century Japan," *Economic History Review*, 2d ser., 18.2 (1965): 258.

11. Matsuyoshi, "Katsura," p. 168 (1598/8/7); Haga Kōshirō, *Azuchi Momoyama jidai no bunka* (Tokyo, 1964), p. 99; *DNK, 8: Mōri ke monjo* (Tokyo, 1920-24), 3: 234-35, doc. 954 (1585 or 1586/9/18); Toyoda Takeshi, "Shokuhō seiken," in Rekishigaku kenkyūkai and Nihonshi kenkyūkai, eds., *Nihon rekishi kōza 3, chūsei-kinsei* (Tokyo, 1956), p. 197; *DNK, 2: Asano ke monjo* (Tokyo, 1906), pp. 478-80, doc. 266 (1595/8/3, art. 1); Kodama et al., *Azuchi Momoyama jidai*, pp. 210-11.

12. Kodama et al., *Azuchi Momoyama jidai*, p. 161 (1588/9/9); Tsuji Zennosuke, *Nihon bukkyō shi, kinsei 1* (Tokyo, 1952), pp. 325ff; *Hōkō ibun*, p. 209 (1589/10/14); *DNK, 2: Asano ke monjo*, pp. 478-80, doc. 266 (1595/8/3, art. 2); *Shiryō sōran*, ed. Tokyo daigaku shiryō hensanjo, 17 vols. (Tokyo, 1965-66), 13: 56 (1594/4/?).

13. *TKR*, 1: 349, chart; Brown, *Money Economy*, p. 88; Okada Akio et al., eds., *Tenka tōitsu* (*Nihon no rekishi*, no. 7; Tokyo, 1959), p. 110; *Shiryō ni yoru*, p. 47 (1584/5/1); Tsuji, *Nihon bukkyō shi*, p. 362.

14. Sansom, *History of Japan*, pp. 343-45, 363; *Hōkō ibun*, p. 384 (1592/6/20); Kuwata Tadachika, *Taikō no tegami* (Tokyo, 1959), p. 191; Matsudaira Tadaaki(?), *Tōdaiki* (c. 1620), in *Shiseki zassan*, 2 (Tokyo, 1911): book 2, p. 56.

15. Haga, *Azuchi Momoyama jidai*, pp. 56-58; Tsuji, *Nihon bukkyō shi*, pp. 373ff.

16. *Sekai rekishi daijiten 22, shiryō hen Nihon* (Tokyo, 1955), p. 255, doc. 288 (1583/8/1); Boscaro, ed., *101 Letters of Hideyoshi*, pp. 10-11.

17. *Tenshōki*, book 3, pp. 62-64; book 6, pp. 97-99; Ōta Gyūichi, *Taikōsama gunki no uchi* (c. 1600), ed. Kuwata Tadachika, *Taikō shiryōshū*, pp. 186-87; Fujino Tamotsu, *Bakuhan taisei shi no kenkyū* (Tokyo, 1961), pp. 61ff, 94ff.

18. Boxer, *Christian Century*, pp. 173-74; *Iezusu-kai Nihon nempō*, trans. Murakami Naojirō, ed. Yanagiya Takeo, 2 vols. (*Shin ikoku sōsho*, nos. 3-4; Tokyo, 1969), 2: 145, 224ff; Nakabe Yoshiko, *Kinsei toshi no seiritsu to kōzō* (Tokyo, 1967), pp. 281-83 (chart); Imai Rintarō, *Ishida Mi-*

tsunari (Jimbutsu sōsho, no. 74; Tokyo, 1961), pp. 8off; *Hōkō ibun*, pp. 444-45 (1593/5/1); *SJJ*, pp. 42, 79, 100, 218.

19. *TKR*, 1: 356; Fujino, *Bakuhan taisei*, p. 96; Yamaguchi Keiji, "Han taisei no seiritsu," in *IKNR 10, kinsei 2* (2d ser., 1963): 114ff.

20. Kuwata Tadachika, "Toyotomo Hideyoshi no shirowari," *Kokugakuin zasshi*, 59.6 (1958): 1-5; Takayanagi Mitsutoshi and Kuwata Tadachika, eds., *Nihon no kassen*, 9 vols. (Tokyo, 1965), 6: 43ff; *DNK, 11: Kobayakawa ke monjo* (Tokyo, 1971), 1: 355-57, doc. 407 (1582/12/18); Nakabe, *Kinsei toshi*, pp. 367-68; *Tenshōki*, book 3, p. 63.

21. Nakabe, *Kinsei toshi*, p. 361 (chart); Toyoda Takeshi, *Nihon no hōken toshi* (Tokyo, 1952), p. 95.

22. *Tenshōki*, book 6, p. 99; *DNS*, ser. 11, 3: 119-20 (1582/12/17); *DNK, 8: Mōri ke monjo*, 3: 265-69, doc. 980 (1583/5/15, art. 16); *Gifu kenshi*, ed. Gifu ken, 17 vols. (Gifu, 1965-), *Shiryō hen kinsei*, 2: 4-5 (1584/11/13); *TKR*, 3: 361, doc. 53 (1591/8/24).

23. *Nihon no komonjo*, ed. Aida Nirō, 2 vols. (Tokyo, 1949-54), 2: 228 (1585/6/18); *Morioka shishi, dai-ni bunsatsu, chūsei-ki*, ed. Morioka shi (Morioka, 1949-51), pp. 162-63 (1590/7/27); *Akita kenshi*, ed. Akita ken, 15 vols. (Akita, 1960-66), *Shiryō, kinsei hen 1*, p. 36, doc. 108 (1590/7/29); *Hōkō ibun*, pp. 138-39 (1587/5/29); Moriyama Tsuneo, "Higo-no-kuni no Toyotomi-shi kurairichi to Katō-shi shoryō," in Takeuchi Rizō, ed., *Kyūshū shi kenkyū* (Tokyo, 1968), p. 224 (1589/5/25); *DNK, 2: Asano ke monjo*, pp. 81-82, doc. 59 (1590/8/12); Asakawa Kan'ichi, *The Documents of Iriki* (Tokyo, 1955), [Japanese] p. 254, doc. 36, [English] pp. 324-25, doc. 148 (1591/10/2); *DNK, 3: Date ke monjo* (Tokyo, 1969), 2: 166-67, doc. 665.

24. Eishun et al., *Tamon'in nikki* (1478-1617), ed. Tsuji Zennosuke, 6 vols. (2d ed., Tokyo, 1967), 4: 194, entry for 1589/9/1; Iwasawa, *Maeda Toshiie*, p. 205; Asakawa, *Documents of Iriki*, [J] p. 254, doc. 36, [E] pp. 324-25, doc. 148.

25. Kobata, "Production and Uses of Gold," p. 260; Wakita Osamu, "Shokuhō seiken ron," in Rekishigaku Kenkyūkai and Nihonshi Kenkyūkai, eds., *Kōza Nihonshi 4, bakuhansei shakai* (Tokyo, 1970), p. 54.

26. *Uesugi nempu*, cited in *Shiga kenshi*, ed. Shiga ken, 6 vols. (Ōtsu, 1928), 3: 613-14.

27. Asao Naohiro, "Toyotomi seiken ron," in *IKNR 9, kinsei 1* (2d ser., 1963): 162; [Kyū] Sambō hombu, *Nihon no senshi*, ed. Kuwata Tadachika and Yamaoka Shōhachi, 11 vols. (Tokyo, 1965), 4 and 5, *passim*.

28. Asao, "Toyotomi seiken ron," pp. 161ff; Okuno, *Nobunaga to Hideyoshi*, p. 29; Asao, "Toyotomi Hideyoshi," pp. 77-78; Marius B. Jansen, "Tosa in the Sixteenth Century: The 100 Article Code of Chōsokabe Motochika," in Hall and Jansen, eds., *Studies in the Institutional History*, pp. 93-94.

29. Asao, "Toyotomi Hideyoshi," pp. 81-82, but see *DNK, 2: Asano ke monjo*, p. 540, doc. 321 (1593/11/20); Fujino, *Bakuhan taisei*, p. 112.

30. *DNK, 2: Asano ke monjo*, pp. 23-38, docs. 11-12 (1584); Miki Seiichirō, "Chōsen eki ni okeru gunyaku taikei ni tsuite," *Shigaku zasshi*, 75.2 (1966): 133-34; *Hōkō ibun*, pp. 212-31.

31. Sasaki Junnosuke, "Gunyaku ron no mondaiten," *Rekishi hyōron*,

146 (1962) and 147 (1962): 71ff; Sasaki, *Bakuhan kenryoku no kiso kōzō* (Tokyo, 1964), pp. 216ff; Sasaki, "Some Remarks on the Economic Foundation of Military Service under the Tokugawa Shogunate System," *Hitotsubashi Journal of Social Studies*, 2.1 (1964): 36-53.

32. See, e.g., *Gifu kenshi, tsūshi hen, kinsei*, 1: 100 (1589/11/21), where 20,000 *koku* out of 70,000 is *muyaku*.

33. Asao, "Toyotomi seiken ron," pp. 183-85; *TKR*, 1: 355-56.

34. Miki, "Chōsen eki," *passim*; *Hōkō ibun*, pp. 212-19 (1589/11). [Kyū] Sambō hombu, *Nihon no senshi*, 4: 172-73, 224-29; *Taikōki*, book 13, p. 344; *Tōdaiki*, book 2, pp. 53-54.

35. Fujiki Hisashi, "Toyotomi-ki daimyō ron jōsetsu," *Rekishigaku kenkyū*, 287 (1964): 33; Yamaguchi Keiji, "Toyotomi seiken no seiritsu to ryōshu keizai no kōzō," in Furushima Toshio, ed., *Kinsei 1 (Nihon keizai shi taikei*, no. 3; Tokyo, 1965): 93, 99.

36. Yamaguchi, "Toyotomi seiken no seiritsu," p. 75; Takayanagi Mitsutoshi, "Toyotomi Hideyoshi no Ōsaka chakujō," *Rekishi kōron*, 5.10 (1936): 267-80; *Hōkō ibun*, p. 36 (1583/5/17), and pp. 198-201 (1588/7/5); *DNK, 8: Mōri ke monjo*, 3: 218-19, doc. 936 (1591/1/15); *Tōdaiki*, book 2, pp. 62-66; *Kyōto no rekishi*, 4: 328; *DNK, 12: Uesugi ke monjo* (Tokyo, 1931-63), 2: 234, doc. 858 (1594/1/19); Fujiki Hisashi, "Toyotomi seiken ron no 2, 3 no mondai," *Kokushi danwakai zasshi*, 6 (1963): 37.

37. Fujino, *Bakuhan taisei*, p. 121, n. 185; *Hōkō ibun*, p. 238 (1589/12/8); Miki, "Chōsen eki," p. 142.

38. *Kyōto no rekishi*, 4: 360; Okamoto Yoshitomo, *Toyotomi Hideyoshi* (*Chūō shinsho*, no. 28; Tokyo, 1963), pp. 40ff, 78-79; *Iezusu-kai Nihon nempō*, 1: 269, and 2: 145-47; Yamaguchi, "Toyotomi seiken no seiritsu," pp. 93-94.

39. Hayami Seiko, "Taikō kenchi no jisshi katei," *Chihōshi kenkyū*, 13.5 (1963): 30-48; see also Guy Moréchand, " 'Taiko Kenchi' le cadastre de Hideyoshi Toyotomi," *Bulletin de l'Ecole Française d'Extrême-Orient*, 53.1 (1966): 7-69.

40. Suzuki Ryōichi, "Oda-Toyotomi jidai no jidai kubun ni tsuite," *Rekishi kyōiku*, 11.10 (1963): 23; Hall, *Government and Local Power*, p. 291; *TKR*, 1: 313ff.

41. *Shiryō ni yoru*, pp. 50-51 (1587/6/18); *DNK, 16: Shimazu ke monjo* (Tokyo, 1966-71), 2: 232-36, doc. 958 (1595/6/3); *Hōkō ibun*, p. 67 (1585/10/2); Hayashiya, *Tenka ittō*, pp. 411-13.

42. Asao, "Toyotomi seiken ron," p. 207.

43. *Ibid.*, pp. 195-96. Examples of grants based on the results of a survey: (a) *DNK, 8: Mōri ke monjo*, 3: 236-38, docs. 956-57 (1591/3/13); Nakabe, *Kinsei toshi*, pp. 409ff; (b) *TKR*, 3: 385, doc. 104 (1595/6/19); *Mito shishi*, ed. Itō Tasaburō, 1 (Mito, 1963): 754ff; (c) *TKR*, 3: 386, doc. 106 (1595/12/1); *Fukuoka kenshi*, vol. 1ge, ed. Fukuoka ken (Fukuoka, 1962): 871-76; (d) *TKR*, 3: 387, doc. 108 (1598/8/5). For an example of *gunyaku* based on *kokudaka*, see Asakawa, *Documents of Iriki*, [J] pp. 258-59, doc. 42, [E] pp. 333-35, doc. 150B (1596/12/5).

44. *TKR*, 1: 349ff; Nagashima Fukutarō, "Hideyoshi no shaji seisaku," *Rekishi kōron*, 5.10 (1936): 159-60; *TKR*, 3: 377, doc. 78 (1583/8/10), 384,

doc. 101 (1593/11/3), 380, doc. 88 (1585/10/15); *Hōkō ibun*, pp. 272-73 (1590/8/21); *Ōita ken shiryō*, ed. Ōita ken shiryō kankōkai (Ōita, 1960-), 12: 375, doc. 463 (1593/i9/15); *Shin Ōtsu shishi, bekkan*, ed. Komaki Saneshige (Ōtsu, 1963), pp. 233-34 (1596/12/3); Takayanagi Mitsutoshi, "Toyotomi Hideyoshi no kenchi," in *IKNR 18* (1st ser., 1935): 33-34; *Kashiwara chōshi*, ed. Kashiwara chōshi kankōkai (Kashiwara, 1955), pp. 310-17; [Niigata ken] *Kariba gun kyūseiki shi*, ed. Kuwayama Naojirō, 2 vols. (Kariba, 1909), 2: 345 (1594/7/23); Kobayashi Keiichirō, "Zenkōji ryō no kenchi," *Shinano*, 8.2 (1956): 61ff; Nakagawa Senzō, "Tenshō kenchi no ichi shiryō," *Rekishi chiri*, 62.1 (1933): 62-66.

45. Asao, "Toyotomi seiken ron," p. 187; *TKR*, 3: 390, doc. 118, and 403, doc. 159; *Echizen Wakasa komonjo sen*, ed. Makino Shinnosuke (Tokyo, 1933), pp. 748-49; *Akita kenshi*, 2: 20ff; Kanai Kikuichirō, "Kita Shinano ni okeru hansei kakuritsu izen no kenchi," *Shinano*, 8, 10, 12 (1956): 780ff; Furukawa Sadao, "Shinano ni okeru Toyotomi-shi no kurairichi to kinzan," *Shinano*, 20.6-9 (1968): 460-69, 517-33, 328-41, 651-63 *passim*.

46. Araki Moriaki, *Taikō kenchi to kokudaka-sei (NHK Bukkusu*, no. 93; Tokyo, 1969), pp. 195ff; Asao, " 'Bakuhan-sei dai'ichidan' ni okeru seisanryoku to kokudaka-sei," *Rekishigaku kenkyū*, 264 (1962): 53-54; Hidemura Senzō, "Kokudaka-sei ni kansuru futatsu no mondai," *Keizaigaku kenkyū*, 39.2 (1963): 93-104 *passim*; Matsuo Hisashi, "Taikō kenchi no tōdai ni tsuite," *Shirin*, 52.1 (1969): 1-32 *passim*; Miyagawa Mitsuru, "Kokudaka kettei ni kansuru ikkōsatsu," in Kobata Atsushi kyōju taikan kinen jigyōkai, ed., *Kobata Atsushi kyōju taikan kinen kokushi ronshū* (Kyoto, 1970), pp. 639-54 *passim*; Nakamura Kichiji, "Kokudaka-sei to hōken-sei," *Shigaku zasshi*, 69.7-8 (1960): 817-24, 965-79 *passim*.

47. Kitajima Masamoto, "Heinō bunri to bakuhan taisei," *Shisō*, 472 (1963): 1418ff; Niizuma Toshitsugi, "Shokuhō seiken no hō-teki seikaku," *Shikai*, 5 (1958), 19; *Hōjō godaiki*, book 2, sec. 7, in *Kaitei shiseki shūran*, ed. Kondō Keizō, 32 vols. (reprint, Tokyo, 1967-69), 5: 638ff; Cooper, *They Came to Japan*, p. 53.

48. *Hōjō godaiki*, book 7, sec. 1, 744; Hagihara Tatsuo, "Sengoku daimyō kashindan no kōsei," *Rekishi kyōiku*, 7.8 (1959): 11; Araki, *Taikō kenchi to kokudaka-sei*, pp. 96ff.

49. Haraguchi Torao et al., *The Status System and Social Organization of Satsuma* (Tokyo, 1975), pp. 14ff; Itō Tadao, "Kinsei shoki hitotsu shōnin no seikaku," *Shigaku zasshi*, 70.1 (1961): 46-47.

50. Nakamura Kichiji, *Kinsei shoki nōseishi kenkyū* (1938; reprint, Tokyo, 1970), pp. 60ff; Sugiyama Hiroshi, *Sengoku daimyō (Nihon no rekishi*, no. 11; Tokyo, 1965), p. 167; Asakawa, *Documents of Iriki*, [E] p. 207, n. 14; Asakawa Kan'ichi, *Land and Society in Medieval Japan*, Committee for the Publication of Dr. K. Asakawa's Works (Tokyo, 1965), pp. 174-75, 191-92, 214.

51. *DNS*, ser. 11, 3: 814 (1583/3/15); *Tokugawa Ieyasu monjo no kenkyū*, ed. Nakamura Kōya, 5 vols. (Tokyo, 1958-71), 1: 641-42 (1584/8/26); *DNK*, 2: *Asano ke monjo*, pp. 48-51, doc. 25 (1590/5/20); Nakagawa Senzō, "Nagahama jidai no Hideyoshi," *Rekishi kōron*, 5.10 (1936): 305-6 (1574/6/6, 7).

52. Hayashiya Tatsusaburō, *Machishū* (*Chūō shinsho*, no. 59; Tokyo, 1964), pp. 12-13; Matsumoto Toyotoshi, *Jōkamachi no rekishi chirigaku-teki kenkyū* (rev. ed., Tokyo, 1971), p. 205; Harada Tomohiko, *Chūsei ni okeru toshi no kenkyū* (Tokyo, 1942), p. 255.

53. Kuwata, *Taikō no tegami*, pp. 28-29 (1574/12/22); *Echizen Wakasa komonjo sen*, pp. 53-54, 99 (1583/4). *DNS*, ser. 11, 7: 682 (1584/6). *TKR*, 3: 356-57, doc. 45 (1586/1/19), 357-58, doc. 46 (1586/3/21), 366-68, doc. 62 (1596/3/1); *Shiga kenshi*, 3: 428 (1588/5/25); *DNK, 11: Kobayakawa ke monjo*, 1: 468-69, doc. 496 (1588/5/25); *Higashiasai gunshi*, ed. Higashiasai gun kyōiku iinkai, 4 vols. (Higashiasai gun, 1927), 2: 735-37, 4: 514, doc. 8 (1590/12/5); Komai Shigekatsu, *Komai nikki* (1593-95), in *Kaitei shiseki shūran*, 25: 505-6, entry for 1593/i9/25, and 519-21, entry for 1592/12/14; *DNK, 16: Shimazu ke monjo*, 2: 252, doc. 968 (1593?/8/29); *Hōkō ibun*, pp. 558-61 (1596/3/1); *Shiryō ni yoru*, pp. 40-41 (1591/8/21).

54. *Echizen Wakasa komonjo sen*, pp. 167-68 (1583/4/24); Aida Nirō, "Toyotomi Hideyoshi no dokō chōsa," *Rekishi chiri*, 46.6 (1925): 520-35, and 47.4 (1926): 302-16; Nakamura Kichiji, "Toyotomi Hideyoshi no nōmin seisaku," in *Kenkyū hōkoku*, ed. Nihon shogaku shinkō iinkai, 5 (keizaigaku) (1939): 224-28; *Hōkō ibun*, pp. 329-31 (1592? and 1592/2/2); *DNK, 9: Kikkawa ke monjo* (Tokyo, 1970), 2: 137-39, doc. 975 (1591/3/6); *DNK, 2: Asano ke monjo*, pp. 126-28, doc. 98 (1594/3/4).

55. *Shiryō ni yoru*, pp. 40-41 (1591/8/21); *DNK, 8: Mōri ke monjo*, 3: 366-68, doc. 1115 (1597/3/7); Nakabe, *Kinsei toshi*, pp. 290ff; *TKR*, 3: 438-39, doc. 207 (1591/8/21).

56. Maki Hidemasa, "Hideyoshi zengo no jinshin baibai hō," *Ōsaka shiritsu daigaku hogaku zasshi*, 5.1 (1958): 44-78 and 6.2 (1959): 1-44, see pp. 16ff; Araki, *Taikō kenchi to kokudaka-sei*, pp. 115, 170ff; *Shinano shiryō*, ed. Shinano shiryō kankōkai, 30 vols. (Nagano, 1956-67) 17: 129 (1590/4/29); *DNK, 12: Uesugi ke monjo*, 2: 222-23, doc. 838 (1590/4/27).

57. Kuwata Tadachika, "Toyotomi Hideyoshi no katanagari," *Shigaku zasshi*, 54.1 (1943): 57-89 *passim*; Nakamura, *Kinsei shoki nōseishi*, pp. 259ff.

58. E. Herbert Norman, *Soldier and Peasant in Japan: The Origins of Conscription* (Vancouver, British Columbia, 1965), pp. 10ff; Tsunoda Ryusaku, William Theodore de Bary, and Donald Keene, eds., *Sources of Japanese Tradition* (New York, 1958), pp. 391-92; J. R. McEwan, *The Political Writings of Ogyū Sorai* (London, 1962), pp. 35, 59-61.

59. *CHS*, 1: 139, no. 200; Kuwata, "Hideyoshi no katanagari," pp. 63-64.

60. *DNK, 1: Kōyasan monjo* (Tokyo, 1968), vol. 2: 603, doc. 336 (1585/10/23), 605-7, doc. 338 (1591/10/24), 611-12, doc. 343 (1584/8/4), and vol. 3: 679-80, doc. 821 (1585/4/10); Kuwata, "Hideyoshi no katanagari," pp. 73, 76; *Tamon'in nikki*, 3: 443, entry for 1585/i8/25.

61. *Kii zoku fudoki*, ed. Niita Kōko, 5 vols. (Wakayama, 1910), 3: *furoku*: 50 (1585/4/22).

62. *Hōkō ibun*, pp. 201-2 (1588/7/8); Kuwata, "Hideyoshi no katanagari," p. 79; *CHS*, 1: 139, no. 200.

63. *Tamon'in nikki*, 3: 443, entry for 1585/i8/24, and 4: 137-38, entries for 1588/7/17, 21; *Gifu kenshi, tsūshi hen, kinsei*, 1: 67.

64. Translation by James Murdoch, in *A History of Japan*, 3 vols. (1903-26; reprint ed., New York, 1964), 2: 369, n. 4.

65. *DNK, 11: Kobayakawa ke monjo*, 1: 468, doc. 495 (1588/5/25); Kuwata, "Hideyoshi no katanagari," p. 73; Okuno, *Nobunaga to Hideyoshi*, p. 90; Watanabe Yosuke, *Kokushi ronsō* (Tokyo, 1956), pp. 471-73 (1592/10/10, art. 15).

66. *Hirado Matsuura ke shiryō*, ed. Kyōto daigaku bungakubu kokushi kenkyūshitsu (Kyoto, 1951), p. 121, doc. 68 (1593/4/5); Delmer M. Brown, "The Impact of Firearms on Japanese Warfare, 1543-98," *Far Eastern Quarterly*, 7.3 (1948): 240-41; *Tōdaiki*, book 2, p. 58.

67. *Hōkō ibun*, pp. 249-50 (1590/4/18), p. 272 (1590/8/18); Kuwata, "Hideyoshi no katanagari," pp. 86-87.

68. *Hirado Matsuura ke shiryō*, pp. 117-18, doc. 56 (1589/4/15); Kuwata, "Hideyoshi no katanagari," p. 84; *Higashiasai gunshi*, 2: 735-37, 4: 514, doc. 8 (1590/12/5); *Kokushi shiryōshū*, ed. Kokumin seishin bunka kenkyūjo, 4 vols. (Tokyo, 1940-43), 3*jō*: 276-77 (1588/8/21).

69. *Nihon no komonjo*, 2: 337-38 (1590/8/10).

70. *DNK, 9: Kikkawa ke monjo*, 2: 137-39, doc. 975 (1591/3/6); *DNK, 11: Kobayakawa ke monjo*, 1: 481-82, doc. 504 (1591/8/21).

71. *TKR*, 3: 395, doc. 135 (1588/8/18); Kuwata, "Hideyoshi no katanagari," pp. 81, 83 (1589/1/11); *DNK, 16: Shimazu ke monjo*, 2: 115, doc. 780 (1589?/7/10); *Shinano shiryō*, 17: 186-87 (1590/10/20).

72. Kuwata, "Hideyoshi no katanagari," pp. 73ff; Iwasawa Yoshihiko, "Yamashiro-Ōmi ni okeru Toyotomi shi no kurairichi ni tsuite," *Rekishigaku kenkyū*, 288 (1964): 18; *Higashiasai gunshi*, 2: 735-37, and 4: 514, doc. 8 (1590/12/5).

73. *TKR*, 3: 400, doc. 150 (1588 or 1589/8/7); *Hirado Matsuura ke shiryō*, pp. 117-18, doc. 56 (1589/4/15); Kuwata, "Hideyoshi no katanagari," pp. 84-86.

74. *Hōkō ibun*, pp. 249-50 (1590/4/18), p. 272 (1590/8/18); Kuwata, "Hideyoshi no katanagari," pp. 86-87.

75. Letters of congratulations: *Saga ken shiryō shūsei*, ed. Saga kenshi hensan iinkai (Saga, 1958), 3: 137-38, doc. 189 (1588/9/18); *DNK, 16: Shimazu ke monjo*, 2: 115, doc. 780 (1589?/7/10). Receipts: *TKR*, 3: 395, doc. 135 (1588/8/18); Kuwata, "Hideyoshi no katanagari," pp. 81ff. Toda and Ryūzōji: *Echizen Wakasa komonjo sen*, pp. 612-13 (1589/11/3). Maeda: *Kaga han shiryō*, ed. Kōshaku Maeda ke henshūbu (Tokyo, 1929), 1: 376 (1588/11/6); Iwasawa, *Maeda Toshiie*, p. 153. Mōri: Kuwata, "Hideyoshi no katanagari," p. 83. Shimazu: *Kokushi shiryōshū*, 3*jō*: 277 (1589/1/23).

76. *TKR*, 3: 395, doc. 135 (1588/8/18); *Kokushi shiryōshū*, 3*jō*: 276-77 (1588/8/21); Kodama Kōta, "Kinsei shotō no nōson ni kansuru ikkōsatsu," *Rekishi chiri*, 61.5, 6 (1933): 546.

77. Kuwata, "Hideyoshi no katanagari," pp. 82-83; *Kaga-han shiryō*, p. 376 (1588/11/6).

78. Kuwata, "Hideyoshi no katanagari," pp. 81, 83; *Seishi kakei daijiten*, ed. Ōta Akira, 3 vols. (Tokyo, 1934-36), 2: 2552-53.

79. Robert K. Sakai, "Feudal Society and Modern Leadership in Satsuma-Han," *Journal of Asian Studies*, 16.3 (1957): 366-67; *Kokushi shiryōshū*, 3*jō*: 277 (1589/1/23); Toyoda, "Shokuhō seiken," p. 202.

80. See note 71 above.

81. *Fukuoka kenshi shiryō*, ed. Itō Bishirō, 12 vols. (Fukuoka, 1932-40), 4:171-72 (1588/9/16); *Echizen Wakasa komonjo sen*, pp. 612-13 (1589/11/3); *Shizuoka ken shiryō*, ed. Shizuoka ken, 5 vols. (Shizuoka, 1932-41), 1: 337-38 (1590/4/18); *Higo kokushi*, ed. Gotō Zezan, 2 vols. (Kumamoto, 1916-17), 2: 427 (1587/5/25).

82. In Kuwata, ed., *Taikō shiryōshū*, pp. 149-50; Nakabe, *Kinsei toshi*, pp. 284ff.

83. *Hōkō ibun*, p. 206 (1589/3/28); Kodama et al., *Azuchi Momoyama jidai*, p. 172.

84. Miyamoto Mataji, *Nihon hōken shugi no saishuppatsu* (Kyoto, 1948), pp. 253-56; Kodama et al., *Azuchi Momoyama jidai*, pp. 180-82; Toyoda Takeshi, *[Zōtei] Chūsei Nihon shōgyō shi no kenkyū* (Tokyo, 1952), p. 405; Yamashina Tokitsune, *Tokitsune-kyō ki*, ed. Tokyo daigaku shiryō hensanjo (*Dai Nihon kokiroku*; Tokyo, 1959-), 1: 310, entry for 1582/10/13; *DNK, 8: Mōri ke monjo*, 3: 227-28, doc. 949 (1586/4/10).

85. *Ōsaka shishi*, ed. Ōsaka shi, 8 vols. (Osaka, 1911-15), 1: 174-75; *Hōkō ibun*, pp. 263-64 (1590/7/3); *DNK, 2: Asano ke monjo*, pp. 77-78, doc. 54.

86. Toyoda, *Chūsei Nihon shōgyō shi*, pp. 420-22; Nakabe, *Kinsei toshi*, pp. 245ff; *DNS*, ser. 11, 4: 594 (1583/6/4), 10: 147 (1584/11/10); *Kyōto no rekishi*, 4: 376-77 (1583/6/25).

87. *Tenshōki*, book 6, p. 100; Okuno, *Nobunaga to Hideyoshi*, p. 122; Nakabe, *Kinsei toshi*, pp. 266, 289; Nagashima Fukutarō, "Toyotomi Hideyoshi no toshi seisaku ippan," *Shigaku zasshi*, 59.4 (1950): 61; Kodama et al., *Azuchi Momoyama jidai*, p. 161 (1588/9/9); *Tamon'in nikki*, 4: 327, entry for 1591/12/28; *Dai Nihon sōsei shi*, ed. Nonaka Jun, 3 vols. (1885; Tokyo, 1926), 2: 285-87 (1598/8); Wakita Osamu, *Kinsei hōken shakai no keizai kōzō* (Tokyo, 1963), p. 39; Kuwata Tadachika, *Rikyū no shokan* (Kyoto, 1961), pp. 387-92, doc. 168.

88. *DNK, 2: Asano ke monjo*, pp. 460-63, doc. 261 (1592/11/1); Moriyama Tsuneo, "Kyūshū ni okeru Toyotomi-shi chokkatsuryō no ikkeitai," *Tōkai shigaku*, 2 (1966): 20-39, and 3 (1967): 36-50, esp. 3: 39-40 (1593/1/?).

89. Wakita, *Kinsei hōken shakai*, pp. 15ff. But see Nakabe, *Kinsei toshi*, pp. 226ff, 263ff.

90. Watanabe Nobuo, *Bakuhan-sei kakuritsuki no shōhin ryūtsū* (Tokyo, 1966), pp. 49ff; Yamaguchi Tetsu, "Obama, Tsuruga ni okeru kinsei shoki gōshō no sonzai keitai," *Rekishigaku kenkyū*, 248 (1960): 6-8.

91. Norman Jacobs and Cornelius C. Vermeule III, *Japanese Coinage* (New York, 1953), pp. 19-22; Asao, "Toyotomi seiken ron," p. 170; Kobata, "Production and Uses of Gold," pp. 263-64.

92. *Shiryō ni yoru*, p. 51 (1587/6/19), art. 5; C. R. Boxer, *The Great Ship from Amacon* (Lisbon, 1963), pp. 319ff; *Hōkō ibun*, pp. 234-35 (1591/8/9); Asao, "Toyotomi Hideyoshi," pp. 85-86; Katō Eiichi, "Seiritsuki no ito wappu ni kansuru ikkōsatsu," in Hōgetsu Keigo Sensei kanreki kinenkai, ed., *Nihon shakai keizai shi kenkyū, kinsei hen* (Tokyo, 1967), pp. 88-89; Iwao Seiichi, *Sakoku* (*Nihon no rekishi*, no. 14; Tokyo, 1966), pp. 116ff;

DNK, 16: Shimazu ke monjo, 1: 377, doc. 384 (1589/8/27); *Echizen Wakasa komonjo sen*, p. 664 (1594/12/11); *Taikōki*, book 16, pp. 451-52.

93. *Hōkō ibun*, p. 202 (1588/7/8), and p. 83 (1586/9/8); *Shiryō ni yoru*, pp. 56-57 (1591/7/25).

94. Iwao Seiichi, "Sakoku," in *IKNR 10, kinsei 2* (2d ser., 1963), pp. 64-65; Moriyama Tsuneo, "Toyotomi-ki kaigai bōeki no ikkeitai," *Tōkai daigaku bungakubu kiyō*, 8 (1967): 14-15; Iwao, *Sakoku*, p. 196.

95. Arnoldus Montanus, *Atlas Japannensis: Being Remarkable Adresses by Way of Embassy from the East-India Company of the United Provinces to the Emperor of Japan* (London, 1670), p. 183.

96. McEwan, *Political Writings of Ogyū Sorai*, p. 75; *TKR*, 1: 357-58.

97. Jansen, "Tosa in the Sixteenth Century," pp. 98-99; see also Boxer, *Christian Century*, pp. 173ff.

98. *Tokugawa jikki*, cited in *TKR*, 1: 357; Kitajima Masamoto, *Edo bakufu no kenryoku kozō* (Tokyo, 1964), p. 190; Yamaguchi, "Han taisei no seiritsu," pp. 114ff.

99. Kobayashi Seiji, *Date Masamune (Jimbutsu sōsho, no. 28; Tokyo, 1959)*, pp. 90-91; *DNK, 12: Uesugi ke monjo*, 2: 238, doc. 863 (1598/1/10); *TKR*, 3: 396, doc. 138 (1598/4/2); Miyamoto, *Nihon hōken shugi*, p. 245; Nakabe, *Kinsei toshi*, pp. 375, 421; Tsukamoto Manabu, "Mikawa no kenchi shikō katei," *Shinano*, 19.1 (1967): 23; Toshioka Toshiaki, "Mōri shi no ryōkoku shihai to heinō bunri no shinten jōkyō ni tsuite," *Yamaguchi ken chihōshi kenkyū*, 8 (1962): 17.

100. David John Lu, *Sources of Japanese History*, 2 vols. (New York, 1974), 1: 173.

101. Nakabe, *Kinsei toshi*, pp. 99-100, 358ff; Owada Tetsuo, "Heinō bunri no rekishi-teki zentei," *Shikan*, 80 (1969): 2-20 passim; *Morioka shishi*, pp. 162-63 (1590/7/27); *Zōho teisei hennen Ōtomo shiryō*, ed. Takita Manabu, 33 vols. (Ōita, 1962-71), 28: 116, doc. 215; *Komai nikki*, pp. 519-21, entry for 1593/12/14; Asao, "Toyotomi seiken ron," pp. 190-91, 201; Fujino, *Bakuhan taisei*, pp. 619-20 (1587/6); *DNK, 8: Mōri ke monjo*, 3: 365-66, doc. 1114 (1587/6/5, art. 8).

102. *DNK, 2: Asano ke monjo*, p. 534, doc. 313 (1583/8/1); Miki Seiichirō, "Toyotomi seiken no chigyō taikei," *Nihonshi kenkyū*, 118 (1971): 118-33 passim; *Hōkō ibun*, pp. 146-47 (1587/6/28); *SJJ*, p. 253; *Gifu kenshi, tsūshi hen, kinsei*, 1: 98-101; *Nakatsugawa shishi, tsūshi 1*, ed. Nakatsugawa shi (Nakatsugawa, 1968), p. 645; *Shirakawa chōshi*, ed. Shirakawa chōshi hensan iinkai (Gifu ken, Kamo gun, Shirakawa chō, 1968), pp. 102ff.

103. Yamaguchi, "Han taisei no seiritsu," pp. 117-19; Yamaguchi, "Toyotomi seiken no seiritsu," pp. 95ff; Fujiki, "Toyotomi ki daimyō ron jōsetsu," p. 34; Fujiki, "Toyotomi seiken ron," p. 37.

104. Murata Senzō, "Sengoku daimyo Mōri shi no kenryoku kōzō," *Nihonshi kenkyū*, 73 (1964): 21-22; Fujino, *Bakuhan taisei*, pp. 563-64; Yamaguchi, "Toyotomi seiken no seiritsu," pp. 99-101; Iwasawa, *Maeda Toshiie*, p. 196; Kimura Tadao, "Sengoku daimyo to Taikō kenchi," *Kyūshū shigaku*, 33-34 (1967): 10; Asao, "Toyotomi seiken ron," p. 174.

105. Yamaguchi, "Toyotomi seiken no seiritsu," p. 100.

106. Fujino, *Bakuhan taisei*, pp. 524 and 530, n. 21, cited from *Ma-*

tsuura monjo, doc. 86 (1597/1/3); *Taikōki*, book 14, p. 401 (1594/9); Asao, "Toyotomi seiken ron," p. 187; *TKR*, 1: 355, 363, n. 19; Miki, "Chōsen eki," pp. 19, 24, n. 1; Iwasawa, *Maeda Toshiie*, pp. 176-77; *Tamon'in nikki*, 4: 337, entry for 1592/2/25; [Kyū] Sambō hombu, *Nihon no senshi*, 4: 224.

107. Fujiki, "Toyotomi ki daimyō ron jōsetsu," p. 38; Hansei shi kenkyūkai, ed., *Hansei seiritsu shi no sōgō kenkyū: Yonezawa han* (Tokyo, 1963), pp. 138-39; Okumura Tetsu, "Maeda Toshiie kanshindan no tenkai," *Chihōshi kenkyū*, 18.3 (1968): 34ff; Fujino, *Bakuhan taisei*, pp. 622-23; Itō Tasaburō, "Echigo Uesugi shi ryōkoku kenkyū no 2 shiryō," *Nihon rekishi*, 138 (1959): 12ff; *Mito shishi*, 1: 735-36, 754; Araki Moriaki, *Bakuhan taisei shakai no seiritsu to kōzō* (rev. ed., Tokyo, 1964), pp. 230ff.

108. Nishimura Keiko, "Azuchi Momoyama jidai ni okeru Kita-Kyūshū no dōkō," *Rekishi kyōiku*, 11.10 (1963): 55; Araki, *Taikō kenchi to kokudaka sei*, pp. 132ff; Imai, *Ishida Mitsunari*, pp. 108ff; Asakawa, *Documents of Iriki*, [J] pp. 254-58, [E] pp. 325-32, doc. 149; *Kagoshima kenshi*, ed. Kagoshima ken, 5 vols. (Kagoshima, 1939-43), 1: 767ff; *DNK, 16: Shimazu ke monjo*, 2: 395-410, docs. 1096-1104; Kanai Madoka, "Shokuhō ki ni okeru Bizen," *Chihōshi kenkyū*, 9.6 (1959): 17; Wakabayashi Kisaburō, *Kaga han nōsei shi no kenkyū*, 2 vols. (Tokyo, 1970), 1: 65.

109. Kawana Noboru, *Nansō no gōyū—Satomi Yoshitaka* (*Nihon no bushō*, no. 36; Tokyo, 1968), pp. 256-57; Sasaki Keiichi, "Kinsei shoki no Date shi kenchi," *Tōhoku gakuin daigaku ronshū*, 48 (1967): 5ff; Kuwanami Tadaoki, "Satsuma han no Manji naiken," in Hidemura Senzō, ed., *Satsuma-han no kiso kōzō* (Tokyo, 1970), pp. 31-32; Robert Sakai, "The Consolidation of Power in Satsuma han," in Hall and Jansen, eds., *Studies in the Institutional History*, pp. 136-37.

110. Asao, "Toyotomi seiken ron," pp. 172ff; Asao, "Toyotomi Hideyoshi," pp. 106-7.

111. *DNK, 8: Mōri ke monjo*, 3: 227-28, doc. 949 (1586/4/10); Fujiki, "Toyotomi seiken ron," *passim*; Fujiki, "Toyotomi ki daimyō ron jōsetsu," pp. 31-32 (1590/7/16).

112. Yamaguchi, "Toyotomi seiken no seiritsu," p. 114 (1591/1/17) and pp. 110ff, 122; Fujiki, "Toyotomi ki daimyō ron jōsetsu," *passim*.

113. *DNK, 16: Shimazu ke monjo*, 1: 360-61, doc. 368 (1592/11/5).

114. *Ibid.*, 2: 353-54, doc. 1061 (1595/4/14); Asakawa, *Documents of Iriki*, [E] p. 331.

Hauser, "Osaka Castle and Tokugawa Authority in Western Japan"

During the research and writing stages of this paper I was aided by an Independent Study and Research Fellowship from the National Endowment for the Humanities (NEH Grant number FA-21695-82), a short-term Professional Fellowship from the Japan Foundation, and a supplementary grant for research materials from the Social Science Research Council, all during the academic year 1982-83. I am grateful to Jeffrey P. Mass and James L. McClain for their critical comments, which assisted me at the revision stage.

1. John W. Hall, *Government and Local Power in Japan, 500 to 1700: A Study Based on Bizen Province* (Princeton, N.J., 1966), p. 331.
2. *Ibid.*, p. 332.
3. For a more detailed discussion of the process of Tokugawa consolidation, see *ibid.*, pp. 341-74.
4. Harold Bolitho, *Treasures among Men: The Fudai Daimyo in Tokugawa Japan* (New Haven, Conn., 1974), p. 8.
5. *Ibid.*, pp. 10-11.
6. *Ibid.*, pp. 13-14; Toshio G. Tsukahira, *Feudal Control in Tokugawa Japan: The Sankin Kōtai System* (Cambridge, Mass., 1966); Hall, *Government and Local Power*, pp. 363-64.
7. Asao Naohiro with Marius B. Jansen, "Shogun and Tennō," in John W. Hall, Nagahara Keiji, and Kozo Yamamura, eds., *Japan Before Tokugawa: Political Consolidation and Economic Growth, 1500-1650* (Princeton, N.J., 1981), p. 261.
8. *Ibid.*, pp. 261-62.
9. In fact, as we know, Ieyasu remained active. Thus in 1614-15, whereas Hidetada called and commanded the daimyo forces from eastern Japan, those from the west were summoned by Ieyasu, since their residual loyalties were to Hideyoshi and his heir, Hideyori. Not until the Battle of Shimabara in 1637 were problems of divided loyalty totally eliminated. See *ibid.*, p. 264.
10. *Ibid.*, pp. 264-65.
11. Yamori Kazuhiko, "Ōsakashi no shizenchiriteki kisō," *Ōsaka no rekishi to fūdo* (Mainichi Hōsō bunka sōsho, no. 1; Osaka, 1973): 3-8.
12. Imai Shuhei, "Ishiyama Honganji jinaimachi ni kansuru ikkosatsu," *Machikaneyama ronsō shigakuhen*, 6 (1973): 3-5; Nakabe Yoshiko, *Kinsei toshi no seiritsu to kōzō* (Tokyo, 1967), pp. 180-81; Fujimoto Atsushi, *Ōsakafu no rekishi* (Tokyo, 1969), pp. 112-16. *Jinaimachi* is read *jinaichō* by some scholars. Historical dictionaries and reference works do not offer consistent guidance on which reading is correct, but since in western Japan *jinaimachi* is more common, I have used it throughout.
13. Nakabe, *Kinsei toshi*, pp. 194-204.
14. *Ibid.*, pp. 205-6.
15. *Ōsaka shishi*, ed. Ōsaka Shisangikai (Osaka, 1965), 1: 165.
16. Nakabe, *Kinsei toshi*, p. 217; Fujimoto, *Ōsakafu no rekishi*, pp. 120-26.
17. *Ōsaka shishi*, 1: 166-67.
18. Nakabe Yoshiko, "Shokuhō seiken no toshi seisaku," *Historia*, 43 (1966): 14-15.
19. *Ibid.*, pp. 14-16; Wakita Osamu and Kobayashi Shigeru, *Ōsaka no seisan to kōtsū* (Mainichi Hōsō bunka sōsho, no. 4; Osaka, 1973): 16-17.
20. Nakabe, "Shokuhō seiken," pp. 16-18.
21. *Ibid.*, pp. 15-16.
22. Wakita and Kobayashi, *Ōsaka no seisan to kōtsū*, pp. 17-18; Yamori Kazuhiko, *Jōkamachi* (Tokyo, 1972), p. 214; Wakita Osamu, *Kinsei hōken shakai no keizai kōzō* (Tokyo, 1963), pp. 43-44; and Wakita, "Kinsei shoki no Ōsaka," *Rekishi kagaku*, 67 (1977): 1-5.

23. Wakita and Kobayashi, *Ōsaka no seisan to kōtsū*, pp. 18-20; *Ōsaka shishi*, 1: 208; Yamori, *Jōkamachi*, pp. 214-15. See Fujimoto, *Ōsakafu no rekishi*, pp. 128-53, for a detailed account of Toyotomi period Osaka and the fall of the city to the Tokugawa in 1615.

24. *Ōsaka hennenshi*, ed. Ōsaka Shiritsu Chūō Toshokan (Osaka, 1967-79), 4: 373.

25. *Ōsaka shishi*, 1: 249-52; Fujimoto, *Ōsakafu no rekishi*, pp. 153-56; *Ōsaka hennenshi*, 4: 409-10; Yasuoka Shigeaki, "Edo chūki no Ōsaka ni okeru torihiki soshiki," pt. 1, *Dōshisha shōgaku*, 16.3 (1964): 294-96.

26. *Ōsaka shishi*, 1: 253-56; *Ōsaka hennenshi*, 4: 406; Yasuoka, "Edo chūki," p. 296; Yamori, *Jōkamachi*, pp. 203-8, 215-17; Wakita Osamu, "Kinsei toshi no kensetsu to gōshō," in *IKNR, kinsei 1* (3d ser., 1975), 9: 175. For the treatment of temples and shrines in Kanazawa, see James L. McClain, *Kanazawa: A Seventeenth-Century Japanese Castle Town* (New Haven, Conn., 1982), pp. 37-38.

27. Fujimoto, *Ōsakafu no rekishi*, pp. 154-55.

28. For a further discussion see Wakita Osamu, "Kinsei shoki no toshi keizai," *Nihonshi kenkyū*, 200 (1979): 52-75.

29. Wakita, "Kinsei shoki no toshi keizai," pp. 54-55; Okamoto Ryōichi, *Ōsaka-jō* (Tokyo, 1970), pp. 128-31; *Ōsaka hennenshi*, 4: 435-39. A compilation of sources on the first phase of construction in 1620 appears in *Ōsaka hennenshi*, 1: 435-66. Documents on later aspects of the castle construction are in *Ōsaka hennenshi*, 5: 1-4, 13-16, 31-36, 51-58, 64, 66-86.

30. Okamoto, *Ōsaka-jō*, p. 137.

31. Wakita, "Kinsei shoki no toshi keizai," pp. 55-57; Okamoto, *Ōsaka-jō*, p. 136. Precise data on the price of rice in 1620 are not available. The use of 20 *monme* silver per *koku* is based on the data from Miyamoto Mataji, ed., *Kinsei Ōsaka no bukka to rishi* (Osaka, 1963), table 2, pp. 66-68, and is a low estimate. Wakita gives a figure of 10.64 *monme* for 1620 in the article cited above (p. 66), but this seems unrealistically low in comparison with data from other years. Elsewhere, he uses a figure of 25 *monme* per *koku*, and this value would reduce the value of outlays in *koku* by 20 percent. See Wakita Osamu, "Kinsei shoki no Ōsaka," *Rekishi kagaku*, 67 (1977): 1-5. I have chosen the figure of 20 *monme* per *koku* because it is on the low end of the prices quoted in the Miyamoto volume between 1616 and 1630. In only two of those years, 1624 and 1628, for which data are extant, did the price of rice meet or exceed 25 *monme* per *koku*. For the Kuroda levy see *Ōsaka hennenshi*, 4: 448-49.

32. Wakita, "Kinsei shoki no toshi keizai," p. 55.

33. Okamoto, *Ōsaka-jō*, pp. 132-33. See *Ōsaka hennenshi*, 4: 444-45, for the Hosokawa request for a lower assessment. See also *ibid.*, 475-77.

34. Okamoto, *Ōsaka-jō*, pp. 136-38; Wakita, "Kinsei shoki no toshi keizai," pp. 58-60.

35. Okamoto, *Ōsaka-jō*, pp. 159-60; Wakita, "Kinsei shoki no toshi keizai," pp. 60-61.

36. Okamoto, *Ōsaka-jō*, pp. 159-60; Wakita, "Kinsei shoki no toshi keizai," pp. 61-62.

37. Wakita, "Kinsei shoki no toshi keizai," pp. 62-63.

38. *Ibid.*, pp. 65-67. Wakita gives a rice price of 10.64 *monme* per *koku* for 1620, but since this figure seems unrealistically low, I have used an estimate of 20 *monme* per *koku*. See note 33 above. The income estimate is from Wakita.

39. Bolitho, *Treasures among Men*, p. 12.

40. Okamoto, *Ōsaka-jō*, p. 144.

41. *Ōsaka shishi*, 1: 258; *Ōsaka hennenshi*, 4: 425. Initially Hidetada planned to ask the northern daimyo to assist building Nijō castle in Kyoto and the western daimyo to assist with Osaka castle, but Tōdō convinced him that the Osaka project was more important and that to undertake both simultaneously would be unmanageable.

42. *Ōsaka hennenshi*, 4: 171-73, 5: 57-59, 106-30.

43. *Ōsaka shishi*, 1: 258; *Ōsaka hennenshi*, 4: 435-37.

44. *Ōsaka shishi*, 1: 260. For a detailed map of the castle with sections assigned to specific daimyo houses for construction, see Ono Kiyoshi, *Ōsaka jōshi* (Tokyo, 1973), foldout between pp. 264 and 265.

45. *Ōsaka shishi*, 1: 261-63.

46. *Ibid.*, pp. 263-64; *Ōsaka hennenshi*, 5: 2-4.

47. *Ōsaka shishi*, 1: 266-67.

48. *Ibid.*, 1: 269-72, 274.

49. Bolitho, *Treasures among Men*, pp. 6-8, 16-17, 37, 102.

Bolitho, "Abe Masahiro and the New Japan"

Earlier versions of this paper were read at the Australian National University, and at Harvard, Princeton, and Yale universities. I am grateful to Albert Craig, Bob Wakabayashi, and John Weik for their comments.

1. In Watanabe Shūjirō, *Abe Masahiro jiseki*, 2 vols. (2d ed., Tokyo, 1978), 2: 825.

2. Kawabata Tahei, *Matsudaira Shungaku* (Tokyo, 1967), p. 29.

3. Watanabe, *Abe Masahiro jiseki*, 1: 53; for a similar appraisal, see also Conrad Totman, *The Collapse of the Tokugawa Bakufu* (Honolulu, Hawaii, 1980).

4. Watanabe, *Abe Masahiro jiseki*, 2: 503-4.

5. Kawaji Kandō, ed., *Kawaji Toshiakira no shōgai* (2d ed., Tokyo, 1970), p. 334.

6. Watanabe, *Abe Masahiro jiseki*, 1: 143-45.

7. Inoue Kiyoshi, *Saigō Takamori*, 2 vols. (Tokyo, 1970), 1: 41.

8. Naitō Chisō, *Tokugawa jūgodai-shi*, 6 vols. (Tokyo, 1969), 6: 3000, 3002, 3014, 3035; Watanabe, *Abe Masahiro jiseki*, 1: 253, 356.

9. Watanabe, *Abe Masahiro jiseki*, 1: 39.

10. *Ibid.*, p. 349; Matsuura Rei, *Katsu Kaishū* (Tokyo, 1968), p. 50; *Nanki Tokugawa-shi*, ed. Nanki Tokugawa shi kanko-kai, 18 vols. (Wakayama, 1931), 3: 32; Arima Seiho, "The Western Influence on Japanese Military Science," in The Centre for East Asian Cultural Studies, ed., *Acceptance of Western Cultures in Japan* (Tokyo, 1964), p. 131.

11. Takeda Kusuo, *Ishin to kagaku* (Tokyo, 1972), p. 12.

12. Matsuura, *Katsu Kaishū*, p. 50; H. J. Jones, "*Bakumatsu* Foreign Employees," in *Monumenta Nipponica*, 29.3 (1974): 307-8.
13. Takeda, *Ishin to kagaku*, p. 85.
14. Watanabe, *Abe Masahiro jiseki*, 1: 375.
15. *Ibid.*, 2: 479, 483.
16. Arima Seiho, *Takashima Shūhan* (Tokyo, 1958), pp. 163ff.
17. Watanabe, *Abe Masahiro jiseki*, 1: 279.
18. *Ibid.*, pp. 387, 392; Kawabata, *Matsudaira Shungaku*, p. 59.
19. Watanabe, *Abe Masahiro jiseki*, 1: 399-401.
20. *Ibid.*, p. 116.
21. Kawabata, *Matsudaira Shungaku*, p. 50.
22. Watanabe, *Abe Masahiro jiseki*, 1: 349.
23. Kawabata, *Matsudaira Shungaku*, pp. 30, 60.
24. Watanabe, *Abe Masahiro jiseki*, 1: 109, 2: 447-49, 451.
25. *Ibid.*, 1: 321-22, 240, 418; Naitō, *Tokugawa jūgodai-shi*, 6: 3005.
26. Watanabe, *Abe Masahiro jiseki*, 1: 323-24; Inoue, *Saigō Takamori*, 1: 48; Kawaji, ed., *Kawaji Toshiakira no shōgai*, pp. 510-11; Ōkubo Toshiaki, *Iwakura Tomomi* (Tokyo, 1973), p. 25.
27. Watanabe, *Abe Masahiro jiseki*, 1: 139-41.
28. Kawaji, ed., *Kawaji Toshiakira no shōgai*, p. 517.
29. Watanabe, *Abe Masahiro jiseki*, 1: 37, 73; Arima, *Takashima*, pp. 139ff.
30. *Ishin shiryō kōyō*, ed. Ishin shiryō kōyō hensan jimukyoku, 10 vols. (Tokyo, 1937), 1: 6.
31. Kuroita Katsumi, ed., *Zoku Tokugawa jikki*, vols. 48-52 of (Shintei zōhō) *Kokushi Taikei* (Tokyo, 1966-67), 49: 579, 586.
32. Naitō, *Tokugawa jūgodai-shi*, 6: 3000.
33. Watanabe, *Abe Masahiro jiseki*, 1: 119. One can understand why the firing of the *Powhatan*'s nine o'clock gun, a 64-pounder, should "apparently have created something of a commotion" among the Japanese at Uraga. See Sidney Wallach, ed., *Narrative of the Expedition of an American Squadron to the China Seas and Japan*, by Francis L. Hawks (London, 1954), p. 52.
34. Naitō, *Tokugawa jūgodai-shi*, 6: 302.
35. Shinagawa Machi-yakuba, ed., *Shinagawa machi-shi*, 3 vols. (Tokyo, 1932), 1: 104, 106, 128, 146; Naitō, *Tokugawa jūgodai-shi*, 6: 3043.
36. Ii Masahiro, ed., *(Ii-ke shiryō) Bakumatsu fūbun tansaku sho*, 3 vols. (Tokyo, 1967), 1: 34-37.
37. *Ishin shiryō kōyō*, 1: 260, 372.
38. Wallach, ed., *Narrative of the Expedition*, p. 48.
39. Watanabe, *Abe Masahiro jiseki*, 1: 169.
40. *Ibid.*, p. 169, 2: 458, 461.   41. *Ibid.*, 1: 156-57.
42. *Ibid.*, pp. 116-19.   43. *Ibid.*, p. 142.
44. *Ibid.*, pp. 162-63, 250.   45. *Ibid.*, pp. 66, 79, 271.
46. *Ibid.*, p. 344.   47. *Ibid.*, p. 253.
48. Harold Bolitho, *Treasures among Men: The Fudai Daimyo in Tokugawa Japan* (New Haven, Conn., 1974), pp. 213-14.
49. Watanabe, *Abe Masahiro jiseki*, 1: 343.
50. Matsuura, *Katsu Kaishū*, p. 52.

51. Watanabe, *Abe Masahiro jiseki*, 2: 413.

52. Hirao Michio, *Yamauchi Yōdō* (Tokyo, 1961), pp. 44-45.

53. Watanabe, *Abe Masahiro jiseki*, 2: 418. Abe Masahiro was known variously as Lord Ise or Lord Fukuyama, among his other titles.

54. *Ibid.*, p. 434.

55. Inoue, *Saigō Takamori*, 1: 26ff.

56. Iwata Masakazu, *Ōkubo Toshimichi, the Bismarck of Japan* (Berkeley, Calif., 1964), p. 113.

57. *Ibid.*, p. 132.

58. Kawabata, *Matsudaira Shungaku*, p. 378.

Index

Through the Muromachi period, all personal names are listed by given name; the surname follows in parentheses. Where known, a brief identification is given for individuals. The following abbreviations are used: KB (Kamakura Bakufu); MB (Muromachi Bakufu); TH (era of Hideyoshi); TB (Tokugawa Bakufu).

Library of Congress Cataloging in Publication Data
Main entry under title:

The Bakufu in Japanese history.

  Bibliography: p.
  Includes index.
    1. Japan—Politics and government—1185–1600.
2. Japan—Politics and government—1600–1868.   3. Local
government—Japan—History.   4. Feudalism—Japan.
5. Samurai—History.   I. Mass, Jeffrey P.   II. Hauser,
William B.
JQ1624.B35   1985   952'.02   84-51768
ISBN 0-8047-1278-6 (alk. paper)